Table of Conten

Operations and Algebraic Thinking

▶ Write and interpret numerical expressions.

▶ Analyze patterns and relationships.

Number and Operations in Base Ten

▶ Understand the place value system.

▶ **Perform operations with multi-digit whole numbers and with decimals to hundredths.**

Number and Operations – Fractions

▶ **Use equivalent fractions as a strategy to add and subtract fractions.**

▶ **Apply and extend previous understandings of multiplication and division to multiply and divide fractions.**

Measurement and Data

▶ Convert like measurement units within a given measurement system.

▶ Represent and interpret data.

▶ Geometric measurement: understand concepts of volume and relate volume to multiplication and to addition.

Geometry

▶ **Graph points on the coordinate plane to solve real-world and mathematical problems.**

▶ **Classify two-dimensional figures into categories based on their properties.**

Introduction

Core Standards for Math offers two-page lessons for every content standard in the *Common Core State Standards for Mathematics*. The first page of each lesson introduces the concept or skill being taught by providing step-by-step instruction and modeling and checks students' understanding through open-ended practice items. The second page includes multiple-choice practice items as well as problem-solving items.

Common Core State Standards for Mathematics: Content Standards

Content Standards define what students should understand and be able to do. These standards are organized into clusters of related standards to emphasize mathematical connections. Finally, domains represent larger groups of related standards. At the elementary (K–6) level, there are ten content domains. Each grade addresses four or five domains. The table below shows how the domains are placed across Grades K–6.

Domains	K	1	2	3	4	5	6
Counting and Cardinality (CC)	●						
Operations and Algebraic Thinking (OA)	●	●	●	●	●	●	
Numbers and Operations in Base Ten (NBT)	●	●	●	●	●	●	
Measurement and Data (MD)	●	●	●	●	●	●	
Geometry (G)	●	●	●	●	●	●	●
Numbers and Operations—Fractions (NF)				●	●	●	
Ratios and Proportional Relationships (RP)							●
The Number System (NS)							●
Expressions and Equations (EE)							●
Statistics and Probability (SP)							●

The lessons in **Core Standards for Math** are organized by content standard. The content standard is listed at the top right-hand corner of each page. The entire text of the standards is provided on pages 251–256. The lesson objective listed below the content standard number indicates what part of the standard is emphasized in the lesson. You may choose to have students complete all the lessons for a particular standard or select lessons based on the more focused objectives.

Name _____

Lesson 1

COMMON CORE STANDARD CC.5.OA.1
Lesson Objective: Use the order of
operations to evaluate numerical expressions.

Algebra • Evaluate Numerical Expressions

A **numerical expression** is a mathematical phrase that includes only numbers and operation symbols.

You **evaluate** the expression when you perform all the computations to find its value.

To evaluate an expression, use the **order of operations.**

Order of Operations
1. Parentheses
2. Multiply and Divide
3. Add and Subtract

Evaluate the expression $(10 + 6 \times 6) - 4 \times 10$.

Step 1 Start with computations inside the parentheses.

$10 + 6 \times 6$

Step 2 Perform the order of operations inside the *parentheses*.

Multiply and divide from left to right.

$10 + 6 \times 6 = 10 + \underline{36}$

Add and subtract from left to right.

$10 + 36 = \underline{46}$

Step 3 Rewrite the expression with the parentheses evaluated.

$46 - 4 \times 10$

Step 4 *Multiply and divide* from left to right.

$46 - 4 \times 10 = 46 - \underline{40}$

Step 5 *Add and subtract* from left to right.

$46 - 40 = \underline{6}$

So, $(10 + 6 \times 6) - 4 \times 10 = 6$.

Evaluate the numerical expression.

1. $8 - (7 \times 1)$

2. $5 - 2 + 12 \div 4$

3. $8 \times (16 \div 2)$

4. $4 \times (28 - 20 \div 2)$

5. $(30 - 9 \div 3) \div 9$

6. $(6 \times 6 - 9) - 9 \div 3$

7. $11 \div (8 + 9 \div 3)$

8. $13 \times 4 - 65 \div 13$

9. $9 + 4 \times 6 - 65 \div 13$

1. Mr. Perkins used the expression $20 - 10 - 3 \times 2$ to find how much change he should receive. How much change should he receive?

   (A) $2

   (B) $4

   (C) $6

   (D) $14

2. Randy used the expression $2 \times 3 + 3 \times 6 + 1$ to find the number of points the Jaguars scored in all. How many points did the Jaguars score in all?

   (A) 25

   (B) 55

   (C) 73

   (D) 74

3. Amanda used the expression $8 + 25 \times 2 - 45$ to find how many beads she has. How many beads does she have?

   (A) 3

   (B) 13

   (C) 21

   (D) 103

4. Arlene used the expression $3 \times 6 + 2 \times 8 + 1$ to find the number of drinks she bought altogether. How many drinks did she buy altogether?

   (A) 215

   (B) 195

   (C) 36

   (D) 35

Problem Solving REAL WORLD

5. Sandy has several pitchers to hold lemonade for the school bake sale. Two pitchers can hold 64 ounces each, and four pitchers can hold 48 ounces each. How many total ounces can Sandy's pitchers hold?

   _____

6. At the bake sale, Jonah sold 4 cakes for $8 each and 36 muffins for $2 each. What was the total amount, in dollars, that Jonah received from these sales?

   _____

Name _____

Lesson 2

COMMON CORE STANDARD CC.5.OA.1

Lesson Objective: Evaluate numerical expressions with parentheses, brackets, and braces.

Algebra • Grouping Symbols

Parentheses ( ), *brackets* [ ], and *braces* { }, are different grouping symbols used in expressions. To evaluate an expression with different grouping symbols, perform the operation in the innermost set of grouping symbols first. Then evaluate the expression from the inside out.

Evaluate the expression $2 \times [(9 \times 4) - (17 - 6)]$.

Step 1 Perform the operations in the *parentheses* first.

$$2 \times [(9 \times 4) - (17 - 6)]$$

$$2 \times [\ \underline{36}\ -\ \underline{11}\ ]$$

Step 2 Next perform the operations in the *brackets*.

$$2 \times [\ 36 - 11\ ]$$

$$2 \times\ \underline{25}$$

Step 3 Then multiply.

$$2 \times 25 = \underline{50}$$

So, $2 \times [(9 \times 4) - (17 - 6)] = \underline{50}$

Evaluate the numerical expression.

1. $4 \times [(15 - 6) \times (7 - 3)]$

   $4 \times [9 \times \text{_____}]$

   $4 \times [\text{_____}]$

   _____

2. $40 - [(8 \times 7) - (5 \times 6)]$

   _____

3. $60 \div [(20 - 6) + (14 - 8)]$

   _____

4. $5 + [(10 - 2) + (4 - 1)]$

   _____

5. $3 \times [(9 + 4) - (2 \times 6)]$

   _____

6. $32 \div [(7 \times 2) - (2 \times 5)]$

   _____

1. Meredith and her brother Liam are saving to buy a basketball hoop that costs $75. Meredith earns $15 per week for babysitting and spends $6 of it. Liam earns $10 per week for walking dogs and spends $4 of it. Which expression can be used to find out how many weeks it will take to save for the basketball hoop?

   Ⓐ $75 \div [(15 - 6) + (10 - 4)]$

   Ⓑ $75 \div [(15 + 6) - (10 + 4)]$

   Ⓒ $75 \div [(15 - 6) + (10 + 4)]$

   Ⓓ $75 \div [(15 - 6) - (10 - 4)]$

2. A hotel costs $89 per night. Sally will receive a $5 per night discount for paying in advance. A rental car costs $35 per day plus taxes that total $4 per day. Which expression can Sally use to find how much she will pay for the hotel and rental car for 5 days?

   Ⓐ $5 \times (89 - 5) - (35 + 4)$

   Ⓑ $[5 \times (89 - 5)] + (35 + 4)$

   Ⓒ $5 \times [(89 - 5) - (35 + 4)]$

   Ⓓ $5 \times [(89 - 5) + (35 + 4)]$

3. Of the 90 trading cards Yoshi has, 55 are baseball cards and 35 are football cards. He gives Henry 10 football cards and Henry gives Yoshi 8 baseball cards. Which expression can be used to find the number of trading cards Yoshi has now?

   Ⓐ $(55 + 8) - (35 + 10)$

   Ⓑ $(55 - 8) - (35 + 10)$

   Ⓒ $(55 - 8) + (35 - 10)$

   Ⓓ $(55 + 8) + (35 - 10)$

4. Jonah is a baker. Each morning, he makes 60 cupcakes. He gives away 5 and sells the rest. Each morning, he also makes 48 brownies. He gives away 4 and sells the rest. Which expression can be used to find how many cupcakes and brownies Jonah sells in 7 days?

   Ⓐ $7 \times [(60 - 5) - (48 - 4)]$

   Ⓑ $7 \times [(60 - 5) + (48 - 4)]$

   Ⓒ $[7 \times (60 - 5)] + (48 - 4)$

   Ⓓ $7 \times (60 - 5) + (48 - 4)$

Problem Solving

Use the information at the right for 9 and 10.

> Joan has a cafe. Each day, she bakes 24 muffins. She gives away 3 and sells the rest. Each day, she also bakes 36 cupcakes. She gives away 4 and sells the rest.

5. Write an expression to represent the total number of muffins and cupcakes Joan sells in 5 days.

6. Evaluate the expression to find the total number of muffins and cupcakes Joan sells in 5 days.

Algebra • Numerical Expressions

Write words to match the expression.

$$6 \times (12 - 4)$$

Think: Many word problems involve finding the cost of a store purchase.

Step 1 Examine the expression.

• What operations are in the expression?   <u>multiplication and subtraction</u>

Step 2 Describe what each part of the expression can represent when finding the cost of a store purchase.

• What can multiplying by 6 represent?   <u>buying 6 of the same item</u>

Step 3 Write the words.

• Joe buys 6 DVDs. Each DVD costs $12. If Joe receives a $4 discount on each DVD, what is the total amount of money Joe spends?

---

1. What is multiplied and what is subtracted?

   _____

2. What part of the expression is the price of the item?

   _____

3. What can subtracting 4 from 12 represent?

   _____

Write words to match the expression.

4. $4 \times (10 - 2)$

   _____

   _____

   _____

5. $3 \times (6 - 1)$

   _____

   _____

   _____

1. Jamie baked 24 cupcakes. Her sister Mia ate 3 cupcakes, and her brother David ate 2 cupcakes. Which expression can Jamie use to find how many cupcakes are left?

   (A) $24 + (3 - 2)$

   (B) $24 - (3 + 2)$

   (C) $(24 - 3) + 2$

   (D) $24 - (3 - 2)$

2. Paul displays his sports trophies on shelves in his room. He has 5 trophies on each of 3 shelves and 2 trophies on another shelf. Which expression could Paul use to find the total number of trophies displayed?

   (A) $(5 \times 3) - 2$

   (B) $5 \times (3 + 2)$

   (C) $5 + (3 \times 2)$

   (D) $(5 \times 3) + 2$

3. William won 50 tickets at the arcade. He redeemed 30 tickets for a prize and gave 5 tickets to Katelyn. Which expression can William use to find how many tickets he has left?

   (A) $50 - (30 + 5)$

   (B) $50 + (30 - 5)$

   (C) $(50 + 30) + 5$

   (D) $50 - (30 - 5)$

4. Rupal poured muffin batter into 3 muffin tins. Each muffin tin holds 8 muffins. She kept 6 muffins and took the rest to school for the bake sale. Which expression could be used to find the total number of muffins Rupal took to school for the bake sale?

   (A) $(3 \times 8) + 6$

   (B) $(3 + 8) - 6$

   (C) $(3 \times 8) - 6$

   (D) $3 \times (8 - 6)$

Problem Solving REAL WORLD

5. Kylie has 14 polished stones. Her friend gives her 6 more stones. Write an expression to match the words.

   _____

6. Rashad had 25 stamps. He shared them equally among himself and 4 friends. Then Rashad found 2 more stamps in his pocket. Write an expression to match the words.

   _____

Numerical Patterns

A soccer league has 5 teams. How many players are needed for 5 teams? How many soccer balls are needed by the 5 teams?

	Number of Teams	1	2	3	4	7
Add _8_.	**Number of Players**	8	16	24	32	56
Add _4_.	**Number of Soccer Balls**	4	8	12	16	28

Step 1 Find a rule that could be used to find the number of players for the number of teams.

Think: In the pattern 8, 16, 24, 32, you add 8 to get the next term.

As the number of teams increases by 1, the number of players increases by 8. So the rule is to add 8.

Step 2 Find a rule that could be used to find the number of soccer balls for the number of teams.

Think: In the pattern 4, 8, 12, 16, you add 4 to get the next term.

As the number of teams increases by 1, the number of soccer balls needed increases by 4. So the rule is to add 4.

Step 3 For 7 teams, multiply the number of players by $\frac{1}{2}$ to find the number of soccer balls.

So, for 7 teams, 56 players will need __28__ soccer balls.

Complete the rule that describes how one sequence is related to the other. Use the rule to find the unknown term.

Number of Teams	1	2	3	4	8	10
Number of Players	15	30	45	60	120	
Number of Bats	5	10	15	20		50

1. Divide the number of players by _____ to find the number of bats.

2. Multiply the number of bats by _____ to find the number of players.

Use the table for 1–2.

Jawan made a table to figure out how much he earns at his job.

Job Earnings

Days	1	2	3	4
Hours Worked	6	12	18	24
Amount Earned ($)	54	108	162	216

1. What rule relates the hours worked to the amount earned?

   (A) Add 6.   (C) Multiply by 2.

   (B) Add 54.   (D) Multiply by 9.

2. Suppose Jawan works 6 days. Using the rule that relates the hours worked to the amount earned, find the total number of hours he will work in 6 days and how much money he will earn in all.

   (A) 36 hours, $648

   (B) 36 hours, $324

   (C) 30 hours, $300

   (D) 30 hours, $270

3. What is the unknown number in Sequence 2 in the chart?

Sequence Number	1	2	3	5	7
Sequence 1	3	6	9	15	21
Sequence 2	15	30	45	75	?

   (A) 63   (C) 105
   (B) 90   (D) 150

4. Wanda made a table to show the number of ounces of flour she uses to make cupcakes.

Flour in Cupcakes

Batches	1	2	3	4	6
Ounces of Flour	8	16	24	32	48
Cupcakes	16	32	48	64	96

What rule relates the number of ounces of flour to the number of cupcakes?

   (A) Add 8.   (C) Multiply by 2.

   (B) Add 12.   (D) Multiply by 8.

5. Mrs. Marston determined how many tubes of paint she would need for the students in her art classes to complete their projects. How many tubes of paint will she need for the class with 20 students? Explain how you found the answer.

Students	4	8	12	16	20
Tubes	8	16	24	32	

_____

_____

_____

_____

_____

Name _____

Lesson 5
COMMON CORE STANDARD CC.5.OA.3
Lesson Objective: Solve problems using
the strategy *solve a simpler problem.*

Problem Solving • Find a Rule

Samantha is making a scarf with fringe around it. Each section of fringe
is made of 4 pieces of yarn with 2 beads holding them together. There are
42 sections of fringe on Samantha's scarf. How many wooden beads and
how many pieces of yarn are on Samantha's scarf?

Read the Problem	Solve the Problem
What do I need to find? Possible answer: I need to find the number of beads and the number of pieces of yarn on Samantha's scarf.	(table below)

Sections of Fringe	1	2	3	4	6	42
Number of Beads	2	4	6	8	12	84
Pieces of Yarn	4	8	12	16	24	168

What information do I need to use?
Possible answer: I need to use the number of sections on the scarf, and that each section has 4 pieces of yarn and 2 beads.

Possible answer: I can multiply the number of sections by 2 to find the number of beads. Then, I can multiply the number of sections by 4, or the number of beads by 2, to find the number of pieces of yarn. So, Samantha's scarf has 2 × 42, or 84 beads, and 4 × 42, or 168 pieces of yarn.

How will I use the information?
I will use the information to search for patterns to solve a simpler problem.

1. A rectangular tile has a decorative pattern of 3 equal-sized squares, each of which is divided into 2 same-sized triangles. If Marnie uses 36 of these tiles on the wall behind her kitchen stove, how many triangles are displayed?

2. Leta is making strawberry-almond salad for a party. For every head of lettuce that she uses, she adds 5 ounces of almonds and 10 strawberries. If she uses 75 ounces of almonds, how many heads of lettuce and how many strawberries does Leta use?

1. Nomi is making a pattern of square tiles, as shown below. The side lengths of the tiles are 2 centimeters.

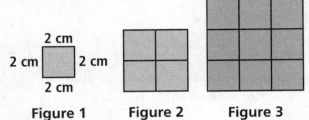

Figure 1   Figure 2   Figure 3

Suppose Nomi continues the pattern. What will be the distance around Figure 7?

Ⓐ 14 centimeters

Ⓑ 49 centimeters

Ⓒ 56 centimeters

Ⓓ 98 centimeters

2. Leroy starts to work at a part-time job. He saves $25 of his earnings each month. By the end of the second month, he saves $50 in all. How much will he save by the end of 24 months?

Ⓐ $75   Ⓒ $1,200

Ⓑ $600   Ⓓ $1,800

Use the table for 3–4.

The table shows the number of tickets needed for rides at an amusement park.

Amusement Park Rides

Number of Rides	1	2	3	7
Number of Tickets	4	8	12	?

3. Which rule relates the number of tickets to the number of rides?

Ⓐ Multiply the number of rides by 4.

Ⓑ Multiply the number of rides by 3.

Ⓒ Add 3 for each ride.

Ⓓ Add 4 for each ride.

4. Jared buys 40 tickets and goes on 7 rides. How many tickets does he have left after the 7 rides?

Ⓐ 33   Ⓒ 24

Ⓑ 28   Ⓓ 12

Problem Solving REAL WORLD

5. A restaurant manager has 10 tables that are 3 feet wide and 4 feet long. Suppose the manager places the 10 tables side-by-side so the 4-foot sides match up. What will be the perimeter of the larger table that is formed? Explain how you know.

3 ft

4 ft

_____

_____

_____

Graph and Analyze Relationships

The scale on a map is 1 in. = 4 mi. Two cities are 5 inches apart on the map. What is the actual distance between the two cities?

Step 1 Make a table that relates the map distances to the actual distances.

Map Distance (in.)	1	2	3	4	5
Actual Distance (mi)	4	8	12	16	?

Step 2 Write the number pairs in the table as ordered pairs.

(1, 4), (2, 8), (3, 12), (4, 16), (5, ?)

Step 3 Graph the ordered pairs. Connect the points with a line from the origin.

Possible rule: Multiply the map distance by <u>4</u> to get the actual distance.

Step 4 Use the rule to find the actual distance between the two cities.

So, two cities that are 5 inches apart on the map are actually 5 × 4, or <u>20</u> miles apart.

Plot the point (5, 20) on the graph.

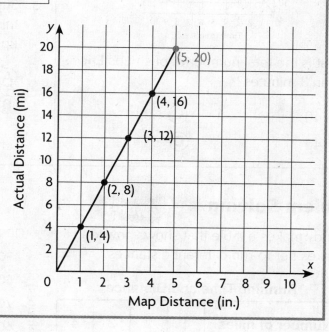

Graph and label the related number pairs as ordered pairs. Then complete and use the rule to find the unknown term.

1. Multiply the number of yards by _____ to find the number of feet.

Number of Yards	1	2	3	4	5
Number of Feet	3	6	9	12	

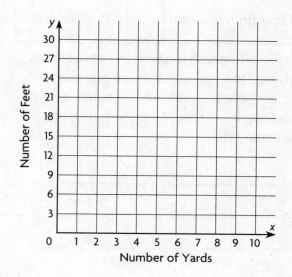

Name _____

Use the graph for 1–3.

The graph shows the relationship between the time and the number of push ups Eric did.

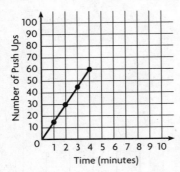

1. What is the total number of push ups Eric did in 3 minutes?

   (A) 40

   (B) 45

   (C) 50

   (D) 55

2. What rule relates the number of push ups to the time?

   (A) Multiply the number of minutes by $\frac{1}{15}$.

   (B) Multiply the number of minutes by $\frac{1}{10}$.

   (C) Multiply the number of minutes by 10.

   (D) Multiply the number of minutes by 15.

3. Suppose Eric continues to do push ups at this rate. What is the total number of push ups he will do in 5 minutes?

   (A) 50

   (B) 65

   (C) 75

   (D) 90

Problem Solving REAL WORLD

4. Randy makes a table that shows how long it takes her to run different distances.

Running Time and Distance

Number of miles	1	2	3	4
Time (in minutes)	10	20	30	40

Draw a line graph to show the relationship between the number of miles and the time. Explain how you can use the graph to find how long it will take Randy to run 5 miles at the same rate.

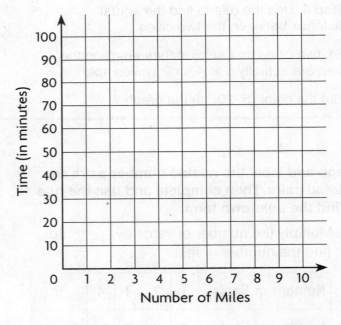

_____

_____

_____

Lesson 7

COMMON CORE STANDARD CC.5.NBT.1
Lesson Objective: Recognize the 10 to 1 relationship among place-value positions.

Place Value and Patterns

You can use a place-value chart and patterns to write numbers that are 10 times as much as or $\frac{1}{10}$ of any given number.

Each place to the right is $\frac{1}{10}$ of the value of the place to its left.

$\frac{1}{10}$ of the hundred thousands place	$\frac{1}{10}$ of the ten thousands place	$\frac{1}{10}$ of the thousands place	$\frac{1}{10}$ of the hundreds place	$\frac{1}{10}$ of the tens place
Hundred Thousands	**Ten Thousands**	**Thousands**	**Hundreds**	**Tens**	**Ones**
10 times the ten thousands place	10 times the thousands place	10 times the hundreds place	10 times the tens place	10 times the ones place

Each place to the left is 10 times the value of the place to its right.

Find $\frac{1}{10}$ of 600.

$\frac{1}{10}$ of 6 hundreds is 6 __tens__ .

So, $\frac{1}{10}$ of 600 is __60__ .

Find 10 times as much as 600.

10 times as much as 6 hundreds is 6 __thousands__.

So, 10 times as much as 600 is __6,000__ .

Use place-value patterns to complete the table.

Number	10 times as much as	$\frac{1}{10}$ of
1. 200		
2. 10		
3. 700		
4. 5,000		

Number	10 times as much as	$\frac{1}{10}$ of
5. 900		
6. 80,000		
7. 3,000		
8. 40		

1. A math workbook contains 50 pages. The number of problems in the book is 10 times as many as the number of pages. How many problems are in the math workbook?

Ⓐ   5

Ⓑ   500

Ⓒ   5,000

Ⓓ   50,000

2. Cara has saved $4,000 to buy a car. Rick wants to buy a new television set. He has saved $\frac{1}{10}$ as much as Cara. How much has Rick saved?

Ⓐ $4

Ⓑ $40

Ⓒ $400

Ⓓ $40,000

3. Riva lives 300 miles from her grandparents. George lives 10 times that distance from his grandparents. How many miles does George live from his grandparents?

Ⓐ   30

Ⓑ   3,000

Ⓒ   30,000

Ⓓ 300,000

4. The Davis family pays $200,000 for a new house. They make a down payment that is $\frac{1}{10}$ of the price of the house. How much is the down payment?

Ⓐ $20

Ⓑ $200

Ⓒ $2,000

Ⓓ $20,000

Problem Solving REAL WORLD

5. The Eatery Restaurant has 200 tables. On a recent evening, there were reservations for $\frac{1}{10}$ of the tables. How many tables were reserved?

6. Mr. Wilson has $3,000 in his bank account. Ms. Nelson has 10 times as much money in her bank account as Mr. Wilson has in his bank account. How much money does Ms. Nelson have in her bank account?

Name _____

Lesson 8
COMMON CORE STANDARD CC.5.NBT.1
Lesson Objective: Read and write whole numbers through hundred millions.

Place Value of Whole Numbers

You can use a place-value chart to help you understand whole numbers and the value of each digit. A **period** is a group of three digits within a number separated by a comma.

Millions Period			Thousands Period			Ones Period		
Hundreds	Tens	Ones	Hundreds	Tens	Ones	Hundreds	Tens	Ones
		2,	3	6	7,	0	8	9

Standard form: 2,367,089

Expanded Form: Multiply each digit by its place value, and then write an addition expression.

$(2 \times 1,000,000) + (3 \times 100,000) + (6 \times 10,000) + (7 \times 1,000) + (8 \times 10) + (9 \times 1)$

Word Form: Write the number in words. Notice that the millions and the thousands periods are followed by the period name and a comma.

two million, three hundred sixty-seven thousand, eighty-nine

To find the value of an underlined digit, multiply the digit by its place value. In 2,367,089, the value of 2 is $2 \times 1,000,000$, or 2,000,000.

Write the value of the underlined digit.

1. 1_5_3,732,991

2. 2_3_6,143,802

3. 264,_8_07

4. 78,_2_09,146

Write the number in two other forms.

5. 701,245

6. 40,023,032

1. A publisher reports that it sold 2,419,386 children's magazines. What is the value of the digit 2 in 2,419,386?

   Ⓐ 200,000,000
   Ⓑ 20,000,000
   Ⓒ 2,000,000
   Ⓓ 200,000

2. The diameter of Saturn at its equator is about 120,540,000 meters. What is 120,540,000 written in word form?

   Ⓐ twelve thousand, five hundred forty
   Ⓑ twelve million, five hundred forty thousand
   Ⓒ one hundred twenty million, fifty-four thousand
   Ⓓ one hundred twenty million, five hundred forty thousand

3. A printing company used 1,896,432 sheets of tag board last year. What is the value of the digit 8 in 1,896,432?

   Ⓐ 800
   Ⓑ 8,000
   Ⓒ 80,000
   Ⓓ 800,000

4. A company manufactured forty-eight million, seven hundred fifty thousand toothpicks last month. What is this number written in standard form?

   Ⓐ 48,750,000
   Ⓑ 48,700,050
   Ⓒ 48,000,750
   Ⓓ 48,750

Problem Solving REAL WORLD

5. The U.S. Census Bureau has a population clock on the Internet. On a recent day, the United States population was listed as 310,763,136. Write this number in word form.

   _____

   _____

   _____

6. In 2008, the population of 10- to 14-year-olds in the United States was 20,484,163. Write this number in expanded form.

   _____

   _____

   _____

Thousandths

Thousandths are smaller parts than hundredths. If one hundredth is divided into 10 equal parts, each part is one **thousandth**.

Write the decimal shown by the shaded parts of the model.

One column of the decimal model is shaded.
It represents one tenth, or __0.1__.

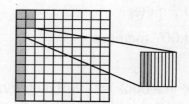

Two small squares of the decimal model are shaded.
They represent two hundredths, or __0.02__.

A one-hundredth square is divided into 10 equal parts, or thousandths. Three columns of the thousandth square are shaded. They represent __0.003__.

So, 0.123 of the decimal model is shaded.

The relationship of a digit in different place-value positions is the same for decimals as for whole numbers.

Write the decimals in a place-value chart.

Ones	•	Tenths	Hundredths	Thousandths
0	•	8		
0	•	0	8	
0	•	0	0	8

0.08 is $\frac{1}{10}$ of __0.8__.

0.08 is 10 times as much as __0.008__.

1. Write the decimal shown by the shaded parts of the model.

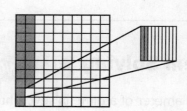

_____

Use place-value patterns to complete the table.

Decimal	10 times as much as	$\frac{1}{10}$ of
2. 0.1		
3. 0.03		
4. 0.5		

Decimal	10 times as much as	$\frac{1}{10}$ of
5. 0.02		
6. 0.4		
7. 0.06		

1. A calculator is 0.07 meter wide. Sam made a model that was $\frac{1}{10}$ the size of the actual calculator. How wide was Sam's model?

   (A) 70 meters

   (B) 7 meters

   (C) 0.7 meter

   (D) 0.007 meter

2. A word in a book is 0.009 meter long. Kai looked at the word with a lens that made it look 10 times as large as the actual word. How long did the word look?

   (A) 0.0009 meter

   (B) 0.09 meter

   (C) 0.9 meter

   (D) 9 meters

3. What is the relationship between 0.008 and 0.08?

   (A) 0.008 is $\frac{1}{10}$ of 0.08.

   (B) 0.08 is $\frac{1}{10}$ of 0.008.

   (C) 0.008 is 10 times as much as 0.08.

   (D) 0.008 is equal to 0.08.

4. Valerie made a model for a decimal. What decimal is shown by Valerie's model?

   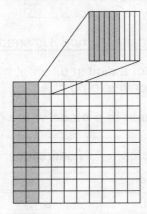

   (A) 0.026   (C) 0.216

   (B) 0.206   (D) 0.26

Problem Solving

5. The diameter of a dime is seven hundred five thousandths of an inch. Complete the table by recording the diameter of a dime.

6. What is the value of the 5 in the diameter of a half dollar?

   _____

7. Which coins have a diameter with a 5 in the hundredths place?

   _____

U.S. Coins	
Coin	**Diameter (in inches)**
Penny	0.750
Nickel	0.835
Dime	
Quarter	0.955
Half dollar	1.205

Lesson 10
COMMON CORE STANDARD CC.5.NBT.2
Lesson Objective: Write and evaluate
repeated factors in exponent form.

Algebra • Powers of 10 and Exponents

You can represent repeated factors with a base and an exponent.

Write 10 × 10 × 10 × 10 × 10 × 10 in exponent form.

10 is the repeated factor, so 10 is the **base**.

The base is repeated 6 times, so 6 is the **exponent**.

$10 \times 10 \times 10 \times 10 \times 10 \times 10 = 10^6$

A base with an exponent can be written in words.

$10^6 \longleftarrow$ exponent

$\uparrow$

base

Write 10^6 in words.

The exponent 6 means "the sixth power."

10^6 in words is "the sixth power of ten."

You can read 10^2 in two ways: "ten squared" or "the second power of ten."

You can also read 10^3 in two ways: "ten cubed" or "the third power of ten."

Write in exponent form and in word form.

1. $10 \times 10 \times 10 \times 10 \times 10 \times 10 \times 10$

   exponent form: _____   word form: _____

2. $10 \times 10 \times 10$

   exponent form: _____   word form: _____

3. $10 \times 10 \times 10 \times 10 \times 10$

   exponent form: _____   word form: _____

Find the value.

4. 10^4

5. 2×10^3

6. 6×10^2

_____   _____   _____

1. A Coast Guard ship is responsible for searching an area that is 5,000 square miles. Which shows 5,000 as a whole number multiplied by a power of ten?

   (A) 5×10^1

   (B) 5×10^2

   (C) 5×10^3

   (D) 5×10^4

2. Martin is going mountain climbing at Snowmass Mountain in Colorado. He looked up the height of the mountain and found it to be about 14×10^3 feet high. What is the height of Snowmass Mountain written as a whole number?

   (A)   140 feet

   (B)   1,400 feet

   (C)   14,000 feet

   (D)   140,000 feet

3. Patel hopes to be one of the first fans to get into the stadium for the baseball game because the first 30,000 fans will receive a baseball cap. Which shows 30,000 as a whole number multiplied by a power of ten?

   (A) 3×10^1

   (B) 3×10^2

   (C) 3×10^3

   (D) 3×10^4

4. Trisha is writing a report about Guam for Social Studies. She looked up the population of Guam and found it to be about 18×10^4. What is the population of Guam written as a whole number?

   (A) 180,000

   (B)   18,000

   (C)   1,800

   (D)   180

Problem Solving REAL WORLD

5. The moon is about 240,000 miles from Earth. What is this distance written as a whole number multiplied by a power of ten?

6. The sun is about 93×10^6 miles from Earth. What is this distance written as a whole number?

COMMON CORE STANDARD CC.5.NBT.2

Lesson Objective: Use a basic fact and a pattern to multiply mentally by multiples of 10, 100, and 1,000.

Algebra • Multiplication Patterns

You can use basic facts, patterns, and powers of 10 to help you multiply whole numbers by multiples of 10, 100, and 1,000.

Use mental math and a pattern to find 90 × 6,000.

- 9×6 is a basic fact. $9 \times 6 = 54$

- Use basic facts, patterns, and powers of 10 to find $90 \times 6,000$.

$$9 \times 60 = (9 \times 6) \times 10^1$$
$$= 54 \times 10^1$$
$$= 54 \times 10$$
$$= 540$$

$$9 \times 600 = (9 \times 6) \times 10^2$$
$$= 54 \times 10^2$$
$$= 54 \times 100$$
$$= 5,400$$

$$9 \times 6,000 = (9 \times 6) \times 10^3$$
$$= 54 \times 10^3$$
$$= 54 \times 1,000$$
$$= 54,000$$

$$90 \times 6,000 = (9 \times 6) \times (10 \times 1,000)$$
$$= 54 \times 10^4$$
$$= 54 \times 10,000$$
$$= 540,000$$

So, $90 \times 6,000 = 540,000$.

Use mental math to complete the pattern.

1. $3 \times 1 = 3$

   $3 \times 10^1 = $ _____

   $3 \times 10^2 = $ _____

   $3 \times 10^3 = $ _____

2. $8 \times 2 = 16$

   $(8 \times 2) \times 10^1 = $ _____

   $(8 \times 2) \times 10^2 = $ _____

   $(8 \times 2) \times 10^3 = $ _____

3. $4 \times 5 = 20$

   $(4 \times 5) \times $ _____ $= 200$

   $(4 \times 5) \times $ _____ $= 2,000$

   $(4 \times 5) \times $ _____ $= 20,000$

4. $7 \times 6 = $ _____

   $(7 \times 6) \times $ _____ $= 420$

   $(7 \times 6) \times $ _____ $= 4,200$

   $(7 \times 6) \times $ _____ $= 42,000$

1. A country music concert will be held at a local park. The promoters have already sold 3,000 concert tickets. Each ticket costs $20. How much money have the promoters already collected?

   Ⓐ $60
   Ⓑ $600
   Ⓒ $60,000
   Ⓓ $600,000

2. Clinton decided to buy 300 shares of stock in an electronics company. Each share costs $60. Which of the following could he use to find the total amount he will pay for the stock?

   Ⓐ $(6 \times 3) \times 10^2 = 1,800$
   Ⓑ $(6 \times 3) \times 10^3 = 18,000$
   Ⓒ $(6 \times 3) \times 10^4 = 180,000$
   Ⓓ $(6 \times 3) \times 10^5 = 1,800,000$

3. Sam is using a microscope to look at a plant specimen. The microscope magnifies the specimen 4×10^2 times. If the specimen is 3 centimeters long, how long will the magnified specimen appear to be?

   Ⓐ   70 centimeters
   Ⓑ   120 centimeters
   Ⓒ   700 centimeters
   Ⓓ 1,200 centimeters

4. So far the fifth-grade students at Silver Run Elementary School have raised $200 toward their class trip. They need to raise 8 times as much to pay for the whole trip. How much money do the fifth-grade students need to raise in all?

   Ⓐ $16
   Ⓑ $1,600
   Ⓒ $16,000
   Ⓓ $160,000

Problem Solving REAL WORLD

5. The Florida Everglades welcomes about 2×10^3 visitors per day. Based on this, about how many visitors come to the Everglades per week?

6. The average person loses about 8×10^1 strands of hair each day. About how many strands of hair would the average person lose in 9 days?

Algebra • Multiplication Patterns with Decimals

You can use patterns and place value to help you place the decimal point.

To multiply a number by a power of 10, you can use the exponent to determine how the position of the decimal point changes in the product.

	Exponent	Move decimal point:
$10^0 \times 5.18 =$ **5.18**	0	0 places to the right
$10^1 \times 5.18 =$ **51.8**	1	1 place to the right
$10^2 \times 5.18 =$ **518**	2	2 places to the right
$10^3 \times 5.18 =$ **5,180**	3	3 places to the right

You can use place-value patterns to find the product of a number and the decimals 0.1 and 0.01.

	Multiply by:	Move decimal point:
$1 \times 2,457 =$ **2,457**	1	0 places to the left
$0.1 \times 2,457 =$ **245.7**	0.1	1 place to the left
$0.01 \times 2,457 =$ **24.57**	0.01	2 places to the left

Complete the pattern.

1. $10^0 \times 25.89 =$ _____

   $10^1 \times 25.89 =$ _____

   $10^2 \times 25.89 =$ _____

   $10^3 \times 25.89 =$ _____

2. $1 \times 182 =$ _____

   $0.1 \times 182 =$ _____

   $0.01 \times 182 =$ _____

1. Ganesh is making a scale model of the Space Needle in Seattle, Washington, for a report on the state of Washington. The Space Needle is 605 feet tall. If the model is $\frac{1}{100}$ of the actual size of the Space Needle, how tall is the model?

   (A)   0.605 foot

   (B)   6.05 feet

   (C)   6.5 feet

   (D) 60.5 feet

2. Madison needs to buy enough meat to make 1,000 hamburgers for the company picnic. Each hamburger will weigh 0.25 pound. How many pounds of hamburger meat should Madison buy?

   (A)   2.5 pounds

   (B)   25 pounds

   (C)   250 pounds

   (D) 2,500 pounds

3. Kareem was doing research for a report about the longest rivers on Earth. He read that the Nile River is 4.16×10^3 miles long. How should Kareem write the length of the Nile River in standard form on his report?

   (A)   4.16 miles

   (B)   41.6 miles

   (C)   416 miles

   (D) 4,160 miles

4. The school store expects to sell a lot of sweatshirts because the football team won the championship. The store ordered 100 sweatshirts. Each sweatshirt cost $8.95. How much did the order of sweatshirts cost the store?

   (A) $89.50

   (B) $895

   (C) $8,950

   (D) $89,500

Problem Solving

5. Nathan plants equal-sized squares of sod in his front yard. Each square has an area of 6 square feet. Nathan plants a total of 1,000 squares in his yard. What is the total area of the squares of sod?

6. Three friends are selling items at a bake sale. May makes $23.25 selling bread. Inez sells gift baskets and makes 100 times as much as May. Carolyn sells pies and makes one tenth of the money Inez makes. How much money does each friend make?

Name _____

Lesson 13
COMMON CORE STANDARD CC.5.NBT.2
Lesson Objective: Find patterns in
quotients when dividing by powers of 10.

Algebra • Division Patterns with Decimals

To divide a number by 10, 100, or 1,000, use the number of zeros in the divisor to determine how the position of the decimal point changes in the quotient.

	Number of zeros:	Move decimal point:
$147 \div 1 = \underline{147}$	0	0 places to the left
$147 \div 10 = \underline{14.7}$	1	1 place to the left
$147 \div 100 = \underline{1.47}$	2	2 places to the left
$147 \div 1,000 = \underline{0.147}$	3	3 places to the left

To divide a number by a power of 10, you can use the exponent to determine how the position of the decimal point changes in the quotient.

	Exponent	Move decimal point:
$97.2 \div 10^0 = \underline{97.2}$	0	0 places to the left
$97.2 \div 10^1 = \underline{9.72}$	1	1 place to the left
$97.2 \div 10^2 = \underline{0.972}$	2	2 places to the left

Complete the pattern.

1. $358 \div 10^0 = $ _____

$358 \div 10^1 = $ _____

$358 \div 10^2 = $ _____

$358 \div 10^3 = $ _____

2. $102 \div 10^0 = $ _____

$102 \div 10^1 = $ _____

$102 \div 10^2 = $ _____

$102 \div 10^3 = $ _____

3. $99.5 \div 1 = $ _____

$99.5 \div 10 = $ _____

$99.5 \div 100 = $ _____

1. Lori is running in a marathon, which is 26.2 miles long. So far, she has run one-tenth of the marathon. How far has Lori run?

   (A) 262 miles

   (B) 2.62 miles

   (C) 0.262 mile

   (D) 0.00262 mile

2. A school bought 1,000 erasers as part of an order for supplies. The total cost of the erasers was $30. What was the cost of 1 eraser?

   (A) $0.03

   (B) $0.30

   (C) $300

   (D) $3,000

3. Tanya baked 100 cupcakes one morning in a bakery. She used 64 ounces of frosting to decorate the cupcakes. If each cupcake had the same amount of frosting, how much frosting did Tanya put on each cupcake?

   (A) 0.0064 ounce

   (B) 0.064 ounce

   (C) 0.64 ounce

   (D) 6.4 ounces

4. A counselor at Sleepy Hollow Camp has 225 yards of lanyard to give to 100 campers to make lanyard key chains. Each camper will get the same amount of lanyard. How much lanyard will each camper get?

   (A) 0.0225 yard

   (B) 0.225 yard

   (C) 2.25 yards

   (D) 22.5 yards

Problem Solving REAL WORLD

5. The local café uses 510 cups of mixed vegetables to make 1,000 quarts of beef barley soup. Each quart of soup contains the same amount of vegetables. How many cups of vegetables are in each quart of soup?

6. The same café uses 18.5 cups of flour to make 100 servings of pancakes. How many cups of flour are in one serving of pancakes?

Place Value of Decimals

You can use a place-value chart to find the value of each digit in a decimal.
Write whole numbers to the left of the decimal point.
Write decimals to the right of the decimal point.

Ones	Tenths	Hundredths	Thousandths
3	8	4	7
3×1	$8 \times \frac{1}{10}$	$4 \times \frac{1}{100}$	$7 \times \frac{1}{1,000}$
3.0	0.8	0.04	0.007

Value

The place value of the digit 8 in 3.847 is tenths.

The value of 8 in 3.847 is $8 \times \frac{1}{10}$, or 0.8.

You can write a decimal in different forms.

Standard Form: <u>3.847</u>

Expanded Form: <u>3</u> $\times 1 +$ <u>8</u> $\times \frac{1}{10} +$ <u>4</u> $\times (\frac{1}{100}) +$ <u>7</u> $\times (\frac{1}{1,000})$

When you write the decimal in word form, write "and" for the decimal point.

Word Form: three <u>and</u> eight hundred forty-seven <u>thousandths</u>

1. Complete the place-value chart to find the value of each digit.

Ones	Tenths	Hundredths	Thousandths
2	6	9	5
2×1		$9 \times \frac{1}{100}$	
	0.6		

Value

Write the value of the underlined digit.

2. 0.7<u>9</u>2

3. 4.<u>6</u>91

4. 3.80<u>5</u>

_____   _____   _____

1. A scientist measured a grain of sand. It had a diameter of 0.049 millimeter. What is 0.049 written in word form?

   (A) forty-nine
   (B) forty-nine tenths
   (C) forty-nine hundredths
   (D) forty-nine thousandths

2. The diamond in Alma's necklace weighs 0.258 carat. What digit is in the hundredths place of 0.258?

   (A) 0
   (B) 2
   (C) 5
   (D) 8

3. The mass of an ant is about 0.003 gram. What is the value of the digit 3 in 0.003?

   (A) 3 ones
   (B) 3 tenths
   (C) 3 hundredths
   (D) 3 thousandths

4. A penny has a diameter of 0.019 meter. What is 0.019 written in word form?

   (A) nineteen thousandths
   (B) nineteen hundredths
   (C) nineteen tenths
   (D) nineteen

Problem Solving REAL WORLD

5. In a gymnastics competition, Paige's score was 37.025. What is Paige's score written in word form?

   _____

   _____

6. Jake's batting average for the softball season is 0.368. What is Jake's batting average written in expanded form?

   _____

   _____

Name _____

Lesson 15
COMMON CORE STANDARD CC.5.NBT.3b
Lesson Objective: Compare and order
decimals to thousandths using place value.

Compare and Order Decimals

You can use a place-value chart to compare decimals.

Compare. Write <, >, or =.

4.375 ◯ 4.382

Write both numbers in a place-value chart. Then compare the digits,
starting with the highest place value. Stop when the digits are different
and compare.

Ones	Tenths	Hundredths	Thousandths
4	3	7	5
4	3	8	2

↑ The ones digits are the same. ↑ The tenths digits are the same. ↑ The hundredths digits are different.

The digits are different in the hundredths place.

Since 7 hundredths < 8 hundredths, 4.375 ◯< 4.382.

1. Use the place-value chart to compare the
two numbers. What is the greatest place-
value position where the digits differ?

Ones	Tenths	Hundredths	Thousandths
2	8	6	5
2	8	6	1

_____

Compare. Write <, >, or =.

2. 5.37 ◯ 5.370   3. 9.425 ◯ 9.417   4. 7.684 ◯ 7.689

Name the greatest place-value position where the digits differ.
Name the greater number.

5. 8.675; 8.654   6. 3.086; 3.194   7. 6.243; 6.247

_____ _____ _____

_____ _____ _____

Order from least to greatest.

8. 5.04; 5.4; 5.406; 5.064   9. 2.614; 2.146; 2.46; 2.164

_____ _____

1. Harry kept a record of how far he ran each day last week.

Day	Distance (in miles)
Monday	4.5
Tuesday	3.9
Wednesday	4.25
Thursday	3.75
Friday	4.2

On which day did Harry run the greatest number of miles?

(A) Monday

(B) Tuesday

(C) Thursday

(D) Friday

2. The four highest scores on the floor exercise at a gymnastics meet were 9.675, 9.25, 9.325, and 9.5. Which shows the order of the scores from least to greatest?

(A) 9.5, 9.25, 9.325, 9.675

(B) 9.25, 9.5, 9.325, 9.675

(C) 9.675, 9.5, 9.325, 9.25

(D) 9.25, 9.325, 9.5, 9.675

3. The table shows the fastest times for the 100-meter hurdles event.

Name	Times (in seconds)
Shakira	15.45
Jameel	15.09
Lindsay	15.6
Nicholas	15.3

Who had the fastest time?

(A) Shakira   (C) Lindsay

(B) Jameel   (D) Nicholas

4. Mary Ann kept a record of how long she practiced the piano each week for a month.

Week	Hours Practiced
Week 1	4.75
Week 2	4.5
Week 3	5.1
Week 4	5.75

During which week did Mary Ann practice the greatest amount of time?

(A) Week 1   (C) Week 3

(B) Week 2   (D) Week 4

Problem Solving REAL WORLD

5. The completion times for three runners in a 100-yard dash are 9.75 seconds, 9.7 seconds, and 9.675 seconds. Which is the winning time?

6. In a discus competition, an athlete threw the discus 63.37 meters, 62.95 meters, and 63.7 meters. Order the distances from least to greatest.

Name _____

Lesson 16

COMMON CORE STANDARD CC.5.NBT.4
Lesson Objective: Round decimals to any place.

Round Decimals

Rounding decimals is similar to rounding whole numbers.

Round 4.682 to the nearest tenth.

Step 1 Write 4.682 in a place-value chart.

Ones	•	Tenths	Hundredths	Thousandths
4	•	⑥	8̲	2

Step 2 Find the digit in the place to which you want to round. Circle that digit.

The digit ___6___ is in the tenths place, so circle it.

Step 3 Underline the digit to the right of the circled digit.

The digit ___8___ is to the right of the circled digit, so underline it.

Step 4 If the underlined digit is less than 5, the circled digit stays the same. If the underlined digit is 5 or greater, round up the circled digit.

___8___ > 5, so round 6 up to 7.

Step 5 After you round the circled digit, drop the digits to the right of the circled digit.

So, 4.682 rounded to the nearest tenth is ___4.7___.

Write the place value of the underlined digit. Round each number to the place of the underlined digit.

1. 0.39̲2

2. 5.7̲14

3. 16̲.908

_____

_____

_____

Name the place value to which each number was rounded.

4. 0.825 to 0.83

5. 3.815 to 4

6. 1.546 to 1.5

_____

_____

_____

1. It takes the dwarf planet Pluto 247.68 years to revolve once around the sun. What is 247.68 years rounded to the nearest whole number of years?

   (A) 247 years

   (B) 247.6 years

   (C) 247.7 years

   (D) 248 years

2. The flagpole in front of Silver Pines Elementary School is 18.375 feet tall. What is 18.375 rounded to the nearest tenth?

   (A) 18

   (B) 18.38

   (C) 18.4

   (D) 20

3. Michelle records the value of one Euro in U.S. dollars each day for her social studies project. The table shows the data she has recorded so far.

Day	Value of 1 Euro (In U.S. dollars)
Monday	1.448
Tuesday	1.443
Wednesday	1.452
Thursday	1.458

   On which day does the value of 1 Euro round to $1.46 to the nearest hundredth?

   (A) Monday   (C) Wednesday

   (B) Tuesday   (D) Thursday

4. Jackie found a rock that has a mass of 78.852 grams. What is the mass of the rock rounded to the nearest tenth?

   (A) 78.85 grams   (C) 79 grams

   (B) 78.9 grams   (D) 80 grams

Problem Solving REAL WORLD

5. The population density of Montana is 6.699 people per square mile. What is the population density per square mile of Montana rounded to the nearest whole number?

6. Alex's batting average is 0.346. What is his batting average rounded to the nearest hundredth?

Name _____

Lesson 17
COMMON CORE STANDARD CC.5.NBT.5
Lesson Objective: Multiply by 1-digit numbers.

Multiply by 1-Digit Numbers

You can use place value to help you multiply by 1-digit numbers.

Estimate. Then find the product. 378 × 6

Estimate: 400 × 6 = 2,400

Step 1 Multiply the ones.

Thousands	Hundreds	Tens	Ones
	3	⁴7	8
×			6
			8

Step 2 Multiply the tens.

Thousands	Hundreds	Tens	Ones
	⁴3	⁴7	8
×			6
		6	8

Step 3 Multiply the hundreds.

Thousands	Hundreds	Tens	Ones
	⁴3	⁴7	8
×			6
2,	2	6	8

So, 378 × 6 = 2,268.

Complete to find the product.

1. 7 × 472   Estimate: 7 × _____ = _____

Multiply the ones.   Multiply the tens.   Multiply the hundreds.

```
  472                  1                 51
×   7               472               472
  ───              ×   7             ×   7
```

Estimate. Then find the product.

2. Estimate: _____

```
  863
×   8
```

3. Estimate: _____

```
  809
×   8
```

4. Estimate: _____

```
  932
×   7
```

5. Estimate: _____

```
2,767
×    7
```

1. A bus driver travels 234 miles every day. How many miles does the bus driver travel in 5 days?

   (A) 1,050 miles

   (B) 1,150 miles

   (C) 1,170 miles

   (D) 1,520 miles

2. Hector does 165 sit-ups every day. How many sit-ups does he do in 7 days?

   (A) 1,155

   (B) 1,145

   (C) 1,125

   (D) 725

3. Lara and Chad are both saving to buy cars. So far, Chad has saved $1,235. Lara has saved 5 times as much as Chad. How much has Lara saved?

   (A) $5,055

   (B) $6,055

   (C) $6,075

   (D) $6,175

4. Mavis drives 634 miles to visit her grandmother in Philadelphia. How many miles does Mavis drive if she visits her grandmother 4 times?

   (A) 2,426 miles

   (B) 2,436 miles

   (C) 2,536 miles

   (D) 2,836 miles

Problem Solving REAL WORLD

5. Mr. and Mrs. Dorsey and their three children are flying to Springfield. The cost of each ticket is $179. Estimate how much the tickets will cost. Then find the exact cost of the tickets.

   _____

   _____

   _____

6. Ms. Tao flies roundtrip twice yearly between Jacksonville and Los Angeles on business. The distance between the two cities is 2,150 miles. Estimate the distance she flies for both trips. Then find the exact distance.

   _____

   _____

   _____

Name _____

Lesson 18
COMMON CORE STANDARD CC.5.NBT.5
Lesson Objective: Multiply by 2-digit numbers.

Multiply by 2-Digit Numbers

You can use place value and regrouping to multiply.

Find 29 × 63.

Step 1 Write the problem vertically.
Multiply by the ones.

$$\begin{array}{r} \overset{2}{63} \\ \times\ 29 \\ \hline 567 \end{array}$$ ← $63 \times 9 = (\underline{60} \times 9) + (\underline{3} \times 9)$
$= \underline{540} + \underline{27}$, or $\underline{567}$

Step 2 Multiply by the tens.

$$\begin{array}{r} \overset{2}{63} \\ \times\ 29 \\ \hline 567 \\ 1{,}260 \end{array}$$ ← $63 \times 20 = (\underline{60} \times 20) + (\underline{3} \times 20)$
$= \underline{1{,}200} + \underline{60}$, or $\underline{1{,}260}$

Step 3 Add the partial products.

$$\begin{array}{r} 63 \\ \times\ 29 \\ \hline 567 \\ +\ 1{,}260 \\ \hline 1{,}827 \end{array}$$

So, $63 \times 29 = 1{,}827$.

Complete to find the product.

1.
$$\begin{array}{r} 57 \\ \times\ 14 \end{array}$$
← 57 × _____
+ _____ ← 57 × _____

2.
$$\begin{array}{r} 76 \\ \times\ 45 \end{array}$$
← 76 × _____
+ _____ ← 76 × _____

3.
$$\begin{array}{r} 139 \\ \times\ 12 \end{array}$$
← 139 × _____
+ _____ ← 139 × _____

4. Find 26 × 69. Estimate first.
$$\begin{array}{r} 69 \\ \times\ 26 \end{array}$$

Estimate: _____

1. Chen burns 354 calories in 1 hour swimming. He swam for 28 hours last month. How many calories did Chen burn in all last month from swimming?

Ⓐ 3,010 calories
Ⓑ 8,482 calories
Ⓒ 9,912 calories
Ⓓ 10,266 calories

2. Rachel earns $27 per hour at work. She worked 936 hours last year. How much did Rachel earn working last year?

Ⓐ $7,584
Ⓑ $24,932
Ⓒ $25,272
Ⓓ $25,332

3. A company manufactures 295 toy cars each day. How many toy cars do they manufacture in 34 days?

Ⓐ 3,065
Ⓑ 7,610
Ⓒ 10,065
Ⓓ 10,030

4. Raul earns $24 per hour painting houses. If he works for 263 hours, how much will Raul earn in all?

Ⓐ $6,312
Ⓑ $6,112
Ⓒ $5,102
Ⓓ $1,578

Problem Solving REAL WORLD

5. A company shipped 48 boxes of canned dog food. Each box contains 24 cans. How many cans of dog food did the company ship in all?

6. There were 135 cars in a rally. Each driver paid a $25 fee to participate in the rally. How much money did the drivers pay in all?

Name _____

Lesson 19
COMMON CORE STANDARD CC.5.NBT.6
Lesson Objective: Use properties of
operations to solve problems.

Algebra • Properties

Properties of operations are characteristics of the operations that are always true.

Property	Examples
Commutative Property of Addition or Multiplication	Addition: $3 + 4 = 4 + 3$ Multiplication: $8 \times 2 = 2 \times 8$
Associative Property of Addition or Multiplication	Addition: $(1 + 2) + 3 = 1 + (2 + 3)$ Multiplication: $6 \times (7 \times 2) = (6 \times 7) \times 2$
Distributive Property	$8 \times (2 + 3) = (8 \times 2) + (8 \times 3)$
Identity Property of Addition	$9 + 0 = 9$ $\qquad$ $0 + 3 = 3$
Identity Property of Multiplication	$54 \times 1 = 54$ $\qquad$ $1 \times 16 = 16$

Use properties to find $37 + 24 + 43$.

$37 + 24 + 43 = 24 + \underline{37} + 43$ $\qquad$ Use the <u>Commutative</u> Property of Addition
to reorder the addends.

$= 24 + (37 + 43)$ $\qquad$ Use the Associative Property of <u>Addition</u>
to group the addends.

$= 24 + \underline{80}$ $\qquad$ Use mental math to add.

$= \underline{104}$

Grouping 37 and 43 makes the problem easier to solve
because their sum, $\underline{80}$, is a multiple of 10.

Use properties to find the sum or product.

1. $31 + 27 + 29$ $\qquad$ 2. $41 \times 0 \times 3$ $\qquad$ 3. $4 + (6 + 21)$

_____ $\qquad$ _____ $\qquad$ _____

Complete the equation, and tell which property you used.

4. $(2 \times \underline{\quad}) + (2 \times 2) = 2 \times (5 + 2)$ $\qquad$ 5. $\underline{\quad} \times 1 = 15$

_____ $\qquad$ _____

_____ $\qquad$ _____

1. Sherry's family is going to a beach resort. Sherry bought 7 beach towels that cost $13 each to take to the resort. To find the total cost, she added the products of 7×10 and 7×3, for a total of $91. What property did Sherry use?

   (A) Commutative Property of Multiplication

   (B) Commutative Property of Addition

   (C) Associative Property of Multiplication

   (D) Distributive Property

2. Chen bought a basketball for $23, a pair of running shoes for $35, and a baseball cap for $7. He wrote the equation $23 + 35 + 7 = 23 + 7 + 35$. What property did Chen use?

   (A) Associative Property of Addition

   (B) Commutative Property of Addition

   (C) Distributive Property

   (D) Identity Property of Multiplication

3. Nicole baked 9 trays of cookies. Each tray had 5 rows with 4 cookies in each row. Nicole wrote the equation $(9 \times 5) \times 4 = 9 \times (5 \times 4)$. What property did Nicole use?

   (A) Commutative Property of Multiplication

   (B) Associative Property of Addition

   (C) Associative Property of Multiplication

   (D) Distributive Property

4. Ramon has a large collection of marbles. He has 150 clear marbles, 214 blue marbles, and 89 green marbles. Ramon wrote this equation about his marble collection:

   $(150 + 214) + 89 = 150 + (214 + 89)$

   What property did Ramon use?

   (A) Associative Property of Addition

   (B) Commutative Property of Addition

   (C) Identity Property of Addition

   (D) Distributive Property

Problem Solving REAL WORLD

5. The Metro Theater has 20 rows of seats with 18 seats in each row. Tickets cost $5. The theater's income in dollars if all seats are sold is $(20 \times 18) \times 5$. Use properties to find the total income.

6. The numbers of students in the four sixth-grade classes at Northside School are 26, 19, 34, and 21. Use properties to find the total number of students in the four classes.

Lesson 20
COMMON CORE STANDARD CC.5.NBT.6
Lesson Objective: Use multiplication to
solve division problems.

Relate Multiplication to Division

Use the Distributive Property to find the quotient of 56 ÷ 4.

Step 1
Write a related multiplication sentence
for the division problem.

$56 ÷ 4 = \Box$

$4 × \Box = 56$

Step 2
Use the Distributive Property to break apart
the product into lesser numbers that are
multiples of the divisor in the division problem.
Use a multiple of 10 for one of the multiples.

$(40 + 16) = 56$

$(4 × 10) + (4 × 4) = 56$

$4 × (10 + 4) = 56$

Step 3
To find the unknown factor, find the sum of the numbers
inside the parentheses.

$10 + 4 = 14$

Step 4
Write the multiplication sentence with the unknown
factor you found. Then, use the multiplication sentence
to complete the division sentence.

$4 × 14 = 56$

$56 ÷ 4 = 14$

Use multiplication and the Distributive Property to find the quotient

1. $68 ÷ 4 =$ _____

2. $75 ÷ 3 =$ _____

3. $96 ÷ 6 =$ _____

4. $80 ÷ 5 =$ _____

5. $54 ÷ 3 =$ _____

6. $105 ÷ 7 =$ _____

1. Francine took 42 photos with her digital camera. She stored an equal number of photos in each of 3 folders on her computer. Which multiplication sentence could Francine use to find the number of photos in each folder?

   (A) $3 \times 14 = 42$

   (B) $3 \times 40 = 120$

   (C) $3 \times 42 = 126$

   (D) $4 \times 42 = 168$

2. Amber baked 120 cookies to give to 5 friends. She wants to put the same number of cookies in each bag. Which of the following can she use to find how many cookies to put in each bag?

   (A) $(5 \times 20) + (5 \times 4)$

   (B) $(5 \times 10) + (5 \times 8)$

   (C) $(5 \times 60) + (5 \times 2)$

   (D) $(5 \times 15) + (5 \times 5)$

3. Shari sent a total of 64 text messages to 4 friends. Each friend received the same number of text messages. Which multiplication sentence could Shari use to find the number of text messages she sent to each friend?

   (A) $4 \times 64 = 256$

   (B) $60 \times 4 = 240$

   (C) $5 \times 64 = 320$

   (D) $4 \times 16 = 64$

4. Jared has 96 books to arrange on 6 shelves of a bookcase. He wants each shelf to have the same number of books. Which of the following **cannot** be used to find how many books Jared can put on each shelf?

   (A) $(6 \times 10) + (6 \times 6)$

   (B) $(6 \times 8) + (6 \times 8)$

   (C) $(6 \times 4) + (6 \times 4)$

   (D) $(6 \times 15) + (6 \times 1)$

Problem Solving REAL WORLD

5. Ken is making gift bags for a party. He has 64 colored pens and wants to put the same number in each bag. How many bags will Ken make if he puts 4 pens in each bag?

   _____

6. Maritza is buying wheels for her skateboard shop. She ordered a total of 92 wheels. If wheels come in packages of 4, how many packages will she receive?

   _____

Name _____

Lesson **21**
COMMON CORE STANDARD CC.5.NBT.6
Lesson Objective: Use the strategy *solve a simpler problem* to solve problems.

Problem Solving • Multiplication and Division

In Brett's town, there are 128 baseball players on 8 different teams. Each team has an equal number of players. How many players are on each team?

Read the Problem	Solve the Problem
What do I need to find? I need to find **how many players are on each team in Brett's town**. **What information do I need to use?** There are **8 teams** with a total of **128 players**. **How will I use the information?** I can **divide** the total number of players by the number of teams. I can use a simpler problem to **divide**.	• First, I use the total number of players. **128 players** • To find the number of players on each team, I will need to solve this problem. $128 \div 8 =$ ___**?**___ • To find the quotient, I break 128 into two simpler numbers that are easier to divide. $128 \div 8 = (80 + \underline{48}) \div 8$ $= (\underline{80} \div 8) + (\underline{48} \div 8)$ $= \underline{10} + 6$ $= \underline{16}$ So, there are **16** players on each team.

1. Susan makes clay pots. She sells 125 pots per month to 5 stores. Each store buys the same number of pots. How many pots does each store buy?

    $125 \div 5 = (100 + \underline{\hspace{1cm}}) \div 5$

    $= (100 \div 5) + (\underline{\hspace{1cm}} \div 5)$

    $= \underline{\hspace{1cm}} + 5$

    $= \underline{\hspace{1cm}}$

    _____

2. Lou grows 112 rosemary plants. He ships an equal number of plants to customers in 8 states. How many rosemary plants does he ship to each customer?

    $112 \div 8 = (80 + \underline{\hspace{1cm}}) \div 8$

    $= (\underline{\hspace{1cm}} \div 8) + (\underline{\hspace{1cm}} \div 8)$

    $= \underline{\hspace{1cm}} + 4$

    $= \underline{\hspace{1cm}}$

    _____

1. Marta has 16 postcards from each of 8 different cities in Pennsylvania. She can fit 4 postcards on each page of her scrapbook. How many pages in the scrapbook can Marta fill with postcards?

  Ⓐ 32
  Ⓑ 41
  Ⓒ 128
  Ⓓ 512

2. Nathan's orchestra has 18 string musicians, 9 percussion musicians, 15 brass musicians, and 12 woodwind musicians. Six of the musicians cannot play in the next performance. If the remaining musicians plan to sit in rows of 6 chairs, how many rows of chairs are needed?

  Ⓐ 4
  Ⓑ 6
  Ⓒ 8
  Ⓓ 9

3. There are 6 buses transporting students to a baseball game, with 32 students on each bus. Each row at the baseball stadium seats 8 students. If the students fill up all of the rows, how many rows of seats will the students need altogether?

  Ⓐ 22
  Ⓑ 23
  Ⓒ 24
  Ⓓ 1,536

4. Laura has 24 stamps from each of 6 different countries. She can fit 4 stamps on each display sheet of an album. How many display sheets can Laura fill with stamps?

  Ⓐ 576
  Ⓑ 36
  Ⓒ 34
  Ⓓ 16

Problem Solving REAL WORLD

5. Ming's DVD collection includes 16 adventure movies, 7 comedies, 12 westerns, and 8 mysteries. He wants to keep 2 of each type of DVD and give away the rest. Ming says that if he gives an equal number of DVDs to 5 friends, he will give each friend 7 DVDs. Do you agree? Support your answer.

_____

_____

_____

_____

Place the First Digit

When you divide, you can use estimation or place value to place the first digit of the quotient.

Divide.

6)1,266

- Estimate. 1,200 ÷ 6 = 200, so the first digit of the quotient is in the hundreds place.
- Divide the hundreds.
- Divide the tens.
- Divide the ones.

So, 1,266 ÷ 6 = 211.

Since 211 is close to the estimate, 200, the answer is reasonable.

```
    211
6)1,266
   -12↓
    06↓
    -6
    06
    -6
     0
```

Divide.

8,895 ÷ 8

- Use place value to place the first digit.
- Look at the first digit.
    If the first digit is less than the divisor, then the first digit of the quotient will be in the hundreds place.
    If the first digit is greater than or equal to the divisor, then the first digit of the quotient will be in the thousands place.
- Since 8 thousands can be shared among 8 groups, the first digit of the quotient will be in the thousands place. Now divide.

So, 8,895 ÷ 8 is 1,111 r7.

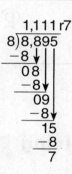

```
  1,111 r7
8)8,895
  -8↓
   08↓
   -8↓
    09↓
    -8↓
     15
     -8
      7
```

Divide.

1. 3)627

2. 5)7,433

3. 4)5,367

4. 9)6,470

5. 8)2,869

6. 6)1,299

7. 4)893

8. 7)4,418

1. Caleb needs to solve the problem
   2,406 ÷ 6. In what place is the first
   digit of the quotient for the problem
   2,406 ÷ 6?

   (A) ones   (C) hundreds

   (B) tens   (D) thousands

2. Mrs. Tao has 154 books on 7 shelves in her
   classroom. Each shelf has the same number
   of books on it. She wants to find out the
   number of books on each shelf. In what place
   should Mrs. Tao write the first digit of the
   quotient for the problem 154 ÷ 7?

   (A) ones   (C) hundreds

   (B) tens   (D) thousands

3. The last problem on Jacob's math test was
   9,072 ÷ 9. In what place should Jacob
   write the first digit of the quotient for the
   problem 9,072 ÷ 9?

   (A) ones   (C) hundreds

   (B) tens   (D) thousands

4. Raul has 486 baseball cards in 9 albums.
   Each album has the same number of
   baseball cards. He wants to find the
   number of baseball cards in each album.
   In what place should Raul write the first
   digit of the quotient for the problem
   486 ÷ 9?

   (A) ones   (C) hundreds

   (B) tens   (D) thousands

Problem Solving REAL WORLD

5. The school theater department made $2,142
   on ticket sales for the three nights of their
   play. The department sold the same number
   of tickets each night and each ticket cost $7.
   How many tickets did the theater department
   sell each night?

   _____

6. Andreus made $625 mowing yards. He
   worked for 5 consecutive days and earned the
   same amount of money each day. How much
   money did Andreus earn per day?

   _____

Name _____

Lesson 23

COMMON CORE STANDARD CC.5.NBT.6

Lesson Objective: Divide 3- and 4-digit dividends by 1-digit divisors.

Divide by 1-Digit Divisors

You can use compatible numbers to help you place the first digit in the quotient. Then you can divide and check your answer.

Divide. $4\overline{)757}$

Step 1 Estimate with compatible numbers to decide where to place the first digit.

$757 \div 4$

$\downarrow$

$800 \div 4 = 200$

The first digit of the quotient is in the hundreds place.

Step 2 Divide.

$$
\begin{array}{r}
189\ r1 \\
4\overline{)757} \\
-4\downarrow \\
\overline{35} \\
-32\downarrow \\
\overline{37} \\
-36 \\
\overline{1}
\end{array}
$$

Step 3 Check your answer.

$$
\begin{array}{r}
189 \leftarrow \text{quotient} \\
\times\ 4 \leftarrow \text{divisor} \\
\overline{756} \\
+\ 1 \leftarrow \text{remainder} \\
\overline{757} \leftarrow \text{dividend}
\end{array}
$$

Since 189 is close to the estimate of 200, the answer is reasonable.

So, $757 \div 4$ is 189 r1.

Divide. Check your answer.

1. $8\overline{)136}$

2. $7\overline{)297}$

3. $5\overline{)8,126}$

4. $7\overline{)4,973}$

5. $3\overline{)741}$

6. $7\overline{)456}$

1. During a school fund raiser, the fifth-grade classes sold rolls of wrapping paper. The table shows how many rolls each class sold. The rolls were sold in packages of 4.

Wrapping Paper Sold

Class	Total Rolls
Ms. Lane	672
Mr. Milner	184
Mrs. Jackson	228

How many packages of wrapping paper did Ms. Lane's class sell?

(A) 2,688   (C) 168
(B) 173   (D) 143

2. Sophia wants to buy collector boxes that can hold 6 dolls each. How many boxes will Sophia need to buy for her collection of 168 dolls?

(A) 21   (C)   34
(B) 28   (D) 1,008

3. On a standard week-long space shuttle flight, 175 servings of fresh food are shared equally among 7 crewmembers. How many servings of fresh food does each crewmember receive?

(A) 25   (C) 32
(B) 26   (D) 33

4. A bakery sold croissants to local restaurants. The table shows how many croissants were sold to each restaurant. The croissants were sold 6 to a box.

Croissants Sold

Restaurant	Number of Croissants
The Coffee Counter	546
La Claudette	768
Bon Jour	858

How many boxes of croissants did the bakery sell to La Claudette?

(A)   4,608   (C) 128
(B)   143   (D) 96

Problem Solving REAL WORLD

5. Randy has 128 ounces of dog food. He feeds his dog 8 ounces of food each day. How many days will the dog food last?

6. Angelina bought a 64-ounce can of lemonade mix. She uses 4 ounces of mix for each pitcher of lemonade. How many pitchers of lemonade can Angelina make from the can of mix?

Name _____

Lesson 24
COMMON CORE STANDARD CC.5.NBT.6
Lesson Objective: Model division with 2-digit divisors using base-ten blocks.

Division with 2-Digit Divisors

You can use base-ten blocks to model division with 2-digit divisors.

Divide. 154 ÷ 11

Step 1 Model 154 with base-ten blocks.

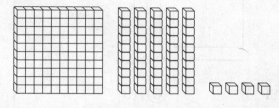

Step 2 Make equal groups of 11. Each group

should contain ___1___ ten and ___1___ one.

You can make 4 groups of 11 without regrouping.

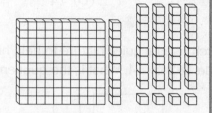

Step 3 Regroup 1 hundred as __10 tens__.

Regroup 1 ten as __10 ones__.

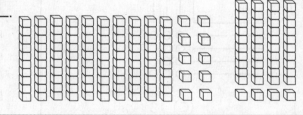

Step 4 Use the regrouped blocks to make as many groups of 11 as possible. Then count the total number of groups.

There are ___14___ groups. So, 154 ÷ 11 = ___14___.

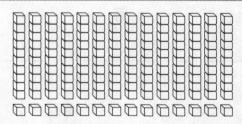

Divide. Use base-ten blocks.

1. 192 ÷ 12 _____

2. 182 ÷ 14 _____

1. Emma used a quick picture to help her divide 154 by 11. What is the quotient?

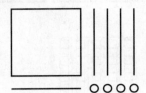

(A) 11   (C) 13
(B) 12   (D) 14

2. Garrett used a quick picture to help him divide 182 by 14. What is the quotient?

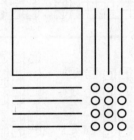

(A) 11   (C) 13
(B) 12   (D) 14

3. Latoya drew a quick picture to solve a division problem. Which division problem does the quick picture show?

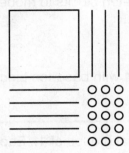

(A) 195 ÷ 15 = 13
(B) 169 ÷ 13 = 13
(C) 180 ÷ 15 = 12
(D) 165 ÷ 15 = 11

4. Ling has 168 baseball cards. He put the same number of cards into each of 14 piles. How many baseball cards did Ling put in each pile?

(A) 11   (C) 13
(B) 12   (D) 14

Problem Solving REAL WORLD

5. There are 182 seats in a theater. The seats are evenly divided into 13 rows. How many seats are in each row?

6. There are 156 students at summer camp. The camp has 13 cabins. An equal number of students sleep in each cabin. How many students sleep in each cabin?

Name _____

Lesson 25

COMMON CORE STANDARD CC.5.NBT.6

Lesson Objective: Use partial quotients to divide by 2-digit divisors.

Partial Quotients

Divide. Use partial quotients.

$858 \div 57$

		Quotient
	858	
	−570	10
	288	

Step 1 Estimate the number of groups of 57 that are in 858. You know $57 \times 10 = 570$. Since $570 < 858$, at least 10 groups of 57 are in 858. Write 10 in the quotient column, because 10 groups of the divisor, 57, are in the dividend, 858.

	288	
	−228	4
	60	

Step 2 Now estimate the number of groups of 57 that are in 288. You know $60 \times 4 = 240$. So at least 4 groups of 57 are in 288. Subtract 228 from 288, because $57 \times 4 = 228$. Write 4 in the quotient column, because 4 groups of the divisor, 57, are in 288.

	60	
	−57	+ 1
remainder →	3	15

Step 3 Identify the number of groups of 57 that are in 60. $57 \times 1 = 57$, so there is 1 group of 57 in 60. Write 1 in the quotient column.

Step 4 Find the total number of groups of the divisor, 57, that are in the dividend, 858, by adding the numbers in the quotient column. Include the remainder in your answer.

Answer: 15 r3

Divide. Use partial quotients.

1. $17\overline{)476}$

2. $14\overline{)365}$

3. $25\overline{)753}$

4. $462 \div 11$

5. $1,913 \div 47$

6. $1,085 \div 32$

1. Jacob divided 976 by 28 using partial quotients. What is missing from Jacob's work?

$$
\begin{array}{r}
34\ r24 \\
28\overline{)976} \\
-280 \quad \leftarrow 10 \times 28 \qquad 10 \\
\overline{696} \\
-280 \quad \leftarrow 10 \times 28 \qquad 10 \\
\overline{416} \\
-280 \quad \leftarrow 10 \times 28 \qquad 10 \\
\overline{136} \\
-\square \quad \leftarrow 4 \times 28 \quad +\ 4 \\
\overline{24} \qquad\qquad\qquad 34
\end{array}
$$

(A) 24

(C) 112

(B) 34

(D) 280

2. Orah takes an 18-day bike tour. She rides 756 miles in all. What is the average number of miles she rides each day?

(A) 32

(C) 90

(B) 42

(D) 92

3. Paloma divided 1,292 by 31 using partial quotients. What is the quotient?

$$
\begin{array}{r}
31\overline{)1,292} \\
-930 \quad \leftarrow 30 \times 31 \qquad 30 \\
\overline{362} \\
-310 \quad \leftarrow 10 \times 31 \qquad 10 \\
\overline{52} \\
-31 \quad \leftarrow 1 \times 31 \qquad +\ 1 \\
\overline{21} \qquad\qquad\qquad 41
\end{array}
$$

(A) 21

(C) 41

(B) 21 r41

(D) 41 r21

4. The school library has 2,976 books on its shelves. Each shelf has 48 books on it. How many shelves are in the library?

(A) 42

(B) 52

(C) 62

(D) 192

Problem Solving REAL WORLD

5. A factory processes 1,560 ounces of olive oil per hour. The oil is packaged into 24-ounce bottles. How many bottles does the factory fill in one hour?

_____

6. A pond at a hotel holds 4,290 gallons of water. The groundskeeper drains the pond at a rate of 78 gallons of water per hour. How long will it take to drain the pond?

_____

Name _____

Lesson 26
COMMON CORE STANDARD CC.5.NBT.6
Lesson Objective: Estimate quotients using compatible numbers.

Estimate with 2-Digit Divisors

You can use *compatible numbers* to estimate quotients. Compatible numbers are numbers that are easy to compute with mentally.

To find two estimates with compatible numbers, first round the divisor. Then list multiples of the rounded divisor until you find the two multiples that are closest to the dividend. Use the one less than and the one greater than the dividend.

Use compatible numbers to find two estimates. $4,125 \div 49$

Step 1 Round the divisor to the nearest ten.
49 rounds to __50__.

Step 2 List multiples of 50 until you get the two closest to the dividend, 4,125.
Some multiples of 50 are:

500   1,000   1,500   2,000   2,500   3,000   3,500   4,000   4,500
__4,000__ and __4,500__ are closest to the dividend.

Step 3 Divide the compatible numbers to estimate the quotient.
$4,000 \div 50 =$ __80__ $4,500 \div 50 =$ __90__

The more reasonable estimate is $4,000 \div 50 = 80$, because __4,000__ is closer to 4,125 than 4,500 is.

Use compatible numbers to find two estimates.

1. $42\overline{)1,578}$

2. $73\overline{)4,858}$

3. $54\overline{)343}$

4. $4,093 \div 63$

5. $4,785 \div 79$

6. $7,459 \div 94$

Use compatible numbers to estimate the quotient.

7. $847 \div 37$

8. $6,577 \div 89$

9. $218 \div 29$

1. Lauren bought a television that cost $805. She plans to make equal payments of $38 each month until the television is paid in full. About how many payments will Lauren make?

   (A) 20
   (B) 30
   (C) 38
   (D) 40

2. Miss Roja plans to sell tote bags at the art festival for $33 each. She will need to make $265 to pay the rent for the space at the festival. About how many tote bags will she need to sell to pay the rent?

   (A) 3
   (B) 7
   (C) 9
   (D) 30

3. Mrs. Ortega bought a dishwasher that cost $579. She will make monthly payments in the amount of $28 until the dishwasher is paid in full. About how many payments will Mrs. Ortega make?

   (A) 12
   (B) 20
   (C) 28
   (D) 30

4. Doug plans to sell mugs at the craft fair for $21 each. He will need to make $182 to pay the rent for the space at the fair. About how many mugs will he need to sell to pay the rent?

   (A) 2
   (B) 6
   (C) 9
   (D) 20

Problem Solving REAL WORLD

5. A cubic yard of topsoil weighs 4,128 pounds. About how many 50-pound bags of topsoil can you fill with one cubic yard of topsoil?

   _____

6. An electronics store places an order for 2,665 USB flash drives. One shipping box holds 36 flash drives. About how many boxes will it take to hold all the flash drives?

   _____

Name _____

Lesson 27
COMMON CORE STANDARD CC.5.NBT.6
Lesson Objective: Divide by 2-digit divisors.

Divide by 2-Digit Divisors

When you divide by a 2-digit divisor, you can use estimation to help you place the first digit in the quotient. Then you can divide.

Divide. $53\overline{)2{,}369}$

Step 1 Use compatible numbers to estimate the quotient. Then use the estimate to place the first digit in the quotient.

$$\begin{array}{r} 40 \\ 50\overline{)2{,}000} \end{array}$$

The first digit will be in the tens place.

Step 2 Divide the tens.

$$\begin{array}{r} 4 \\ 53\overline{)2{,}369} \\ -\underline{212} \\ 24 \end{array}$$

Think:

Divide: 236 tens ÷ 53

Multiply: 53 × 4 tens = 212 tens

Subtract: 236 tens − 212 tens

Compare: 24 < 53, so the first digit of the quotient is reasonable.

Step 3 Bring down the 9 ones. Then divide the ones.

$$\begin{array}{r} 44\ r37 \\ 53\overline{)2{,}369} \\ -\underline{212}\downarrow \\ 249 \\ -\underline{212} \\ 37 \end{array}$$

Think:

Divide: 249 ones ÷ 53

Multiply: 53 × 4 ones = 212 ones

Subtract: 249 ones − 212 ones

Compare: 37 < 53, so the second digit of the quotient is reasonable.

Write the remainder to the right of the whole number part of the quotient.

So, 2,369 ÷ 53 is <u>44 r37</u>.

Divide. Check your answer.

1. $52\overline{)612}$

2. $63\overline{)917}$

3. $89\overline{)1{,}597}$

4. $43\overline{)641}$

5. $27\overline{)4{,}684}$

6. $64\overline{)8{,}455}$

1. The local concert hall has 48 concerts scheduled this season. Each concert has the same number of tickets available for sale. There is a total of 4,560 tickets. How many tickets are available for each concert?

(A) 1,140
(B) 950
(C) 105
(D) 95

2. The director of a pet shelter received a shipment of 1,110 puppy blankets. He put the same number of blankets in each of 27 boxes and put the leftover blankets in the puppy kennels. How many blankets were put in the puppy kennels?

(A) 3
(B) 18
(C) 28
(D) 41

3. An airplane has 416 seats arranged in 52 rows. If there is the same number of seats in each row, how many seats are in one row?

(A) 21,632
(B) 364
(C) 8
(D) 6

4. Mr. Stephens needs to haul 1,518 tons of rock from a construction site. His dump truck can hold 26 tons per load. How many tons will Mr. Stephens need to haul in the last load to move all of the rock?

(A) 10
(B) 58
(C) 68
(D) 1,492

Problem Solving REAL WORLD

5. The factory workers make 756 machine parts in 36 hours. Suppose the workers make the same number of machine parts each hour. How many machine parts do they make each hour?

6. One bag holds 12 bolts. Several bags filled with bolts are packed into a box and shipped to the factory. The box contains a total of 2,760 bolts. How many bags of bolts are in the box?

Name _____

Lesson 28

COMMON CORE STANDARD CC.5.NBT.6

Lesson Objective: Adjust the quotient if the
estimate is too high or too low.

Adjust Quotients

When you divide, you can use the first digit of your estimate as
the first digit of your quotient. Sometimes the first digit will be
too high or too low. Then you have to adjust the quotient by
increasing or decreasing the first digit.

Estimate Too High		**Estimate Too Low**	
Divide. 271 ÷ 48		**Divide.** 2,462 ÷ 27	
Estimate. 300 ÷ 50 = 6		**Estimate.** 2,400 ÷ 30 = 80	
Try 6 ones. 6 $48)\overline{271}$ $\underline{-288}$	Try 5 ones. $5\ r31$ $48)\overline{271}$ $\underline{-240}$ 31	Try 8 tens. 8 $27)\overline{2,462}$ $\underline{-2\ 16}$ 30	Try 9 tens. $91\ r5$ $27)\overline{2,462}$ $\underline{-2\ 43}$ 32 $\underline{-27}$ 5
You cannot subtract 288 from 271. So, the estimate is too high.	So, 271 ÷ 48 is 5 r31.	30 is greater than the divisor. So, the estimate is too low.	So, 2,462 ÷ 27 is 91 r5.

Adjust the estimated digit in the quotient, if needed. Then divide.

1. $\overset{2}{58)\overline{1,325}}$

2. $\overset{6}{37)\overline{241}}$

3. $\overset{8}{29)\overline{2,276}}$

Divide.

4. $16)\overline{845}$

5. $24)\overline{217}$

6. $37)\overline{4,819}$

1. To solve the division problem below, Kyle estimates that 2 is the first digit in the quotient.

$$\begin{array}{r} 2 \\ 29\overline{)556} \\ -58 \end{array}$$

Which of the following is correct?

(A) 2 is the correct first digit of the quotient.

(B) 2 is too low. The first digit should be adjusted to 4.

(C) 2 is too low. The first digit should be adjusted to 3.

(D) 2 is too high. The first digit should be adjusted to 1.

2. Alex is saving up to buy a guitar that costs $855. He plans to save $45 a month. How many months will it take him to save enough money to buy the guitar?

(A) 19 months

(B) 21 months

(C) 23 months

(D) 25 months

3. An auditorium has 1,224 seats. There are 36 seats in each row. How many rows of seats are in the auditorium?

(A) 32

(B) 34

(C) 42

(D) 44

4. Diego estimates that 3 is the first digit in the quotient of the problem below.

$$\begin{array}{r} 3 \\ 16\overline{)4272} \\ -48 \end{array}$$

Which of the following is correct?

(A) 3 is the correct first digit of the quotient.

(B) 3 is too low. The first digit should be adjusted to 4.

(C) 3 is too low. The first digit should be adjusted to 5.

(D) 3 is too high. The first digit should be adjusted to 2.

Problem Solving REAL WORLD

5. A copier prints 89 copies in one minute. How long does it take the copier to print 1,958 copies?

6. Erica is saving her money to buy a dining room set that costs $580. If she saves $29 each month, how many months will she need to save to have enough money to buy the set?

Name _____

Lesson 29
COMMON CORE STANDARD CC.5.NBT.6
Lesson Objective: Solve problems by using the strategy *Draw a Diagram.*

Problem Solving • Division

Sara and Sam picked apples over the weekend. Sam picked nine times as many apples as Sara. Together, they picked 310 apples. How many apples did each person pick?

Read the Problem		
What do I need to find I need to find **the number of apples each person picked.**	**What information do I need to use?** I need to know that Sam and Sara picked a total of **310** apples. I need to know that Sam picked **9** times as many apples as Sara.	**How will I use the information?** I can use the strategy **draw a diagram** to organize the information. I can draw and use a bar model to write the division problem that will help me find the number of apples Sam and Sara each picked.

Solve the Problem

My bar model needs to have one box for the number of apples Sara picked and nine boxes for the number of apples Sam picked. I can divide the total number of apples picked by the total number of boxes.

Sara | 31 |

Sam | 31 | 31 | 31 | 31 | 31 | 31 | 31 | 31 | 31 |

310

$$\begin{array}{r} 31 \\ 10)\overline{310} \\ -30 \\ \hline 10 \\ -10 \\ \hline 0 \end{array}$$

So, Sara picked ____31____ apples and Sam picked ____279____ apples.

Solve each problem. To help, draw a bar model on a separate sheet of paper.

1. Kai picked 11 times as many blueberries as Nico. Together, they picked 936 blueberries. How many blueberries did each boy pick?

2. Jen wrote 10 times as many pages of a school report as Tom. They wrote 396 pages altogether. How many pages did each student write?

1. Ricardo's dog weighs 6 times as much as his cat. The total weight of his two pets is 98 pounds. How much does Ricardo's dog weigh?

   (A) 92 pounds
   (B) 84 pounds
   (C) 16 pounds
   (D) 14 pounds

2. The number of children at the library was 3 times the number of adults. The total number of people at the library was 48. How many children were at the library?

   (A) 12
   (B) 24
   (C) 32
   (D) 36

3. Sarah baby-sat 7 times as many hours during summer break as she did during spring break. She baby-sat a total of 56 hours during both breaks. How many hours did Sarah baby-sit during spring break?

   (A) 49 hours
   (B) 9 hours
   (C) 8 hours
   (D) 7 hours

4. Melanie is 3 times as old as her cousin. The total of their ages is 36 years. How old is Melanie's cousin?

   (A) 9 years old
   (B) 12 years old
   (C) 27 years old
   (D) 33 years old

Problem Solving REAL WORLD

5. Ian and Joe took their younger sister Michelle to pick strawberries. Ian picked 5 times as many strawberries as Michelle. Joe picked 7 times as many strawberries as Michelle. Ian and Joe picked a total of 192 strawberries. How many strawberries did Joe pick? Use a diagram to help find the answer. Explain how you used the diagram to answer the question.

   _____

   _____

   _____

   _____

   _____

Name _____

Lesson 30
COMMON CORE STANDARD CC.5.NBT.7
Lesson Objective: Model decimal addition
using base-ten blocks.

Decimal Addition

You can use decimal models to help you add decimals.

Add. 1.25 + 0.85

Step 1 Shade squares to represent 1.25.

Step 2 Shade additional squares to
represent adding 0.85.

Remember:
Since there are only 75 squares
left in the second model, you need to
add another whole model for the
remaining 10 squares.

Step 3 Count the total number of shaded squares.
There are 2 whole squares and 10 one-hundredths
squares shaded. So, 2.10 wholes in all are shaded.

So, 1.25 + 0.85 = __2.10__.

**Add. Use decimal models. Draw a picture
to show your work.**

1. 2.1 + 0.59

_____

2. 1.4 + 0.22

_____

3. 1.27 + 1.15

_____

4. 0.81 + 0.43

_____

1. Ken used a quick picture to model
   $1.77 + 1.19$. Which picture shows
   the sum?

   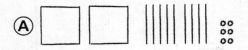
   (A)

   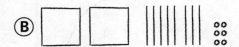
   (B)

   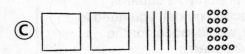
   (C)

   (D)

2. It took Margo 0.5 hour to do her science
   homework and 0.9 hour to do her math
   homework. How long did it take Margo to
   do her science and math homework?

   (A) 0.14 hour   (C) 1.04 hours

   (B) 0.45 hour   (D) 1.4 hours

3. It took Ray 0.45 hour to rake the leaves
   and 0.75 hour to mow the lawn. How long
   did it take Ray to rake the leaves and mow
   the lawn?

   (A) 0.12 hour   (C) 1.2 hours

   (B) 1.1 hours   (D) 1.21 hours

Problem Solving REAL WORLD

4. Draco bought 0.6 pound of bananas and
   0.9 pound of grapes at the farmers' market.
   What is the total weight of the fruit?

   _____

5. Nancy biked 2.65 miles in the morning
   and 3.19 miles in the afternoon. What total
   distance did she bike?

   _____

Name _____

Lesson 31
COMMON CORE STANDARD CC.5.NBT.7
Lesson Objective: Model decimal subtraction using base-ten blocks.

Decimal Subtraction

You can use decimal models to help you subtract decimals.

Subtract. 1.85 − 0.65

Step 1 Shade squares to represent 1.85.

Step 2 Circle and cross out 65 of the shaded squares to represent subtracting 0.65.

Remember:
By circling and crossing out shaded squares, you can see how many squares are taken away, or subtracted.

Step 3 Count the shaded squares that are not crossed out. Altogether, 1 whole square and 20 one-hundredths squares, or 1.20 wholes, are NOT crossed out.

So, 1.85 − 0.65 = _1.20_.

Subtract. Use decimal models. Draw a picture to show your work.

1. 1.4 − 0.61

2. 1.6 − 1.08

3. 0.84 − 0.17

4. 1.39 − 1.14

1. Taryn used a quick picture to model 2.34 − 1.47. Which picture shows the difference?

   Ⓐ

   Ⓑ

   Ⓒ

   Ⓓ

2. Jasmine lives 1.25 miles from school and 0.82 mile from the library. How much farther does Jasmine live from school than from the library?

   Ⓐ 0.33 mile   Ⓒ 2.07 miles

   Ⓑ 0.43 mile   Ⓓ 4.3 miles

3. Avery bought 3.45 pounds of red apples and 1.57 pounds of green apples. How many more pounds of red apples than green apples did Avery buy?

   Ⓐ 5.02 pounds

   Ⓑ 1.98 pounds

   Ⓒ 1.88 pounds

   Ⓓ 1.12 pounds

Problem Solving

4. Yelina made a training plan to run 5.6 miles per day. So far, she has run 3.1 miles today. How much farther does she have to run to meet her goal for today?

   _____

5. Tim cut a 2.3-foot length of pipe from a pipe that was 4.1 feet long. How long is the remaining piece of pipe?

   _____

Lesson **32**

COMMON CORE STANDARD CC.5.NBT.7
Lesson Objective: Make reasonable estimates of decimal sums and differences.

Estimate Decimal Sums and Differences

You can use rounding to help you estimate sums and differences.

Use rounding to estimate 1.24 + 0.82 + 3.4.

Round to the nearest whole number. Then add.

$$1.24 \longrightarrow 1$$
$$0.82 \longrightarrow 1$$
$$+\ 3.4 \longrightarrow +\ 3$$
$$\overline{5}$$

So, the sum is about ___5___.

Remember:

If the digit to the right of the place you are rounding to is:
- less than 5, the digit in the rounding place stays the same.
- greater than or equal to 5, the digit in the rounding place increases by 1.

Use benchmarks to estimate 8.78 − 0.30.

$$8.78 \longrightarrow 8.75$$
$$-\ 0.30 \longrightarrow -\ 0.25$$
$$\overline{8.5}$$

Think: 0.78 is between 0.75 and 1.
It is closer to 0.75.

Think: 0.30 is between 0.25 and 0.50.
It is closer to 0.25.

So, the difference is about ___8.5___.

Use rounding to estimate.

1. 51.23
    −28.4

2. $29.38
    +$42.75

3. 7.6
    −2.15

4. 0.74
    +0.20

5. 2.08
    0.56
    +0.41

Use benchmarks to estimate.

6. 6.17
    −3.5

7. 1.73
    1.4
    +3.17

8. 3.28
    −0.86

9. 15.27
    +41.8

10. $23.07
     −$ 7.83

11. 0.427 + 0.711

12. 61.05 − 18.63

13. 40.51 + 30.39

_____ _____ _____

1. Julie has $16.73. She buys a purse that costs $4.12. About how much money will Julie have left?

(A) $3

(B) $13

(C) $21

(D) $23

2. A vet measured the mass of two birds. The mass of the robin was 76.64 grams. The mass of the blue jay was 81.54 grams. Which is the best estimate of the difference in the masses of the birds?

(A) 5 grams

(B) 10 grams

(C) 15 grams

(D) 20 grams

3. A town plans to add a 3.88-kilometer extension to a road that is currently 5.02 kilometers long. Which is the best estimate of the length of the road after the extension is added?

(A) 1 kilometer

(B) 2 kilometers

(C) 4 kilometers

(D) 9 kilometers

4. Denise has $78.22. She wants to buy a computer game that costs $29.99. About how much money will Denise have left?

(A) $40

(B) $50

(C) $60

(D) $110

Problem Solving REAL WORLD

5. Elian bought 1.87 pounds of chicken and 2.46 pounds of turkey at the deli. About how much meat did he buy altogether?

_____

6. Jenna bought a gallon of milk at the store for $3.58. About how much change did she receive from a $20 bill?

_____

Name _____

Lesson 33
COMMON CORE STANDARD CC.5.NBT.7
Lesson Objective: Add decimals using place value.

Add Decimals

Add. 4.37 + 9.8

Step 1 Estimate the sum.

$$4.37 + 9.8$$

Estimate: 4 + 10 = 14

Step 2 Line up the place values for each number in a place-value chart. Then add.

	Ones	Tenths	Hundredths
	4	3	7
+	9	8	
	14	1	7	←sum

Step 3 Use your estimate to determine if your answer is reasonable.

Think: 14.17 is close to the estimate, 14. The answer is reasonable.

So, 4.37 + 9.8 = __14.17__.

Estimate. Then find the sum

1. Estimate: _____

```
  1.20
+ 0.34
```

2. Estimate: _____

```
  1.52
+ 1.21
```

3. Estimate: _____

```
  12.25
+ 11.25
```

4. Estimate: _____

```
  10.75
+  1.11
```

5. Estimate: _____

```
  22.65
+ 18.01
```

6. Estimate: _____

```
  34.41
+ 15.37
```

1. Yolanda's sunflower plant was 64.34 centimeters tall in July. During August, the plant grew 58.7 centimeters. How tall was Yolanda's sunflower plant at the end of August?

   (A) 702.1 centimeters

   (B) 123.04 centimeters

   (C) 70.21 centimeters

   (D) 58.7 centimeters

2. Malcolm read that 2.75 inches of rain fell on Saturday. He read that 1.6 inches of rain fell on Sunday. How much rain fell on the two days?

   (A) 1.15 inches

   (B) 2.91 inches

   (C) 3.81 inches

   (D) 4.35 inches

3. Olivia bought a beach towel for $9.95 and a beach bag for $13.46. What is the total amount of money Olivia spent on the two items?

   (A) $12.31

   (B) $23.41

   (C) $112.96

   (D) $144.55

4. Jon walked 1.75 kilometers on Monday and 3.2 kilometers on Wednesday. What was the total distance that Jon walked on Monday and Wednesday?

   (A) 33.75 kilometers

   (B) 20.7 kilometers

   (C) 4.95 kilometers

   (D) 2.07 kilometers

Problem Solving REAL WORLD

5. Marcela's dog gained 4.1 kilograms in two months. Two months ago, the dog's mass was 5.6 kilograms. What is the dog's current mass?

   _____

6. During last week's storm, 2.15 inches of rain fell on Monday and 1.68 inches of rain fell on Tuesday. What was the total amount of rainfall on both days?

   _____

Name _____

Lesson 34
COMMON CORE STANDARD CC.5.NBT.7
Lesson Objective: Subtract decimals using place value.

Subtract Decimals

Subtract. 12.56 − 4.33

Step 1 Estimate the difference.

$$12.56 − 4.33$$

Estimate: 13   −   4 = 9

Step 2 Line up the place values for each number in a place-value chart. Then subtract.

Ones	Tenths	Hundredths
12	5	6
− 4	3	3
8	2	3	← difference

Step 3 Use your estimate to determine if your answer is reasonable.

Think: 8.23 is close to the estimate, 9. The answer is reasonable.

So, 12.56 − 4.33 = __8.23__.

Estimate. Then find the difference.

1. Estimate: _____

```
   1.97
 − 0.79
 _____
```

2. Estimate: _____

```
   4.42
 − 1.26
 _____
```

3. Estimate: _____

```
  10.25
 − 8.25
 _____
```

Find the difference. Check your answer.

4.
```
   5.75
 − 1.11
 _____
```

5.
```
   25.21
 − 19.05
 _____
```

6.
```
   42.14
 − 25.07
 _____
```

1. Juan had a 10.75-pound block of clay. He used 4.6 pounds of clay to make a sculpture of a horse. How much clay does Juan have left?

(A) 6.1 pounds
(B) 6.15 pounds
(C) 10.29 pounds
(D) 15.35 pounds

2. Ella and Nick are meeting at the library. The library is 4.61 kilometers from Ella's house and 3.25 kilometers from Nick's house. How much farther does Ella live from the library than Nick?

(A) 1.36 kilometers
(B) 1.46 kilometers
(C) 7.86 kilometers
(D) 42.85 kilometers

3. Rafael bought 3.26 pounds of potato salad and 2.8 pounds of macaroni salad to bring to a picnic. How much more potato salad than macaroni salad did Rafael buy?

(A) 6.06 pounds
(B) 2.98 pounds
(C) 0.98 pound
(D) 0.46 pound

4. Salvador had 3.25 pounds of dry cement. He used 1.7 pounds to make a paver for his lawn. How many pounds of dry cement does Salvador have left?

(A) 1.55 pounds
(B) 2.08 pounds
(C) 3.08 pounds
(D) 4.95 pounds

Problem Solving REAL WORLD

5. The width of a tree was 3.15 inches last year. This year, the width is 5.38 inches. How much did the width of the tree increase?

6. The temperature decreased from 71.5°F to 56.8°F overnight. How much did the temperature drop?

Lesson 35
COMMON CORE STANDARD CC.5.NBT.7
Lesson Objective: Identify, describe, and
create numeric patterns with decimals.

Algebra • Patterns with Decimals

Marla wants to download some songs from the Internet. The first
song costs $1.50, and each additional song costs $1.20. How much
will 2, 3, and 4 songs cost?

1 song
$1.50

2 songs
?

3 songs
?

4 songs
?

Step 1 Identify the first term in the sequence.
   Think: The cost of 1 song is $1.50. The first term is $1.50.

Step 2 Identify whether the sequence is increasing or decreasing
   from one term to the next.
   Think: Marla will pay $1.20 for each additional song.
   The sequence is increasing.

Step 3 Write a rule that describes the sequence. Start with $1.50 and add $1.20.

Step 4 Use your rule to find the unknown terms in the sequence.

Number of Songs	1	2	3	4
Cost	$1.50	1.50 + 1.20 = $2.70	2.70 + 1.20 = $3.90	3.90 + 1.20 = $5.10

So, 2 songs cost $2.70, 3 songs cost $3.90, and 4 songs cost $5.10.

Write a rule for the sequence.

1. 0.4, 0.7, 1.0, 1.3, …

   Rule: _____

2. 5.25, 5.00, 4.75, 4.50, …

   Rule: _____

**Write a rule for the sequence, then find
the unknown term.**

3. 26.1, 23.8, 21.5, _____, 16.9

4. 4.62, 5.03, _____, 5.85, 6.26

_____

_____

1. Students are selling muffins at a school bake sale. One muffin costs $0.25, 2 muffins cost $0.37, 3 muffins cost $0.49, and 4 muffins cost $0.61. If this pattern continues, how much will 6 muffins cost?

   (A) $0.73

   (B) $0.83

   (C) $0.85

   (D) $0.97

2. Bob and Ling are playing a number sequence game. Bob wrote the following sequence.

   28.9, 26.8, 24.7, __?__, 20.5

   What is the unknown term in this sequence?

   (A) 21.6

   (B) 22.6

   (C) 22.7

   (D) 25.8

3. Students are selling handmade magnets at the school craft fair. One magnet costs $0.30, 2 magnets cost $0.43, 3 magnets cost $0.56, and 4 magnets cost $0.69. If this pattern continues, how much will 6 magnets cost?

   (A) $0.82

   (B) $0.93

   (C) $0.95

   (D) $1.02

4. Kevin and Yasuko are writing number sequences. Yasuko wrote the following number sequence.

   35.9, 34.7, 33.5, __?__, 31.1

   What is the unknown term in this sequence?

   (A) 32.3

   (B) 32.2

   (C) 32

   (D) 31.2

Problem Solving REAL WORLD

5. The Ride-It Store rents bicycles. The cost is $8.50 for 1 hour, $13.65 for 2 hours, $18.80 for 3 hours, and $23.95 for 4 hours. If the pattern continues, how much will it cost Nate to rent a bike for 6 hours?

   _____

6. Lynne walks dogs every day to earn money. The fees she charges per month are 1 dog, $40; 2 dogs, $37.25 each; 3 dogs, $34.50 each; 4 dogs, $31.75 each. A pet store wants her to walk 8 dogs. If the pattern continues, how much will Lynne charge to walk each of the 8 dogs?

   _____

Name _____

Lesson 36
COMMON CORE STANDARD CC.5.NBT.7
Lesson Objective: Solve problems using the strategy *make a table*.

Problem Solving •
Add and Subtract Money

At the end of April, Mrs. Lei had a balance of $476.05. Since then she has written checks for $263.18 and $37.56, and made a deposit of $368.00. Her checkbook balance currently shows $498.09. Find Mrs. Lei's correct balance.

Read the Problem	Solve the Problem
What do I need to find? I need to find <u>Mrs. Lei's</u> <u>correct checkbook balance</u>.	**Balancing Mrs. Lei's Checkbook**

What information do I need to use?
I need to use the <u>April balance, and</u> <u>the check and deposit amounts</u>

How will I use the information?
I need to make a table and use the information to <u>subtract the checks</u> <u>and add the deposit to find the</u> <u>correct balance</u>

Balancing Mrs. Lei's Checkbook			
April balance			$476.05
Deposit		$368.00	+$368.00
			$844.05
Check	$263.18		−$263.18
			$580.87
Check	$37.56		−$37.56
			$543.31

Mrs. Lei's correct balance is
<u>$543.31</u>

1. At the end of June, Mr. Kent had a balance of $375.98. Since then he has written a check for $38.56 and made a deposit of $408.00. His checkbook shows a balance of $645.42. Find Mr. Kent's correct balance.

2. Jordan buys a notebook for himself and each of 4 friends. Each notebook costs $1.85. Make a table to find the cost of 5 notebooks.

Name _____

1. At the end of October, Mr. Diamond had a balance of $367.38 in his checking account. Since then, he has written two checks for $136.94 and $14.75 and made a deposit of $185.00. What is the balance in Mr. Diamond's checking account now?

   (A) $30.69

   (B) $334.07

   (C) $400.69

   (D) $704.07

2. Mario has $15. If he spends $6.25 on admission to the ice skating rink, $2.95 to rent skates, and $1.65 each for 2 hot chocolates, how much money will he have left?

   (A) $2.50

   (B) $3.50

   (C) $4.15

   (D) $10.85

3. Miguel has $20 to spend on going to a movie. If he spends $7.25 on a movie ticket, $3.95 for snacks, and $1.75 for bus fare each way, how much money will he have left?

   (A) $14.70

   (B) $7.05

   (C) $6.30

   (D) $5.30

4. At the end of November, Mrs. Gold had a balance of $426.83 in her checking account. Since then, she has written two checks for $163.49 and $16.85 and made a deposit of $195.00. What is the balance in Mrs. Gold's checking account now?

   (A) $51.49

   (B) $412.17

   (C) $441.49

   (D) $802.17

Problem Solving REAL WORLD

5. Each package of stickers that Olivia wants to buy costs $1.25. Olivia has $10. Explain how you can find the number of packages of stickers Olivia can buy.

   _____

   _____

   _____

   _____

   _____

Choose a Method

There is more than one way to find the sums and differences of whole numbers and decimals. You can use properties, mental math, place value, a calculator, or paper and pencil.

Choose a method. Find the sum or difference.

- Use mental math for problems with fewer digits or rounded numbers.

$$\begin{array}{r} 2.86 \\ -\ 1.2 \\ \hline 1.66 \end{array}$$

- Use a calculator for difficult numbers or very large numbers.

- Use place value for larger numbers.

$$\begin{array}{r} \overset{1\ 1}{\$15.79} \\ +\ \$32.81 \\ \hline \$48.60 \end{array}$$

| 3 | 8 | . | 4 | 4 | − | 2 | 5 | . | 8 | 6 | = | 12.58 |

Find the sum or difference.

1. $\begin{array}{r} 73.9 \\ +\ 4.37 \\ \hline \end{array}$
2. $\begin{array}{r} 127.35 \\ +\ 928.52 \\ \hline \end{array}$
3. $\begin{array}{r} 10 \\ +\ 2.25 \\ \hline \end{array}$
4. $\begin{array}{r} 0.36 \\ +\ 1.55 \\ \hline \end{array}$

5. $\begin{array}{r} 71.4 \\ +\ 11.5 \\ \hline \end{array}$
6. $\begin{array}{r} 90.4 \\ +\ 88.76 \\ \hline \end{array}$
7. $\begin{array}{r} 3.3 \\ +\ 5.6 \\ \hline \end{array}$
8. $\begin{array}{r} 14.21 \\ 1.79 \\ +\ 15.88 \\ \hline \end{array}$

9. $68.20 - 42.10$
10. $2.25 - 1.15$
11. $875.33 - 467.79$
12. $97.26 - 54.90$

_____   _____   _____   _____

1. Della's cats weigh 9.8 and 8.25 pounds, and her dog weighs 25 pounds. How much more does her dog weigh than the total weight of both of her cats?

   (A) 6.95 pounds

   (B) 15.2 pounds

   (C) 16.75 pounds

   (D) 18.05 pounds

2. Rob used 4.25 ounces of peanuts, 3.4 ounces of pecans, and 2.75 ounces of walnuts to make a trail mix. How many ounces of nuts did Rob use in the trail mix?

   (A) 4.1 ounces

   (B) 4.865 ounces

   (C) 7.34 ounces

   (D) 10.4 ounces

3. Gina is training for a marathon. She ran 4.6 miles on Friday and 6.75 miles on Saturday. On Sunday, she ran 13 miles. How much farther did she run on Sunday than she did on Friday and Saturday combined?

   (A) 1.65 miles

   (B) 6.25 miles

   (C) 11.35 miles

   (D) 24.35 miles

4. Paul used 1.75 pounds of grapes, 2.6 pounds of bananas, and 3.25 pounds of apples to make fruit salad. How many pounds of fruit did Paul use in the salad?

   (A) 5.26 pounds

   (B) 6.6 pounds

   (C) 7.6 pounds

   (D) 8.6 pounds

Problem Solving REAL WORLD

5. Jill bought 6.5 meters of blue lace and 4.12 meters of green lace. What was the total length of lace she bought?

   _____

6. Zack bought a coat for $69.78. He paid with a $100 bill and received $26.73 in change. How much was the sales tax?

   _____

Name _____

Multiply Decimals and Whole Numbers

You can draw a quick picture to help multiply a decimal and a whole number.

Find the product. 4 × 0.23

Draw a quick picture. Each bar represents one tenth, or 0.1.
Each circle represents one hundredth, or 0.01.

Step 1
Draw ____4____ groups of ____2____
tenths and ____3____ hundredths.

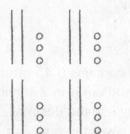

So, 4 × 0.23 = __0.92__

Step 2
Combine the tenths. Then combine the hundredths.

Step 3
There are ____12____ hundredths.
Rename ____10____ hundredths
as ____1____ tenth. Then you
will have ____9____ tenths and
____2____ hundredths.

Find the product. Use a quick picture.

1. 2 × 0.19 = _____

2. 3 × 0.54 = _____

3. 4 × 0.07 = _____

4. 3 × 1.22 = _____

1. Callie used a decimal model to help her multiply a decimal by a whole number. What equation does the model show?

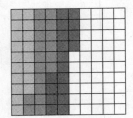

Ⓐ 3 × 0.18 = 0.54
Ⓑ 3 × 0.18 = 5.4
Ⓒ 18 × 0.3 = 0.54
Ⓓ 18 × 0.3 = 5.4

2. The weight of a dime is 0.08 ounce. Amad used a model to find the weight of 7 dimes. What is the weight of 7 dimes?

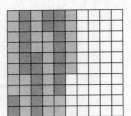

Ⓐ 0.54 ounce   Ⓒ 0.58 ounce
Ⓑ 0.56 ounce   Ⓓ 0.78 ounce

3. Miguel used a quick picture to help him multiply a decimal by a whole number. What equation does the model show?

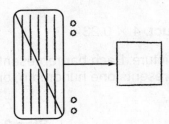

Ⓐ 2 × 5.2 = 1.04
Ⓑ 2 × 5.2 = 10.4
Ⓒ 2 × 0.52 = 10.4
Ⓓ 2 × 0.52 = 1.04

4. One serving of soup contains 0.45 gram of sodium. How much sodium is in 2 servings of the soup? You may use the decimal model to help you answer the question.

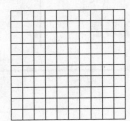

Ⓐ 0.09 gram   Ⓒ 9 grams
Ⓑ 0.9 gram   Ⓓ 90 grams

Problem Solving REAL WORLD

5. In physical education class, Sonia walks a distance of 0.12 mile in 1 minute. At that rate, how far can she walk in 9 minutes?

6. A certain tree can grow 0.45 meter in one year. At that rate, how much can the tree grow in 3 years?

Name _____

Lesson 39

COMMON CORE STANDARD CC.5.NBT.7

Lesson Objective: Multiply a decimal and a whole number using drawings and place value.

Multiplication with Decimals and Whole Numbers

To find the product of a one-digit whole number and a decimal, multiply as you would multiply whole numbers. To find the number of decimal places in the product, add the number of decimal places in the factors.

To multiply 6 × 4.25, multiply as you would multiply 6 × 425.

Step 1
Multiply the ones.

$$\begin{array}{r} {}^{3} \\ 425 \\ \times6 \\ \hline 0 \end{array}$$

So, 6 × 4.25 = __25.50__.

Step 2
Multiply the tens.

$$\begin{array}{r} {}^{1\,3} \\ 425 \\ \times6 \\ \hline 50 \end{array}$$

Step 3
Multiply the hundreds. Then place the decimal point in the product.

$$\begin{array}{r} {}^{1\,3} \\ 4.25 \longleftarrow \\ \times6 \longleftarrow \\ \hline 25.50 \longleftarrow \end{array}$$

2 decimal places
+ 0 decimal places
2 decimal places

Place the decimal point in the product.

1. $\begin{array}{r} 8.23 \\ \times6 \\ \hline 4\,9.3\,8 \end{array}$ **Think:** The place value of the decimal factor is hundredths.

2. $\begin{array}{r} 6.3 \\ \times4 \\ \hline 2\,5\,2 \end{array}$

3. $\begin{array}{r} 16.82 \\ \times5 \\ \hline 8\,4\,1\,0 \end{array}$

Find the product.

4. $\begin{array}{r} 5.19 \\ \times3 \\ \hline \end{array}$

5. $\begin{array}{r} 7.2 \\ \times8 \\ \hline \end{array}$

6. $\begin{array}{r} 37.46 \\ \times7 \\ \hline \end{array}$

1. Marci mailed 9 letters at the post office. Each letter weighed 3.5 ounces. What was the total weight of the letters that Marci mailed?

   (A) 33.5 ounces

   (B) 32.5 ounces

   (C) 31.5 ounces

   (D) 27.5 ounces

2. Laurie is in training for a race. When she trains, Laurie runs on a path that is 1.45 miles long. Last week, Laurie ran on this path 6 times. How many miles did Laurie run on the path last week?

   (A) 0.87 mile

   (B) 8.7 miles

   (C) 87 miles

   (D) 870 miles

3. Mari and Rob are making a science poster. They need to write how much a rock that weighs 7 pounds on Earth would weigh on Mars. They know they can multiply weight on Earth by 0.38 to find weight on Mars. What number should they write on their poster?

   (A) 0.266 pound

   (B) 2.66 pounds

   (C) 26.6 pounds

   (D) 266 pounds

4. Rhianna made a shelf to store her collection of rocks and shells. She used 5 pieces of wood that were each 3.25 feet long. How much wood did Rhianna use in all to make the shelf?

   (A) 6.25 feet

   (B) 15.05 feet

   (C) 15.25 feet

   (D) 16.25 feet

Problem Solving REAL WORLD

5. A half-dollar coin issued by the United States Mint measures 30.61 millimeters across. Mikk has 9 half dollars. He lines them up end to end in a row. What is the total length of the row of half dollars?

6. One pound of grapes costs $3.49. Linda buys exactly 3 pounds of grapes. How much will the grapes cost?

Multiply Using Expanded Form

You can use a model and partial products to help you find the product of a two-digit whole number and a decimal.

Find the product. 13×6.8

Step 1 Draw a large rectangle. Label its longer side __13__ and its shorter side __6.8__. The area of the large rectangle represents the product, __13__ $\times$ __6.8__.

Step 2 Rewrite the factors in expanded form. Divide the large rectangle into four smaller rectangles. Use the expanded forms to label the smaller rectangles.

$13 = $ __10__ $+$ __3__ $6.8 = $ __6__ $+$ __0.8__

Step 3 Multiply to find the area of each small rectangle.

$10 \times 6 = $ __60__ $10 \times 0.8 = $ __8__ $3 \times 6 = $ __18__ $3 \times 0.8 = $ __2.4__

Step 4 Add to find the total area.

__60__ $+$ __8__ $+$ __18__ $+$ __2.4__ $=$ __88.4__

So, $13 \times 6.8 = $ __88.4__.

Draw a model to find the product.

1. $18 \times 0.25 = $ _____

2. $26 \times 7.2 = $ _____

Find the product.

3. $17 \times 9.3 = $ _____   4. $21 \times 43.5 = $ _____   5. $48 \times 4.74 = $ _____

1. Ari is setting up a fish tank for his goldfish. The tank holds 15 gallons of water. The weight of a gallon of water rounded to the nearest tenth is 8.3 pounds. Ari used this weight to calculate the weight of the water in his fish tank. Which is the weight that Ari would find for the water in the fish tank?

   (A) 12.45 pounds

   (B) 16.5 pounds

   (C) 124.5 pounds

   (D) 165 pounds

2. Paul works at the local grocery store. He worked 15 hours this week. Last week, he worked 2.5 times as many hours as he worked this week. How many hours did Paul work last week?

   (A) 30.5 hours

   (B) 32.5 hours

   (C) 35 hours

   (D) 37.5 hours

3. The Barbers are keeping track of their family energy costs. It costs the Barbers $0.16 per week to run their dishwasher. How much will it cost them to run their dishwasher for 52 weeks?

   (A) $8.64

   (B) $8.32

   (C) $3.64

   (D) $1.92

4. Mrs. Green needs to store 21 math books on a shelf during school vacation. Each math book is 2.4 centimeters thick. If Mrs. Green stacks the math books on top of each other, how tall does the shelf have to be?

   (A) 12.6 centimeters

   (B) 40.4 centimeters

   (C) 50.4 centimeters

   (D) 54 centimeters

Problem Solving REAL WORLD

5. An object that weighs one pound on the moon will weigh about 6.02 pounds on Earth. Suppose a moon rock weighs 11 pounds on the moon. How much will the same rock weigh on Earth?

6. Tessa is on the track team. For practice and exercise, she runs 2.25 miles each day. At the end of 14 days, how many total miles will Tessa have run?

Lesson **41**
COMMON CORE STANDARD CC.5.NBT.7
Lesson Objective: Solve problems using the
strategy *draw a diagram* to multiply money.

Problem Solving • Multiply Money

Three students in the garden club enter a pumpkin-growing contest.
Jessie's pumpkin is worth $12.75. Mara's pumpkin is worth 4 times
as much as Jessie's. Hayden's pumpkin is worth $22.25 more than
Mara's. How much is Hayden's pumpkin worth?

Read the Problem	Solve the Problem
What do I need to find? I need to find __how much__ __Hayden's pumpkin is worth__.	The amount that Hayden's and Mara's pumpkins are worth depends on how much Jessie's pumpkin is worth. Draw a diagram to compare the amounts without calculating. Then use the diagram to find how much each person's pumpkin is worth.
What information do I need to use? I need to use the worth of __Jessie's__ pumpkin to find how much __Mara's__ and __Hayden's__ pumpkins are worth.	Jessie [$12.75] Mara [$12.75][$12.75][$12.75][$12.75] Hayden [$12.75][$12.75][$12.75][$12.75][$22.25]
How will I use the information: I can draw a diagram to show __how__ __much Jessie's and Mara's__ __pumpkins are worth to__ __find how much Hayden's__ __pumpkin is worth.__	**Jessie:** $12.75 **Mara:** $4 \times$ __$12.75__ = __$51.00__ **Hayden:** __$51.00__ + $22.25 = __$73.25__

So Hayden's pumpkin is worth __$73.25__.

1. Three friends go to the local farmers' market. Latasha spends $3.35. Helen spends 4 times as much as Latasha. Dee spends $7.50 more than Helen. How much does Dee spend?

2. Alexia raises $75.23 for a charity. Sue raises 3 times as much as Alexia. Manuel raises $85.89. How much money do the three friends raise for the charity in all?

1. At a dry cleaning store, it costs $1.79 to clean a man's dress shirt and $8.25 to clean a suit. Thomas brought in 4 shirts and 1 suit to be cleaned. How much will he be charged for the dry cleaning?

   (A) $15.41

   (B) $10.04

   (C) $8.95

   (D) $7.16

2. Mandy, Jeremy, and Lily went to an amusement park during their summer vacation. Mandy spent $16.25 at the amusement park. Jeremy spent $3.40 more than Mandy spent. Lily spent 2 times as much money as Jeremy spent. How much money did Lily spend at the amusement park?

   (A) $6.80   (C) $32.50

   (B) $19.65   (D) $39.30

3. Tim wants to rent a bike at the state park. It costs $3.95 per hour for the first 4 hours. After 4 hours, the cost is $2.50 per hour. How much would it cost Tim to rent a bike for 5 hours?

   (A) $19.75

   (B) $18.30

   (C) $15.80

   (D) $12.50

4. Peter spent $32.50 at the ballpark. Marty spent 5 times as much money as Peter spent. Callie spent $27.25 more than Marty. How much did Callie spend at the ballpark?

   (A) $59.75

   (B) $136.25

   (C) $162.50

   (D) $189.75

Problem Solving REAL WORLD

5. Chris collected $25.65 for a fundraiser. Remy collected $15.87 more than Chris did. Sandy collected 3 times as much as Remy. How much did Sandy collect for the fundraiser? Draw a diagram to solve. Then explain how you found your answer.

   _____

   _____

   _____

Name _____

Lesson **42**
COMMON CORE STANDARD CC.5.NBT.7
Lesson Objective: Model multiplication by decimals.

Decimal Multiplication

You can use decimal squares to multiply decimals.

Multiply. 0.2 × 0.9

Step 1 Draw a square with 10 equal rows and 10 equal columns.

Step 2 Shade 9 columns to represent ___0.9___.

Step 3 Shade 2 rows to represent ___0.2___.

Step 4 Count the number of small squares where the shadings overlap: ___18___ squares, or 0.18.

So, 0.2 × 0.9 = ___0.18___.

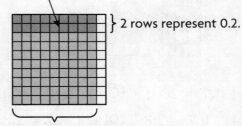

The shadings overlap in 18 squares, or 0.18.

} 2 rows represent 0.2.

9 columns represent 0.9.

Multiply. Use the decimal model.

1. 0.3 × 0.2 = _____

2. 0.9 × 0.5 = _____

3. 0.1 × 1.8 = _____

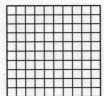 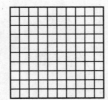 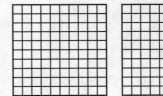

4. 0.4 × 0.4 = _____

5. 0.6 × 0.5 = _____

6. 0.4 × 1.2 = _____

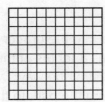 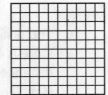 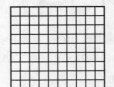 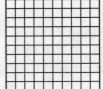

1. Keisha used this decimal model to help her multiply. What equation does the model show?

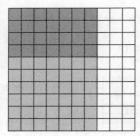

   (A) $4 \times 7 = 28$ (C) $0.4 \times 0.7 = 0.28$

   (B) $4 \times 0.7 = 2.8$ (D) $0.4 \times 7 = 2.8$

2. Lorenzo had a piece of wire that was 0.6 meter long. He used 0.5 of the wire. How much wire did Lorenzo use?

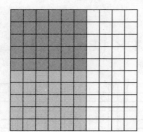

   (A) 0.03 meter   (C) 0.3 meter

   (B) 0.1 meter   (D) 1.1 meters

3. Mickey used a decimal model to help him multiply 0.3×0.8. What is the product of 0.3 and 0.8?

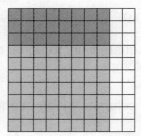

   (A) 0.024   (C) 2.4

   (B) 0.24   (D) 24

4. One serving of a dried fruit mix contains 0.9 gram of potassium. How much potassium is in 0.5 serving of the dried fruit mix? You may use the decimal model to help you answer the question.

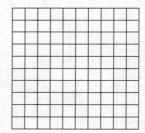

   (A) 0.45 gram   (C) 4.5 grams

   (B) 1.4 grams   (D) 45 grams

Problem Solving REAL WORLD

5. A certain bamboo plants grow 1.2 feet in 1 day. At that rate, how many feet could the plant grow in 0.5 day?

6. The distance from the park to the grocery store is 0.9 mile. Ezra runs 8 tenths of that distance and walks the rest of the way. How far does Ezra run from the park to the grocery store?

Lesson **43**
COMMON CORE STANDARD CC.5.NBT.7
Lesson Objective: Place the decimal point
in decimal multiplication.

Multiply Decimals

Multiply. 9.3 × 5.27

Step 1 Multiply as with whole numbers.

$$
\begin{array}{r}
{\scriptstyle 2\ 6} \\
{\scriptstyle 2} \\
527 \\
\times\ \ \ 93 \\
\hline
1{,}581 \\
+\ 47{,}430 \\
\hline
49{,}011
\end{array}
$$

Step 2 Add the number of decimal places in the factors
to place the decimal point in the product.

$$
\begin{array}{r}
5.27 \longleftarrow \underline{\mathbf{2}}\ \text{decimal places} \\
\times\ \ 9.3 \longleftarrow +\ \underline{\mathbf{1}}\ \text{decimal place} \\
\hline
1{,}581 \\
+\ 47{,}430 \\
\hline
49.011 \longleftarrow \underline{\mathbf{3}}\ \text{decimal places}
\end{array}
$$

So, 9.3 × 5.27 = **49.011**.

Place the decimal point in the product.

1. $\begin{array}{r} 1.6 \\ \times\ 0.7 \\ \hline 1\ 1\ 2 \end{array}$

2. $\begin{array}{r} 14.2 \\ \times\ 7.6 \\ \hline 1\ 0\ 7\ 9\ 2 \end{array}$

3. $\begin{array}{r} 3.59 \\ \times\ 4.8 \\ \hline 1\ 7\ 2\ 3\ 2 \end{array}$

Find the product.

4. $\begin{array}{r} 5.7 \\ \times\ 0.8 \\ \hline \end{array}$

5. $\begin{array}{r} 35.1 \\ \times\ 8.4 \\ \hline \end{array}$

6. $\begin{array}{r} 2.19 \\ \times\ 6.3 \\ \hline \end{array}$

1. A scientist at a giant panda preserve in China measured the length of a newborn cub as 15.5 centimeters. The cub's mother was 9.5 times as tall as the length of the cub. How tall is the mother?

    (A)   14.725 centimeters

    (B)   25 centimeters

    (C)   147.25 centimeters

    (D) 1,472.5 centimeters

2. Emily stopped at a produce stand to buy some tomatoes. Tomatoes cost $1.25 per pound at the stand. Emily bought 5 tomatoes that weighed a total of 1.8 pounds. How much did Emily pay for the tomatoes?

    (A) $2.25

    (B) $3.05

    (C) $6.25

    (D) $22.50

3. Mel's father asked Mel to mow his lawn while he was on vacation. Mel bought 1.6 gallons of gas for the lawn mower. The gas cost $2.85 per gallon. How much money did Mel pay for the gas?

    (A) $45.60

    (B) $4.56

    (C) $4.45

    (D) $4.13

4. Mr. Harris has 54.8 acres of land. Mr. Fitz has 0.35 times as many acres as Mr. Harris has. How many acres of land does Mr. Fitz have?

    (A) 4.384 acres

    (B) 19.108 acres

    (C) 19.18 acres

    (D) 43.84 acres

Problem Solving REAL WORLD

5. Aretha runs a marathon in 3.25 hours. Neal takes 1.6 times as long to run the same marathon. How many hours does it take Neal to run the marathon?

    _____

6. Tiffany catches a fish that weighs 12.3 pounds. Frank catches a fish that weighs 2.5 times as much as Tiffany's fish. How many pounds does Frank's fish weigh?

    _____

Zeros in the Product

Sometimes when you multiply two decimals, there are not enough digits in the product to place the decimal point.

Multiply. 0.9×0.03

Step 1 Multiply as with whole numbers.

$$\begin{array}{r} 3 \\ \times\ 9 \\ \hline 27 \end{array}$$

Step 2 Find the number of decimal places in the product by adding the number of decimal places in the factors.

$$\begin{array}{r} 0.03 \longleftarrow \underline{\ 2\ } \text{ decimal places} \\ \times\ 0.9 \longleftarrow +\underline{\ 1\ } \text{ decimal place} \\ \hline \longleftarrow \underline{\ 3\ } \text{ decimal places} \end{array}$$

Step 3 Place the decimal point.

0.027   There are not enough digits in the product to place the decimal point. Write zeros as needed to the left of the product to place the decimal point.

So, $0.9 \times 0.03 =$ ___0.027___ .

Write zeros in the product.

1. $\begin{array}{r} 0.8 \\ \times\ 0.1 \\ \hline \boxed{}8 \end{array}$

2. $\begin{array}{r} 0.04 \\ \times\ 0.7 \\ \hline \boxed{}28 \end{array}$

3. $\begin{array}{r} 0.03 \\ \times\ 0.3 \\ \hline \boxed{}9 \end{array}$

Find the product.

4. $\begin{array}{r} \$0.06 \\ \times\quad 0.5 \\ \hline \end{array}$

5. $\begin{array}{r} 0.09 \\ \times\ 0.8 \\ \hline \end{array}$

6. $\begin{array}{r} 0.05 \\ \times\ 0.7 \\ \hline \end{array}$

1. Denise, Keith, and Tim live in the same neighborhood. Denise lives 0.3 mile from Keith. The distance that Tim and Keith live from each other is 0.2 times longer than the distance between Denise and Keith. How far from each other do Tim and Keith live?

   (A) 0.6 mile

   (B) 0.5 mile

   (C) 0.1 mile

   (D) 0.06 mile

2. Tina is making a special dessert for her brother's birthday. Tina's recipe calls for 0.5 kilogram of flour. The recipe also calls for an amount of sugar that is 0.8 times as much as the amount of flour. How much sugar will Tina need to make the dessert?

   (A) 4 kilograms

   (B) 0.4 kilogram

   (C) 0.04 kilogram

   (D) 0.004 kilogram

3. The information booklet for a video console says that the console uses about 0.2 kilowatt of electricity per hour. If electricity costs $0.15 per kilowatt hour, how much does it cost to run the console for an hour?

   (A) $0.03

   (B) $0.30

   (C) $3.00

   (D) $30.00

4. Bruce is getting materials for a chemistry experiment. His teacher gives him a container that holds 0.25 liter of a blue liquid. Bruce needs to use 0.4 of this liquid for the experiment. How much blue liquid will Bruce use?

   (A) 0.001 liter

   (B) 0.01 liter

   (C) 0.1 liter

   (D) 1 liter

Problem Solving  REAL WORLD

5. A beaker contains 0.5 liter of a solution. Jordan uses 0.08 of the solution for an experiment. How much of the solution does Jordan use?

6. A certain type of nuts are on sale at $0.35 per pound. Tamara buys 0.2 pound of nuts. How much will the nuts cost?

Divide Decimals by Whole Numbers

You can draw a quick picture to help you divide a decimal by a whole number.

In a decimal model, each large square represents one, or 1. Each bar represents one-tenth, or 0.1.

Divide. 1.2 ÷ 3

Step 1 Draw a quick picture to represent the dividend, _1.2_.

Step 2 Draw 3 circles to represent the divisor, _3_.

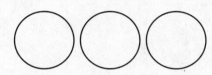

Step 3 You cannot evenly divide 1 into 3 groups. Regroup 1 as 10 tenths. There are _12_ tenths in 1.2.

Step 4 Share the tenths equally among 3 groups.

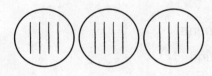

Each group contains _0_ ones and _4_ tenths.

So, 1.2 ÷ 3 = _0.4_.

Divide. Draw a quick picture.

1. 2.7 ÷ 9 = _____

2. 4.8 ÷ 8 = _____

3. 2.8 ÷ 7 = _____

4. 7.25 ÷ 5 = _____

5. 3.78 ÷ 3 = _____

6. 8.52 ÷ 4 = _____

1. Emilio used a model to help him divide 2.46 by 2. What is the quotient?

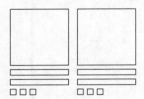

Ⓐ 1.23
Ⓑ 1.32
Ⓒ 3.21
Ⓓ 12.3

2. Heath bought 1.2 pounds of potato salad. He divided it into 4 containers, each with the same amount. How much potato salad was in each container?

Ⓐ 0.03 pound
Ⓑ 0.3 pound
Ⓒ 0.8 pound
Ⓓ 4.8 pounds

3. Theo made a model to represent a division statement. What division statement does the model show?

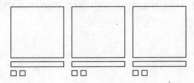

Ⓐ 3.12 ÷ 3 = 1.12
Ⓑ 3.63 ÷ 3 = 1.21
Ⓒ 2.24 ÷ 2 = 1.12
Ⓓ 3.36 ÷ 3 = 1.12

4. Maya practiced the piano for 3.75 hours last week. If she practiced the same amount of time each of 5 days, how long did she practice each day?

Ⓐ 0.25 hour
Ⓑ 0.5 hour
Ⓒ 0.75 hour
Ⓓ 1.25 hours

Problem Solving

5. In PE class, Carl runs a distance of 1.17 miles in 9 minutes. At that rate, how far does Carl run in one minute?

6. Marianne spends $9.45 on 5 greeting cards. Each card costs the same amount. What is the cost of one greeting card?

Lesson **46**

COMMON CORE STANDARD CC.5.NBT.7
Lesson Objective: Estimate decimal quotients.

Estimate Quotients

You can use multiples and compatible numbers to estimate decimal quotients.

Estimate. $249.7 \div 31$

Step 1 Round the divisor, 31, to the nearest 10.

31 rounded to the nearest 10 is __30__.

Step 2 Find the multiples of 30 that the dividend, 249.7, is between.

249.7 is between __240__ and __270__.

Step 3 Divide each multiple by the rounded divisor, 30.

$240 \div 30 = $ __8__ $270 \div 30 = $ __9__

So, two possible estimates are __8__ and __9__.

Use compatible numbers to estimate the quotient.

1. $23.6 \div 7$

2. $469.4 \div 62$

_____ ÷ _____ = _____   _____ ÷ _____ = _____

Estimate the quotient.

3. $338.7 \div 49$ 4. $75.1 \div 9$ 5. $674.8 \div 23$

6. $61.9 \div 7$ 7. $96.5 \div 19$ 8. $57.2 \div 8$

1. Ashleigh rode her bicycle 26.5 miles in 4 hours. Which gives the **best** estimate of how far Ashleigh rode in 1 hour?

   (A) 0.5 mile

   (B) 0.6 mile

   (C) 5 miles

   (D) 7 miles

2. Ellen drove 357.9 miles. Her car gets about 21 miles per gallon. Which is the **best** estimate of how many gallons of gas Ellen used?

   (A) 17 gallons

   (B) 16 gallons

   (C) 1.7 gallons

   (D) 0.17 gallon

3. Landon bought a box of plants for $8.79. There were 16 plants in the box. If Landon had bought only 1 plant, about how much would it have cost?

   (A) about $0.40

   (B) about $0.50

   (C) about $0.60

   (D) about $0.70

4. Josh bought a 34.6-pound bag of dry dog food to feed his dogs. The bag lasted 8 days. About how much dog food did his dogs eat each day?

   (A) about 0.4 pound

   (B) about 0.5 pound

   (C) about 4 pounds

   (D) about 5 pounds

Problem Solving REAL WORLD

5. Taylor uses 645.6 gallons of water in 7 days. Suppose he uses the same amount of water each day. About how much water does Taylor use each day?

6. On a road trip, Sandy drives 368.7 miles. Her car uses a total of 18 gallons of gas. About how many miles per gallon does Sandy's car get?

92

Name _____

Lesson **47**
COMMON CORE STANDARD CC.5.NBT.7
Lesson Objective: Divide decimals by whole numbers.

Division of Decimals by Whole Numbers

Divide. 19.61 ÷ 37

Step 1 Estimate the quotient.
2,000 hundredths ÷ 40 = __50__ hundredths, or 0.50.
So, the quotient will have a zero in the ones place.

$$37\overline{)19.61} \quad 0$$

Step 2 Divide the tenths.
Use the estimate. Try 5 in the tenths place.

Multiply. __5__ × 37 = __185__

Subtract. 196 − __185__ = __11__

Check. __11__ < 37

$$37\overline{)19.61}$$
$$\begin{array}{r} 0\ 5 \\ -18\ 5 \\ \hline 1\ 1 \end{array}$$

Step 3 Divide the hundredths.
Estimate: 120 hundredths ÷ 40 = 3 hundredths.

Multiply. __3__ × 37 = __111__

Subtract. __111__ − __111__ = __0__

Check. __0__ < 37

Place the decimal point in the quotient.

So, 19.61 ÷ 37 = __0.53__.

$$37\overline{)19.61}$$
$$\begin{array}{r} 0.53 \\ -18\ 5 \\ \hline 1\ 11 \\ -1\ 11 \\ \hline 0 \end{array}$$

Write the quotient with the decimal point placed correctly.

1. 5.94 ÷ 3 = 198 _____

2. 48.3 ÷ 23 = 21 _____

Divide.

3. $9\overline{)61.2}$

4. $17\overline{)83.3}$

5. $9\overline{)7.38}$

1. Grant is making small bags of dried fruit from a large bag of dried fruit that weighs 5.46 pounds. If he puts the same amount of dried fruit in each of 6 bags, how much will each bag weigh?

Ⓐ 0.0091 pound

Ⓑ 0.091 pound

Ⓒ 0.91 pound

Ⓓ 9.1 pounds

2. Mia has a piece of ribbon that is 30.5 yards long. The length is just enough ribbon to make 5 bows that are the same size. How long is the ribbon that she uses for each bow?

Ⓐ 6.01 yards

Ⓑ 6.1 yards

Ⓒ 6.2 yards

Ⓓ 6.5 yards

3. A plumber has a piece of copper tubing that is 112.8 inches long. He needs to cut the tubing into 12 equal pieces to repair some leaky pipes. How long will each piece of tubing be?

Ⓐ 0.094 inch

Ⓑ 0.94 inch

Ⓒ 9.4 inches

Ⓓ 94 inches

4. Matthew bought 13 used video games that were on sale in a store. He paid $84.37 for the games. If each video game cost the same price, how much did 1 video game cost?

Ⓐ $6.09

Ⓑ $6.19

Ⓒ $6.39

Ⓓ $6.49

Problem Solving  REAL WORLD

5. On Saturday, 12 friends go ice skating. Altogether, they pay $83.40 for admission. They share the cost equally. How much does each person pay?

_____

6. A team of 4 people participates in a 400-yard relay race. Each team member runs the same distance. The team completes the race in a total of 53.2 seconds. What is the average running time for each person?

_____

Name _____

Decimal Division

You can use decimal models to divide tenths.

Divide. 1.8 ÷ 0.3.

Step 1 Shade 18 tenths to represent

the dividend, __1.8__.

Step 2 Divide the 18 tenths into groups

of __3__ tenths to represent the divisor, __0.3__.

Step 3 Count the groups.

There are __6__ groups of 0.3 in 1.8. So, 1.8 ÷ 0.3 = __6__.

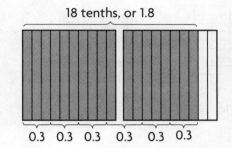

18 tenths, or 1.8

0.3 0.3 0.3   0.3 0.3 0.3

You can use decimal models to divide hundredths.

Divide. 0.42 ÷ 0.06

Step 1 Shade 42 squares to represent

the dividend, __0.42__.

Step 2 Divide the 42 small squares into groups

of __6__ hundredths to represent the

divisor, __0.06__.

Step 3 Count the groups.

There are __7__ groups of 0.06 in 0.42. So, 0.42 ÷ 0.06 = __7__.

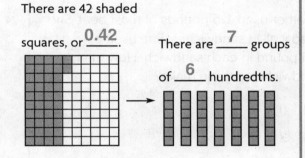

There are 42 shaded
squares, or __0.42__.

There are __7__ groups
of __6__ hundredths.

Use the model to complete the number sentence.

1. 1.4 ÷ 0.7 = _____

2. 0.15 ÷ 0.03 = _____

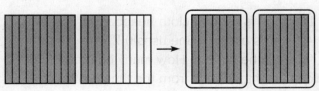

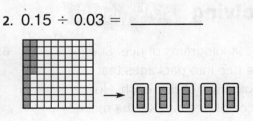

Divide. Use decimal models.

3. 2.7 ÷ 0.3 = _____

4. 0.52 ÷ 0.26 = _____

5. 0.96 ÷ 0.16 = _____

1. Peter used a model to help him divide 0.28 by 0.07. What is the quotient?

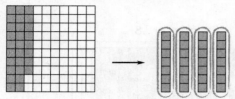

   (A) 0.04
   (B) 0.4
   (C) 4
   (D) 28

2. Heather used 1.5 pounds of roast beef. She used it all in sandwiches. She used 0.5 pound in each sandwich. How many sandwiches did she make?

   (A) 0.3
   (B) 3
   (C) 4.5
   (D) 30

3. Fiona made the model below to represent a division statement. What division statement does the model show?

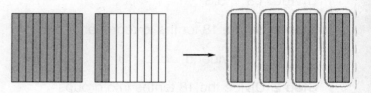

   (A) $1.2 \div 0.3 = 4$
   (B) $1.2 \div 0.4 = 3$
   (C) $1.6 \div 0.4 = 4$
   (D) $0.9 \div 0.3 = 3$

4. Tyrone used 3.75 cups of hot water to make hot chocolate. He poured 0.75 cup of hot water into each mug of chocolate. How many mugs of hot chocolate did he make?

   (A) 3
   (B) 4
   (C) 5
   (D) 6

Problem Solving

5. Keisha buys 2.4 kilograms of rice. She separates the rice into packages that contain 0.4 kilogram of rice each. How many packages of rice can Keisha make?

6. Leighton is making cloth headbands. She has 4.2 yards of cloth. She uses 0.2 yard of cloth for each headband. How many headbands can Leighton make from the length of cloth she has?

Divide Decimals

You can multiply the dividend and the divisor by the same power of 10 to make the divisor a whole number. As long as you multiply both the dividend and the divisor by the same power of 10, the quotient stays the same.

Example 1: Divide. $0.84 \div 0.07$

Multiply the dividend, __0.84__, and the divisor, __0.07__, by the

power of 10 that makes the __divisor__ a whole number.

Since $84 \div 7 = 12$, you know that $0.84 \div 0.07 = $ __12__.

$$0.84 \div 0.07 = ?$$
$$\times 100 \quad \times 100$$
$$84 \div 7 = 12$$

Example 2: Divide. $4.42 \div 3.4$

Multiply both the dividend and the divisor by 10 to make the divisor a whole number.

$3.4\overline{)4.42}$ —— Multiply 3.4 and 4.42 both by 10 —→ $34\overline{)44.2}$

Divide as you would whole numbers. Place the decimal point in the quotient, above the decimal point in the dividend.

So, $4.42 \div 3.4 = $ __1.3__.

$$\begin{array}{r} 1.3 \\ 34\overline{)44.2} \\ -34 \\ \hline 102 \\ -102 \\ \hline 0 \end{array}$$

Copy and complete the pattern.

1. $54 \div 6 = $ _____

   $5.4 \div $ _____ $= 9$

   _____ $\div 0.06 = 9$

2. $184 \div 23 = $ _____

   $18.4 \div $ _____ $= 8$

   _____ $\div 0.23 = 8$

3. $138 \div 2 = $ _____

   $13.8 \div $ _____ $= 69$

   _____ $\div 0.02 = 69$

Divide.

4. $1.4\overline{)9.8}$

5. $0.3\overline{)0.6}$

6. $3.64 \div 1.3$

1. Leilani bought tomatoes that cost $0.84 per pound. She paid $3.36 for the tomatoes. How many pounds of tomatoes did she buy?

Ⓐ 0.004 pound

Ⓑ 0.04 pound

Ⓒ 0.4 pound

Ⓓ 4 pounds

2. Carly has a piece of yarn that is 7.2 yards long. She needs to cut the yarn into pieces of fringe that each measure 0.3 yard long. How many pieces of fringe can she cut from the piece of yarn?

Ⓐ 2,400

Ⓑ 240

Ⓒ 24

Ⓓ 2.4

3. Latisha hiked along a trail that was 9.66 miles long last Saturday. It took her 4.2 hours to complete the trail. What was Latisha's average speed per hour?

Ⓐ 0.23 mile per hour

Ⓑ 2.3 miles per hour

Ⓒ 20.3 miles per hour

Ⓓ 23 miles per hour

4. Quan records that his hamster can turn the wheel in its cage to make 1 revolution in 0.5 minute. How many revolutions can the hamster make in 20.5 minutes?

Ⓐ   4.1

Ⓑ   41

Ⓒ   410

Ⓓ 4,100

Problem Solving  REAL WORLD

5. At the market, grapes cost $0.85 per pound. Clarissa buys grapes and pays a total of $2.55. How many pounds of grapes does she buy?

6. Damon kayaks on a river near his home. He plans to kayak a total of 6.4 miles. Damon kayaks at an average speed of 1.6 miles per hour. How many hours will it take Damon to kayak the 6.4 miles?

Name _____

Lesson 50

COMMON CORE STANDARD CC.5.NBT.7

Lesson Objective: Write a zero in the dividend to find a quotient.

Write Zeros in the Dividend

When there are not enough digits in the dividend to complete the division, you can write zeros to the right of the last digit in the dividend. Writing zeros will not change the value of the dividend or the quotient.

Divide. $5.2 \div 8$

Step 1 Divide as you would whole numbers. Place the decimal point in the quotient above the decimal point in the dividend.

The decimal point in the quotient is directly above the decimal point in the dividend.

```
   0.6
8)5.2
  -48
    4
```

Step 2 The difference is less than the divisor. Write a 0 in the dividend and continue to divide.

The difference, 4, is less than the divisor.

```
   0.65
8)5.20
  -48
    40
   -40
     0
```

Write a 0 in the dividend. Then continue to divide.

So, $5.2 \div 8 = \underline{0.65}$.

Write the quotient with the decimal point placed correctly.

1. $3 \div 0.4 = 75$ 　　 2. $25.2 \div 8 = 315$ 　　 3. $60 \div 25 = 24$ 　　 4. $8.28 \div 0.72 = 115$

Divide.

5. $6)\overline{43.5}$ 　　　　 6. $1.4)\overline{7.7}$ 　　　　 7. $30)\overline{72}$ 　　　　 8. $0.18)\overline{0.63}$

1. Tony collected 16.2 pounds of pecans from the trees at his farm. He will give the same weight of pecans to each of 12 friends. How many pounds of pecans will each friend get?

   Ⓐ 0.135 pound

   Ⓑ 1.35 pounds

   Ⓒ 13.5 pounds

   Ⓓ 135 pounds

2. Trevor drove 202 miles to visit his grandparents. It took him 4 hours to get there. What was the average speed that Trevor drove?

   Ⓐ 5.05 miles per hour

   Ⓑ 5.5 miles per hour

   Ⓒ 50.5 miles per hour

   Ⓓ 55 miles per hour

3. Denise's mother bought some zucchini for $0.78 per pound. If she paid $2.73 for the zucchini, how many pounds of zucchini did she buy?

   Ⓐ 0.35 pound

   Ⓑ 3.5 pounds

   Ⓒ 35 pounds

   Ⓓ 350 pounds

4. The students at Winwood Elementary School collected 574 cans of food in 20 days for a food drive. What was the average number of cans of food collected each day?

   Ⓐ 2.87

   Ⓑ 27

   Ⓒ 28

   Ⓓ 28.7

Problem Solving  REAL WORLD

5. Mark has a board that is 12 feet long. He cuts the board into 8 pieces that are the same length. How long is each piece?

6. Josh pays $7.59 for 2.2 pounds of ground turkey. What is the price per pound of the ground turkey?

Name _____

Lesson 51

COMMON CORE STANDARD CC.5.NBT.7

Lesson Objective: Solve multistep decimal problems using the strategy *work backward*.

Problem Solving • Decimal Operations

Rebecca spent $32.55 for a photo album and three identical candles. The photo album cost $17.50 and the sales tax was $1.55. How much did each candle cost?

Read the Problem

What do I need to find	What information do I need to use?	How will I use the information?
I need to find <u>the cost of each</u> <u>candle</u> .	Rebecca spent <u>$32.55</u> for a photo album and <u>3</u> candles. The photo album cost <u>$17.50</u> The sales tax was <u>$1.55</u>.	I can <u>use a flowchart and</u> <u>work backward from the total</u> <u>amount Rebecca spent to</u> <u>find the cost of each candle</u>

Solve the Problem

• Make a flowchart to show the information. Then work backward to solve.

Cost of 3 candles	plus	Cost of photo album	plus	Sales tax	equals	Total spent
3 × cost of each candle	+	$17.50	+	$1.55	=	$32.55

Total spent	minus	Sales tax	minus	Cost of photo album	equals	Cost of 3 candles
$32.55	−	$1.55	−	$17.50	=	$13.50

• Divide the cost of 3 candles by 3 to find the cost of each candle.

$13.50 ÷ 3 = $4.50

So, each candle cost $4.50.

Use a flowchart to help you solve the problem.

1. Maria spent $28.69 on one pair of jeans and two T-shirts. The jeans cost $16.49. Each T-shirt cost the same amount. The sales tax was $1.62. How much did each T-shirt cost?

2. At the skating rink, Sean and Patrick spent $17.45 on admission and snacks. They used one coupon for $2 off the admission cost. The snacks cost $5.95. What is the admission cost for one?

1. Reshawn is buying 3 books in a set for $24.81. He will save $6.69 by buying the set instead of buying individual books. If each book costs the same amount, how much does each of the 3 books cost when purchased individually?

   Ⓐ $2.23
   Ⓑ $6.04
   Ⓒ $8.27
   Ⓓ $10.50

2. Mackenzie spent a total of $17.50 on Saturday afternoon. She bought a movie ticket for $7.25 and snacks for $4.95. She spent the rest of the money on bus fare to get to the movie and back home. How much was the bus fare each way if each trip cost the same amount?

   Ⓐ $2.60   Ⓒ $5.20
   Ⓑ $2.65   Ⓓ $5.30

3. Corey and Nicole spent $17.00, including sales tax, on 2 sandwiches and 3 slices of pizza. The sandwiches cost $5.25 each and the total sales tax was $0.92. How much did each slice of pizza cost?

   Ⓐ $1.86
   Ⓑ $2.47
   Ⓒ $2.79
   Ⓓ $5.58

4. Jocelyn bought 2 sweaters for the same price. She paid $23.56, including sales tax of $1.36 and a $5.00 coupon. What was the price of one sweater before the tax and coupon?

   Ⓐ $8.60
   Ⓑ $19.96
   Ⓒ $13.60
   Ⓓ $14.96

Problem Solving REAL WORLD

5. Samantha bought flowers at a craft store for $14.02. She also bought 4 packages of glass beads and 2 vases. The vases cost $3.59 each and the total sales tax was $1.34. The total amount she paid was $28.50, including sales tax. Explain a strategy you would use to find the cost of one package of glass beads.

_____

_____

_____

_____

Name _____

Lesson 52
COMMON CORE STANDARD CC.5.NF.1
Lesson Objective: Find a common denominator or a least common denominator to write equivalent fractions.

Common Denominators and Equivalent Fractions

You can find a common denominator of two fractions.

A **common denominator** of two fractions is a common multiple of their denominators.

Find a common denominator of $\frac{1}{6}$ and $\frac{7}{10}$. Rewrite the pair of fractions using a common denominator.

Step 1	Identify the denominators. The denominators are 6 and 10.
Step 2	List the multiples of the greater denominator, 10. Multiples of 10: 10, 20, 30, 40, 50, 60, ...
Step 3	Check if any of the multiples of the greater denominator are evenly divisible by the other denominator. Both 30 and 60 are evenly divisible by 6. Common denominators of $\frac{1}{6}$ and $\frac{7}{10}$ are 30 and 60.
Step 4	Rewrite the fractions with a denominator of 30. Multiply the numerator and the denominator of each fraction by the same number so that the denominator results in 30.

$$\frac{1}{6} = \frac{1 \times 5}{6 \times 5} = \frac{5}{30} \qquad \frac{7}{10} = \frac{7 \times 3}{10 \times 3} = \frac{21}{30}$$

Use a common denominator to write an equivalent fraction for each fraction.

1. $\frac{5}{12}, \frac{2}{9}$

   common denominator: _____

   _____

2. $\frac{3}{8}, \frac{5}{6}$

   common denominator: _____

   _____

3. $\frac{2}{9}, \frac{1}{6}$

   common denominator: _____

   _____

4. $\frac{3}{4}, \frac{9}{10}$

   common denominator: _____

   _____

1. Arturo wants to find the amount of time he spent on his math and science homework combined. He worked $\frac{2}{5}$ hour on math and $\frac{1}{3}$ hour on science. Which is the **best** strategy to find the least common denominator so he can add the time he spent on his homework?

   (A) Multiply denominators since they share no common factors other than 1.

   (B) Find all the multiples of each denominator.

   (C) One denominator is the multiple of the other, so the multiple is the least common denominator.

   (D) Add the denominators to find the least common multiple.

2. Francine wants to find the total of $\frac{2}{3}$ cup of blueberries and $\frac{5}{8}$ cup of raspberries. What is the least common denominator of the fractions?

   (A) 10   (C) 18

   (B) 11   (D) 24

3. Alana bought $\frac{3}{8}$ pound of Swiss cheese and $\frac{1}{4}$ pound of American cheese. Which pair of fractions **cannot** be used to find how many pounds of cheese she bought in all?

   (A) $\frac{6}{16}$ and $\frac{4}{16}$

   (B) $\frac{9}{24}$ and $\frac{6}{24}$

   (C) $\frac{24}{64}$ and $\frac{8}{64}$

   (D) $\frac{15}{40}$ and $\frac{10}{40}$

4. Charles bought $\frac{7}{8}$ foot of electrical wire and $\frac{5}{6}$ foot of copper wire for his science project. What is the least common denominator of the fractions?

   (A) 14

   (B) 18

   (C) 24

   (D) 48

Problem Solving REAL WORLD

5. Ella spends $\frac{2}{3}$ hour practicing the piano each day. She also spends $\frac{1}{2}$ hour jogging. What is the least common denominator of the fractions?

6. In a science experiment, a plant grew $\frac{3}{4}$ inch one week and $\frac{1}{2}$ inch the next week. Use a common denominator to write an equivalent fraction for each fraction.

Name _____

Lesson 53
COMMON CORE STANDARD CC.5.NF.1
Lesson Objective: Use equivalent fractions to add and subtract fractions.

Add and Subtract Fractions

To add or subtract fractions with unlike denominators, you need to rename them as fractions with like denominators. You can do this by making a list of equivalent fractions.

Add. $\frac{5}{12} + \frac{1}{8}$

Step 1 Write equivalent fractions for $\frac{5}{12}$. $\frac{5}{12}, \frac{10}{24}, \frac{15}{36}, \frac{20}{48}$

Step 2 Write equivalent fractions for $\frac{1}{8}$. $\frac{1}{8}, \frac{2}{16}, \frac{3}{24}$

Step 3 Rewrite the problem using the equivalent fractions. Then add.

$\frac{5}{12} + \frac{1}{8}$ becomes $\frac{10}{24} + \frac{3}{24} = \frac{13}{24}$.

> Stop when you find two fractions with the same denominator.

Subtract. $\frac{9}{10} - \frac{1}{2}$

Step 1 Write equivalent fractions for $\frac{9}{10}$. $\frac{9}{10}, \frac{18}{20}, \frac{27}{30}, \frac{36}{40}$

Step 2 Write equivalent fractions for $\frac{1}{2}$. $\frac{1}{2}, \frac{2}{4}, \frac{3}{6}, \frac{4}{8}, \frac{5}{10}$

Step 3 Rewrite the problem using the equivalent fractions. Then subtract.

$\frac{9}{10} - \frac{1}{2}$ becomes $\frac{9}{10} - \frac{5}{10} = \frac{4}{10}$. Written in simplest form, $\frac{4}{10} = \frac{2}{5}$.

Find the sum or difference. Write your answer in simplest form.

1. $\frac{2}{9} + \frac{1}{3}$ 2. $\frac{1}{2} + \frac{2}{5}$ 3. $\frac{1}{4} + \frac{1}{6}$ 4. $\frac{1}{5} + \frac{3}{4}$

_____ _____ _____ _____

5. $\frac{7}{8} - \frac{1}{4}$ 6. $\frac{3}{4} - \frac{2}{3}$ 7. $\frac{9}{10} - \frac{4}{5}$ 8. $\frac{8}{9} - \frac{5}{6}$

_____ _____ _____ _____

1. Brady used $\frac{2}{3}$ gallon of yellow paint and $\frac{1}{4}$ gallon of white paint to paint his dresser. How many gallons of paint did Brady use?

   (A) $\frac{3}{7}$ gallon

   (B) $\frac{3}{4}$ gallon

   (C) $\frac{5}{6}$ gallon

   (D) $\frac{11}{12}$ gallon

2. Mr. Barber uses $\frac{7}{9}$ yard of wire to put up a ceiling fan. He uses $\frac{1}{3}$ yard of wire to fix a switch. How much more wire does he use to put up the fan than to fix the switch?

   (A) $1\frac{1}{9}$ yards

   (B) $\frac{6}{9}$ yard

   (C) $\frac{4}{9}$ yard

   (D) $\frac{1}{3}$ yard

3. Tom jogged $\frac{3}{5}$ mile on Monday and $\frac{2}{6}$ mile on Tuesday. How much farther did Tom jog on Monday than on Tuesday?

   (A) $\frac{1}{30}$ mile

   (B) $\frac{3}{15}$ mile

   (C) $\frac{8}{30}$ mile

   (D) $\frac{14}{15}$ mile

4. Mindy bought $\frac{1}{6}$ pound of almonds and $\frac{3}{4}$ pound of walnuts. How many pounds of nuts did she buy in all?

   (A) $\frac{1}{3}$

   (B) $\frac{7}{12}$

   (C) $\frac{2}{3}$

   (D) $\frac{11}{12}$

Problem Solving REAL WORLD

5. Kaylin mixed two liquids for a science experiment. One container held $\frac{7}{8}$ cup and the other held $\frac{9}{10}$ cup. What is the total amount of the mixture?

6. Henry bought $\frac{1}{4}$ pound of screws and $\frac{2}{5}$ pound of nails to build a skateboard ramp. What is the total weight of the screws and nails?

Lesson 54

COMMON CORE STANDARD CC.5.NF.1

Lesson Objective: Add and subtract mixed numbers with unlike denominators.

Add and Subtract Mixed Numbers

When you add or subtract mixed numbers, you may need to rename the fractions as fractions with a common denominator.

Find the sum. Write the answer in simplest form. $5\frac{3}{4} + 2\frac{1}{3}$

Step 1   Model $5\frac{3}{4}$ and $2\frac{1}{3}$.

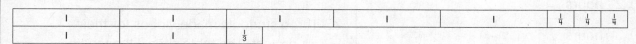

Step 2   A common denominator for $\frac{3}{4}$ and $\frac{1}{3}$ is 12,
so rename $5\frac{3}{4}$ as $5\frac{9}{12}$ and $2\frac{1}{3}$ as $2\frac{4}{12}$.

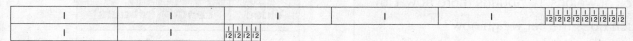

Step 3   Add the fractions.

$$\frac{9}{12} + \frac{4}{12} = \frac{13}{12}$$

Step 4   Add the whole numbers

$$5 + 2 = 7$$

Add the sums. Write the answer in simplest form.

$$\frac{13}{12} + 7 = 7\frac{13}{12}, \text{ or } 8\frac{1}{12}$$

So, $5\frac{3}{4} + 2\frac{1}{3} = 8\frac{1}{12}$.

Find the sum or difference. Write your answer in simplest form.

1. $2\frac{2}{9} + 4\frac{1}{6}$

2. $10\frac{5}{6} + 5\frac{3}{4}$

3. $11\frac{7}{8} - 9\frac{5}{6}$

4. $18\frac{3}{5} - 14\frac{1}{2}$

_____   _____   _____   _____

1. David practices piano for $1\frac{1}{3}$ hours on Monday and $3\frac{1}{2}$ hours on Tuesday. How much longer does he practice piano on Tuesday than on Monday?

   (A) $1\frac{1}{5}$ hours

   (B) $2\frac{1}{6}$ hours

   (C) $2\frac{2}{5}$ hours

   (D) $2\frac{5}{6}$ hours

2. Roberto's cat weighed $6\frac{3}{4}$ pounds last year. The cat weighs $1\frac{1}{2}$ pounds more now. How much does the cat weigh now?

   (A) $5\frac{1}{4}$ pounds

   (B) $7\frac{1}{4}$ pounds

   (C) $7\frac{3}{4}$ pounds

   (D) $8\frac{1}{4}$ pounds

3. Ken bought $3\frac{3}{4}$ pounds of apples at the farmers' market. Abby bought $2\frac{1}{8}$ pounds of apples. How many pounds of apples did Ken and Abby buy in all?

   (A) $5\frac{1}{8}$ pounds   (C) $5\frac{7}{8}$ pounds

   (B) $5\frac{1}{3}$ pounds   (D) $6\frac{1}{4}$ pounds

4. Three students made videos for their art project. The table shows the length of each video.

   Art in Nature

Video	Length (in hours)
1	$4\frac{3}{4}$
2	$2\frac{7}{12}$
3	$2\frac{1}{6}$

   How much longer is video 1 than video 3?

   (A) $1\frac{5}{12}$ hours   (C) $2\frac{5}{12}$ hours

   (B) $1\frac{7}{12}$ hours   (D) $2\frac{7}{12}$ hours

Problem Solving REAL WORLD

5. Jacobi bought $7\frac{1}{2}$ pounds of meatballs. He decided to cook $1\frac{1}{4}$ pounds and freeze the rest. How many pounds did he freeze?

   _____

6. Jill walked $8\frac{1}{8}$ miles to a park and then $7\frac{2}{5}$ miles home. How many miles did she walk in all?

   _____

Name _____

Lesson 55
COMMON CORE STANDARD CC.5.NF.1
Lesson Objective: Rename to find the difference of two mixed numbers.

Subtraction with Renaming

You can use a common denominator to find the difference of two mixed numbers.

Estimate. $9\frac{1}{6} - 2\frac{3}{4}$

Step 1 Estimate by using 0, $\frac{1}{2}$, and 1 as benchmarks.

$$9\frac{1}{6} - 2\frac{3}{4} \rightarrow 9 - 3 = 6$$

So, the difference should be close to 6.

Step 2 Identify a common denominator.

$9\frac{1}{6} - 2\frac{3}{4}$ A common denominator of 6 and 4 is 12.

Step 3 Write equivalent fractions using the common denominator.

$$9\frac{1}{6} = 9 + \frac{1 \times 2}{6 \times 2} = 9\frac{2}{12}$$
$$2\frac{3}{4} = 2 + \frac{3 \times 3}{4 \times 3} = 2\frac{9}{12}$$

Step 4 Rename if needed. Then subtract.

Since $\frac{2}{12} < \frac{9}{12}$, rename $9\frac{2}{12}$ as $8\frac{14}{12}$.

Subtract. $8\frac{14}{12} - 2\frac{9}{12} = 6\frac{5}{12}$

So, $9\frac{1}{6} - 2\frac{3}{4} = 6\frac{5}{12}$.

Since the difference of $6\frac{5}{12}$ is close to 6, the answer is reasonable.

Estimate. Then find the difference and write it in simplest form.

1. Estimate: _____

   $5\frac{1}{3} - 3\frac{5}{6}$ _____

2. Estimate: _____

   $7\frac{1}{4} - 2\frac{5}{12}$ _____

3. Estimate: _____

   $8\frac{2}{3} - 2\frac{7}{9}$ _____

4. Estimate: _____

   $9\frac{2}{5} - 3\frac{3}{4}$ _____

5. Estimate: _____

   $7\frac{3}{16} - 1\frac{5}{8}$ _____

6. Estimate: _____

   $2\frac{4}{9} - 1\frac{11}{18}$ _____

1. Kyle is hanging wallpaper in his bedroom. A roll of wallpaper is $18\frac{3}{8}$ feet long. Kyle cut off a piece of wallpaper $2\frac{5}{6}$ feet long. How much wallpaper is left on the roll?

   (A) $15\frac{13}{24}$ feet

   (B) $15\frac{7}{12}$ feet

   (C) $16\frac{13}{24}$ feet

   (D) $17\frac{3}{8}$ feet

2. Giselle made $24\frac{1}{8}$ ounces of lemonade. She sampled $1\frac{1}{2}$ ounces to make sure it is not too sour. How much lemonade is left?

   (A) $23\frac{9}{8}$ ounces

   (B) $23\frac{5}{8}$ ounces

   (C) $22\frac{5}{8}$ ounces

   (D) $22\frac{5}{16}$ ounces

3. Maria needs a piece of string $4\frac{2}{3}$ feet long for a science project. She cuts it from a piece that is $7\frac{1}{12}$ feet long. How much string does she have left?

   (A) $11\frac{3}{4}$ feet

   (B) $3\frac{5}{12}$ feet

   (C) $2\frac{7}{12}$ feet

   (D) $2\frac{5}{12}$ feet

4. Taylor saw an American alligator at a zoo that measured $12\frac{11}{12}$ feet long. The record length of an American alligator is $19\frac{1}{6}$ feet long. How much longer is the record alligator than the alligator Taylor saw?

   (A) $5\frac{5}{8}$ feet

   (B) $5\frac{7}{8}$ feet

   (C) $6\frac{1}{4}$ feet

   (D) $6\frac{1}{3}$ feet

Problem Solving REAL WORLD

5. Carlene bought $8\frac{1}{16}$ yards of ribbon to decorate a shirt. She only used $5\frac{1}{2}$ yards. How much ribbon does she have left over?

6. During his first vet visit, Pedro's puppy weighed $6\frac{1}{8}$ pounds. On his second visit, he weighed $9\frac{1}{16}$ pounds. How much weight did he gain between visits?

Algebra • Patterns with Fractions

You can find an unknown term in a sequence by finding a rule for the sequence.

Find the unknown term in the sequence.

$1\frac{2}{5}, 1\frac{7}{10}, 2, \underline{\hspace{1cm}}, 2\frac{3}{5}$

Step 1 Find equivalent fractions with a common denominator for all of the terms.

The denominators are 5 and 10. A common denominator is 10.

$1\frac{2}{5} = 1\frac{4}{10}$ and $2\frac{3}{5} = 2\frac{6}{10}$

Step 2 Write the terms in the sequence using the common denominator.

$1\frac{4}{10}, 1\frac{7}{10}, 2, \underline{\hspace{1cm}}, 2\frac{6}{10}$

Step 3 Write a rule that describes the pattern.

The sequence increases. To find the difference between terms, subtract at least two pairs of consecutive terms.

$1\frac{7}{10} - 1\frac{4}{10} = \frac{3}{10}$ $\qquad$ $2 - 1\frac{7}{10} = \frac{3}{10}$

So, a rule is to add $\frac{3}{10}$.

Step 4 Use the rule to find the unknown term.

Add $\frac{3}{10}$ to the third term to find the unknown term.

$2 + \frac{3}{10} = 2\frac{3}{10}$

Write a rule for the sequence. Then, find the unknown term.

1. $2\frac{2}{3}, 3\frac{1}{2}, \underline{\hspace{1cm}}, 5\frac{1}{6}, 6$

2. $4\frac{1}{2}, 3\frac{7}{8}, 3\frac{1}{4}, \underline{\hspace{1cm}}, 2$

Rule: _____

Rule: _____

1. Carrie is given a plant. After one week, it grows to $\frac{7}{8}$ foot tall, and after two weeks it grows to $1\frac{1}{2}$ feet tall. If it keeps growing at the same pace, how tall will it be after 3 weeks?

   (A) $2\frac{1}{4}$ feet

   (B) $2\frac{1}{8}$ feet

   (C) $1\frac{7}{8}$ feet

   (D) $1\frac{5}{8}$ feet

2. Chan ran a race course in $1\frac{3}{5}$ hours. The following month, he ran the same course in $1\frac{3}{10}$ hours. If his time improves by the same amount each month, how long will it take to run the course after another month?

   (A) $\frac{4}{5}$ hour

   (B) $\frac{9}{10}$ hour

   (C) 1 hour

   (D) $1\frac{1}{5}$ hours

3. When Bruce started bowling, he won $\frac{1}{4}$ of the games he played. Within six months, he was winning $\frac{7}{16}$ of his games. If he improves at the same rate, what fraction of his games should he expect to win after another six months?

   (A) $\frac{1}{2}$

   (B) $\frac{9}{16}$

   (C) $\frac{5}{8}$

   (D) $\frac{11}{16}$

4. A farm produced $1\frac{1}{8}$ tons of corn in its first year, $1\frac{3}{8}$ tons in its second year, and $1\frac{10}{16}$ tons in its third year. If the pattern continues each year, how much corn did the farm produce in the fourth year?

   (A) $1\frac{12}{16}$ tons

   (B) $1\frac{7}{8}$ tons

   (C) $1\frac{3}{4}$ tons

   (D) $1\frac{5}{16}$ tons

Problem Solving REAL WORLD

5. Jarett's puppy weighed $3\frac{3}{4}$ ounces at birth. At one week old, the puppy weighed $5\frac{1}{8}$ ounces. At two weeks old, the puppy weighed $6\frac{1}{2}$ ounces. If the weight gain continues in this pattern, how much will the puppy weigh at three weeks old?

6. A baker started out with 12 cups of flour. She had $9\frac{1}{4}$ cups of flour left after the first batch of batter she made. She had $6\frac{1}{2}$ cups of flour left after the second batch of batter she made. If she makes two more batches of batter, how many cups of flour will be left?

Algebra • Use Properties of Addition

You can use the properties of addition to help you add fractions with unlike denominators.

Use the Commutative Property and the Associative Property.

Add. $\left(3\frac{2}{5} + 1\frac{7}{15}\right) + 2\frac{1}{5}$

$\left(3\frac{2}{5} + 1\frac{7}{15}\right) + 2\frac{1}{5} = \left(1\frac{7}{15} + 3\frac{2}{5}\right) + 2\frac{1}{5}$ ← Use the Commutative Property to order fractions with like denominators.

$= 1\frac{7}{15} + \left(3\frac{2}{5} + 2\frac{1}{5}\right)$ ← Use the Associative Property to group fractions with like denominators.

$= 1\frac{7}{15} + 5\frac{3}{5}$ ← Use mental math to add the fractions with like denominators.

$= 1\frac{7}{15} + 5\frac{9}{15}$ ← Write equivalent fractions with like denominators. Then add.

$= 6\frac{16}{15} = 7\frac{1}{15}$ ← Rename and simplify.

Use the properties and mental math to solve. Write your answer in simplest form.

1. $\left(\frac{5}{7} + \frac{3}{14}\right) + \frac{4}{7}$ _____

2. $\left(\frac{2}{5} + \frac{5}{9}\right) + \frac{7}{9}$ _____

3. $\left(3\frac{7}{10} + 5\frac{3}{4}\right) + \frac{3}{4}$ _____

4. $2\frac{5}{12} + \left(4\frac{2}{3} + 3\frac{7}{12}\right)$ _____

5. $3\frac{3}{8} + \left(2\frac{1}{5} + 5\frac{1}{8}\right)$ _____

6. $\left(4\frac{3}{7} + 2\frac{1}{6}\right) + 3\frac{5}{7}$ _____

1. Ava hiked a trail that has three sections that are $4\frac{7}{8}$ miles, $3\frac{3}{4}$ miles, and $5\frac{1}{8}$ miles long. Ava wrote this expression to show the total distance that she hiked.

$$\left(4\frac{7}{8} + 3\frac{3}{4}\right) + 5\frac{1}{8}$$

Which shows another way to write the expression using only the Commutative Property of Addition?

Ⓐ $4\frac{7}{8} + \left(3\frac{3}{4} + 5\frac{1}{8}\right)$

Ⓑ $\left(5\frac{1}{8} + 4\frac{7}{8}\right) + 3\frac{3}{4}$

Ⓒ $\left(3\frac{3}{4} + 4\frac{7}{8}\right) + 5\frac{1}{8}$

Ⓓ $(4 + 3 + 5) + \left(\frac{7}{8} + \frac{3}{4} + \frac{1}{8}\right)$

2. Shelley wove three rugs with geometric designs. She wrote this expression to show the total length in feet of all three rugs.

$$\left(8\frac{7}{16} + 11\frac{7}{8}\right) + 15\frac{1}{4}$$

Which shows another way to write the expression using the Associative Property of Addition?

Ⓐ $8\frac{7}{16} + \left(15\frac{7}{8} + 11\frac{1}{4}\right)$

Ⓑ $8\frac{7}{16} + \left(11\frac{7}{8} + 15\frac{1}{4}\right)$

Ⓒ $\left(8\frac{7}{16} + 11\frac{7}{8}\right) + \left(8\frac{7}{16} + 15\frac{1}{4}\right)$

Ⓓ $(8 + 11 + 15) + \left(\frac{7}{16} + \frac{7}{8} + \frac{1}{4}\right)$

3. Larry wrote this expression to show the total number of hours he spent driving during the last three weeks.

$$\left(5\frac{2}{5} + 7\frac{4}{10}\right) + 9\frac{1}{10}$$

Which shows another way to write the expression using the Associative Property of Addition?

Ⓐ $5\frac{2}{5} + \left(7\frac{4}{10} + 9\frac{1}{10}\right)$

Ⓑ $5\frac{2}{5} + \left(9\frac{1}{10} + 7\frac{4}{10}\right)$

Ⓒ $\left(7\frac{4}{10} + 9\frac{1}{10}\right) + 5\frac{2}{5}$

Ⓓ $(5 + 9 + 4) + \left(\frac{2}{5} + \frac{4}{10} + \frac{1}{10}\right)$

4. Marco wrote the following expression to find the total amount of gasoline he bought last month.

$$8\frac{1}{5} + 6\frac{1}{8} + 7\frac{3}{5}$$

Which expression will help make the addition easier for Marco?

Ⓐ $\left(8\frac{1}{5} + 6\frac{1}{8}\right) + 7\frac{3}{5}$

Ⓑ $\left(7\frac{3}{5} + 6\frac{1}{8}\right) + 8\frac{1}{5}$

Ⓒ $\left(8\frac{1}{5} + 7\frac{3}{5}\right) + 6\frac{1}{8}$

Ⓓ $\left(8\frac{1}{5} + 7\frac{3}{5}\right) + 6\frac{1}{5}$

Problem Solving REAL WORLD

5. Elizabeth rode her bike $6\frac{1}{2}$ miles from her house to the library and then another $2\frac{2}{5}$ miles to her friend Milo's house. If Carson's house is $2\frac{1}{2}$ miles beyond Milo's house, how far would she travel from her house to Carson's house?

_____

6. Hassan made a vegetable salad with $2\frac{3}{8}$ pounds of tomatoes, $1\frac{1}{4}$ pounds of asparagus, and $2\frac{7}{8}$ pounds of potatoes. How many pounds of vegetables did he use altogether?

_____

Lesson 58
COMMON CORE STANDARD CC.5.NF.2
Lesson Objective: Use models to add
fractions with unlike denominators.

Addition with Unlike Denominators

Karen is stringing a necklace with beads. She puts green beads on $\frac{1}{2}$ of the string and purple beads on $\frac{3}{10}$ of the string. How much of the string does Karen cover with beads?

You can use fraction strips to help you add fractions with unlike denominators. Trade fraction strips of fractions with unlike denominators for equivalent strips of fractions with like denominators.

Use fraction strips to find the sum. Write your answer in simplest form.

$\frac{1}{2} + \frac{3}{10}$

Step 1   Use a $\frac{1}{2}$ strip and three $\frac{1}{10}$ strips to model fractions with unlike denominators.

Step 2   Trade the $\frac{1}{2}$ strip for five $\frac{1}{10}$ strips.

$$\frac{1}{2} + \frac{3}{10} = \frac{5}{10} + \frac{3}{10}$$

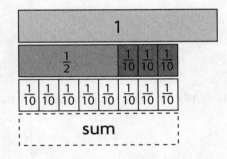

Step 3   Add the fractions with like denominators.

$$\frac{5}{10} + \frac{3}{10} = \frac{8}{10}$$

Step 4   Write the answer in simplest form.

$$\frac{8}{10} = \frac{4}{5}$$

So, Karen covers $\frac{4}{5}$ of the string with beads.

Use fraction strips to find the sum Write your answer in simplest form.

1. $\frac{3}{8} + \frac{3}{4}$

2. $\frac{2}{3} + \frac{1}{4}$

3. $\frac{5}{6} + \frac{7}{12}$

Use the information for 1-2.

Addison used $\frac{5}{6}$ yard of ribbon to decorate a photo frame. She used $\frac{1}{3}$ yard of ribbon to decorate her scrapbook.

1

$\frac{1}{6}$	$\frac{1}{6}$	$\frac{1}{6}$	$\frac{1}{6}$	$\frac{1}{6}$	$\frac{1}{3}$

1. Which fraction strips should Addison trade for the $\frac{1}{3}$ strip in order to find how many yards of ribbon she used in all?

   (A) $\frac{1}{2}$ (C) $\frac{1}{4}$

   (B) $\frac{1}{3}$ (D) $\frac{1}{6}$

2. How many yards of ribbon did Addison use in all?

   (A) $1\frac{1}{6}$ yards   (C) $\frac{5}{9}$ yard

   (B) 1 yard   (D) $\frac{1}{2}$ yard

Use the information for 3-4.

Gabrielle paints a flower pot to sell at the craft fair. She paints $\frac{2}{5}$ of the pot teal, $\frac{3}{10}$ of the pot yellow, and the rest of the pot white.

1

$\frac{1}{5}$	$\frac{1}{5}$	$\frac{1}{10}$	$\frac{1}{10}$	$\frac{1}{10}$

3. Which fraction strips should Gabrielle trade for the $\frac{2}{5}$ strip in order to find how much of the pot is painted teal or yellow?

   (A) $\frac{1}{2}$ (C) $\frac{1}{10}$

   (B) $\frac{1}{5}$ (D) $\frac{1}{15}$

4. How much of the pot is painted teal or yellow?

   (A) $\frac{1}{10}$ (C) $\frac{1}{2}$

   (B) $\frac{5}{15}$ (D) $\frac{7}{10}$

Problem Solving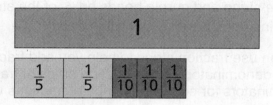

5. Brandus bought $\frac{1}{3}$ pound of ground turkey and $\frac{3}{4}$ pound of ground beef to make sausages. How many pounds of meat did he buy?

6. To make a ribbon and bow for a hat, Stacey needs $\frac{5}{6}$ yard of black ribbon and $\frac{2}{3}$ yard of red ribbon. How much total ribbon does she need?

Name _____

Lesson 59
COMMON CORE STANDARD CC.5.NF.2
Lesson Objective: Use models to subtract fractions with unlike denominators.

Subtraction with Unlike Denominators

You can use fraction strips to help you subtract fractions with unlike denominators. Trade fraction strips of fractions with unlike denominators for equivalent strips of fractions with like denominators.

Use fraction strips to find the difference. Write your answer in simplest form.

$\frac{1}{2} - \frac{1}{10}$

Step 1	Use a $\frac{1}{2}$ fraction strip to model the first fraction.	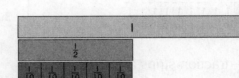
Step 2	Trade the $\frac{1}{2}$ strip for five $\frac{1}{10}$ strips. $\frac{1}{2} - \frac{1}{10} = \frac{5}{10} - \frac{1}{10}$	
Step 3	Subtract by taking away $\frac{1}{10}$. $\frac{5}{10} - \frac{1}{10} = \frac{4}{10}$	

So, $\frac{1}{2} - \frac{1}{10} = \frac{4}{10}$. Written in simplest form, $\frac{4}{10} = \frac{2}{5}$.

Use fraction strips to find the difference. Write your answer in simplest form.

1. $\frac{7}{8} - \frac{1}{2}$

2. $\frac{2}{3} - \frac{1}{4}$

3. $\frac{5}{6} - \frac{1}{3}$

_____

_____

_____

4. $\frac{1}{2} - \frac{1}{3}$

5. $\frac{9}{10} - \frac{4}{5}$

6. $\frac{2}{3} - \frac{5}{12}$

_____

_____

_____

Use the information for 1-2.

Armand lives $\frac{7}{8}$ mile from school. On his way home from school, he rode his skateboard $\frac{5}{16}$ mile and walked the rest of the way.

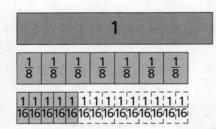

1. How many $\frac{1}{16}$ fraction strips are equal to $\frac{7}{8}$?

   (A) 5   (C) 8

   (B) 7   (D) 14

2. How far did Armand walk?

   (A) $\frac{1}{8}$ mile   (C) $\frac{9}{16}$ mile

   (B) $\frac{1}{2}$ mile   (D) $1\frac{1}{8}$ miles

Use the information for 3-4.

Kim has a piece of cardboard that is $\frac{5}{6}$ inch long. She cut off a $\frac{5}{12}$-inch piece.

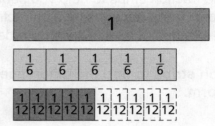

3. How many $\frac{1}{12}$ fraction strips are equal to $\frac{5}{6}$?

   (A) 5   (C) 10

   (B) 6   (D) 12

4. How long is the remaining piece of cardboard?

   (A) $\frac{10}{12}$ inch   (C) $\frac{1}{3}$ inch

   (B) $\frac{5}{12}$ inch   (D) $\frac{1}{6}$ inch

Problem Solving

5. Amber had $\frac{3}{8}$ of a cake left after her party. She wrapped a piece that was $\frac{1}{4}$ of the original cake for her best friend. What fractional part did she have left for herself?

6. Wesley bought $\frac{1}{2}$ pound of nails for a project. When he finished the project, he had $\frac{1}{4}$ pound of the nails left. How many pounds of nails did he use?

Estimate Fraction Sums and Differences

You can round fractions to 0, to $\frac{1}{2}$, or to 1 to estimate sums and differences.

Estimate the sum. $\frac{4}{6} + \frac{1}{9}$

Step 1   Find $\frac{4}{6}$ on the number line. Is it closest to 0, $\frac{1}{2}$, or 1? The fraction $\frac{4}{6}$ is closest to $\frac{1}{2}$.

$$\frac{0}{6} \quad \frac{1}{6} \quad \frac{2}{6} \quad \frac{3}{6} \quad \frac{4}{6} \quad \frac{5}{6} \quad \frac{6}{6}$$

$$0 \qquad\qquad \frac{1}{2} \qquad\qquad 1$$

Step 2   Find $\frac{1}{9}$ on the number line. Is it closest to 0, $\frac{1}{2}$, or 1? The fraction $\frac{1}{9}$ is closest to 0.

$$\frac{0}{9} \quad \frac{1}{9} \quad \frac{2}{9} \quad \frac{3}{9} \quad \frac{4}{9} \quad \frac{5}{9} \quad \frac{6}{9} \quad \frac{7}{9} \quad \frac{8}{9} \quad \frac{9}{9}$$

$$0 \qquad\qquad \frac{1}{2} \qquad\qquad 1$$

Step 3   To estimate the sum $\frac{4}{6} + \frac{1}{9}$, add the two rounded numbers.

$$\frac{1}{2} + 0 = \frac{1}{2}$$

So, $\frac{4}{6} + \frac{1}{9}$ is about $\frac{1}{2}$.

Estimate the sum or difference.

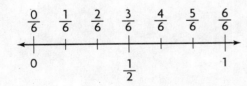

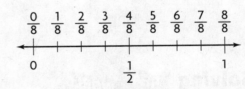

1. $\frac{4}{6} + \frac{1}{8}$ 2. $\frac{2}{6} + \frac{7}{8}$ 3. $\frac{5}{6} - \frac{3}{8}$

_____   _____   _____

4. $\frac{4}{6} + \frac{3}{8}$ 5. $\frac{7}{8} - \frac{5}{6}$ 6. $\frac{1}{6} + \frac{7}{8}$

_____   _____   _____

1. Ron walked $\frac{8}{10}$ mile from his grandmother's house to the store. Then he walked $\frac{9}{10}$ mile to his house. About how far did he walk altogether?

   (A) about $\frac{1}{2}$ mile

   (B) about 1 mile

   (C) about $1\frac{1}{2}$ miles

   (D) about 2 miles

2. Sophia baby-sat for $3\frac{7}{12}$ hours on Friday. She baby-sat $2\frac{5}{6}$ hours on Saturday. Which is the **best** estimate of how many hours Sophia baby-sat altogether?

   (A) about $5\frac{1}{2}$ hours

   (B) about 6 hours

   (C) about $6\frac{1}{2}$ hours

   (D) about 7 hours

3. Three fences on a ranch measure $\frac{15}{16}$ mile, $\frac{7}{8}$ mile, and $\frac{7}{16}$ mile. Which is the **best** estimate of the total length of all three fences?

   (A) $1\frac{1}{2}$ miles

   (B) 2 miles

   (C) $2\frac{1}{2}$ miles

   (D) 3 miles

4. Mr. Krasa poured $\frac{5}{16}$ gallon of white paint into a bucket. He then added $\frac{3}{4}$ gallon of blue paint and $\frac{3}{8}$ gallon of red paint. Which is the **best** estimate of the total amount of paint in the bucket?

   (A) $\frac{3}{4}$ gallon

   (B) 1 gallon

   (C) $1\frac{1}{2}$ gallons

   (D) 3 gallons

Problem Solving  REAL WORLD

5. For a fruit salad recipe, Jenna combined $\frac{3}{8}$ cup of raisins, $\frac{7}{8}$ cup of oranges, and $\frac{3}{4}$ cup of apples. About how many cups of fruit are in the salad?

   _____

6. Tyler had $2\frac{7}{16}$ yards of fabric. He used $\frac{3}{4}$ yard to make a vest. About how much fabric did he have left?

   _____

Name _____

Lesson 61
COMMON CORE STANDARD CC.5.NF.2
Lesson Objective: Solve problems using
the strategy *work backward*.

Problem Solving • Practice Addition and Subtraction

Makayla walks for exercise. She wants to walk a total of 6 miles.
On Monday, she walked $2\frac{5}{6}$ miles. On Tuesday, she walked $1\frac{1}{3}$ miles.
How many more miles does Makayla need to walk to reach her goal?

Read the Problem	Solve the Problem
What do I need to find I need to find <u>the distance that</u> <u>Makayla needs to walk.</u>	• Start with the equation. $$6 = 2\frac{5}{6} + 1\frac{1}{3} + x$$ Subtraction is the inverse operation of addition.
What information do I need to use? I need to use <u>the distance she</u> <u>wants to walk</u> and <u>the distance</u> <u>she has already walked.</u>	• Use subtraction to work backward and rewrite the equation. $$6 - 2\frac{5}{6} - 1\frac{1}{3} = x$$
How will I use the information? First <u>I can write an equation</u> $6 = 2\frac{5}{6} + 1\frac{1}{3} + x$. Then <u>I can work backward to</u> <u>solve the problem.</u>	• Subtract to find the value of *x*. $$\begin{array}{rl} 6 = & 5\frac{6}{6} \\ -2\frac{5}{6} = & -2\frac{5}{6} \\ \hline & 3\frac{1}{6} \end{array} \longrightarrow \begin{array}{rl} 3\frac{1}{6} = & 2\frac{7}{6} \\ -1\frac{1}{3} = & -1\frac{2}{6} \\ \hline & 1\frac{5}{6} \end{array}$$ Estimate to show that your answer is reasonable. $$3 + 1 + 2 = 6$$ So, Makayla has to walk <u>$1\frac{5}{6}$</u> more miles to reach her goal.

1. Ben has $5\frac{3}{4}$ cups of sugar. He uses $\frac{2}{3}$ cup of sugar to make cookies. Then he uses $2\frac{1}{2}$ cups of sugar to make fresh lemonade. How many cups of sugar does Ben have left?

   _____

2. Cheryl has 5 ft of ribbon. She cuts a $3\frac{3}{4}$-ft strip to make a hair bow. Then she cuts a $\frac{5}{6}$-ft strip for a border on a scrapbook page. Is there enough ribbon for Cheryl to cut two $\frac{1}{3}$-ft pieces to put on a picture frame? **Explain.**

   _____

   _____

1. Jacques caught 3 fish weighing a total of $23\frac{1}{2}$ pounds. Two of the fish weighed $9\frac{5}{8}$ and $6\frac{1}{4}$ pounds. How much did the third fish weigh?

   (A) $6\frac{5}{8}$ pounds

   (B) $7\frac{3}{8}$ pounds

   (C) $7\frac{5}{8}$ pounds

   (D) $8\frac{3}{8}$ pounds

2. Maria bought a total of $1\frac{3}{4}$ dozen bagels. Of the total, she bought $\frac{1}{6}$ dozen whole grain bagels, $\frac{3}{4}$ dozen sesame seed bagels, and some plain bagels. How many dozen plain bagels did Maria buy?

   (A) $\frac{5}{6}$ dozen

   (B) 1 dozen

   (C) $\frac{11}{12}$ dozen

   (D) $2\frac{2}{3}$ dozen

3. A squash, an apple, and an orange weigh a total of $2\frac{3}{8}$ pounds. The squash weighs $1\frac{15}{16}$ pounds, and the apple weighs $\frac{1}{4}$ pound. How much does the orange weigh?

   (A) $\frac{1}{8}$ pound

   (B) $\frac{3}{16}$ pound

   (C) $\frac{1}{4}$ pound

   (D) $\frac{5}{16}$ pound

4. Kelsey entered the triathlon at Camp Meadowlark. The total distance was $15\frac{11}{16}$ miles. The bike segment was $12\frac{1}{4}$ miles, and the running segment was $3\frac{1}{16}$ miles. How long was the swimming segment?

   (A) $\frac{3}{16}$ mile

   (B) $\frac{1}{4}$ mile

   (C) $\frac{5}{16}$ mile

   (D) $\frac{3}{8}$ mile

Problem Solving  REAL WORLD

5. In three days this week, Julio worked $18\frac{7}{10}$ total hours. He worked $6\frac{1}{5}$ hours on the first day and $6\frac{2}{5}$ hours on the second day. Explain how you would find the number of hours Julio worked on the third day.

   _____

   _____

   _____

   _____

   _____

Lesson 62

COMMON CORE STANDARD CC.5.NF.3

Lesson Objective: Solve division problems and decide when to write a remainder as a fraction.

Interpret the Remainder

Erin has 87 ounces of trail mix. She puts an equal number of ounces in each of 12 bags. How many ounces does she put in each bag?

$$\begin{array}{r} 7\ r3 \\ 12\overline{)87} \\ -84 \\ \hline 3 \end{array}$$

First, divide to find the quotient and remainder. Then, decide how to use the quotient and the remainder to answer the question.

- The dividend, __87__, represents the total number of ounces of trail mix.
- The divisor, __12__, represents the total number of bags.
- The quotient, __7__, represents the whole-number part of the number of ounces in each bag.
- The remainder, __3__, represents the number of ounces left over.

Divide the 3 ounces in the remainder by the divisor, 12, to write the

remainder as a fraction: __$\frac{3}{12}$__

Write the fraction part in simplest form in your answer.

So, Erin puts __$7\frac{1}{4}$__ ounces of trail mix in each bag.

Interpret the remainder to solve.

1. Harry goes on a canoe trip with his scout troop. They will canoe a total of 75 miles and want to travel 8 miles each day. How many days will they need to travel the entire distance?

_____

2. Hannah and her family want to hike 8 miles per day along a 125-mile-long trail. How many days will Hannah and her family hike exactly 8 miles?

_____

3. There are 103 students eating lunch in the cafeteria. Each table seats 4 students. All the tables are full, except for one table. How many students are sitting at the table that is not full?

_____

4. Emily buys 240 square feet of carpet. She can convert square feet to square yards by dividing the number of square feet by 9. How many square yards of carpet did Emily buy? (Hint: Write the remainder as a fraction.)

_____

123

Name _____

1. Taylor took 560 photographs during summer vacation. She placed 12 photos on each page of her scrapbook, except the last page. She had fewer than 12 photos to put on the last page. How many photos did Taylor place on the last page of the scrapbook?

   (A) 7   (C) 9

   (B) 8   (D) 10

2. Marla filled up her car's gas tank and then went on a trip. After she drove 329 miles, she filled her tank with 14 gallons of gas. If she drove the same number of miles on each gallon of gas, how many miles per gallon did Marla drive?

   (A) 23 miles per gallon

   (B) $23\frac{1}{2}$ miles per gallon

   (C) 24 miles per gallon

   (D) $24\frac{1}{2}$ miles per gallon

3. Kate made 180 ounces of punch for a party. She pours 8 ounces of punch for one serving. How many people can have a full serving?

   (A) 22

   (B) $22\frac{1}{2}$

   (C) 23

   (D) 25

4. The pool director has a list of 123 students who have signed up for swimming lessons. The pool director can register 7 students in each class. What is the **least** number of classes needed for all the students to be registered in a class?

   (A) 16   (C) 18

   (B) 17   (D) 19

Problem Solving  REAL WORLD

5. Fiona bought 212 stickers to make a sticker book. If she places 18 stickers on each page, how many pages will her sticker book have?

6. Jenny has 220 ounces of cleaning solution that she wants to divide equally among 12 large containers. How much cleaning solution should she put in each container?

Connect Fractions to Division

You can write a fraction as a division expression.

$$\frac{4}{5} = 4 \div 5 \qquad \frac{15}{3} = 15 \div 3$$

There are 8 students in a wood-working class and 5 sheets of plywood for them to share equally. What fraction of a sheet of plywood will each student get?

Divide. 5 ÷ 8   **Use a drawing.**

Step 1 Draw ___5___ rectangles to represent 5 sheets of plywood. Since there are 8 students, draw lines to divide each

piece of plywood into __eighths__ .

 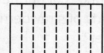  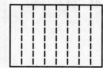 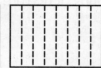

Each student's share of 1 sheet of plywood is $\frac{1}{8}$.

Step 2 Count the total number of eighths each student gets.

Since there are 5 sheets of plywood, each student will

get 5 of the __eighths__ , or $\frac{5}{8}$.

Step 3 Complete the number sentence.

$$5 \div 8 = \frac{5}{8}$$

Step 4 Check your answer.

Since $\frac{5}{8}$ × $\frac{8}{5}$ = ___5___ , the quotient is correct.

So, each student will get $\frac{5}{8}$ of a sheet of plywood.

Complete the number sentence to solve.

1. Ten friends share 6 pizzas equally. What fraction of a pizza does each friend get?

2. Four students share 7 sandwiches equally. How much of a sandwich does each student get?

    6 ÷ 10 = _____   7 ÷ 4 = _____

1. Four friends share 3 apples equally. What fraction of an apple does each friend get?

Ⓐ $\frac{2}{3}$

Ⓑ $\frac{3}{4}$

Ⓒ $1\frac{1}{4}$

Ⓓ $1\frac{1}{3}$

2. Ten pounds of rice are distributed equally into 6 bags to give out at the food bank. How many pounds of rice are in each bag?

Ⓐ $\frac{3}{5}$ pound

Ⓑ $1\frac{1}{3}$ pounds

Ⓒ $1\frac{2}{3}$ pounds

Ⓓ $1\frac{4}{5}$ pounds

3. Twelve friends share 4 pizzas equally. What fraction of a pizza does each friend get?

Ⓐ $\frac{1}{12}$

Ⓑ $\frac{1}{3}$

Ⓒ $\frac{1}{4}$

Ⓓ $\frac{1}{2}$

4. Terry picked 7 pounds of strawberries. She wants to share the strawberries equally among 3 of her neighbors. How many pounds of strawberries will each neighbor get?

Ⓐ $\frac{3}{7}$ pound

Ⓑ $\frac{7}{10}$ pound

Ⓒ $1\frac{3}{7}$ pounds

Ⓓ $2\frac{1}{3}$ pounds

Problem Solving REAL WORLD

5. There are 12 students in a jewelry-making class and 8 sets of charms. What fraction of a set of charms will each student get?

_____

6. Five friends share 6 cheesecakes equally. How many cheesecakes will each friend get?

_____

Lesson **64**

COMMON CORE STANDARD CC.5.NF.4a

Lesson Objective: Model to find the fractional part of a group.

Find Part of a Group

Lauren bought 12 stamps for postcards. She gave Brianna $\frac{1}{6}$ of them. How many stamps did Lauren give to Brianna?

Find $\frac{1}{6}$ of 12.

Step 1 What is the denominator in the fraction of the stamps Lauren gave to Brianna? 6
So, divide the 12 stamps into 6 equal groups. Circle the groups.

Step 2 Each group represents $\frac{1}{6}$ of the stamps.

How many stamps are in 1 group? 2

So, $\frac{1}{6}$ of 12 is __2__, or $\frac{1}{6} \times 12$ is __2__.

So, Lauren gave Brianna __2__ stamps.

Use a model to solve.

1. $\frac{3}{4} \times 12 =$ _____

2. $\frac{1}{3} \times 9 =$ _____

3. $\frac{3}{5} \times 20 =$ _____

4. $\frac{4}{6} \times 18 =$ _____

1. Sophie uses 18 beads to make a necklace. Three-sixths of the beads are purple. How many of Sophie's beads are purple?

   (A) 6
   (B) 9
   (C) 12
   (D) 15

2. Charlotte bought 16 songs. Three-fourths of the songs are pop songs.

   How many of the songs are pop songs?

   (A) 16
   (B) 12
   (C) 8
   (D) 4

3. Mr. Walton ordered 12 pizzas for the art class celebration. One-fourth of the pizzas had only mushrooms.

   How many of the pizzas had only mushrooms?

   (A) 3   (C) 8
   (B) 4   (D) 9

4. Trisha's mom baked 16 muffins. Two-eighths of the muffins have cranberries.

   How many of the muffins have cranberries?

   (A) 12   (C) 4
   (B) 8   (D) 2

Problem Solving

5. Marco drew 20 pictures. He drew $\frac{3}{4}$ of them in art class. How many pictures did Marco draw in art class?

6. Caroline has 10 marbles. One half of them are blue. How many of Caroline's marbles are blue?

Lesson 65

COMMON CORE STANDARD CC.5.NF.4a

Lesson Objective: Model the product of a fraction and a whole number.

Multiply Fractions and Whole Numbers

Find the product. $\frac{3}{8} \times 4$

Step 1 Draw 4 rectangles to represent the factor 4.

Step 2 The denominator of the factor $\frac{3}{8}$ is 8. So, divide the 4 rectangles into 8 equal parts.

Step 3 The numerator of the factor $\frac{3}{8}$ is 3. So, shade 3 of the parts.

Step 4 The 4 rectangles have 3 shaded parts. Each rectangle is divided into 2 equal parts. So, $\frac{3}{2}$ of the rectangles are shaded.

So, $\frac{3}{8} \times 4$ is $\frac{3}{2}$, or $1\frac{1}{2}$.

Find the product.

1. $\frac{5}{12} \times 4 =$ _____

2. $8 \times \frac{3}{4} =$ _____

3. $\frac{7}{9} \times 3 =$ _____

4. $5 \times \frac{4}{7} =$ _____

5. $\frac{9}{10} \times 5 =$ _____

6. $3 \times \frac{3}{4} =$ _____

7. $\frac{7}{12} \times 6 =$ _____

8. $12 \times \frac{2}{9} =$ _____

9. $\frac{2}{9} \times 3 =$ _____

129

1. Gwen uses $\frac{2}{3}$ cup of sugar for one batch of cookies. She used a model to find how much sugar to use in 2 batches of cookies.

How much sugar does Gwen need for 2 batches of cookies?

Ⓐ $1\frac{1}{3}$ cups

Ⓑ $1\frac{2}{3}$ cups

Ⓒ $2\frac{1}{3}$ cups

Ⓓ $2\frac{2}{3}$ cups

2. Brandon used $\frac{3}{4}$ of an 8-ounce package of blueberries to make muffins. How many ounces of blueberries did he use for the muffins? You may use a model to help you solve the problem.

Ⓐ 2 ounces

Ⓑ 4 ounces

Ⓒ 6 ounces

Ⓓ $7\frac{1}{4}$ ounces

3. Yoshi wants $\frac{3}{5}$ of his garden to have red flowers. His garden has an area of 3 square yards. He used a model to find the area of his garden that will have red flowers.

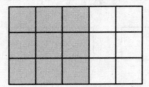

What area of Yoshi's garden will have red flowers?

Ⓐ $1\frac{1}{5}$ square yards

Ⓑ $1\frac{4}{5}$ square yards

Ⓒ $2\frac{1}{5}$ square yards

Ⓓ $3\frac{3}{5}$ square yards

4. Kenya needs $\frac{1}{4}$ yard of material to make a placemat. How much material does she need for 6 placemats? You may use a model to help you solve the problem.

Ⓐ $1\frac{1}{4}$ yards

Ⓑ $1\frac{1}{2}$ yards

Ⓒ $1\frac{3}{4}$ yards

Ⓓ $6\frac{1}{4}$ yards

Problem Solving REAL WORLD

5. Jody has a 5-pound bag of potatoes. She uses $\frac{4}{5}$ of the bag to make potato salad. How many pounds of potatoes does Jody use for the potato salad?

6. Lucas lives $\frac{5}{8}$ mile from school. Kenny lives twice as far as Lucas from school. How many miles does Kenny live from school?

Name _____

Lesson 66

COMMON CORE STANDARD CC.5.NF.4a
Lesson Objective: Multiply fractions and whole numbers.

Fraction and Whole Number Multiplication

Find the product. $3 \times \dfrac{5}{6}$

$3 \times \dfrac{5}{6} = \dfrac{3}{\boxed{1}} \times \dfrac{5}{6}$ Write the whole-number factor, 3, as $\dfrac{3}{1}$.

$= \dfrac{3 \times \boxed{5}}{1 \times 6}$ Multiply the numerators. Then multiply the denominators.

$= \dfrac{\boxed{15}}{6}$

$= \boxed{2}\,\dfrac{3}{6}$, or $2\,\dfrac{\boxed{1}}{\boxed{2}}$ Write the product as a mixed number in simplest form.

So, $3 \times \dfrac{5}{6}$ is $\underline{2\tfrac{1}{2}}$.

Find the product. Write the product in simplest form.

1. $\dfrac{2}{3} \times 8 = \dfrac{2}{3} \times \dfrac{8}{\square}$

     $= \dfrac{\square \times \square}{\square \times \square}$

     $= \dfrac{\square}{\square}$, or _____

2. $4 \times \dfrac{2}{9} =$ _____

3. $6 \times \dfrac{3}{4} =$ _____

4. $\dfrac{4}{9} \times 3 =$ _____

5. $5 \times \dfrac{3}{8} =$ _____

6. $9 \times \dfrac{2}{3} =$ _____

7. $2 \times \dfrac{5}{6} =$ _____

8. $7 \times \dfrac{4}{10} =$ _____

1. Julia has a recipe for salad dressing that calls for $\frac{1}{4}$ cup of sugar. Julia is making 5 batches of the salad dressing. How much sugar will she use?

   (A) $\frac{4}{5}$ cup

   (B) $1\frac{1}{5}$ cups

   (C) $1\frac{1}{4}$ cups

   (D) $5\frac{1}{4}$ cups

2. Taniqua took a test that had 20 questions. She got $\frac{4}{5}$ of the questions correct. How many questions did Taniqua get correct?

   (A) 25

   (B) 16

   (C) 15

   (D) 12

3. In a class book order, $\frac{2}{3}$ of the books are fantasy and $\frac{1}{4}$ of the books are biography. If the order contains 60 books, how many books are either fantasy or biography?

   (A) 15

   (B) 30

   (C) 40

   (D) 55

4. Laurie runs around a track that is $\frac{1}{4}$ mile long. If she does 10 laps around the track, how far does she run?

   (A) $\frac{2}{5}$ mile

   (B) $2\frac{1}{4}$ miles

   (C) $2\frac{1}{2}$ miles

   (D) $10\frac{1}{4}$ miles

Problem Solving REAL WORLD

5. Leah makes aprons to sell at a craft fair. She needs $\frac{3}{4}$ yard of material to make each apron. How much material does Leah need to make 6 aprons?

6. The gas tank of Mr. Tanaka's car holds 15 gallons of gas. He used $\frac{2}{3}$ of a tank of gas last week. How many gallons of gas did Mr. Tanaka use?

Name _____

Lesson 67
COMMON CORE STANDARD CC.5.NF.4a
Lesson Objective: Multiply fractions.

Fraction Multiplication

To multiply fractions, you can multiply the numerators, then multiply the denominators. Write the product in simplest form.

Multiply. $\frac{3}{10} \times \frac{4}{5}$

Step 1 Multiply the numerators. Multiply the denominators.

$$\frac{3}{10} \times \frac{4}{5} = \frac{3 \times 4}{10 \times 5}$$

$$= \frac{12}{50}$$

Step 2 Write the product in simplest form.

$$\frac{12}{50} = \frac{12 \div 2}{50 \div 2}$$

$$= \frac{6}{25}$$

So, $\frac{3}{10} \times \frac{4}{5}$ is $\frac{6}{25}$.

Find the product. Write the product in simplest form.

1. $\frac{3}{4} \times \frac{1}{5}$

2. $\frac{4}{7} \times \frac{5}{12}$

3. $\frac{3}{8} \times \frac{2}{9}$

4. $\frac{4}{5} \times \frac{5}{8}$

_____ _____ _____ _____

5. $\frac{1}{3} \times 4$

6. $\frac{3}{4} \times 8$

7. $\frac{5}{8} \times \frac{2}{3}$

8. $\frac{5}{6} \times \frac{3}{8}$

_____ _____ _____ _____

1. Julia has a recipe for salad dressing that calls for $\frac{3}{4}$ cup of vegetable oil. How much vegetable oil should she use to make $\frac{1}{2}$ of the recipe for salad dressing?

   (A) $1\frac{1}{4}$ cups

   (B) $\frac{2}{3}$ cup

   (C) $\frac{1}{2}$ cup

   (D) $\frac{3}{8}$ cup

2. A scientist had $\frac{3}{4}$ liter of solution. He used $\frac{1}{6}$ of the solution for an experiment. How much solution did the scientist use for the experiment?

   (A) $\frac{1}{8}$ liter

   (B) $\frac{3}{8}$ liter

   (C) $\frac{1}{2}$ liter

   (D) $\frac{7}{12}$ liter

3. Of the flowers on Jill's front lawn, $\frac{2}{5}$ are tulips. Of the tulips, $\frac{5}{8}$ are yellow. What fraction of the flowers on Jill's front lawn are yellow tulips?

   (A) $\frac{7}{13}$

   (B) $\frac{1}{2}$

   (C) $\frac{1}{4}$

   (D) $\frac{1}{8}$

4. Otis bought a total of $\frac{7}{10}$ pound of grapes and cherries. The weight of the grapes is $\frac{2}{3}$ of the total weight. What is the weight of the grapes?

   (A) $\frac{3}{10}$ pound

   (B) $\frac{7}{15}$ pound

   (C) $\frac{9}{13}$ pound

   (D) $\frac{20}{21}$ pound

Problem Solving REAL WORLD

5. Jason ran $\frac{5}{7}$ of the distance around the school track. Sara ran $\frac{4}{5}$ of Jason's distance. What fraction of the total distance around the track did Sara run?

6. A group of students attend a math club. Half of the students are boys and $\frac{4}{9}$ of the boys have brown eyes. What fraction of the group are boys with brown eyes?

Lesson 68

COMMON CORE STANDARD CC.5.NF.4b
Lesson Objective: Multiply fractions using models.

Multiply Fractions

You can use a model to help you multiply two fractions.

Multiply. $\frac{1}{3} \times \frac{4}{5}$

Step 1 Draw a rectangle. Divide it into 5 equal columns.
To represent the factor $\frac{4}{5}$, shade
4 of the 5 columns.

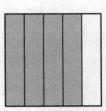

Step 2 Now divide the rectangle into 3 equal rows.
Shade $\frac{1}{3}$ of the $\frac{4}{5}$ you already shaded.

The rectangle is divided into **15** smaller
rectangles. This is the denominator of the
product.

There are 4 smaller rectangles that contain
both types of shading. So, **4** is the numerator
of the product.

So $\frac{4}{15}$ of the rectangles contain both types of shading.

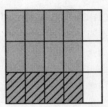

Think: What is $\frac{1}{3}$ of $\frac{4}{5}$?

$\frac{1}{3} \times \frac{4}{5} = \underline{\frac{4}{15}}$.

Find the product. Draw a model.

1.
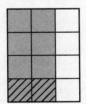

$\frac{1}{4} \times \frac{2}{3} = \underline{\hspace{2cm}}$

2.
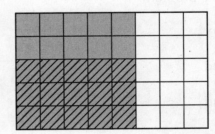

$\frac{3}{5} \times \frac{5}{8} = \underline{\hspace{2cm}}$

3.

$\frac{2}{5} \times \frac{3}{4} = \underline{\hspace{2cm}}$

4.

$\frac{2}{3} \times \frac{3}{8} = \underline{\hspace{2cm}}$

1. Marta breaded $\frac{1}{2}$ of the fish she cooked for dinner. She ate $\frac{1}{3}$ of the breaded fish. She used a model to find how much of the fish she had eaten.

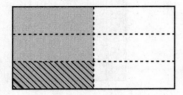

How much of the fish did Marta eat?

Ⓐ $\frac{1}{6}$

Ⓑ $\frac{1}{5}$

Ⓒ $\frac{2}{5}$

Ⓓ $\frac{2}{3}$

2. Lawrence bought $\frac{2}{3}$ pound of roast beef. He used $\frac{3}{4}$ of it to make a sandwich. How much roast beef did Lawrence use for his sandwich? You may use a model to help you solve the problem.

Ⓐ $\frac{5}{12}$ pound

Ⓑ $\frac{1}{2}$ pound

Ⓒ $\frac{5}{7}$ pound

Ⓓ $\frac{6}{7}$ pound

3. Alexa planted tulips in $\frac{2}{5}$ of her garden. Of the tulips, $\frac{2}{3}$ are yellow tulips. She used a model to find what part of her garden has yellow tulips.

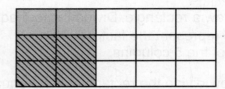

What part of Alexa's garden has yellow tulips?

Ⓐ $\frac{2}{15}$ Ⓒ $\frac{1}{3}$

Ⓑ $\frac{4}{15}$ Ⓓ $\frac{1}{2}$

4. A scientist has a bottle that is $\frac{5}{8}$ full of solution. He uses $\frac{2}{5}$ of the solution in the bottle for an experiment. How much of a full bottle of solution does he use? You may use a model to help you solve the problem.

Ⓐ $\frac{7}{13}$

Ⓑ $\frac{1}{2}$

Ⓒ $\frac{1}{4}$

Ⓓ $\frac{1}{40}$

Problem Solving REAL WORLD

5. Nora has a piece of ribbon that is $\frac{3}{4}$ yard long. She will use $\frac{1}{2}$ of it to make a bow. What length of the ribbon will she use for the bow?

6. Marlon bought $\frac{7}{8}$ pound of turkey at the deli. He used $\frac{2}{3}$ of it to make sandwiches for lunch. How much of the turkey did Marlon use for sandwiches?

Name _____

Lesson 69

COMMON CORE STANDARD CC.5.NF.4b

Lesson Objective: Use a model to multiply two mixed numbers and find the area of a rectangle.

Area and Mixed Numbers

You can use an area model to help you multiply mixed numbers.

Find the area. $1\frac{4}{5} \times 2\frac{1}{3}$

Step 1 Rewrite each mixed-number factor as the sum of a whole number and a fraction.

$$1\frac{4}{5} = 1 + \frac{4}{5} \text{ and } 2\frac{1}{3} = 2 + \frac{1}{3}$$

Step 2 Draw an area model to show the original multiplication problem.

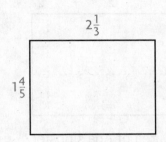

Step 3 Draw dashed lines, and label each section to show how you broke apart the mixed numbers in Step 1.

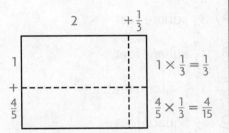

Step 4 Find the area of each section.

$$1 \times 2 = \underline{\quad 2 \quad}$$
$$1 \times \frac{1}{3} = \underline{\quad \frac{1}{3} \quad}$$
$$\frac{4}{5} \times 2 = \underline{\quad \frac{8}{5} \quad}$$
$$\frac{4}{5} \times \frac{1}{3} = \underline{\quad \frac{4}{15} \quad}$$

Step 5 Add the areas of each of the sections to find the total area of the rectangle.

$$2 + \frac{1}{3} + \frac{8}{5} + \frac{4}{15} = \frac{\boxed{30}}{15} + \frac{\boxed{5}}{15} + \frac{\boxed{24}}{15} + \frac{4}{15}$$

$$= \frac{\boxed{63}}{15}, \text{ or } \underline{\quad 4\frac{1}{5} \quad}$$

So, $1\frac{4}{5} \times 2\frac{1}{3}$ is $\underline{\quad 4\frac{1}{5} \quad}$.

Use an area model to solve.

1. $1\frac{2}{3} \times 2\frac{1}{4}$
2. $1\frac{3}{4} \times 2\frac{3}{5}$
3. $2\frac{1}{2} \times 1\frac{1}{3}$

1. Ana has a poster that is $1\frac{2}{3}$ feet high and $2\frac{1}{4}$ feet wide. She used an area model to find the area of the poster.

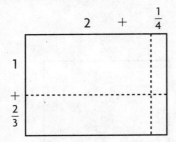

What is the area of Ana's poster?

(A) $3\frac{1}{2}$ square feet

(B) $3\frac{3}{4}$ square feet

(C) $3\frac{11}{12}$ square feet

(D) $4\frac{1}{2}$ square feet

2. The top of Colin's desk is $2\frac{2}{3}$ feet long and $2\frac{1}{4}$ feet wide. What is the area of the top of Colin's desk? You may use an area model to help you.

(A) $4\frac{1}{6}$ square feet

(B) $4\frac{11}{12}$ square feet

(C) $5\frac{11}{12}$ square feet

(D) 6 square feet

3. Eloise is painting a mural that is $1\frac{3}{4}$ yards long and $1\frac{1}{4}$ yards high. She uses a grid to find the area of the mural.

What is the area of the mural?

(A) $2\frac{3}{16}$ square yards

(B) 6 square yards

(C) $8\frac{3}{4}$ square yards

(D) 35 square yards

4. A ping pong table is $2\frac{3}{4}$ meters long and $1\frac{1}{2}$ meters wide. What is the area of the ping pong table? You may use an area model to help you.

(A) $4\frac{1}{8}$ square meters

(B) $4\frac{1}{4}$ square meters

(C) $4\frac{3}{8}$ square meters

(D) $4\frac{1}{2}$ square meters

Problem Solving REAL WORLD

5. Ava's bedroom rug is $2\frac{3}{4}$ feet long and $2\frac{1}{2}$ feet wide. What is the area of the rug?

6. A painting is $2\frac{2}{3}$ feet long and $1\frac{1}{2}$ feet high. What is the area of the painting?

Compare Fraction Factors and Products

You can use a model to determine how the size of the product compares to the size of one factor when multiplying fractions.

The factor is 1: $\frac{2}{3} \times 1$

- Draw a model to represent the factor 1.
  Divide it into 3 equal sections.

- Shade 2 of the 3 sections to represent the factor $\frac{2}{3}$.

$\frac{2}{3}$ of the rectangle is shaded. So, $\frac{2}{3} \times 1$ is ____**equal to**____ $\frac{2}{3}$.

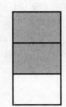

The factor is greater than 1: $\frac{2}{3} \times 2$

- Draw two rectangles to represent the factor 2.
  Divide each rectangle into 3 equal sections.

- Shade 2 of 3 sections in each to represent the factor $\frac{2}{3}$.

In all, 4 sections are shaded, which is greater than the number of sections in one rectangle. So, $\frac{2}{3} \times 2$ is ____**greater than**____ $\frac{2}{3}$.

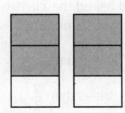

The factor is less than 1: $\frac{2}{3} \times \frac{1}{6}$

- Draw a rectangle. Divide it into 6 equal columns.
  Shade 1 of the 6 columns to represent the factor $\frac{1}{6}$.

- Now divide the rectangle into 3 equal rows. Shade 2 of the
  3 rows of the section already shaded to represent the factor $\frac{2}{3}$.

The rectangle is divided into 18 sections. 2 of the sections are shaded twice. 2 sections is less than the 3 sections that represent $\frac{1}{6}$.

So, $\frac{2}{3} \times \frac{1}{6}$ is ____**less than**____ $\frac{1}{6}$.

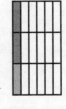

Complete the statement with *equal to*, *greater than*, or *less than*.

1. $\frac{3}{7} \times \frac{2}{5}$ will be _____ $\frac{3}{7}$.

2. $\frac{7}{8} \times 3$ will be _____ $\frac{7}{8}$.

3. $\frac{1}{6} \times \frac{5}{5}$ will be _____ $\frac{1}{6}$.

4. $5 \times \frac{6}{7}$ will be _____ 5.

1. Doreen lives $\frac{3}{4}$ mile from the library. If Sheila lives $\frac{1}{2}$ as far away as Doreen, which statement below is true?

   (A) Sheila lives closer to the library.

   (B) Doreen lives closer to the library.

   (C) Sheila lives twice as far from the library as Doreen.

   (D) They live the same distance from the library.

2. Mrs. Stephens wrote 4 statements on the board and asked the class which one was true. Which statement below is true?

   (A) $\frac{5}{6} \times \frac{5}{6}$ is equal to $\frac{5}{6}$.

   (B) $\frac{2}{3} \times \frac{1}{3}$ is less than $\frac{2}{3}$.

   (C) $\frac{7}{8} \times 8$ is less than $\frac{7}{8}$.

   (D) $\frac{3}{5} \times 5$ is greater than 5.

3. Nadia needs $\frac{3}{4}$ cup of orange juice for a punch recipe. She will double the recipe to make punch for a party. Which statement below is true?

   (A) She will be using the same amount of orange juice.

   (B) She will be using less orange juice.

   (C) She will be using more orange juice.

   (D) She will be using $\frac{3}{4}$ as much orange juice.

4. It took Mary Lou $\frac{5}{6}$ hour to write a report for her English class. It took Heather $\frac{9}{10}$ as much time to write her report as it took Mary Lou. Which statement below is true?

   (A) It took them both the same amount of time.

   (B) Mary Lou spent less time writing her book report than Heather.

   (C) Mary Lou spent more time writing her book report than Heather.

   (D) It took Heather twice as long to write her book report than it took Mary Lou to write her book report.

Problem Solving REAL WORLD

5. Starla is making hot cocoa. She plans to multiply the recipe by 4 to make enough hot cocoa for the whole class. If the recipe calls for $\frac{1}{2}$ teaspoon vanilla extract, will she need more than $\frac{1}{2}$ teaspoon or less than $\frac{1}{2}$ teaspoon of vanilla extract to make all the hot cocoa?

6. Miles is planning to spend $\frac{2}{3}$ as many hours bicycling this week as he did last week. Is Miles going to spend more hours or fewer hours bicycling this week than last week?

Lesson **71**

COMMON CORE STANDARD CC.5.NF.5a
Lesson Objective: Relate the size of the product to the factors when multiplying fractions greater than one.

Name _____

Compare Mixed Number Factors and Products

Complete each statement with *equal to*, *greater than*, or *less than*.

$1 \times 1\frac{3}{4}$ is ____**?**____ $1\frac{3}{4}$.

The Identity Property of Multiplication states that the product of

1 and any number is that number. So, $1 \times 1\frac{3}{4}$ is ____**equal to**____ $1\frac{3}{4}$.

$\frac{1}{2} \times 2\frac{1}{4}$ is ____**?**____ $2\frac{1}{4}$.

Draw three rectangles. Divide each rectangle into 4 equal columns.

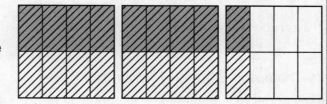

Shade completely the first two rectangles and one column of the last rectangle to represent $\frac{1}{4}$.

Divide the rectangles into 2 rows. Shade one row to represent the factor $\frac{1}{2}$.

18 small rectangles are shaded. 9 rectangles have both types of shading. 9 rectangles is less than the 18 rectangles that represent $2\frac{1}{4}$.

So, $\frac{1}{2} \times 2\frac{1}{4}$ is ____**less than**____ $2\frac{1}{4}$.

When you multiply a mixed number by a fraction less than 1,

the product will be ____**less than**____ the mixed number.

$1\frac{1}{4} \times 1\frac{3}{4}$ is ____**?**____ $1\frac{1}{4}$.

Use what you know about the product of two whole numbers greater than 1 to determine the size of the product of two mixed numbers.

So, $1\frac{1}{4} \times 1\frac{3}{4}$ is ____**greater than**____ $1\frac{1}{4}$ and ____**greater than**____ $1\frac{3}{4}$.

When you multiply two mixed numbers, their product is ____**greater than**____ either factor.

Complete the statement with *equal to*, *greater than*, or *less than*.

1. $\frac{3}{5} \times 1\frac{2}{7}$ is _____ $1\frac{2}{7}$.

2. $\frac{6}{6} \times 3\frac{1}{3}$ is _____ $3\frac{1}{3}$.

3. $2\frac{1}{5} \times 1\frac{1}{4}$ is _____ $1\frac{1}{4}$.

4. $\frac{8}{9} \times 4\frac{3}{4}$ is _____ $4\frac{3}{4}$.

1. Stuart rode his bicycle $6\frac{3}{5}$ miles last week. This week he rode $1\frac{1}{3}$ times as far as he rode last week. Which statement below is true?

   (A) He rode the same number of miles both weeks.

   (B) He rode fewer miles this week.

   (C) He rode more miles this week.

   (D) He rode twice as many miles this week.

2. Mrs. Thompson is buying $1\frac{3}{4}$ pounds of turkey and $\frac{3}{4}$ as much cheese as turkey at a deli. Which statement below is true?

   (A) She is buying the same amount of turkey and cheese.

   (B) She is buying less turkey than cheese.

   (C) She is buying twice as much turkey as cheese.

   (D) She is buying more turkey than cheese.

3. Miss Parks wrote 4 statements on the board and asked the class which one was true. Which statement below is true?

   (A) $3\frac{2}{3} \times \frac{4}{5}$ is greater than $3\frac{2}{3}$.

   (B) $1\frac{7}{8} \times 2\frac{1}{3}$ is greater than $2\frac{1}{3}$.

   (C) $2\frac{5}{6} \times \frac{8}{8}$ is less than $2\frac{5}{6}$.

   (D) $2\frac{3}{8} \times 4$ is less than 4.

4. Diana worked on her science project for $5\frac{1}{3}$ hours. Gabe worked on his science project $1\frac{1}{4}$ times as long as Diana. Which statement below is true?

   (A) Gabe spent more time on his science project than Diana did on hers.

   (B) Diana worked on her science project longer than Gabe worked on his.

   (C) Gabe worked on his science project twice as long as Diana worked on hers.

   (D) They both worked on their science projects the same amount of time.

Problem Solving REAL WORLD

5. Fraser is making a scale drawing of a dog house. The dimensions of the drawing will be $\frac{1}{8}$ of the dimensions of the actual doghouse. The height of the actual doghouse is $36\frac{3}{4}$ inches. Will the dimensions of Fraser's drawing be equal to, greater than, or less than the dimensions of the actual dog house?

6. Jorge has a recipe that calls for $2\frac{1}{3}$ cups of flour. He plans to make $1\frac{1}{2}$ times the recipe. Will the amount of flour Jorge needs be equal to, greater than, or less than the amount of flour his recipe calls for?

Problem Solving • Find Unknown Lengths

Zach built a rectangular deck in his backyard. The area of the deck is 300 square feet. The length of the deck is $1\frac{1}{3}$ times as long as the width. What are the dimensions of the deck?

Read the Problem		
What do I need to find? I need to find __the__ _____ __dimensions of the deck__.	**What information do I need to use?** The deck has an area of __300__ square feet, and the length is __$1\frac{1}{3}$__ as long as the width.	**How will I use the information?** I will __guess__ the length and width of the deck. Then I will __check__ my guess and __revise__ it if it is not correct.

Solve the Problem

I can try different values for the length of the deck, each that is $1\frac{1}{3}$ times as long as the width. Then I can multiply the length and width and compare to the correct area.

Guess		Check	Revise
Width (in feet)	**Length (in feet) ($1\frac{1}{3}$ times the width)**	**Area of Deck (in square feet)**	
12	$1\frac{1}{3} \times 12 =$ __16__	$12 \times 16 =$ __192__ too low	Try a __longer__ width.
18	$1\frac{1}{3} \times 18 =$ __24__	$18 \times 24 =$ __432__ too high	Try a __shorter__ width.
15	$1\frac{1}{3} \times 15 =$ __20__	$15 \times 20 =$ __300__ correct	

So, the dimensions of the deck are __20__ feet by __15__ feet.

1. Abigail made a quilt that has an area of 4,800 square inches. The length of the quilt is $1\frac{1}{3}$ times the width of the quilt. What are the dimensions of the quilt?

2. The width of the mirror in Shannon's bathroom is $\frac{4}{9}$ its length. The area of the mirror is 576 square inches. What are the dimensions of the mirror?

1. Louis wants to carpet the rectangular floor of his basement. The basement has an area of 864 square feet. The width of the basement is $\frac{2}{3}$ its length. What is the length of Louis's basement?

   Ⓐ 24 feet
   Ⓑ 36 feet
   Ⓒ 48 feet
   Ⓓ 576 feet

2. Sally painted a picture that has an area of 480 square inches. The length of the painting is $1\frac{1}{5}$ as long as it is wide. Which of the following could be the dimensions of Sally's painting?

   Ⓐ 20 inches by 24 inches
   Ⓑ 12 inches by 40 inches
   Ⓒ 16 inches by 30 inches
   Ⓓ 15 inches by 32 inches

3. A rectangular park has an area of 6 square miles. The width of the property is $\frac{3}{8}$ the length of the property. What is the width of the property?

   Ⓐ $1\frac{1}{2}$ miles
   Ⓑ $2\frac{1}{4}$ miles
   Ⓒ 3 miles
   Ⓓ 4 miles

4. A pool at a park takes up an area of 540 square yards. The length is $1\frac{2}{3}$ times as long as the width. Which of the following could be the dimensions of the pool?

   Ⓐ 21 yards by 35 yards
   Ⓑ 20 yards by 27 yards
   Ⓒ 15 yards by 36 yards
   Ⓓ 18 yards by 30 yards

Problem Solving REAL WORLD

5. Brianna has a rug that has an area of 24 square feet. The width of the rug is $\frac{2}{3}$ the length of the rug. Explain how you can find the length and the width of the rug.

_____

_____

_____

_____

_____

Multiply Mixed Numbers

You can use a multiplication square to multiply mixed numbers.

Multiply. $1\frac{2}{7} \times 1\frac{3}{4}$ **Write the product in simplest form.**

Step 1 Write the mixed numbers outside the square.

$\times$	1	$\frac{2}{7}$
1		
$\frac{3}{4}$		

Step 2 Multiply the number in each column by the number in each row.

$\times$	1	$\frac{2}{7}$
1	1×1	$\frac{2}{7} \times 1$
$\frac{3}{4}$	$1 \times \frac{3}{4}$	$\frac{2}{7} \times \frac{3}{4}$

Step 3 Write each product inside the square.

$\times$	1	$\frac{2}{7}$
1	1	$\frac{2}{7}$
$\frac{3}{4}$	$\frac{3}{4}$	$\frac{3}{14}$

Step 4 Add the products inside the multiplication square.

Find the least common denominator.

Simplify.

$1 + \frac{2}{7} + \frac{3}{4} + \frac{3}{14}$

$\frac{28}{28} + \frac{8}{28} + \frac{21}{28} + \frac{6}{28} = \frac{63}{28}$

$\frac{63}{28} = 2\frac{7}{28}$, or $2\frac{1}{4}$

So, $1\frac{2}{7} \times 1\frac{3}{4}$ is $\underline{2\frac{1}{4}}$.

Find the product. Write the product in simplest form.

1. $2\frac{5}{8} \times 1\frac{1}{7}$ 2. $3\frac{1}{2} \times 12$ 3. $10\frac{5}{6} \times \frac{3}{5}$ 4. $7\frac{7}{10} \times \frac{10}{11}$

_____   _____   _____   _____

Use the Distributive Property to find the product.

5. $12 \times 2\frac{1}{2}$ 6. $15 \times 5\frac{1}{3}$

_____   _____

1. Jared made $12\frac{3}{4}$ cups of snack mix for a party. His guests ate $\frac{2}{3}$ of the mix. How much snack mix did his guests eat?

   (A) $4\frac{5}{12}$ cups

   (B) $4\frac{1}{2}$ cups

   (C) $8\frac{1}{2}$ cups

   (D) $12\frac{5}{7}$ cups

2. Kayla walks $3\frac{7}{10}$ miles for exercise each day. What is the total number of miles she walks in 31 days?

   (A) $117\frac{4}{10}$ miles

   (B) $114\frac{7}{10}$ miles

   (C) $34\frac{7}{10}$ miles

   (D) $6\frac{4}{5}$ miles

3. Carlos has $7\frac{1}{2}$ acres of farmland. He uses $\frac{1}{3}$ of the acres to graze animals and $\frac{1}{5}$ of the acres to grow vegetables. How many acres does Carlos use for grazing animals or for growing vegetables?

   (A) $1\frac{1}{2}$ acres   (C) 4 acres

   (B) $2\frac{1}{2}$ acres   (D) $6\frac{29}{30}$ acres

4. The table shows how many hours some students worked on their math project.

   Math Project

Name	Hours Worked
Carl	$5\frac{1}{4}$
Sonia	$6\frac{1}{2}$
Tony	$5\frac{2}{3}$

   April worked $1\frac{1}{2}$ times as long on her math project as Carl. For how many hours did April work on her math project?

   (A) $5\frac{3}{8}$ hours   (C) $7\frac{1}{4}$ hours

   (B) $6\frac{1}{3}$ hours   (D) $7\frac{7}{8}$ hours

Problem Solving REAL WORLD

5. Jake can carry $6\frac{1}{4}$ pounds of wood in from the barn. His father can carry $1\frac{5}{7}$ times as much as Jake. How many pounds can Jake's father carry?

6. A glass can hold $3\frac{1}{3}$ cups of water. A bowl can hold $2\frac{3}{5}$ times the amount in the glass. How many cups can a bowl hold?

Lesson 74
COMMON CORE STANDARDS
CC.5.NF.7a, CC.5.NF.7b
Lesson Objective: Divide a whole number by a fraction and divide a fraction by a whole number.

Divide Fractions and Whole Numbers

You can use a number line to help you divide a whole number by a fraction.

Divide. $6 \div \frac{1}{2}$

Step 1 Draw a number line from 0 to 6. Divide the number line into halves. Label each half on your number line, starting with $\frac{1}{2}$.

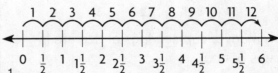

Step 2 Skip count by halves from 0 to 6 to find $6 \div \frac{1}{2}$.

Step 3 Count the number of skips. It takes **12** skips to go from 0 to 6. So the quotient is 12.

$$6 \div \frac{1}{2} = \underline{\ 12\ } \text{ because } \underline{\ 12\ } \times \frac{1}{2} = 6.$$

You can use fraction strips to divide a fraction by a whole number.

Divide. $\frac{1}{2} \div 5$

Step 1 Place a $\frac{1}{2}$ strip under a 1-whole strip.

Step 2 Find 5 fraction strips, all with the same denominator, that fit exactly under the $\frac{1}{2}$ strip.

Each part is $\frac{1}{10}$ of the whole.

Step 3 Record and check the quotient.

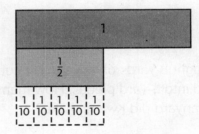

$$\frac{1}{2} \div 5 = \frac{1}{\underline{10}} \text{ because } \frac{1}{\underline{10}} \times 5 = \frac{1}{2}.$$

So, $\frac{1}{2} \div 5 = \frac{1}{\underline{10}}$.

Divide. Draw a number line or use fraction strips.

1. $1 \div \frac{1}{2} =$ _____

2. $2 \div \frac{1}{3} =$ _____

3. $4 \div \frac{1}{4} =$ _____

4. $\frac{1}{5} \div 3 =$ _____

5. $\frac{1}{3} \div 2 =$ _____

6. $4 \div \frac{1}{5} =$ _____

1. Olivia needs to find the number of $\frac{1}{3}$-cup servings in 2 cups of rice. She used the number line below to find $2 \div \frac{1}{3}$.

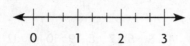

How many $\frac{1}{3}$-cup servings of rice are in 2 cups of rice?

(A) 2

(B) 3

(C) 5

(D) 6

2. Kwami bought 8 yards of lanyard. He cut the lanyard into $\frac{1}{2}$-yard pieces. How many pieces of lanyard did Kwami make?

(A) 2

(B) 8

(C) 16

(D) 64

3. Chris divided $\frac{1}{2}$ pound of nails into 6 small bags with the same amount in each bag. He used fraction strips to find the weight of each bag.

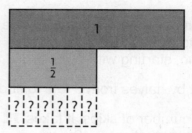

How much does each small bag weigh?

(A) $\frac{1}{2}$ pound

(B) $\frac{1}{3}$ pound

(C) $\frac{1}{6}$ pound

(D) $\frac{1}{12}$ pound

4. Josie filled a watering can with $\frac{1}{3}$ quart of water. She poured the same amount of water from the can onto each of 3 plants. How much water did Josie pour onto each plant?

(A) $\frac{1}{9}$ quart

(B) $2\frac{2}{3}$ quarts

(C) 3 quarts

(D) 9 quarts

Problem Solving REAL WORLD

5. Amy can run $\frac{1}{10}$ mile per minute. How many minutes will it take Amy to run 3 miles?

6. Jeremy has 3 yards of ribbon to use for wrapping gifts. He cuts the ribbon into pieces that are $\frac{1}{4}$ yard long. How many pieces of ribbon does Jeremy have?

Problem Solving • Use Multiplication

Nathan makes 4 batches of soup and divides each batch into halves. How many $\frac{1}{2}$-batches of soup does he have?

Read the Problem	Solve the Problem
What do I need to find? I need to find __the number of__ __$\frac{1}{2}$-batches of soup Nathan__ __has__ .	Since Nathan makes 4 batches of soup, my diagram needs to show 4 circles to represent the 4 batches. I can divide each of the 4 circles in half.
What information do I need to use? I need to use the size of each __batch of__ __soup__ and the total number of __batches__ of soup Nathan makes.	To find the total number of halves in the 4 batches, I can multiply 4 by the number of halves in each circle. $4 \div \frac{1}{2} = 4 \times \underline{\ 2\ } = \underline{\ 8\ }$
How will I use the information? I can __make a diagram__ to organize the information from the problem. Then I can use the diagram to find __the number__ __of $\frac{1}{2}$-batches of soup__ __Nathan has after he divides__ __the 4 batches of soup__ .	So, Nathan has __8__ one-half-batches of soup.

Draw a diagram to help you solve the problem.

1. A nearby park has 8 acres of land to use for gardens. The park divides each acre into fourths. How many $\frac{1}{4}$-acre gardens does the park have?

2. Clarissa has 3 pints of ice tea that she divides into $\frac{1}{2}$-pint servings. How many $\frac{1}{2}$-pint servings does she have?

1. Ben is making a recipe that calls for 5 cups of flour. He only has a $\frac{1}{2}$-cup measuring cup. How many times will Ben need to fill the $\frac{1}{2}$-cup measuring cup to get 5 cups of flour?

   (A) $\frac{2}{5}$

   (B) $2\frac{1}{2}$

   (C) 7

   (D) 10

2. Lily made 3 pounds of coleslaw for a picnic. Each serving of coleslaw is $\frac{1}{8}$ pound. How many $\frac{1}{8}$-pound servings of coleslaw are there?

   (A) $2\frac{2}{3}$

   (B) 12

   (C) 24

   (D) 32

3. Kyle shares 3 bananas with some friends. If each person gets $\frac{1}{2}$ of a banana, how many people can share Kyle's bananas?

   (A) 9

   (B) 6

   (C) $1\frac{1}{2}$

   (D) $\frac{1}{6}$

4. A 6-mile walking trail has a distance marker every $\frac{1}{3}$ mile, beginning at $\frac{1}{3}$ mile. How many distance markers are along the trail?

   (A) 2

   (B) 6

   (C) 9

   (D) 18

Problem Solving REAL WORLD

5. Aya made 2 pans of brownies to give to some families in her neighborhood. Each family will get $\frac{1}{4}$ of a pan. How many families will share Aya's brownies? Explain how to use a diagram to find your answer.

_____
_____
_____
_____

Name _____

Fraction and Whole-Number Division

Lesson 76
COMMON CORE STANDARD CC.5.NF.7c

Lesson Objective: Divide a whole number by a fraction and divide a fraction by a whole number.

You can divide fractions by solving a related multiplication sentence.

Divide. $4 \div \frac{1}{3}$

Step 1 Draw 4 circles to represent the dividend, 4.

Step 2 Since the divisor is $\frac{1}{3}$, divide each circle into thirds.

Step 3 Count the total number of thirds.

When you divide the __4__ circles into thirds, you are finding

the number of thirds in 4 circles, or finding 4 groups of __3__.

There are __12__ thirds.

Step 4 Complete the number sentence.

$4 \div \frac{1}{3} = 4 \times$ __3__ $=$ __12__

Use the model to complete the number sentence.

1.

$3 \div \frac{1}{5} = 3 \times$ _____ $=$ _____

2.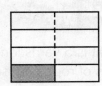

$\frac{1}{4} \div 2 = \frac{1}{4} \times$ _____ $=$ _____

Write a related multiplication sentence to solve.

3. $2 \div \frac{1}{5}$ 4. $\frac{1}{3} \div 3$ 5. $\frac{1}{6} \div 2$ 6. $5 \div \frac{1}{4}$

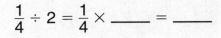

Core Standards for Math, Grade 5

1. Samara solved $\frac{1}{5} \div 10$ by using a related multiplication sentence. Which multiplication sentence could she have used?

   (A) $5 \times 10 = 50$

   (B) $\frac{1}{5} \times 10 = 2$

   (C) $5 \times \frac{1}{10} = \frac{5}{10}$

   (D) $\frac{1}{5} \times \frac{1}{10} = \frac{1}{50}$

2. Jawan solved $8 \div \frac{1}{3}$ by using a related multiplication sentence. Which multiplication sentence could he have used?

   (A) $8 \times \frac{1}{3} = \frac{8}{3}$

   (B) $\frac{1}{8} \times \frac{1}{3} = \frac{1}{24}$

   (C) $8 \times 3 = 24$

   (D) $\frac{1}{8} \times 3 = \frac{3}{8}$

3. Annette has $\frac{1}{4}$ pound of cheese that she is going to cut into 3 chunks of the same size. What fraction of a pound of cheese will each chunk be?

   (A) $\frac{1}{12}$ pound

   (B) $\frac{1}{8}$ pound

   (C) $\frac{1}{2}$ pound

   (D) $\frac{3}{4}$ pound

4. Eli made 2 peanut butter and jelly sandwiches and cut each one into fourths. How many $\frac{1}{4}$-sandwich pieces did Eli have?

   (A) $\frac{1}{8}$

   (B) $2\frac{1}{4}$

   (C) 4

   (D) 8

Problem Solving REAL WORLD

5. Isaac has a piece of rope that is 5 yards long. Into how many $\frac{1}{2}$-yard pieces of rope can Isaac cut the rope?

   _____

6. Two friends share $\frac{1}{2}$ of a pineapple equally. What fraction of a whole pineapple does each friend get?

   _____

Lesson 77

COMMON CORE STANDARD CC.5.NF.7c

Lesson Objective: Represent division by drawing diagrams and writing story problems and equations.

Interpret Division with Fractions

You can draw a diagram or write an equation to represent division with fractions.

Beatriz has 3 cups of applesauce. She divides the applesauce into $\frac{1}{4}$-cup servings. How many servings of applesauce does she have?

One Way Draw a diagram to solve the problem.

Draw 3 circles to represent the 3 cups of applesauce. Since Beatriz divides the applesauce into $\frac{1}{4}$-cup servings, draw lines to divide each "cup" into fourths.

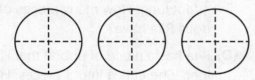

To find $3 \div \frac{1}{4}$, count the total number of fourths in the 3 circles.

So, Beatriz has ___12___ one-fourth-cup servings of applesauce.

Another Way Write an equation to solve.

Write an equation.	$3 \div \dfrac{1}{4} = n$
Write a related multiplication equation.	$3 \times \underline{4} = n$
Then solve.	$\underline{12} = n$

So, Beatriz has ___12___ one-fourth-cup servings of applesauce.

1. Draw a diagram to represent the problem. Then solve.

   Drew has 5 granola bars. He cuts the bars into halves. How many $\frac{1}{2}$-bar pieces does he have?

2. Write an equation to represent the problem. Then solve.

   Three friends share $\frac{1}{4}$ pan of brownies. What fraction of the whole pan of brownies does each friend get?

   _____

   _____

_____

1. Tina has $\frac{1}{2}$ quart of iced tea. She pours the same amount into each of 3 glasses. Which equation represents the fraction of a quart of iced tea, n, that is in each glass?

    (A) $\frac{1}{2} \div \frac{1}{3} = n$

    (B) $\frac{1}{2} \div 3 = n$

    (C) $3 \div \frac{1}{2} = n$

    (D) $3 \div 2 = n$

2. Lucy bought 9 yards of ribbon on a spool. She cut the ribbon into $\frac{1}{2}$-yard pieces. Which equation represents the number of pieces of ribbon, n, Lucy has now?

    (A) $9 \div \frac{1}{2} = n$

    (B) $\frac{1}{2} \div 9 = n$

    (C) $2 \div 9 = n$

    (D) $9 \div 2 = n$

3. Which situation can be represented by $6 \div \frac{1}{3}$?

    (A) Rita has a piece of ribbon that is $\frac{1}{3}$ foot long. She cuts it into 6 pieces, each having the same length. How many feet long is each piece of ribbon?

    (B) Rita has 6 pieces of ribbon. Each piece is $\frac{1}{3}$ foot long. How many feet of ribbon does Rita have in all?

    (C) Rita has a piece of ribbon that is 6 feet long. She cuts it into pieces that are $\frac{1}{3}$ foot long. How many pieces of ribbon does Rita have?

    (D) Rita has a piece of ribbon that is 6 feet long. She cuts it into 3 pieces. How many feet long is each piece of ribbon?

Problem Solving REAL WORLD

4. Spencer has $\frac{1}{3}$ pound of nuts. He divides the nuts equally into 4 bags. What fraction of a pound of nuts is in each bag?

    _____

5. Humma has 3 apples. She slices each apple into eighths. How many $\frac{1}{8}$-apple slices does she have?

    _____

Customary Length

You can convert one customary unit of length to another customary unit of length by multiplying or dividing.

<u>Multiply</u> to change from <u>larger to smaller</u> units of length.

<u>Divide</u> to change from <u>smaller to larger</u> units of length.

Customary Units of Length
1 foot (ft) = 12 inches (in.)
1 yard (yd) = 3 feet
1 mile (mi) = 5,280 feet
1 mile = 1,760 yards

Convert 3 feet to inches.

Step 1
Decide:
(Multiply) or Divide

feet ⟶ inches
larger ⟶ smaller

Step 2
Think:

1 ft = 12 in., so
3 ft = (3 × __12__) in.

Step 3
Multiply.
3 × 12 = 36

So, 3 feet = __36__ inches.

Convert 363 feet to yards.

Step 1
Decide:
Multiply or (Divide)

feet ⟶ yards
smaller ⟶ larger

Step 2
Think:

3 ft = 1 yd,
so 363 ft = (363 ÷ __3__) yd.

Step 3
Divide.
363 ÷ __3__ = __121__

So, 363 feet = __121__ yards.

Convert.

1. 33 yd = _____ ft

2. 300 mi = _____ yd

3. 46 in. = ____ ft ____ in.

4. 96 yd = _____ ft

5. 48 ft = _____ yd

6. 2 mi 20 yd = _____ yd

Compare. Write <, >, or =.

7. 2 yd ◯ 7 ft

8. 67 mi ◯ 117,920 yd

9. 250 yd ◯ 800 ft

10. 14 yd 2 ft ◯ 16 ft

11. 34 ft 10 in. ◯ 518 in.

12. 5 mi 8 ft ◯ 8,800 yd

1. The first stop on a bus route is 4 miles from school. How many yards are in 4 miles?

   (A) 48 yards

   (B) 144 yards

   (C) 7,040 yards

   (D) 21,120 yards

2. Anoki bought 36 yards of fabric to make costumes for the school play. What is that length in inches?

   (A) 3 inches

   (B) 12 inches

   (C) 108 inches

   (D) 1,296 inches

3. Sarah is 53 inches tall. Sarah's brother Luke is 4 inches taller than she is. What is Luke's height in feet and inches?

   (A) 4 feet 7 inches

   (B) 4 feet 9 inches

   (C) 5 feet 7 inches

   (D) 5 feet 8 inches

4. The distance between a football field and a parking lot is 135 feet. What is that length in yards?

   (A) 36 yards

   (B) 45 yards

   (C) 405 yards

   (D) 1,620 yards

Problem Solving REAL WORLD

5. Marita orders 12 yards of material to make banners. If she needs 1 foot of fabric for each banner, how many banners can she make?

   _____

6. Christy bought an 8-foot piece of lumber to trim a bookshelf. Altogether, she needs 100 inches of lumber for the trim. Did Christy buy enough lumber? Explain.

   _____

   _____

Customary Capacity

You can convert one unit of customary capacity to another by multiplying or dividing.

<u>Multiply</u> to change from <u>larger to smaller</u> units.

<u>Divide</u> to change from <u>smaller to larger</u> units.

Customary Units of Capacity
1 cup (c) = 8 fluid ounces (fl oz)
1 pint (pt) = 2 cups
1 quart (qt) = 2 pints
1 quart = 4 cups
1 gallon (gal) = 4 quarts

Convert 8 cups to quarts.

Step 1
Decide:
Multiply or (Divide)

cups ⟶ quarts
smaller ⟶ larger

Step 2
Think:

4 c = 1 qt,
so 8 c = (8 ÷ **4**) qt.

Step 3
Divide.

8 ÷ **4** = **2**

So, 8 cups = **2** quarts.

Convert 19 gallons to quarts.

Step 1
Decide:
(Multiply) or Divide

gallons ⟶ quarts
larger ⟶ smaller

Step 2
Think:

1 gal = 4 qt,
so 19 gal = (19 × **4**) qt.

Step 3
Multiply.

19 × **4** = **76**

So, 19 gallons = **76** quarts.

Convert.

1. 14 pt = _____ qt

2. 32 qt = _____ c

3. 7 c = _____ fl oz

4. 28 c = _____ pt

5. 9 gal = _____ qt

6. 16 c = _____ qt

Compare. Write <, >, or =.

7. 16 qt ◯ 60 c

8. 88 fl oz ◯ 11 c

9. 3 gal ◯ 10 qt

10. 36 qt ◯ 54 c

11. 66 fl oz ◯ 9 c

12. 16 gal ◯ 64 qt

1. Brian filled 72 glasses with apple juice for a school party. If each glass holds 1 cup of juice, how many quarts of apple juice did Brian use?

   (A)   9 quarts

   (B)   18 quarts

   (C)   36 quarts

   (D) 288 quarts

2. Mrs. Davis has 64 bottles of water. If each bottle holds 1 pint of water, how many gallons of water does Mrs. Davis have?

   (A)   4 gallons

   (B)   6 gallons

   (C)   8 gallons

   (D) 32 gallons

3. Isabel bought 3 bottles of liquid soap. Each bottle has 1 quart of soap in it. How many fluid ounces of liquid soap are in the 3 bottles that Isabel bought?

   (A) 16 fluid ounces

   (B) 32 fluid ounces

   (C) 72 fluid ounces

   (D) 96 fluid ounces

4. Mark filled 48 glasses with orange juice for a camp breakfast. If each glass holds 1 cup of juice, how many quarts of orange juice did Mark use?

   (A)   6 quarts

   (B)   12 quarts

   (C)   24 quarts

   (D) 192 quarts

Problem Solving REAL WORLD

5. Vickie made a recipe for 144 fluid ounces of scented candle wax. How many 1-cup candle molds can she fill with the recipe?

   _____

6. A recipe calls for 32 fluid ounces of heavy cream. How many 1-pint containers of heavy cream are needed to make the recipe?

   _____

Weight

You can convert one customary unit of weight to another by multiplying or dividing.

<u>Multiply</u> to change from <u>larger to smaller</u> units.

<u>Divide</u> to change from <u>smaller to larger</u> units.

Customary Units of Weight
1 pound (lb) = 16 ounces (oz)
1 ton (T) = 2,000 pounds

Convert 96 ounces to pounds.

Step 1
Decide:
Multiply or (Divide)

ounces ⟶ pounds
smaller ⟶ larger

Step 2
Think:

16 oz = 1 lb
so 96 oz = (96 ÷ __16__) lb.

Step 3
Divide.

$96 ÷ \underline{16} = \underline{6}$

So, 96 ounces = __6__ pounds.

Convert 4 pounds to ounces.

Step 1
Decide:
(Multiply) or Divide

pounds ⟶ ounces
larger ⟶ smaller

Step 2
Think:

1 lb = 16 oz,
so 4 lb = (4 × __16__) oz.

Step 3
Multiply.

$4 × \underline{16} = \underline{64}$

So, 4 pounds = __64__ ounces.

Convert.

1. 14 lb = _____ oz

2. 12,000 lb = _____ T

3. 2 T = _____ lb

4. 7 lb = _____ oz

5. 22 lb = _____ oz

6. 16 oz = _____ lb

Compare. Write <, >, or =.

7. 1 T ◯ 3,000 lb

8. 3 lb ◯ 43 oz

9. 5 T ◯ 10,000 lb

10. 3 T ◯ 6,000 lb

11. 6 lb ◯ 96 oz

12. 16 T ◯ 6,400 lb

1. Students picked 576 ounces of apples to make apple cider. How many pounds of apples did they pick?

   (A)   16 pounds
   (B)   36 pounds
   (C)   48 pounds
   (D) 9,216 pounds

2. Keiko bought 3 pounds of fruit salad. How many ounces of fruit salad did Keiko buy?

   (A) 16 ounces
   (B) 32 ounces
   (C) 36 ounces
   (D) 48 ounces

3. A female elephant can weigh up to 8,000 pounds. What is this weight in tons?

   (A) 2 tons
   (B) 3 tons
   (C) 4 tons
   (D) 8 tons

4. A truck loaded with concrete weighs about 30 tons. What is this weight in pounds?

   (A)   30,000 pounds
   (B)   60,000 pounds
   (C) 300,000 pounds
   (D) 600,000 pounds

Problem Solving REAL WORLD

5. Mr. Fields ordered 3 tons of gravel for a driveway at a factory. How many pounds of gravel did he order?

   _____

6. Sara can take no more than 22 pounds of luggage on a trip. Her suitcase weighs 112 ounces. How many more pounds can she pack without going over the limit?

   _____

Name _____

Multistep Measurement Problems

An ice cream parlor donated 6 containers of ice cream to a local elementary school. Each container holds 3 gallons of ice cream. If each student is served 1 cup of ice cream, how many students can be served?

Step 1 Record the information you are given.

There are __6__ containers of ice cream.

Each container holds __3__ gallons of ice cream.

Step 2 Find the total amount of ice cream in the 6 containers.

6 × 3 gallons = __18__ gallons of ice cream

Step 3 Convert from gallons to cups.

There are __4__ quarts in 1 gallon, so 18 gallons = __72__ quarts.

There are __2__ pints in 1 quart, so 72 quarts = __144__ pints.

There are __2__ cups in 1 pint, so 144 pints = __288__ cups.

So, __288__ students can be served 1 cup of ice cream.

Solve.

1. A cargo truck weighs 8,750 pounds. The weight limit for a certain bridge is 5 tons. How many pounds of cargo can be added to the truck before it exceeds the weight limit for the bridge?

   _____

2. A plumber uses 16 inches of tubing to connect each washing machine in a laundry to the water source. He wants to install 18 washing machines. How many yards of tubing will he need?

   _____

3. Larry has 9 gallons of paint. He uses 10 quarts to paint his kitchen and 3 gallons to paint his living room. How many pints of paint will be left?

   _____

4. Ketisha is practicing for a marathon by running around a track that is 440 yards long. Yesterday she ran around the track 20 times. How many miles did she run?

   _____

1. At the bulk food store, Stacey bought 7 pounds of nuts. She used 8 ounces of nuts in a recipe and then made small bags to use for snacks. If each small bag contained 4 ounces of nuts, how many small bags of nuts did Stacey make?

   (A) 15
   (B) 19
   (C) 26
   (D) 29

2. Keisha is walking around a track that is 400 yards long. She has walked around the track 5 times so far. How many more yards does she need to walk around the track to do 2 miles?

   (A) 1,520 yards
   (B) 3,120 yards
   (C) 3,280 yards
   (D) 8,560 yards

3. Devon uses 64 inches of ribbon to make 1 bow. How many yards of ribbon does Devon need to make 9 bows?

   (A) 8 yards
   (B) 16 yards
   (C) 24 yards
   (D) 48 yards

4. Brandon bought a 5-gallon container of paint to paint his house. After he finished painting, he had 2 quarts of paint left over. How many quarts of paint did Brandon use?

   (A) 3 quarts
   (B) 8 quarts
   (C) 18 quarts
   (D) 23 quarts

Problem Solving REAL WORLD

5. A pitcher contains 40 fluid ounces of iced tea. Shelby pours 3 cups of iced tea. How many pints of iced tea are left in the pitcher?

6. Olivia ties 2.5 feet of ribbon onto one balloon. How many yards of ribbon does Olivia need for 18 balloons?

Metric Measures

The metric system is based on place value. To convert between units, you multiply or divide by a power of 10. You **multiply** to change larger units to smaller units, such as liters to centiliters. You **divide** to change smaller units to larger units, such as meters to kilometers.

Convert 566 millimeters to decimeters.

• Think about how the two units are related.

1 decimeter = 100 millimeters

• **Think:** Should I multiply or divide?

Millimeters are smaller than decimeters.

So divide, or move the decimal point left for each power of 10.

Metric Units of Length
1 centimeter (cm) = 10 millimeters (mm)
1 decimeter (dm) = 10 centimeters (cm)
1 meter (m) = 1,000 millimeters (mm)
1 kilometer (km) = 1,000 meters (m)

kilo- (k)	hecto- (h)	deka- (da)	meter liter gram	deci- (d)	centi- (c)	milli- (m)
				5	6	6

566	÷	100	= **5.66**
millimeters		*mm in 1 dm*	*total decimeters*

So, 566 mm = **5.66** dm.

Complete the equation to show the conversion.

1. 115 km ◯ 10 = _____ hm

    115 km ◯ 100 = _____ dam

    115 km ◯ 1,000 = _____ m

2. 418 cL ◯ 10 = _____ dL

    418 cL ◯ 100 = _____ L

    418 cL ◯ 1,000 = _____ daL

Convert.

3. 40 cm = _____ mm

4. 500 mL = _____ dL

5. 6 kg = _____ g

6. 5,000 cL = _____ L

7. 4 kg = _____ hg

8. 200 mm = _____ cm

1. Ed bought 3 liters of water, 2,750 milliliters of sports drink, and 2.25 liters of juice. Which statement is true?

   Ⓐ Ed bought 50 milliliters more sports drink than juice.

   Ⓑ Ed bought 1.25 liters more water than juice.

   Ⓒ Ed bought 75 milliliters more water than juice.

   Ⓓ Ed bought 250 milliliters more water than sports drink.

2. Roland's dog has a mass of 2,500 dekagrams. What is the dog's mass in kilograms?

   Ⓐ 0.25 kilogram

   Ⓑ 2.5 kilograms

   Ⓒ 25 kilograms

   Ⓓ 250 kilograms

3. Sofia bought 3.25 meters of fabric to make a costume. How many centimeters of fabric did she buy?

   Ⓐ 0.325 centimeter

   Ⓑ 3.25 centimeters

   Ⓒ 32.5 centimeters

   Ⓓ 325 centimeters

4. Lorena's backpack has a mass of 10,000 grams. What is the mass of Lorena's backpack in kilograms?

   Ⓐ 1 kilogram

   Ⓑ 10 kilograms

   Ⓒ 100 kilograms

   Ⓓ 1,000 kilograms

Problem Solving REAL WORLD

5. Bria ordered 145 centimeters of fabric. Jayleen ordered 1.5 meters of fabric. Who ordered more fabric?

6. Ed fills his sports bottle with 1.2 liters of water. After his bike ride, he drinks 200 milliliters of the water. How much water is left in Ed's sports bottle?

Problem Solving • Customary and Metric Conversions

You can use the strategy *make a table* to help you solve problems about customary and metric conversions.

Jon's faucet is dripping at the rate of 24 centiliters in a day. How many milliliters of water will have dripped from Jon's faucet in 24 hours?

Read the Problem

What do I need to find

I need to find <u>how many milliliters of water will have dripped from Jon's faucet in 24 hours.</u>

What information do I need to use?

I need to use <u>the number of cL that have dripped in 24 hr and the number of mL in a cL.</u>

How will I use the information?

I will make a table to show the relationship between the number of <u>centiliters</u> and the number of <u>milliliters</u>.

Conversion Table

	L	dL	cL	mL
1 L	1	10	100	1,000
1 dL	$\frac{1}{10}$	1	10	100
1 cL	$\frac{1}{100}$	$\frac{1}{10}$	1	10
1 mL	$\frac{1}{1,000}$	$\frac{1}{100}$	$\frac{1}{10}$	1

I can use the Conversion Table to find the number of milliliters in 1 centiliter.

There are <u>10</u> milliliters in 1 centiliter.

cL	1	2	4	24
mL	10	20	40	240

So, <u>240</u> milliliters of water will have dripped from Jon's faucet in 24 hours.

Make a table to help you solve the problems.

1. Fernando has a bucket that holds 3 gallons of water. He is filling the bucket using a 1-pint container. How many times will he have to fill the pint container in order to fill the bucket?

2. Lexi has a roll of shelf paper that is 800 cm long. She wants to cut the paper into 1-m strips to line the shelves in her pantry. How many 1-meter strips can she cut?

1. When it is full, a fish tank holds 15 gallons of water. Jordan is using a 1-pint container to fill the fish tank. How many times will he need to fill the 1-pint container to fill the fish tank?

   (A) 30
   (B) 60
   (C) 90
   (D) 120

2. An art teacher has a roll of art paper 5 meters long. She needs to cut it into 1-decimeter long pieces for a collage project. How many 1-decimeter pieces can she cut from the roll of art paper?

   (A) 5
   (B) 50
   (C) 500
   (D) 5,000

3. Mickey needs to cut pieces of ribbon that are each 1 meter long to tie onto balloons. If he has 8 pieces of ribbon that are each 1 dekameter long, how many 1-meter pieces of ribbon can he cut?

   (A) 80
   (B) 800
   (C) 8,000
   (D) 80,000

4. The largest known carnivorous dinosaur, Spinosaurus, weighed about 18,000 pounds. How many tons did the Spinosaurus dinosaur weigh?

   (A) 9 tons
   (B) 18 tons
   (C) 36 tons
   (D) 90 tons

Problem Solving REAL WORLD

5. A Komodo dragon lizard can grow up to about 30 decimeters in length. Toni says that this is 300 centimeters. Do you agree? Explain how you can use a table to support your answer.

   _____

   _____

   _____

   _____

   _____

Lesson 84

COMMON CORE STANDARD CC.5.MD.1

Lesson Objective: Convert units of time to solve elapsed time problems.

Elapsed Time

You can solve elapsed time problems by converting units of time.

Starting at 4:20 P.M., Connie practiced piano for 90 minutes. At what time did Connie stop practicing piano?

Convert 90 minutes to hours and minutes. Then find the end time.

Units of Time
60 seconds (s) = 1 minute (min)
60 minutes = 1 hour (hr)
24 hours = 1 day (d)
7 days = 1 week (wk)
52 weeks = 1 year (yr)
12 months (mo) = 1 year
365 days = 1 year

Step 1 To convert minutes to hours, divide.

90 ÷ 60 is 1 with a remainder of 30

90 min = _____**1**_____ hr _____**30**_____ min

Step 2 Count forward by hours until you reach 1 hour.

4:20 → 5:20 = 1 hour

Step 3 Count forward by minutes until you reach 30 minutes.

5:20 → 5:30 = 1 hour 10 minutes
5:30 → 5:40 = 1 hour 20 minutes
5:40 → 5:50 = 1 hour 30 minutes

Connie stops practicing piano at **5:50 P.M.** _____

Convert.

1. 480 min = _____ hr

2. 4 d = _____ hr

3. 125 hr = _____ d _____ hr

Find the start, elapsed, or end time.

4. Start time: 7:15 A.M.

   Elapsed time: 2 hr 20 min

   End time: _____

5. Start time: 6:28 A.M.

   Elapsed time: _____

   End time: 10:08 A.M.

6. Start time: _____

   Elapsed time: 5 hr 50 min

   End time: 7:55 P.M.

7. Start time: 5:24 P.M.

   Elapsed time: 6 hr

   End time: _____

1. The high school football game started at 7:15 P.M. and ended at 10:44 P.M. How long did the game last?

   Ⓐ 2 hours 9 minutes

   Ⓑ 2 hours 29 minutes

   Ⓒ 3 hours 9 minutes

   Ⓓ 3 hours 29 minutes

2. Betsy spent 26 days traveling in Europe. How many weeks and days did Betsy travel in Europe?

   Ⓐ 2 weeks 6 days

   Ⓑ 3 weeks 5 days

   Ⓒ 4 weeks 2 days

   Ⓓ 5 weeks 1 day

3. Students arrived at the science museum at 1:15 P.M. They stayed at the museum for 2 hours 51 minutes. What time did the students leave the museum?

   Ⓐ 3:06 P.M.

   Ⓑ 4:00 P.M.

   Ⓒ 4:06 P.M.

   Ⓓ 4:44 P.M.

4. It takes Kate 10 minutes to walk to the bus stop. How many seconds does it take her to walk to the bus stop?

   Ⓐ 6,000 seconds

   Ⓑ 600 seconds

   Ⓒ 60 seconds

   Ⓓ 6 seconds

Problem Solving REAL WORLD

5. Kiera's dance class starts at *4:30* P.M. and ends at *6:15* P.M. How long is her dance class?

   _____

6. Julio watched a movie that started at *11:30* A.M. and ended at *2:12* P.M. How long was the movie?

   _____

Name _____

Lesson 85
COMMON CORE STANDARD CC.5.MD.2
Lesson Objective: Make and use line plots
with fractions to solve problems.

Line Plots

A **line plot** is a graph that shows the shape of a data set by placing Xs above each data value on a number line. You can make a line plot to represent a data set and then use the line plot to answer questions about the data set.

Students measure the lengths of several seeds.
The length of each seed is listed below.

$\frac{1}{2}$ inch, $\frac{3}{4}$ inch, $\frac{1}{2}$ inch, $\frac{1}{4}$ inch, $\frac{3}{4}$ inch, $\frac{3}{4}$ inch, $\frac{3}{4}$ inch, $\frac{1}{4}$ inch, $\frac{1}{2}$ inch

What is the combined length of the seeds that are $\frac{1}{4}$ inch long?

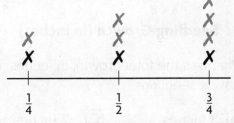

Length of Seeds (in inches)

Step 1 To represent the different lengths of the seeds, draw and label a line plot with the data values $\frac{1}{4}$, $\frac{1}{2}$, and $\frac{3}{4}$. Then use an X to represent each seed. The line plot has been started for you.

Step 2 There are ____2____ Xs above $\frac{1}{4}$ on the line plot.

Multiply to find the combined length of the seeds:

__2__ × __$\frac{1}{4}$__ = __$\frac{2}{4}$__, or $\frac{1}{2}$ ____ inch

The combined length of the seeds that are $\frac{1}{4}$ inch long is $\frac{1}{2}$ inch.

You can use the same process to find the combined lengths of the seeds that are $\frac{1}{2}$ inch long and $\frac{3}{4}$ inch long.

Use the data and the line plot above to answer the questions.

1. What is the total length of all the seeds that the students measured?

2. What is the average length of one of the seeds that the students measured?

_____   _____

Use the line plot for 1–2.

Maya measured the heights of the seedlings she was growing. She made a line plot to record the data.

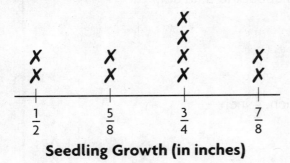

Seedling Growth (in inches)

1. What was the total growth, in inches, of Maya's seedlings?

   (A) 3 inches   (C) 7 inches

   (B) $3\frac{1}{2}$ inches   (D) 10 inches

2. What was the average height, in inches, of the seedlings she measured?

   (A) $\frac{11}{16}$ inch   (C) $\frac{3}{4}$ inch

   (B) $\frac{7}{10}$ inch   (D) $\frac{7}{8}$ inch

Use the line plot for 3–4.

A builder is buying property where she can build new houses. The line plot shows the sizes of the lots for each house.

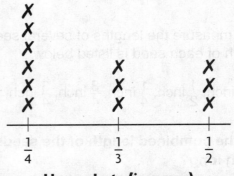

House Lots (in acres)

3. How many acres does the builder buy?

   (A) 3 acres   (C) 6 acres

   (B) 4 acres   (D) 12 acres

4. What is the average size of the lots?

   (A) $\frac{1}{12}$ acre   (C) $\frac{1}{4}$ acre

   (B) $\frac{1}{6}$ acre   (D) $\frac{1}{3}$ acre

Problem Solving REAL WORLD

5. Shia measured the thickness of the buttons in her collection. She graphed the results in a line plot.

   What steps could Shia use to find the average thickness of her buttons?

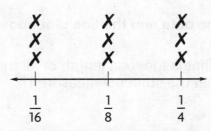

Button Thicknesses (in inches)

_____

_____

Name _____

Three-Dimensional Figures

A **polyhedron** is a solid figure with faces that are polygons. You can identify a polyhedron by the shape of its faces.

A **pyramid** is a polyhedron with one polygon base. The lateral faces of a pyramid are triangles that meet at a common vertex.

triangular pyramid	The base and faces are triangles.	
rectangular pyramid	The base is a rectangle.	
square pyramid	The base is a square.	
pentagonal pyramid	The base is a pentagon.	
hexagonal pyramid	The base is a hexagon.	

A **prism** is a polyhedron with two congruent polygons as bases. The lateral faces of a prism are rectangles.

triangular prism	The two bases are triangles.	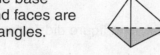
rectangular prism	All faces are rectangles.	
square prism or cube	All faces are squares.	
pentagonal prism	The two bases are pentagons.	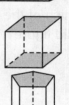
hexagonal prism	The two bases are hexagons.	

A solid figure with curved surfaces is **not a polyhedron**.

cone	The one base is a circle.	
sphere	There is no base.	
cylinder	The two bases are circles.	

Classify the solid figure. Write *prism, pyramid, cone, cylinder,* **or** *sphere.*

The solid figure has one base.

The rest of its faces are triangles.

So, the solid figure is a ___**pyramid**___.

Classify each solid figure. Write *prism, pyramid, cone, cylinder,* **or** *sphere.*

1.   2.   3.   4.

1. Koji is building a tower out of paper. He starts by making 2 congruent circular bases. He then makes 1 curved surface for the body of the tower. What three-dimensional figure does Koji build?

   (A) cone

   (B) cylinder

   (C) prism

   (D) sphere

2. Which of the following **best** classifies this solid figure?

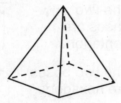

   (A) triangular pyramid

   (B) triangular prism

   (C) square pyramid

   (D) square prism

3. Tanya drew this solid figure on her notebook.

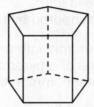

   What solid figure did Tanya draw?

   (A) hexagonal prism

   (B) pentagonal prism

   (C) hexagonal pyramid

   (D) pentagonal pyramid

4. Min Soo is making solid figures in the shape of party hats. He starts by making 1 circular base. He then makes 1 curved surface for the figure. What three-dimensional figure does Min Soo make?

   (A) prism

   (B) sphere

   (C) cylinder

   (D) cone

Problem Solving REAL WORLD

5. Darrien is making a solid figure out of folded paper. His solid figure has six congruent faces that are all squares. What solid figure did Darrien make?

6. Nanako said she drew a square pyramid and that all of the faces are triangles. Is this possible? **Explain.**

COMMON CORE STANDARD CC.5.MD.3a
Lesson Objective: Understand unit cubes and how they can be used to build a solid figure.

Unit Cubes and Solid Figures

A **unit cube** is a cube that has a length, width, and height of 1 unit. You can use unit cubes to build a rectangular prism.

Count the number of cubes used to build the rectangular prism.

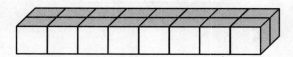

The length of the prism is made up of __8__ unit cubes.

The width of the prism is made up of __2__ unit cubes.

The height of the prism is made up of __1__ unit cube.

The number of unit cubes used to build the rectangular prism is __16__ .

Count the number of unit cubes used to build each solid figure.

1.
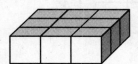

_____ unit cubes

2.

_____ unit cubes

3.
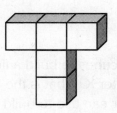

_____ unit cubes

4.
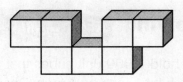

_____ unit cubes

1. Chase built a solid figure with unit cubes. How many unit cubes did he use for his figure?

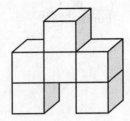

Ⓐ 5
Ⓑ 6
Ⓒ 7
Ⓓ 8

2. Diana used more than one unit cube to build a figure. When she traced around the figure, she drew a square. What is the **least** number of unit cubes she could have used?

Ⓐ 1
Ⓑ 2
Ⓒ 4
Ⓓ 9

3. Ella placed some unit cubes on her desk as shown below. How many unit cubes did Ella use?

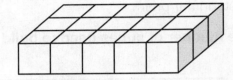

Ⓐ 5
Ⓑ 10
Ⓒ 15
Ⓓ 20

4. Henry stacked these unit cubes. How many unit cubes did Henry stack?

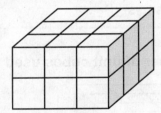

Ⓐ 6
Ⓑ 9
Ⓒ 12
Ⓓ 18

Problem Solving REAL WORLD

5. A carton can hold 1,000 unit cubes that measure 1 inch by 1 inch by 1 inch. Describe the dimensions of the carton using unit cubes.

_____

_____

6. Peter uses unit cubes to build a figure in the shape of the letter X. What is the fewest unit cubes that Peter can use to build the figure?

Understand Volume

The **volume** of a rectangular prism is equal to the number of unit cubes that make up the prism. Each unit cube has a volume of 1 cubic unit.

Find the volume of the prism. 1 unit cube = 1 cubic inch

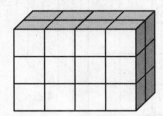

Step 1 Count the number of unit cubes in the bottom layer of the prism.

There are __4__ unit cubes that make up the length of the first layer.

There are __2__ unit cubes that make up the width of the first layer.

There is __1__ unit cube that makes up the height of the first layer.

So, altogether, there are __8__ unit cubes that make up the bottom layer of the prism.

Step 2 Count the number of layers of cubes that make up the prism.

The prism is made up of __3__ layers of unit cubes.

Step 3 Find the total number of cubes that fill the prism.

Multiply the number of layers by the number of cubes in each layer.

$3 \times 8 =$ __24__ unit cubes

Each unit cube has a volume of 1 cubic inch. So, the volume of the prism is 24×1, or __24__ cubic inches.

Use the unit given. Find the volume.

1.

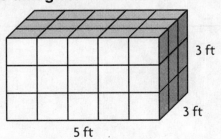

3 ft
3 ft
5 ft

Each cube = 1 cu ft

Volume = _____ cu _____

2.

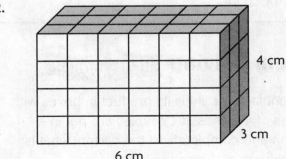

4 cm
3 cm
6 cm

Each cube = 1 cu cm

Volume = _____ cu _____

175

1. Cole stacked 1-foot cube-shaped boxes in a storage bin as shown. What is the volume of the space he filled?

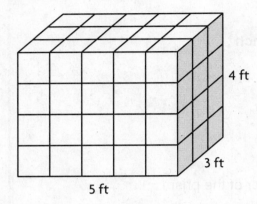

4 ft

3 ft

5 ft

Each cube = 1 cu ft

Ⓐ 20 cu in.

Ⓑ 20 cu ft

Ⓒ 60 cu in.

Ⓓ 60 cu ft

2. A jeweler received a carton of boxes packed with gift boxes. The gift boxes were 2 inches long on each edge. If 12 boxes completely fill the carton, what is the volume of the carton?

Ⓐ 24 cu in.

Ⓑ 48 cu in.

Ⓒ 96 cu in.

Ⓓ 144 cu in.

3. Lindsay filled a box with 1-centimeter cubes. What is the volume of box?

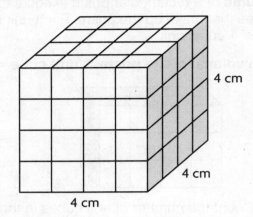

4 cm

4 cm

4 cm

Each cube = 1 cu cm

Ⓐ 16 cu cm   Ⓒ 64 cu cm

Ⓑ 16 cu m   Ⓓ 64 cu m

4. Marina packed 36 1-inch cubes into this box. How many layers of cubes did Marina make?

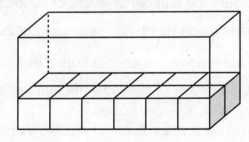

Ⓐ 2   Ⓒ 4

Ⓑ 3   Ⓓ 6

Problem Solving REAL WORLD

5. A manufacturer ships its product in boxes with edges of 4 inches. If 12 boxes are put in a carton and completely fill the carton, what is the volume of the carton?

Estimate Volume

You can estimate the volume of a larger box by filling it
with smaller boxes.

Mario packs boxes of markers into a large box. The volume
of each box of markers is 15 cubic inches. Estimate the
volume of the large box.

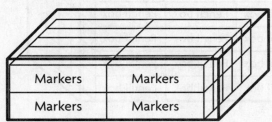

The volume of one box of markers is __15__ cubic inches.

Use the box of markers to estimate the volume of the large box.

• The large box holds __2__ layers of boxes of markers, a top
  layer and a bottom layer. Each layer contains __10__ boxes of markers.
  So, the large box holds about 2 × 10, or __20__ boxes of markers.

• Multiply the volume of 1 box of markers by the estimated
  number of boxes of markers that fit in the large box.

  __20__ × __15__ = __300__

So, the volume of the large box is about 300 cubic inches.

Estimate the volume.

1. Each box of toothpaste has a volume of
   25 cubic inches.

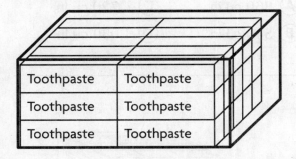

There are _____ boxes of toothpaste in
the large box.

The estimated volume of the large box

is _____ × 25 = _____ cubic inches.

2. Volume of CD case: 80 cu cm

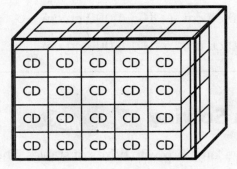

Volume of large box: _____

1. The volume of a box of coloring pencils is 250 cubic centimeters. Which is the best estimate of the volume of the box that the coloring pencils came packed in?

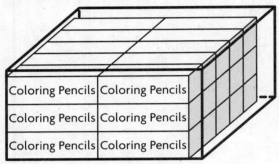

Ⓐ 750 cu cm   Ⓒ 7,500 cu cm

Ⓑ 3,750 cu cm   Ⓓ 75,000 cu cm

2. Joe packed boxes of staplers into a larger box. If the volume of each stapler box is 400 cubic centimeters, which is the best estimate for the volume of the box that Joe packed with staplers?

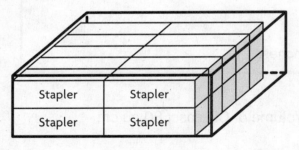

Ⓐ 800 cu cm   Ⓒ 4,000 cu cm

Ⓑ 2,000 cu cm   Ⓓ 8,000 cu cm

3. The volume of a pencil box is 80 cubic inches. Which is the best estimate of the volume of the box that the pencil boxes came packed in?

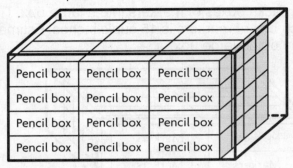

Ⓐ 9,600 cu in.   Ⓒ 960 cu in.

Ⓑ 3,840 cu in.   Ⓓ 384 cu in.

4. Joe packed tissue boxes into a larger box. If the volume of each tissue box is 90 cubic inches, which is the best estimate for the volume of the box that Joe packed with tissue boxes?

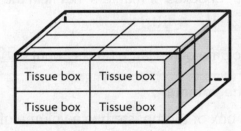

Ⓐ 360 cu in.   Ⓒ 720 cu in.

Ⓑ 540 cu in.   Ⓓ 1,080 cu in.

Problem Solving REAL WORLD

5. Theo fills a large box with boxes of staples. The volume of each box of staples is 120 cu cm. Estimate the volume of the large box.

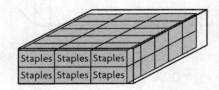

_____

Lesson **90**

COMMON CORE STANDARD CC.5.MD.5a

Lesson Objective: Find the volume of rectangular prisms.

Volume of Rectangular Prisms

Jorge wants to find the volume of this rectangular prism. He can use cubes that measure 1 centimeter on each side to find the volume.

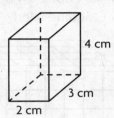

Step 1 The base has a length of 2 centimeters and a width of 3 centimeters. Multiply to find the area of the base.

Base = __2__ × __3__

Base = __6__ cm²

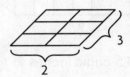

Step 2 The height of the prism is 4 centimeters. Add the number of cubes in each layer to find the volume.

Remember: Each layer has 6 cubes.

Step 3 Count the cubes. __24__ cubes
Multiply the base and the height to check your answer.

Volume = __6__ × __4__

Volume = __24__ cubic centimeters

So, the volume of Jorge's rectangular prism is __24__ cubic centimeters.

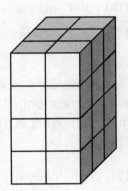

Find the volume.

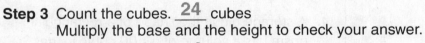

1.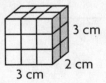

Volume: _____

2.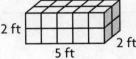

Volume: _____

3.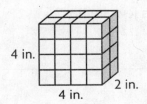

Volume: _____

4.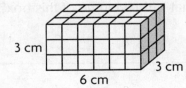

Volume: _____

1. Claudine filled a box with smaller boxes shaped like cubes. What is the volume of the box Claudine filled?

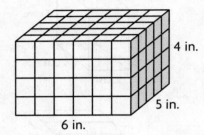

4 in.

5 in.

6 in.

Ⓐ 15 cubic inches

Ⓑ 25 cubic inches

Ⓒ 100 cubic inches

Ⓓ 120 cubic inches

2. Luke keeps his art supplies in a shoe box that is 12 inches long, 7 inches wide, and 5 inches high. What is the volume of the shoe box?

Ⓐ 420 cubic inches

Ⓑ 358 cubic inches

Ⓒ 240 cubic inches

Ⓓ 24 cubic inches

3. Barbie stacked small cubes into a box until it was full. What is the volume of the box?

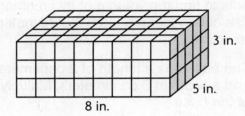

3 in.

5 in.

8 in.

Ⓐ 18 cubic inches

Ⓑ 40 cubic inches

Ⓒ 120 cubic inches

Ⓓ 158 cubic inches

4. A storage bin in the shape of a rectangular prism has a volume of 5,400 cubic inches. The base area of the storage bin is 450 square inches. What is the height of the storage bin?

Ⓐ 9 inches

Ⓑ 11 inches

Ⓒ 12 inches

Ⓓ 15 inches

Problem Solving REAL WORLD

5. Aaron keeps his baseball cards in a cardboard box that is 12 inches long, 8 inches wide, and 3 inches high. What is the volume of this box?

_____

6. Amanda's jewelry box is in the shape of a cube that has 6-inch edges. What is the volume of Amanda's jewelry box?

_____

Algebra • Apply Volume Formulas

You can use a formula to find the volume of a rectangular prism.

$$Volume = length \times width \times height$$
$$V = (l \times w) \times h$$

Find the volume of the rectangular prism.

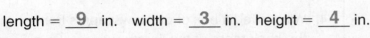

Step 1 Identify the length, width, and height of the rectangular prism.

length = __9__ in.   width = __3__ in.   height = __4__ in.

Step 2 Substitute the values of the length, width, and height into the formula.

$$V = (l \times w) \times h$$
$$V = (\underline{\ 9\ } \times \underline{\ 3\ }) \times \underline{\ 4\ }$$

Step 3 Multiply the length by the width.

$$V = (9 \times 3) \times 4$$
$$V = \underline{\ 27\ } \times 4$$

Step 4 Multiply the product of the length and width by the height.

$$V = 27 \times \underline{\ 4\ }$$
$$= \underline{\ 108\ }$$

So, the volume of the rectangular prism is __108__ cubic inches.

Find the volume.

1.

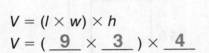

5 ft
4 ft
12 ft

V = _____

2.

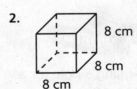

8 cm
8 cm
8 cm

V = _____

1. Antonio found an antique chest in his grandfather's attic.

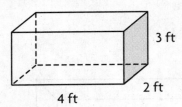

What is the volume of the chest?

(A) 6 cubic feet   (C) 12 cubic feet

(B) 9 cubic feet   (D) 24 cubic feet

2. When Emma went to college, her mother packed up all her old skiing trophies into a box with the dimensions shown.

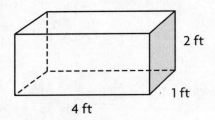

What is the volume of the box?

(A) 7 cubic feet   (C) 9 cubic feet

(B) 8 cubic feet   (D) 10 cubic feet

3. Kristin keeps paper clips in a box that is the shape of a cube. Each edge of the cube is 3 inches. What is the volume of the cube?

(A) 6 cubic inches

(B) 9 cubic inches

(C) 18 cubic inches

(D) 27 cubic inches

4. Will moved a box of old newspapers from the back room of the library.

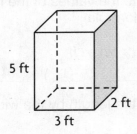

What is the volume of the box?

(A) 10 cubic feet

(B) 15 cubic feet

(C) 30 cubic feet

(D) 40 cubic feet

Problem Solving REAL WORLD

5. A construction company is digging a hole for a swimming pool. The hole will be 12 yards long, 7 yards wide, and 3 yards deep. How many cubic yards of dirt will the company need to remove?

6. Amy rents a storage room that is 15 feet long, 5 feet wide, and 8 feet. What is the volume of the storage room?

Problem Solving • Compare Volumes

A company makes aquariums that come in three sizes of rectangular prisms. The length of each aquarium is three times its width and depth. The depths of the aquariums are 1 foot, 2 feet, and 3 feet. What is the volume of each aquarium?

Read the Problem	Solve the Problem
What do I need to find? I need to find the <u>volume</u> of each aquarium.	**Think:** The depth of an aquarium is the same as the height of the prism formed by the aquarium
What information do I need to use? I can use the formula for volume, <u>$V = l \times w \times h$, or $V = B \times h$</u>. I can use <u>1 ft, 2 ft, and 3 ft</u> as the depths. I can use the clues <u>the length is three times</u> <u>the width and depth</u>.	
How will I use the information? I will use the <u>volume formula</u> and a <u>table</u> to list all of the possible combinations of lengths, widths, and depths.	

Solve the Problem table:

Length (ft)	Width (ft)	Depth, or Height (ft)	Volume (cu ft)
3	1	1	3
6	2	2	24
9	3	3	81

So, the volumes of the aquariums are 3 cubic feet, 24 cubic feet, and 81 cubic feet.

1. Jamie needs a bin for her school supplies. A blue bin has a length of 12 inches, a width of 5 inches, and a height of 4 inches. A green bin has a length of 10 inches, a width of 6 inches, and a height of 5 inches. What is the volume of the bin with the greatest volume?

2. Suppose the blue bin that Jamie found had a length of 5 inches, a width of 5 inches, and a height of 12 inches. Would one bin have a greater volume than the other? **Explain.**

1. Ben is filling a box that has the shape of a rectangular prism with 1-inch cubes. A layer of 7 rows with 8 cubes in each row filled the bottom of the box. The volume of the box is 224 cubic inches. How many layers of cubes can Ben fit in the box?

Ⓐ 2   Ⓒ 8
Ⓑ 4   Ⓓ 10

2. Mary bought a puzzle in a box that has a width of 3 inches, a length of 10 inches, and a height of 8 inches. She put it in a box that has a volume of 576 cubic inches so she could mail it with some other things. How many cubic inches of space were left in the box?

Ⓐ 816 cu in.   Ⓒ 336 cu in.
Ⓑ 597 cu in.   Ⓓ 240 cu in.

3. Sylvia can buy a blue box or a green box to store her markers. Both boxes have a base that measures 8 inches by 4 inches. The height of the blue box is 2 inches. The height of the green box is 1 inch. How much greater is the volume of the blue box than the green box?

Ⓐ 96 cu in.   Ⓒ 35 cu in.
Ⓑ 64 cu in.   Ⓓ 32 cu in.

4. Mr. McDonald is designing a cabinet to store sports equipment in the gym. The length and width of one design cannot be the same as the length or width of another design. He wants the cabinet to be 5 feet high with a volume of 60 cubic feet. How many different designs, all with whole number dimensions, can he make?

Ⓐ 2   Ⓒ 6
Ⓑ 3   Ⓓ 12

Problem Solving REAL WORLD

5. Margie is packing 108 small boxes into a large carton. The small boxes will fill all of the space inside the large carton. Each small box is 3 inches long, 2 inches wide, and 1 inch high. The width of the base and the height of the large carton are the same. The length of the base is less than 36 inches. All of the dimensions are whole numbers. Explain how to find possible dimensions for the large carton.

_____
_____
_____
_____
_____
_____

Lesson 93
COMMON CORE STANDARD CC.5.MD.5c
Lesson Objective: Find the volume of
combined rectangular prisms.

Find Volume of Composed Figures

A composite figure is a solid made up of two or more solids. To find the
volume of a composite figure, first find the volume of each solid that
makes up the figure. Then find the sum of the volumes of the figures.

Find the volume of the composite figure at right.

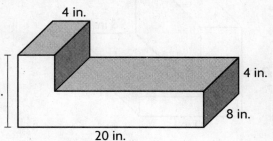

Step 1 Break apart the composite figure into two
rectangular prisms. Label the dimensions
of each prism.

Prism 1   **Prism 2**

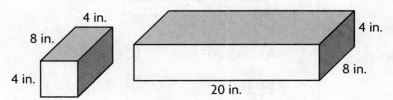

Step 2 Find the volume of each prism.

Prism 1	**Prism 2**
$V = (l \times w) \times h$	$V = (l \times w) \times h$
$V = \underline{4} \times \underline{8} \times \underline{4}$	$V = \underline{20} \times \underline{8} \times \underline{4}$
$V = 128$ in.^{3}	$V = 640$ in.^{3}

Step 3 Find the sum of the volumes of the two prisms.

Volume of Prism 1 + Volume of Prism 2 = Volume of Composite Figure
        <u>128</u>   +   <u>640</u>   = Volume of Composite Figure
                    <u>768</u>   = Volume of Composite Figure

So, the volume of the composite figure is 768 in.^{3}

Find the volume of the composite figure.

1.
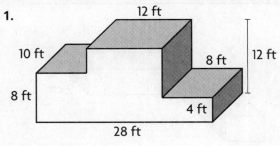

$V = $ _____

2.
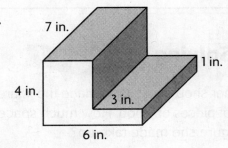

$V = $ _____

1. Dmitri built a step out of blocks. What is the volume of the step?

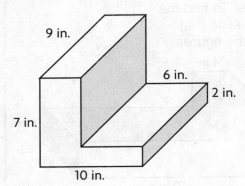

   Ⓐ 360 cu in.   Ⓒ 540 cu in.

   Ⓑ 450 cu in.   Ⓓ 750 cu in.

2. Latoya built some new steps up to the front of her house. What is the volume of the steps?

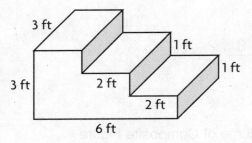

   Ⓐ 18 cu ft   Ⓒ 48 cu ft

   Ⓑ 36 cu ft   Ⓓ 54 cu ft

3. Maksim built a scratching toy for his cat. What is the volume of the scratching toy?

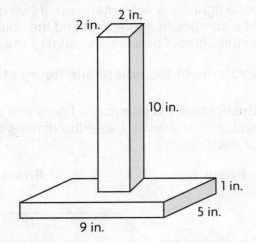

   Ⓐ 85 cu in.   Ⓒ 210 cu in.

   Ⓑ 180 cu in.   Ⓓ 1,800 cu in.

4. Jacinda made some steps for her deck. What is the volume of the steps?

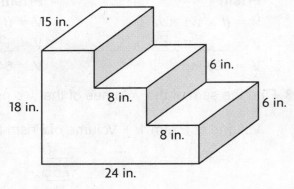

   Ⓐ 432 cu in.   Ⓒ 4,320 cu in.

   Ⓑ 3,240 cu in.   Ⓓ 6,480 cu in.

Problem Solving REAL WORLD

5. As part of her shop class, Jules made the figure below out of pieces of wood. How much space does the figure she made take up?

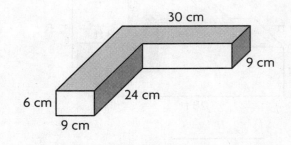

Lesson 94

COMMON CORE STANDARD CC.5.G.1
Lesson Objective: Graph and name points on a coordinate grid using ordered pairs.

Ordered Pairs

A coordinate grid is like a sheet of graph paper bordered at the left and at the bottom by two perpendicular number lines. The **x-axis** is the horizontal number line at the bottom of the grid. The **y-axis** is the vertical number line on the left side of the grid.

An ordered pair is a pair of numbers that describes the location of a point on the grid. An ordered pair contains two coordinates, *x* and *y*. The **x-coordinate** is the first number in the ordered pair, and the **y-coordinate** is the second number.

$(x, y) \longrightarrow (10, 4)$

Plot and label (10, 4) on the coordinate grid.

To graph an ordered pair:

- Start at the origin, (0, 0).

- Think: The letter *x* comes before *y* in the alphabet. Move across the *x*-axis first.

- The *x*-coordinate is 10, so move 10 units right.

- The *y*-coordinate is 4, so move 4 units up.

- Plot and label the ordered pair (10, 4).

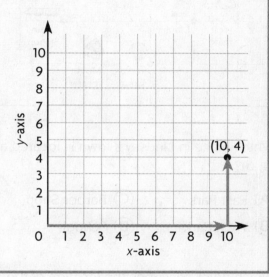

Use the coordinate grid to write an ordered pair for the given point.

1. *G* _____

2. *H* _____

3. *J* _____

4. *K* _____

Plot and label the points on the coordinate grid.

5. *A* (1, 6)

6. *B* (1, 9)

7. *C* (3, 7)

8. *D* (5, 5)

9. *E* (9, 3)

10. *F* (6, 2)

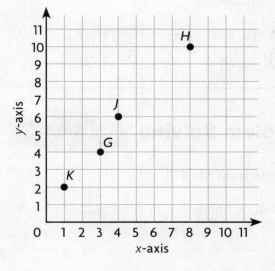

Use the coordinate grid for 1–2.

Lindsey made a map of her town.

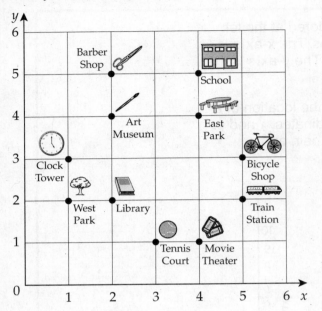

1. Which place in Lindsey's town is located at (4, 5)?

   (A) East Park   (C) Barber Shop
   (B) West Park   (D) School

2. Which point describes the location of the Art Museum?

   (A) (2, 4)   (C) (4, 4)
   (B) (2, 5)   (D) (5, 2)

Use the coordinate grid for 3.

The map shows the location of the attractions in an amusement park.

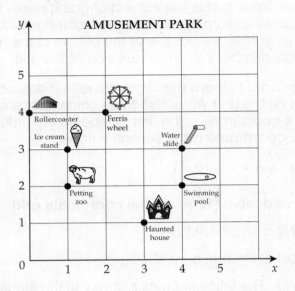

AMUSEMENT PARK

3. Which attraction is located at (2, 4)?

   (A) Rollercoaster
   (B) Ferris Wheel
   (C) Water Slide
   (D) Haunted Houses

Problem Solving REAL WORLD

Use the map for 4-5.

4. Which building is located at (5, 6)?

   _____

5. What is the distance between Kip's Pizza and the bank?

   _____

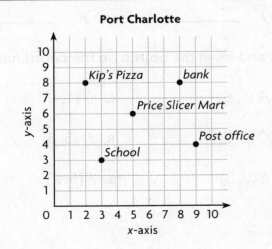

Port Charlotte

Lesson 95

COMMON CORE STANDARD CC.5.G.2
Lesson Objective: Collect and graph data on a coordinate grid.

Graph Data

Graph the data on the coordinate grid.

Plant Growth				
End of Week	1	2	3	4
Height (in inches)	4	7	10	11

- Choose a title for your graph and label it. You can use the data categories to name the *x*- and *y*-axis.

- Write the related pairs of data as ordered pairs.

(__1__, __4__), (__2__, __7__)

(__3__, __10__), (__4__, __11__)

- Plot the point for each ordered pair.

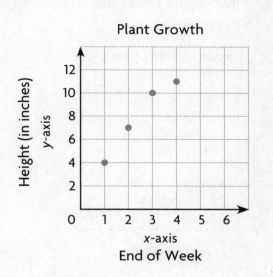

Plant Growth

Graph the data on the coordinate grid. Label the points.

1.

Distance of Bike Ride				
Time (in minutes)	30	60	90	120
Distance (in miles)	9	16	21	27

Write the ordered pair for each point.

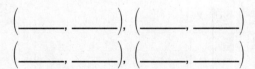

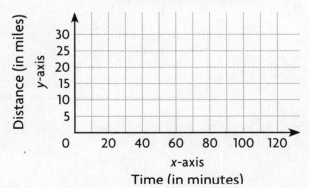

Distance of Bike Ride

2.

Bianca's Writing Progress				
Time (in minutes)	15	30	45	60
Total Pages	1	3	9	11

Write the ordered pair for each point.

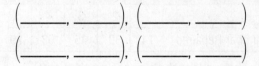

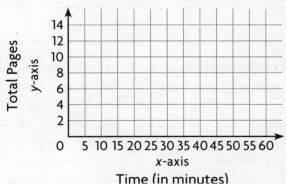

Bianca's Writing Progress

Use the graph for 1–3.

Sunil made this graph to show the weight of his new puppy.

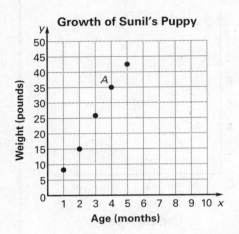

Growth of Sunil's Puppy

1. At what age did the puppy weigh 26 pounds?

   Ⓐ 2 months   Ⓒ 3 months

   Ⓑ 4 months   Ⓓ 5 months

2. What information is represented by the point labeled *A*?

   Ⓐ The puppy weighed 4 pounds at age 35 months.

   Ⓑ The puppy weighed 40 pounds at age 4 months.

   Ⓒ The puppy weighed 35 pounds at age 4 months.

   Ⓓ The puppy weighed 35 pounds at age 5 months.

3. What was the weight of the puppy at age 5 months?

   Ⓐ 40 pounds   Ⓒ 47 pounds

   Ⓑ 43 pounds   Ⓓ 50 pounds

Problem Solving REAL WORLD

4.

Windows Repaired					
Day	1	2	3	4	5
Total Number Repaired	14	30	45	63	79

a. Write the ordered pairs for each point.

_____

_____

b. What does the ordered pair (2, 30) tell you about the number of windows repaired?

_____

_____

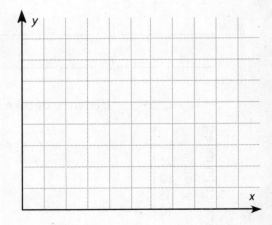

Name _____

Lesson 96

COMMON CORE STANDARD CC.5.G.2

Lesson Objective: Analyze and display data in a line graph.

Line Graphs

A **line graph** uses a series of line segments to show how a set of data changes over time. The **scale** of a line graph measures and labels the data along the axes. An **interval** is the distance between the numbers on an axis.

Use the table to make a line graph.

• Write a title for your graph. In this example, use **Average Monthly High Temperature in Sacramento**.

• Draw and label the axes of the line graph. Label the horizontal axis **Month**. Write the months. Label the vertical axis **Temperature (°F)**.

• Choose a scale and an interval. The range is 53–80, so a possible scale is 0–80, with intervals of 20.

• Write the related pairs of data as ordered pairs: **(Jan, 53); (Feb, 60); (Mar, 65); (April, 71); (May, 80).**

Average Monthly High Temperature in Sacramento, California

Month	Jan.	Feb.	Mar.	April	May
Temperature (°F)	53	60	65	71	80

1. Make a line graph of the data above.

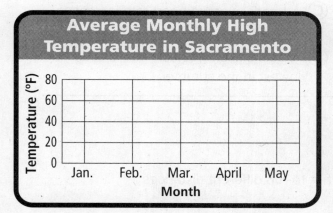

Use the graph to determine between which two months the least change in average high temperature occurs.

2. Make a line graph of the data in the table.

Average Low Temperature in San Diego, California

Month	Mar.	April	May	June	July
Temperature (°F)	51	51	60	62	66

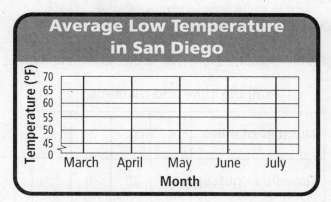

Use the graph to determine between which two months the greatest change in average low temperature occurs.

© Houghton Mifflin Harcourt Publishing Company

Core Standards for Math, Grade 5

Name _____

Lesson 96
CC.5.G.2

1. Kareem made a table showing how much he earned each month mowing lawns.

Lawn Mowing Earnings

Month	April	May	June	July	August
Amount Earned	$40	$55	$60	$75	$50

What are the most appropriate scale and interval for Kareem to use to make a line graph of the data?

(A) Scale: 0 to 50, Interval: 2

(B) Scale: 0 to 50, Interval: 5

(C) Scale: 0 to 100, Interval: 10

(D) Scale: 0 to 100, Interval: 20

2. A scientist made a line graph that showed how a bear's average heart rate changes over time.

CHANGE IN AVERAGE HEART RATE OF BEARS

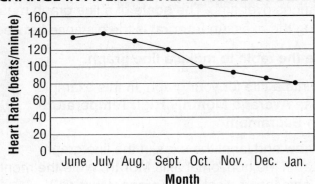

Based on the graph, which statement is true?

(A) A bear's average heart rate rarely changes.

(B) A bear's average heart rate starts to decrease at the end of the summer.

(C) A bear's average heart rate increases over time.

(D) A bear's average heart rate is at its lowest in the summer.

Problem Solving REAL WORLD

3. Randy makes a table that shows how long it takes her to run different distances.

Running Time and Distance

Number of miles	1	2	3	4
Time (in minutes)	10	20	28	35

Randy uses the data to make a line graph. Describe the line graph.

_____

_____

Polygons

A **polygon** is a closed plane figure formed by three or more line segments that meet at points called vertices. You can classify a polygon by the number of sides and the number of angles that it has.

Congruent figures have the same size and shape. In a **regular polygon,** all sides are congruent and all angles are congruent.

Classify the polygon below.

Polygon	Sides	Angles	Vertices
Triangle	3	3	3
Quadrilateral	4	4	4
Pentagon	5	5	5
Hexagon	6	6	6
Heptagon	7	7	7
Octagon	8	8	8
Nonagon	9	9	9
Decagon	10	10	10

How many sides does this polygon have? __**5 sides**__

How many angles does this polygon have? __**5 angles**__

Name the polygon. __**pentagon**__

Are all the sides congruent? __**no**__

Are all the angles congruent? __**no**__

So, the polygon above is a pentagon. It is *not* a regular polygon.

Name each polygon. Then tell whether it is a *regular polygon* or *not a regular polygon*.

1.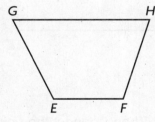

2.

3.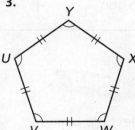

4.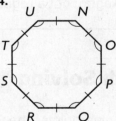

_____

_____

_____

_____

_____

_____

_____

_____

_____

_____

_____

_____

1. Mr. Delgado sees this sign while he is driving.

   Which **best** describes the sign?

   Ⓐ triangle; regular polygon

   Ⓑ triangle; not a regular polygon

   Ⓒ hexagon; regular polygon

   Ⓓ hexagon; not a regular polygon

2. Mr. Diaz is building a fence around his yard. He drew a sketch of the fence line.

   Which **best** describes the fence line?

   Ⓐ pentagon; regular polygon

   Ⓑ pentagon; not a regular polygon

   Ⓒ hexagon; regular polygon

   Ⓓ hexagon; not a regular polygon

3. A stained glass window at the town library is the shape of a regular octagon. Which of the following describes a regular octagon?

   Ⓐ a figure with 6 congruent sides and 6 congruent angles

   Ⓑ a figure with 6 sides that are not congruent

   Ⓒ a figure with 8 sides that are not congruent

   Ⓓ a figure with 8 congruent sides and 8 congruent angles

4. Beth drew four quadrilaterals. Which of the quadrilaterals that she drew is a regular polygon?

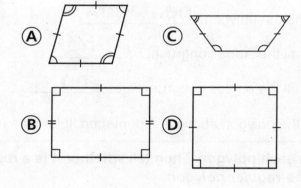

Problem Solving REAL WORLD

5. Sketch nine points. Then, connect the points to form a closed plane figure. What kind of polygon did you draw?

6. Sketch seven points. Then, connect the points to form a closed plane figure. What kind of polygon did you draw?

_____

Name _____

Triangles

Lesson 98
COMMON CORE STANDARD CC.5.G.3
Lesson Objective: Classify and draw triangles using their properties.

You can classify triangles by the length of their sides and by the measure of their angles. **Classify each triangle.**

Use a ruler to measure the side lengths.

- **equilateral triangle**
  All sides are the same length.

- **isosceles triangle**
  Two sides are the same length.

- **scalene triangle**
  All sides are different lengths.

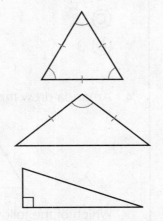

Use the corner of a sheet of paper to classify the angles.

- **acute triangle**
  All three angles are acute.

- **obtuse triangle**
  One angle is obtuse. The other two angles are acute.

- **right triangle**
  One angle is right. The other two angles are acute.

Classify the triangle according to its side lengths.
It has two congruent sides.
The triangle is an isosceles triangle.

Classify the triangle according to its angle measures.
It has one right angle.
The triangle is a right triangle.

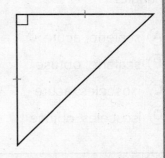

Classify each triangle. Write *isosceles*, *scalene*, or *equilateral*.
Then write *acute*, *obtuse*, or *right*.

1.
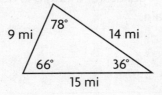
9 mi   78°   14 mi
66°   36°
15 mi

_____

2.
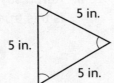
5 in.   5 in.
5 in.

_____

3.
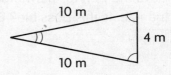
10 m   4 m
10 m

_____

4.
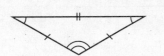

_____

5.
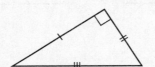

_____

6.

_____

1. Which kind of triangle has no congruent sides?

   Ⓐ equilateral

   Ⓑ horizontal

   Ⓒ isosceles

   Ⓓ scalene

2. Nathan drew this triangle.

   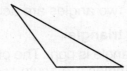

   Which of the following **best** classifies the triangle?

   Ⓐ scalene, acute

   Ⓑ scalene, obtuse

   Ⓒ isosceles, acute

   Ⓓ isosceles, obtuse

3. What is the **least** number of acute angles that a triangle can have?

   Ⓐ 0

   Ⓑ 1

   Ⓒ 2

   Ⓓ 3

4. Amanda drew this triangle.

   Which of the following **best** classifies the triangle?

   Ⓐ equilateral, acute

   Ⓑ isosceles, acute

   Ⓒ scalene, acute

   Ⓓ isosceles, right

Problem Solving REAL WORLD

5. Mary says the pen for her horse is an acute right triangle. Is this possible? **Explain.**

   _____

   _____

6. Karen says every equilateral triangle is acute. Is this true? **Explain.**

   _____

   _____

Problem Solving • Properties of Two-Dimensional Figures

Haley thinks hexagon *ABCDEF* has 6 congruent sides, but she does not have a ruler to measure the sides. Are the 6 sides congruent?

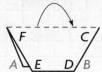

Read the Problem	Solve the Problem
What do I need to find? I need to determine if sides *AB*, *BC*, *CD*, *DE*, *EF*, and *FA* have the **same length** .	Trace the hexagon and cut out the shape. **Step 1** Fold the hexagon to match the sides *AB* and *ED*, sides *FE* and *FA*, and sides *CD* and *CB*. The sides match, so they are congruent.
What information do I need to use? The figure is a **hexagon** with **6** sides and **6 congruent** angles.	**Step 2** Fold along the diagonal between *B* and *E* to match sides *BA* and *BC*, sides *AF* and *CD*, and sides *EF* and *ED*. Fold along the diagonal between *A* and *D* to match sides *AF* and *AB*, sides *FE* and *BC*, and sides *DE* and *DC*.
How will I use the information? I will **act it out by tracing the figure and then folding the figure** to match all the sides to see if they are **congruent** .	**Step 3** Use logic to match sides *AB* and *CD*, sides *AB* and *EF*, sides *BC* and *DE*, and sides *DE* and *FA*. The sides match, so they are congruent.

1. Justin thinks square *STUV* has 4 congruent sides, but he does not have a ruler to measure the sides. Are the sides congruent? **Explain.**

   _____

   _____

   _____

   _____

   _____

2. Esther knows octagon *OPQRSTUV* has 8 congruent angles. How can she determine whether the octagon has 8 congruent sides without using a ruler?

   _____

   _____

   _____

   _____

   _____

1. Keiko drew the shapes of her tables on grid paper. Then she cut them out and used them on a floor plan to help arrange her furniture.

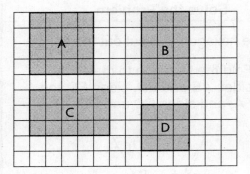

Which two shapes that Keiko drew are congruent?

(A) A and B   (C) B and C

(B) A and C   (D) B and D

2. Ezra drew triangles to make this design.

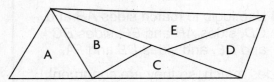

Which of the triangles appear to be congruent?

(A) A and B   (C) C and E

(B) B and D   (D) A and D

3. Fumiko drew the shapes of her neighbors' patios on grid paper.

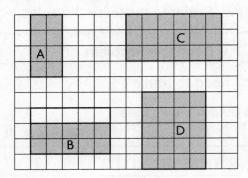

Which two shapes that Fumiko drew are congruent?

(A) A and B   (C) B and C

(B) A and C   (D) B and D

4. Ian drew triangles to make this design.

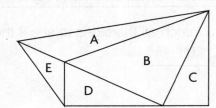

Which of the triangles appear to be congruent?

(A) A and E   (C) B and D

(B) B and C   (D) C and D

Problem Solving REAL WORLD

5. Juanita has a quadrilateral that she thinks is a rhombus, but she does not have a ruler to measure the sides. How can Juanita determine whether the quadrilateral is a rhombus?

_____

_____

_____

_____

Quadrilaterals

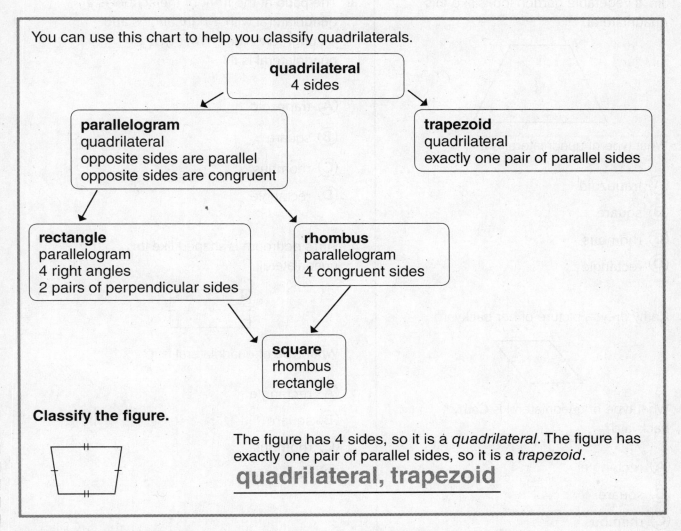

You can use this chart to help you classify quadrilaterals.

quadrilateral
4 sides

parallelogram
quadrilateral
opposite sides are parallel
opposite sides are congruent

trapezoid
quadrilateral
exactly one pair of parallel sides

rectangle
parallelogram
4 right angles
2 pairs of perpendicular sides

rhombus
parallelogram
4 congruent sides

square
rhombus
rectangle

Classify the figure.

The figure has 4 sides, so it is a *quadrilateral*. The figure has exactly one pair of parallel sides, so it is a *trapezoid*.

quadrilateral, trapezoid

Classify the quadrilateral in as many ways as possible. Write *quadrilateral,*
parallelogram, rectangle, rhombus, square, **or** *trapezoid.*

1.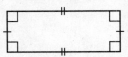

   _____

   _____

2.

   _____

   _____

3.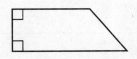

   _____

   _____

4.

   _____

   _____

1. Jim's vegetable garden looks like this quadrilateral.

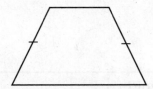

What type of quadrilateral is it?

Ⓐ trapezoid

Ⓑ square

Ⓒ rhombus

Ⓓ rectangle

2. Cathy drew a picture of her backyard.

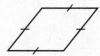

What type of quadrilateral is Cathy's backyard?

Ⓐ rectangle

Ⓑ square

Ⓒ rhombus

Ⓓ trapezoid

3. The patio at the front of the school is a quadrilateral with 4 right angles and 4 congruent sides. What type of quadrilateral is it?

Ⓐ trapezoid

Ⓑ square

Ⓒ rhombus

Ⓓ rectangle

4. Tim's bedroom is shaped like this quadrilateral.

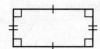

What type of quadrilateral is it?

Ⓐ rectangle

Ⓑ square

Ⓒ rhombus

Ⓓ trapezoid

Problem Solving REAL WORLD

5. Kevin claims he can draw a trapezoid with three right angles. Is this possible? **Explain.**

_____

_____

_____

6. "If a figure is a square, then it is a regular quadrilateral." Is this true or false? **Explain.**

_____

_____

_____

Lesson 1

Name _____

COMMON CORE STANDARD CC.5.OA.1
Lesson Objective: Use the order of operations to evaluate numerical expressions.

Algebra • Evaluate Numerical Expressions

A **numerical expression** is a mathematical phrase that includes only numbers and operation symbols.

You **evaluate** the expression when you perform all the computations to find its value.

To evaluate an expression, use the **order of operations**.

Order of Operations
1. Parentheses
2. Multiply and Divide
3. Add and Subtract

Evaluate the expression (10 + 6 × 6) − 4 × 10.

Step 1 Start with computations inside the parentheses. $10 + 6 × 6$

Step 2 Perform the order of operations inside the *parentheses*.   *Multiply and divide* from left to right.
$10 + 6 × 6 = 10 + \underline{36}$
Add and subtract from left to right.
$10 + 36 = \underline{46}$

Step 3 Rewrite the expression with the parentheses evaluated. $46 − 4 × 10$

Step 4 *Multiply and divide* from left to right. $46 − 4 × 10 = 46 − \underline{40}$

Step 5 *Add and subtract* from left to right. $46 − 40 = \underline{6}$

So, $(10 + 6 × 6) − 4 × 10 = 6.$

Evaluate the numerical expression.

1. $8 − (7 × 1)$ __1__
2. $5 − 2 + 12 ÷ 4$ __6__
3. $8 × (16 ÷ 2)$ __64__

4. $4 × (28 − 20 ÷ 2)$ __72__
5. $(30 − 9 ÷ 3) ÷ 9$ __3__
6. $(6 × 6 − 9) − 9 ÷ 3$ __24__

7. $11 ÷ (8 + 9 ÷ 3)$ __1__
8. $13 × 4 − 65 ÷ 13$ __47__
9. $9 + 4 × 6 − 65 ÷ 13$ __28__

Lesson 1
CC.5.OA.1

Name _____

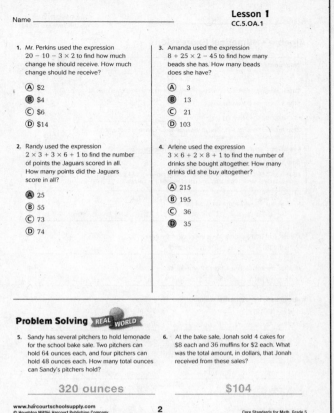

1. Mr. Perkins used the expression $20 − 10 − 3 × 2$ to find how much change he should receive. How much change should he receive?
   - (A) $2
   - (B) $4
   - (C) $6
   - (D) $14

2. Randy used the expression $2 × 3 + 3 × 6 + 1$ to find the number of points the Jaguars scored in all. How many points did the Jaguars score in all?
   - (A) 25
   - (B) 55
   - (C) 73
   - (D) 74

3. Amanda used the expression $8 + 25 × 2 − 45$ to find how many beads she has. How many beads does she have?
   - (A) 3
   - (B) 13
   - (C) 21
   - (D) 103

4. Arlene used the expression $3 × 6 + 2 × 8 + 1$ to find the number of drinks she bought altogether. How many drinks did she buy altogether?
   - (A) 215
   - (B) 195
   - (C) 36
   - (D) 35

Problem Solving REAL WORLD

5. Sandy has several pitchers to hold lemonade for the school bake sale. Two pitchers can hold 64 ounces each, and four pitchers can hold 48 ounces each. How many total ounces can Sandy's pitchers hold?

   __320 ounces__

6. At the bake sale, Jonah sold 4 cakes for $8 each and 36 muffins for $2 each. What was the total amount, in dollars, that Jonah received from these sales?

   __$104__

Lesson 2

Name _____

COMMON CORE STANDARD CC.5.OA.1
Lesson Objective: Evaluate numerical expressions with parentheses, brackets, and braces.

Algebra • Grouping Symbols

Parentheses ( ), *brackets* [ ], and *braces* { }, are different grouping symbols used in expressions. To evaluate an expression with different grouping symbols, perform the operation in the innermost set of grouping symbols first. Then evaluate the expression from the inside out.

Evaluate the expression 2 × [(9 × 4) − (17 − 6)].

Step 1 Perform the operations in the *parentheses* first.
$2 × [(9 × 4) − (17 − 6)]$
$2 × [\ \underline{36}\ −\ \underline{11}\ ]$

Step 2 Next perform the operations in the *brackets*.
$2 × [36 − 11]$
$2 × \underline{25}$

Step 3 Then multiply.
$2 × 25 = \underline{50}$

So, $2 × [(9 × 4) − (17 − 6)] = \underline{50}$

Evaluate the numerical expression.

1. $4 × [(15 − 6) × (7 − 3)]$
   $4 × [9 × \underline{4}\ ]$
   $4 × [\ \underline{36}\ ]$
   __144__
2. $40 − [(8 × 7) − (5 × 6)]$ __14__
3. $60 ÷ [(20 − 6) + (14 − 8)]$ __3__

4. $5 + [(10 − 2) + (4 − 1)]$ __16__
5. $3 × [(9 + 4) − (2 × 6)]$ __3__
6. $32 ÷ [(7 × 2) − (2 × 5)]$ __8__

Lesson 2
CC.5.OA.1

Name _____

1. Meredith and her brother Liam are saving to buy a basketball hoop that costs $75. Meredith earns $15 per week for babysitting and spends $6 of it. Liam earns $10 per week for walking dogs and spends $4 of it. Which expression can be used to find out how many weeks it will take to save for the basketball hoop?
   - (A) $75 ÷ [(15 − 6) + (10 − 4)]$
   - (B) $75 ÷ [(15 + 6) − (10 + 4)]$
   - (C) $75 ÷ [(15 − 6) + (10 + 4)]$
   - (D) $75 ÷ [(15 − 6) − (10 − 4)]$

2. A hotel costs $89 per night. Sally will receive a $5 per night discount for paying in advance. A rental car costs $35 per day plus taxes that total $4 per day. Which expression can Sally use to find how much she will pay for the hotel and rental car for 5 days?
   - (A) $5 × (89 − 5) − (35 + 4)$
   - (B) $[5 × (89 − 5)] + (35 + 4)$
   - (C) $5 × [(89 − 5) − (35 + 4)]$
   - (D) $5 × [(89 − 5) + (35 + 4)]$

3. Of the 90 trading cards Yoshi has, 55 are baseball cards and 35 are football cards. He gives Henry 10 football cards and Henry gives Yoshi 8 baseball cards. Which expression can be used to find the number of trading cards Yoshi has now?
   - (A) $(55 + 8) − (35 + 10)$
   - (B) $(55 − 8) − (35 + 10)$
   - (C) $(55 − 8) + (35 − 10)$
   - (D) $(55 + 8) + (35 − 10)$

4. Jonah is a baker. Each morning, he makes 60 cupcakes. He gives away 5 and sells the rest. Each morning, he also makes 48 brownies. He gives away 4 and sells the rest. Which expression can be used to find how many cupcakes and brownies Jonah sells in 7 days?
   - (A) $7 × [(60 − 5) − (48 − 4)]$
   - (B) $7 × [(60 − 5) + (48 − 4)]$
   - (C) $[7 × (60 − 5)] + (48 − 4)$
   - (D) $7 × (60 − 5) + (48 − 4)$

Problem Solving REAL WORLD

Use the information at the right for 9 and 10.

> Joan has a cafe. Each day, she bakes 24 muffins. She gives away 3 and sells the rest. Each day, she also bakes 36 cupcakes. She gives away 4 and sells the rest.

5. Write an expression to represent the total number of muffins and cupcakes Joan sells in 5 days.

   $5 × [(24 − 3) + (36 − 4)]$

6. Evaluate the expression to find the total number of muffins and cupcakes Joan sells in 5 days.

   __265 muffins and cupcakes__

Answer Key

Name _____

Lesson **3**

COMMON CORE STANDARD CC.5.OA.2
Lesson Objective: Write numerical expressions.

Algebra • Numerical Expressions

Write words to match the expression.

$$6 \times (12 - 4)$$

Think: Many word problems involve finding the cost of a store purchase.

Step 1 Examine the expression.

• What operations are in the expression?   <u>multiplication and subtraction</u>

Step 2 Describe what each part of the expression can represent when finding the cost of a store purchase.

• What can multiplying by 6 represent?   <u>buying 6 of the same item</u>

Step 3 Write the words.

• Joe buys 6 DVDs. Each DVD costs $12. If Joe receives a $4 discount on each DVD, what is the total amount of money Joe spends?

1. What is multiplied and what is subtracted?
   <u>The difference of 12 and 4 is multiplied by 6.</u>

2. What part of the expression is the price of the item?
   <u>the part in the parentheses</u>

3. What can subtracting 4 from 12 represent?
   <u>The original price of the item is $12, and there is a $4 discount.</u>

Write words to match the expression.

4. $4 \times (10 - 2)$
   <u>Possible answer: Pat buys 4 books. Each book costs $10. If Pat receives a $2 discount on each book, what is the total amount Pat spends?</u>

5. $3 \times (6 - 1)$
   <u>Possible answer: Ty buys 3 movie tickets. Each ticket costs $6. If Ty receives a $1 discount on each ticket, what is the total amount Ty spends?</u>

---

1. Jamie baked 24 cupcakes. Her sister Mia ate 3 cupcakes, and her brother David ate 2 cupcakes. Which expression can Jamie use to find how many cupcakes are left?

   Ⓐ $24 + (3 - 2)$
   Ⓑ $24 - (3 + 2)$
   Ⓒ $(24 - 3) + 2$
   Ⓓ $24 - (3 - 2)$

2. Paul displays his sports trophies on shelves in his room. He has 5 trophies on each of 3 shelves and 2 trophies on another shelf. Which expression could Paul use to find the total number of trophies displayed?

   Ⓐ $(5 \times 3) - 2$
   Ⓑ $5 \times (3 + 2)$
   Ⓒ $5 + (3 \times 2)$
   Ⓓ $(5 \times 3) + 2$

3. William won 50 tickets at the arcade. He redeemed 30 tickets for a prize and gave 5 tickets to Katelyn. Which expression can William use to find how many tickets he has left?

   Ⓐ $50 - (30 + 5)$
   Ⓑ $50 + (30 - 5)$
   Ⓒ $(50 + 30) + 5$
   Ⓓ $50 - (30 - 5)$

4. Rupal poured muffin batter into 3 muffin tins. Each muffin tin holds 8 muffins. She kept 6 muffins and took the rest to school for the bake sale. Which expression could be used to find the total number of muffins Rupal took to school for the bake sale?

   Ⓐ $(3 \times 8) + 6$
   Ⓑ $(3 + 8) - 6$
   Ⓒ $(3 \times 8) - 6$
   Ⓓ $3 \times (8 - 6)$

Problem Solving

5. Kylie has 14 polished stones. Her friend gives her 6 more stones. Write an expression to match the words.

   <u>$14 + 6$</u>

6. Rashad had 25 stamps. He shared them equally among himself and 4 friends. Then Rashad found 2 more stamps in his pocket. Write an expression to match the words.

   <u>$(25 \div 5) + 2$</u>

Name _____

Lesson **4**

COMMON CORE STANDARD CC.5.OA.3
Lesson Objective: Use two rules to generate a numerical pattern and identify the relationship between the corresponding terms in the patterns.

Numerical Patterns

A soccer league has 5 teams. How many players are needed for 5 teams? How many soccer balls are needed by the 5 teams?

	Number of Teams	1	2	3	4	7
Add 8	Number of Players	8	16	24	32	56
Add 4	Number of Soccer Balls	4	8	12	16	28

Step 1 Find a rule that could be used to find the number of players for the number of teams.

Think: In the pattern 8, 16, 24, 32, you add 8 to get the next term.

As the number of teams increases by 1, the number of players increases by 8. So the rule is to add 8.

Step 2 Find a rule that could be used to find the number of soccer balls for the number of teams.

Think: In the pattern 4, 8, 12, 16, you add 4 to get the next term.

As the number of teams increases by 1, the number of soccer balls needed increases by 4. So the rule is to add 4.

Step 3 For 7 teams, multiply the number of players by $\frac{1}{2}$ to find the number of soccer balls.

So, for 7 teams, 56 players will need <u>28</u> soccer balls.

Complete the rule that describes how one sequence is related to the other. Use the rule to find the unknown term.

Number of Teams	1	2	3	4	8	10
Number of Players	15	30	45	60	120	150
Number of Bats	5	10	15	20	40	50

1. Divide the number of players by <u>3</u> to find the number of bats.

2. Multiply the number of bats by <u>3</u> to find the number of players.

Use the table for 1–2.

Jawan made a table to figure out how much he earns at his job.

Job Earnings

Days	1	2	3	4
Hours Worked	6	12	18	24
Amount Earned ($)	54	108	162	216

1. What rule relates the hours worked to the amount earned?

   Ⓐ Add 6.
   Ⓑ Add 54.
   Ⓒ Multiply by 2.
   Ⓓ Multiply by 9.

2. Suppose Jawan works 6 days. Using the rule that relates the hours worked to the amount earned, find the total number of hours he will work in 6 days and how much money he will earn in all.

   Ⓐ 36 hours, $648
   Ⓑ 36 hours, $324
   Ⓒ 30 hours, $300
   Ⓓ 30 hours, $270

3. What is the unknown number in Sequence 2 in the chart?

Sequence Number	1	2	3	5	7
Sequence 1	3	6	9	15	21
Sequence 2	15	30	45	75	?

   Ⓐ 63
   Ⓑ 90
   Ⓒ 105
   Ⓓ 150

4. Wanda made a table to show the number of ounces of flour she uses to make cupcakes.

Flour in Cupcakes

Batches	1	2	3	4	6
Ounces of Flour	8	16	24	32	48
Cupcakes	16	32	48	64	96

   What rule relates the number of ounces of flour to the number of cupcakes?

   Ⓐ Add 8.
   Ⓑ Add 12.
   Ⓒ Multiply by 2.
   Ⓓ Multiply by 8.

5. Mrs. Marston determined how many tubes of paint she would need for the students in her art classes to complete their projects. How many tubes of paint will she need for the class with 20 students? Explain how you found the answer.

Students	4	8	12	16	20
Tubes	8	16	24	32	40

   <u>40 tubes of paint; I could see that a rule is multiply the number of students by 2 to find the number of tubes; $20 \times 2 = 40$.</u>

Left top panel

Name _____

Lesson 5
COMMON CORE STANDARD CC.5.OA.3
Lesson Objective: Solve problems using the strategy *solve a simpler problem.*

Problem Solving • Find a Rule

Samantha is making a scarf with fringe around it. Each section of fringe is made of 4 pieces of yarn with 2 beads holding them together. There are 42 sections of fringe on Samantha's scarf. How many wooden beads and how many pieces of yarn are on Samantha's scarf?

Read the Problem	Solve the Problem

What do I need to find?
Possible answer: I need to find the number of beads and the number of pieces of yarn on Samantha's scarf.

Sections of Fringe	1	2	3	4	6	42
Number of Beads	2	4	6	8	12	84
Pieces of Yarn	4	8	12	16	24	168

What information do I need to use?
Possible answer: I need to use the number of sections on the scarf, and that each section has 4 pieces of yarn and 2 beads.

Possible answer: I can multiply the number of sections by 2 to find the number of beads. Then, I can multiply the number of sections by 4, or the number of beads by 2, to find the number of pieces of yarn. So, Samantha's scarf has 2 × 42, or 84 beads, and 4 × 42, or 168 pieces of yarn.

How will I use the information?
I will use the information to search for patterns to solve a simpler problem.

1. A rectangular tile has a decorative pattern of 3 equal-sized squares, each of which is divided into 2 same-sized triangles. If Marnie uses 36 of these tiles on the wall behind her kitchen stove, how many triangles are displayed?

216 triangles

2. Leta is making strawberry-almond salad for a party. For every head of lettuce that she uses, she adds 5 ounces of almonds and 10 strawberries. If she uses 75 ounces of almonds, how many heads of lettuce and how many strawberries does Leta use?

15 heads of lettuce; 150 strawberries

Right top panel

Name _____

Lesson 5
CC.5.OA.3

1. Nomi is making a pattern of square tiles, as shown below. The side lengths of the tiles are 2 centimeters.

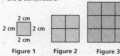

Figure 1   Figure 2   Figure 3

Suppose Nomi continues the pattern. What will be the distance around Figure 7?

- (A) 14 centimeters
- (B) 49 centimeters
- (C) 56 centimeters
- (D) 98 centimeters

2. Leroy starts to work at a part-time job. He saves $25 of his earnings each month. By the end of the second month, he saves $50 in all. How much will he save by the end of 24 months?

- (A) $75
- (B) $600
- (C) $1,200
- (D) $1,800

Use the table for 3–4.

The table shows the number of tickets needed for rides at an amusement park.

Amusement Park Rides

Number of Rides	1	2	3	7
Number of Tickets	4	8	12	?

3. Which rule relates the number of tickets to the number of rides?

- (A) Multiply the number of rides by 4.
- (B) Multiply the number of rides by 3.
- (C) Add 3 for each ride.
- (D) Add 4 for each ride.

4. Jared buys 40 tickets and goes on 7 rides. How many tickets does he have left after the 7 rides?

- (A) 33   (C) 24
- (B) 28   (D) 12

Problem Solving REAL WORLD

5. A restaurant manager has 10 tables that are 3 feet wide and 4 feet long. Suppose the manager places the 10 tables side-by-side so the 4-foot sides match up. What will be the perimeter of the larger table that is formed? Explain how you know.

3 ft
4 ft

The perimeter of the larger table will be 68 feet. I know because the perimeter of 1 small table is 14 feet. Each time a small table is added, 6 feet is added to the perimeter. With 9 small tables added, that would be 9 × 6 or 54 feet added. So the perimeter of the larger table is 14 + 54 = 68 feet.

Left bottom panel

Name _____

Lesson 6
COMMON CORE STANDARD CC.5.OA.3
Lesson Objective: Graph the relationship between two numerical patterns on a coordinate grid.

Graph and Analyze Relationships

The scale on a map is 1 in. = 4 mi. Two cities are 5 inches apart on the map. What is the actual distance between the two cities?

Step 1 Make a table that relates the map distances to the actual distances.

Map Distance (in.)	1	2	3	4	5
Actual Distance (mi)	4	8	12	16	?

Step 2 Write the number pairs in the table as ordered pairs.

(1, 4), (2, 8), (3, 12), (4, 16), (5, ?)

Step 3 Graph the ordered pairs. Connect the points with a line from the origin.

Possible rule: Multiply the map distance by 4 to get the actual distance.

Step 4 Use the rule to find the actual distance between the two cities.

So, two cities that are 5 inches apart on the map are actually 5 × 4, or 20 miles apart.

Plot the point (5, 20) on the graph.

Check students' graphs.

Graph and label the related number pairs as ordered pairs. Then complete and use the rule to find the unknown term.

1. Multiply the number of yards by **3** to find the number of feet.

Number of Yards	1	2	3	4	5
Number of Feet	3	6	9	12	15

Right bottom panel

Name _____

Lesson 6
CC.5.OA.3

Use the graph for 1–3.

The graph shows the relationship between the time and the number of push ups Eric did.

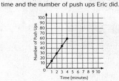

1. What is the total number of push ups Eric did in 3 minutes?

- (A) 40   (C) 50
- (B) 45   (D) 55

2. What rule relates the number of push ups to the time?

- (A) Multiply the number of minutes by $\frac{1}{15}$
- (B) Multiply the number of minutes by $\frac{1}{10}$
- (C) Multiply the number of minutes by 10.
- (D) Multiply the number of minutes by 15.

3. Suppose Eric continues to do push ups at this rate. What is the total number of push ups he will do in 5 minutes?

- (A) 50   (C) 75
- (B) 65   (D) 90

Problem Solving REAL WORLD

4. Randy makes a table that shows how long it takes her to run different distances.

Running Time and Distance

Number of miles	1	2	3	4
Time (in minutes)	10	20	30	40

Draw a line graph to show the relationship between the number of miles and the time. Explain how you can use the graph to find how long it will take Randy to run 5 miles at the same rate.

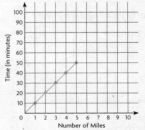

It will take Randy 50 minutes to run 5 miles. I know because the line on my graph goes through (5, 50). The 5 in the ordered pair stands for 5 miles, and the 50 stands for 50 minutes.

Answer Key

Name _____

Place Value and Patterns

You can use a place-value chart and patterns to write numbers that are 10 times as much as or $\frac{1}{10}$ of any given number.

Each place to the right is $\frac{1}{10}$ of the value of the place to its left.

$\frac{1}{10}$ of the hundred thousands place	$\frac{1}{10}$ of the ten thousands place	$\frac{1}{10}$ of the thousands place	$\frac{1}{10}$ of the hundreds place	$\frac{1}{10}$ of the tens place	
Hundred Thousands	Ten Thousands	Thousands	Hundreds	Tens	Ones
10 times the ten thousands place	10 times the thousands place	10 times the hundreds place	10 times the tens place	10 times the ones place	

Each place to the left is 10 times the value of the place to its right.

Find $\frac{1}{10}$ of 600.

$\frac{1}{10}$ of 6 hundreds is 6 __tens__.

So, $\frac{1}{10}$ of 600 is __60__.

Find 10 times as much as 600.

10 times as much as 6 hundreds is 6 __thousands__.

So, 10 times as much as 600 is __6,000__.

Use place-value patterns to complete the table.

Number	10 times as much as	$\frac{1}{10}$ of		Number	10 times as much as	$\frac{1}{10}$ of
1. 200	2,000	20		5. 900	9,000	90
2. 10	100	1		6. 80,000	800,000	8,000
3. 700	7,000	70		7. 3,000	30,000	300
4. 5,000	50,000	500		8. 40	400	4

Name _____

1. A math workbook contains 50 pages. The number of problems in the book is 10 times as many as the number of pages. How many problems are in the math workbook?

   (A) 5
   (B) 500
   (C) 5,000
   (D) 50,000

2. Cara has saved $4,000 to buy a car. Rick wants to buy a new television set. He has saved $\frac{1}{10}$ as much as Cara. How much has Rick saved?

   (A) $4
   (B) $40
   (C) $400
   (D) $40,000

3. Riva lives 300 miles from her grandparents. George lives 10 times that distance from his grandparents. How many miles does George live from his grandparents?

   (A) 30
   (B) 3,000
   (C) 30,000
   (D) 300,000

4. The Davis family pays $200,000 for a new house. They make a down payment that is $\frac{1}{10}$ of the price of the house. How much is the down payment?

   (A) $20
   (B) $200
   (C) $2,000
   (D) $20,000

Problem Solving REAL WORLD

5. The Eatery Restaurant has 200 tables. On a recent evening, there were reservations for $\frac{1}{10}$ of the tables. How many tables were reserved?

   __20 tables__

6. Mr. Wilson has $3,000 in his bank account. Ms. Nelson has 10 times as much money in her bank account as Mr. Wilson has in his bank account. How much money does Ms. Nelson have in her bank account?

   __$30,000__

Name _____

Place Value of Whole Numbers

You can use a place-value chart to help you understand whole numbers and the value of each digit. A **period** is a group of three digits within a number separated by a comma.

Millions Period			Thousands Period			Ones Period		
Hundreds	Tens	Ones	Hundreds	Tens	Ones	Hundreds	Tens	Ones
		2,	3	6	7,	0	8	9

Standard form: 2,367,089

Expanded Form: Multiply each digit by its place value, and then write an addition expression.

$(2 \times 1,000,000) + (3 \times 100,000) + (6 \times 10,000) + (7 \times 1,000) + (8 \times 10) + (9 \times 1)$

Word Form: Write the number in words. Notice that the millions and the thousands periods are followed by the period name and a comma.

two million, three hundred sixty-seven thousand, eighty-nine

To find the value of an underlined digit, multiply the digit by its place value. In 2,367,089, the value of 2 is $2 \times 1,000,000$, or 2,000,000.

Write the value of the underlined digit.

1. 153,732,991
   __100,000,000__

2. 236,143,802
   __30,000,000__

3. 264,807
   __4,000__

4. 78,209,146
   __200,000__

Write the number in two other forms.

5. 701,245
   $(7 \times 100,000) + (1 \times 1,000) + (2 \times 100) + (4 \times 10) + (5 \times 1)$; seven hundred one thousand, two hundred forty-five

6. 40,023,032
   $(4 \times 10,000,000) + (2 \times 10,000) + (3 \times 1,000) + (3 \times 10) + (2 \times 1)$; forty million, twenty-three thousand, thirty-two

---

Name _____

1. A publisher reports that it sold 2,419,386 children's magazines. What is the value of the digit 2 in 2,419,386?

   (A) 200,000,000
   (B) 20,000,000
   (C) 2,000,000
   (D) 200,000

2. The diameter of Saturn at its equator is about 120,540,000 meters. What is 120,540,000 written in word form?

   (A) twelve thousand, five hundred forty
   (B) twelve million, five hundred forty thousand
   (C) one hundred twenty million, fifty-four thousand
   (D) one hundred twenty million, five hundred forty thousand

3. A printing company used 1,896,432 sheets of tag board last year. What is the value of the digit 8 in 1,896,432?

   (A) 800
   (B) 8,000
   (C) 80,000
   (D) 800,000

4. A company manufactured forty-eight million, seven hundred fifty thousand toothpicks last month. What is this number written in standard form?

   (A) 48,750,000
   (B) 48,700,050
   (C) 48,000,750
   (D) 48,750

Problem Solving REAL WORLD

5. The U.S. Census Bureau has a population clock on the Internet. On a recent day, the United States population was listed as 310,763,136. Write this number in word form.

   three hundred ten million, seven hundred sixty-three thousand, one hundred thirty-six

6. In 2008, the population of 10- to 14-year-olds in the United States was 20,484,163. Write this number in expanded form.

   $(2 \times 10,000,000) + (4 \times 100,000) + (8 \times 10,000) + (4 \times 1,000) + (1 \times 100) + (6 \times 10) + (3 + 1)$

Lesson 9

Name _____

COMMON CORE STANDARD CC.5.NBT.1
Lesson Objective: Model, read, and write decimals to thousandths.

Thousandths

Thousandths are smaller parts than hundredths. If one hundredth is divided into 10 equal parts, each part is one **thousandth**.

Write the decimal shown by the shaded parts of the model.

One column of the decimal model is shaded. It represents one tenth, or _0.1_.

Two small squares of the decimal model are shaded. They represent two hundredths, or _0.02_.

A one-hundredth square is divided into 10 equal parts, or thousandths. Three columns of the thousandth square are shaded. They represent _0.003_.

So, 0.123 of the decimal model is shaded.

The relationship of a digit in different place-value positions is the same for decimals as for whole numbers.

Write the decimals in a place-value chart.

Ones	Tenths	Hundredths	Thousandths
0	8		
0	0	8	
0	0	0	8

0.08 is $\frac{1}{10}$ of _0.8_

0.08 is 10 times as much as _0.008_

1. Write the decimal shown by the shaded parts of the model.

_0.182_

Use place-value patterns to complete the table.

Decimal	10 times as much as	$\frac{1}{10}$ of
2. 0.1	1.0	0.01
3. 0.03	0.3	0.003
4. 0.5	5.0	0.05

Decimal	10 times as much as	$\frac{1}{10}$ of
5. 0.02	0.2	0.002
6. 0.4	4.0	0.04
7. 0.06	0.6	0.006

Lesson 9

Name _____

CC.5.NBT.1

1. A calculator is 0.07 meter wide. Sam made a model that was $\frac{1}{10}$ the size of the actual calculator. How wide was Sam's model?
   - (A) 70 meters
   - (B) 7 meters
   - (C) 0.7 meter
   - (D) 0.007 meter

2. A word in a book is 0.009 meter long. Kai looked at the word with a lens that made it look 10 times as large as the actual word. How long did the word look?
   - (A) 0.0009 meter
   - (B) 0.09 meter
   - (C) 0.9 meter
   - (D) 9 meters

3. What is the relationship between 0.008 and 0.08?
   - (A) 0.008 is $\frac{1}{10}$ of 0.08.
   - (B) 0.08 is $\frac{1}{10}$ of 0.008.
   - (C) 0.008 is 10 times as much as 0.08.
   - (D) 0.008 is equal to 0.08.

4. Valerie made a model for a decimal. What decimal is shown by Valerie's model?
   - (A) 0.026   (C) 0.216
   - (B) 0.206   (D) 0.26

Problem Solving REAL WORLD

5. The diameter of a dime is seven hundred five thousandths of an inch. Complete the table by recording the diameter of a dime.

6. What is the value of the 5 in the diameter of a half dollar?

   5 thousandths, or 0.005

U.S. Coins	
Coin	**Diameter (in inches)**
Penny	0.750
Nickel	0.835
Dime	0.705
Quarter	0.955
Half dollar	1.205

7. Which coins have a diameter with a 5 in the hundredths place?

   penny and quarter

Lesson 10

Name _____

COMMON CORE STANDARD CC.5.NBT.2
Lesson Objective: Write and evaluate repeated factors in exponent form.

Algebra • Powers of 10 and Exponents

You can represent repeated factors with a base and an exponent.

Write $10 \times 10 \times 10 \times 10 \times 10 \times 10$ in exponent form.

10 is the repeated factor, so 10 is the **base**.

The base is repeated 6 times, so 6 is the **exponent**.

10^6 ← exponent

$10 \times 10 \times 10 \times 10 \times 10 \times 10 = 10^6$

base

A base with an exponent can be written in words.

Write 10^6 in words.

The exponent 6 means "the sixth power."

10^6 in words is "the sixth power of ten."

You can read 10^2 in two ways: "ten squared" or "the second power of ten."

You can also read 10^3 in two ways: "ten cubed" or "the third power of ten."

Write in exponent form and in word form.

1. $10 \times 10 \times 10 \times 10 \times 10 \times 10 \times 10$

   exponent form: 10^7 word form: _the seventh power of ten_

2. $10 \times 10 \times 10$

   exponent form: 10^3 word form: _the third power of ten_

3. $10 \times 10 \times 10 \times 10 \times 10$

   exponent form: 10^5 word form: _the fifth power of ten_

Find the value.

4. 10^4

   _10,000_

5. 2×10^3

   _2,000_

6. 6×10^2

   _600_

Lesson 10

Name _____

CC.5.NBT.2

1. A Coast Guard ship is responsible for searching an area that is 5,000 square miles. Which shows 5,000 as a whole number multiplied by a power of ten?
   - (A) 5×10^1
   - (B) 5×10^2
   - (C) 5×10^3
   - (D) 5×10^4

2. Martin is going mountain climbing at Snowmass Mountain in Colorado. He looked up the height of the mountain and found it to be about 14×10^3 feet high. What is the height of Snowmass Mountain written as a whole number?
   - (A) 140 feet
   - (B) 1,400 feet
   - (C) 14,000 feet
   - (D) 140,000 feet

3. Patel hopes to be one of the first fans to get into the stadium for the baseball game because the first 30,000 fans will receive a baseball cap. Which shows 30,000 as a whole number multiplied by a power of ten?
   - (A) 3×10^1
   - (B) 3×10^2
   - (C) 3×10^3
   - (D) 3×10^4

4. Trisha is writing a report about Guam for Social Studies. She looked up the population of Guam and found it to be about 18×10^4. What is the population of Guam written as a whole number?
   - (A) 180,000
   - (B) 18,000
   - (C) 1,800
   - (D) 180

Problem Solving REAL WORLD

5. The moon is about 240,000 miles from Earth. What is this distance written as a whole number multiplied by a power of ten?

   24×10^4 miles

6. The sun is about 93×10^6 miles from Earth. What is this distance written as a whole number?

   93,000,000 miles

Answer Key

Algebra • Multiplication Patterns

You can use basic facts, patterns, and powers of 10 to help you multiply whole numbers by multiples of 10, 100, and 1,000.

Use mental math and a pattern to find $90 \times 6,000$.

- 9×6 is a basic fact. $9 \times 6 = 54$
- Use basic facts, patterns, and powers of 10 to find $90 \times 6,000$.

$$9 \times 60 = (9 \times 6) \times 10^1$$
$$= 54 \times 10^1$$
$$= 54 \times 10$$
$$= 540$$

$$9 \times 600 = (9 \times 6) \times 10^2$$
$$= 54 \times 10^2$$
$$= 54 \times 100$$
$$= 5,400$$

$$9 \times 6,000 = (9 \times 6) \times 10^3$$
$$= 54 \times 10^3$$
$$= 54 \times 1,000$$
$$= 54,000$$

$$90 \times 6,000 = (9 \times 6) \times (10 \times 1,000)$$
$$= 54 \times 10^4$$
$$= 54 \times 10,000$$
$$= 540,000$$

So, $90 \times 6,000 = 540,000$.

Use mental math to complete the pattern.

1. $3 \times 1 = 3$
   $3 \times 10^1 = \underline{30}$
   $3 \times 10^2 = \underline{300}$
   $3 \times 10^3 = \underline{3,000}$

2. $8 \times 2 = 16$
   $(8 \times 2) \times 10^1 = \underline{160}$
   $(8 \times 2) \times 10^2 = \underline{1,600}$
   $(8 \times 2) \times 10^3 = \underline{16,000}$

3. $4 \times 5 = 20$
   $(4 \times 5) \times \underline{10^1} = 200$
   $(4 \times 5) \times \underline{10^2} = 2,000$
   $(4 \times 5) \times \underline{10^3} = 20,000$

4. $7 \times 6 = \underline{42}$
   $(7 \times 6) \times \underline{10^1} = 420$
   $(7 \times 6) \times \underline{10^2} = 4,200$
   $(7 \times 6) \times \underline{10^3} = 42,000$

---

1. A country music concert will be held at a local park. The promoters have already sold 3,000 concert tickets. Each ticket costs $20. How much money have the promoters already collected?
   - (A) $60
   - (B) $600
   - **(C) $60,000**
   - (D) $600,000

2. Clinton decided to buy 300 shares of stock in an electronics company. Each share costs $60. Which of the following could he use to find the total amount he will pay for the stock?
   - (A) $(6 \times 3) \times 10^2 = 1,800$
   - (B) $(6 \times 3) \times 10^3 = 18,000$
   - **(C) $(6 \times 3) \times 10^4 = 180,000$**
   - (D) $(6 \times 3) \times 10^5 = 1,800,000$

3. Sam is using a microscope to look at a plant specimen. The microscope magnifies the specimen 4×10^2 times. If the specimen is 3 centimeters long, how long will the magnified specimen appear to be?
   - (A) 70 centimeters
   - (B) 120 centimeters
   - (C) 700 centimeters
   - **(D) 1,200 centimeters**

4. So far the fifth-grade students at Silver Run Elementary School have raised $200 toward their class trip. They need to raise 8 times as much to pay for the whole trip. How much money do the fifth-grade students need to raise in all?
   - (A) $16
   - (B) $1,600
   - **(C) $16,000**
   - (D) $160,000

Problem Solving REAL WORLD

5. The Florida Everglades welcomes about 2×10^3 visitors per day. Based on this, about how many visitors come to the Everglades per week?

   about 14,000 visitors

6. The average person loses about 8×10^1 strands of hair each day. About how many strands of hair would the average person lose in 9 days?

   about 720 strands

Algebra • Multiplication Patterns with Decimals

You can use patterns and place value to help you place the decimal point.

To multiply a number by a power of 10, you can use the exponent to determine how the position of the decimal point changes in the product.

	Exponent	Move decimal point:
$10^0 \times 5.18 = \underline{5.18}$	0	0 places to the right
$10^1 \times 5.18 = \underline{51.8}$	1	1 place to the right
$10^2 \times 5.18 = \underline{518}$	2	2 places to the right
$10^3 \times 5.18 = \underline{5,180}$	3	3 places to the right

You can use place-value patterns to find the product of a number and the decimals 0.1 and 0.01.

	Multiply by:	Move decimal point:
$1 \times 2,457 = \underline{2,457}$	1	0 places to the left
$0.1 \times 2,457 = \underline{245.7}$	0.1	1 place to the left
$0.01 \times 2,457 = \underline{24.57}$	0.01	2 places to the left

Complete the pattern.

1. $10^0 \times 25.89 = \underline{25.89}$
   $10^1 \times 25.89 = \underline{258.9}$
   $10^2 \times 25.89 = \underline{2,589}$
   $10^3 \times 25.89 = \underline{25,890}$

2. $1 \times 182 = \underline{182}$
   $0.1 \times 182 = \underline{18.2}$
   $0.01 \times 182 = \underline{1.82}$

---

1. Ganesh is making a scale model of the Space Needle in Seattle, Washington, for a report on the state of Washington. The Space Needle is 605 feet tall. If the model is $\frac{1}{100}$ of the actual size of the Space Needle, how tall is the model?
   - (A) 0.605 foot
   - (B) 6.05 feet
   - **(C) 6.5 feet**
   - (D) 60.5 feet

2. Madison needs to buy enough meat to make 1,000 hamburgers for the company picnic. Each hamburger will weigh 0.25 pound. How many pounds of hamburger meat should Madison buy?
   - (A) 2.5 pounds
   - (B) 25 pounds
   - **(C) 250 pounds**
   - (D) 2,500 pounds

3. Kareem was doing research for a report about the longest rivers on Earth. He read that the Nile River is 4.16×10^3 miles long. How should Kareem write the length of the Nile River in standard form on his report?
   - (A) 4.16 miles
   - (B) 41.6 miles
   - (C) 416 miles
   - **(D) 4,160 miles**

4. The school store expects to sell a lot of sweatshirts because the football team won the championship. The store ordered 100 sweatshirts. Each sweatshirt cost $8.95. How much did the order of sweatshirts cost the store?
   - (A) $89.50
   - (B) $895
   - **(C) $8,950**
   - (D) $89,500

Problem Solving REAL WORLD

5. Nathan plants equal-sized squares of sod in his front yard. Each square has an area of 6 square feet. Nathan plants a total of 1,000 squares in his yard. What is the total area of the squares of sod?

   6,000 square feet

6. Three friends are selling items at a bake sale. May makes $23.25 selling bread. Inez sells gift baskets and makes 100 times as much as May. Carolyn sells pies and makes one tenth of the money Inez makes. How much money does each friend make?

   May: $23.25; Inez: $2,325; Carolyn: $232.50

Answer Key

Name _____

Algebra • Division Patterns with Decimals

Lesson 13
COMMON CORE STANDARD CC.5.NBT.2
Lesson Objective: Find patterns in quotients when dividing by powers of 10.

To divide a number by 10, 100, or 1,000, use the number of zeros in the divisor to determine how the position of the decimal point changes in the quotient.

	Number of zeros:	Move decimal point:
147 ÷ 1 = __147__	0	0 places to the left
147 ÷ 10 = __14.7__	1	1 place to the left
147 ÷ 100 = __1.47__	2	2 places to the left
147 ÷ 1,000 = __0.147__	3	3 places to the left

To divide a number by a power of 10, you can use the exponent to determine how the position of the decimal point changes in the quotient.

	Exponent	Move decimal point:
$97.2 ÷ 10^0$ = __97.2__	0	0 places to the left
$97.2 ÷ 10^1$ = __9.72__	1	1 place to the left
$97.2 ÷ 10^2$ = __0.972__	2	2 places to the left

Complete the pattern.

1. $358 ÷ 10^0$ = __358__
   $358 ÷ 10^1$ = __35.8__
   $358 ÷ 10^2$ = __3.58__
   $358 ÷ 10^3$ = __0.358__

2. $102 ÷ 10^0$ = __102__
   $102 ÷ 10^1$ = __10.2__
   $102 ÷ 10^2$ = __1.02__
   $102 ÷ 10^3$ = __0.102__

3. 99.5 ÷ 1 = __99.5__
   99.5 ÷ 10 = __9.95__
   99.5 ÷ 100 = __0.995__

www.harcourtschoolsupply.com
© Houghton Mifflin Harcourt Publishing Company
25
Core Standards for Math, Grade 5

Name _____

Lesson 13
CC.5.NBT.2

1. Lori is running in a marathon, which is 26.2 miles long. So far, she has run one-tenth of the marathon. How far has Lori run?
   - Ⓐ 262 miles
   - Ⓑ 2.62 miles
   - Ⓒ 0.262 mile
   - Ⓓ 0.00262 mile

2. A school bought 1,000 erasers as part of an order for supplies. The total cost of the erasers was $30. What was the cost of 1 eraser?
   - Ⓐ $0.03
   - Ⓑ $0.30
   - Ⓒ $300
   - Ⓓ $3,000

3. Tanya baked 100 cupcakes one morning in a bakery. She used 64 ounces of frosting to decorate the cupcakes. If each cupcake had the same amount of frosting, how much frosting did Tanya put on each cupcake?
   - Ⓐ 0.0064 ounce
   - Ⓑ 0.064 ounce
   - Ⓒ 0.64 ounce
   - Ⓓ 6.4 ounces

4. A counselor at Sleepy Hollow Camp has 225 yards of lanyard to give to 100 campers to make lanyard key chains. Each camper will get the same amount of lanyard. How much lanyard will each camper get?
   - Ⓐ 0.0225 yard
   - Ⓑ 0.225 yard
   - Ⓒ 2.25 yards
   - Ⓓ 22.5 yards

Problem Solving

5. The local café uses 510 cups of mixed vegetables to make 1,000 quarts of beef barley soup. Each quart of soup contains the same amount of vegetables. How many cups of vegetables are in each quart of soup?

   __0.51 cup__

6. The same café uses 18.5 cups of flour to make 100 servings of pancakes. How many cups of flour are in one serving of pancakes?

   __0.185 cup__

www.harcourtschoolsupply.com
© Houghton Mifflin Harcourt Publishing Company
26
Core Standards for Math, Grade 5

Name _____

Place Value of Decimals

Lesson 14
COMMON CORE STANDARD CC.5.NBT.3a
Lesson Objective: Read and write decimals through thousandths.

You can use a place-value chart to find the value of each digit in a decimal. Write whole numbers to the left of the decimal point. Write decimals to the right of the decimal point.

Ones	Tenths	Hundredths	Thousandths
3	8	4	7
3 × 1	8 × $\frac{1}{10}$	4 × $\frac{1}{100}$	7 × $\frac{1}{1,000}$
3.0	0.8	0.04	0.007	Value

The place value of the digit 8 in 3.847 is tenths.
The value of 8 in 3.847 is 8 × $\frac{1}{10}$, or 0.8.
You can write a decimal in different forms.

Standard Form: __3.847__

Expanded Form: __3__ × 1 + __8__ × $\frac{1}{10}$ + __4__ × $(\frac{1}{100})$ + __7__ × $(\frac{1}{1,000})$

When you write the decimal in word form, write "and" for the decimal point.

Word Form: three __and__ eight hundred forty-seven __thousandths__

1. Complete the place-value chart to find the value of each digit.

Ones	Tenths	Hundredths	Thousandths
2	6	9	5
2 × 1	6 × $\frac{1}{10}$	9 × $\frac{1}{100}$	5 × $\frac{1}{1000}$
2	0.6	0.09	0.005	Value

Write the value of the underlined digit.

2. 0.7<u>9</u>2   __9 hundredths, or 0.09__

3. 4.<u>6</u>91   __6 tenths, or 0.6__

4. 3.80<u>5</u>   __5 thousandths, or 0.005__

www.harcourtschoolsupply.com
© Houghton Mifflin Harcourt Publishing Company
27
Core Standards for Math, Grade 5

Name _____

Lesson 14
CC.5.NBT.3a

1. A scientist measured a grain of sand. It had a diameter of 0.049 millimeter. What is 0.049 written in word form?
   - Ⓐ forty-nine
   - Ⓑ forty-nine tenths
   - Ⓒ forty-nine hundredths
   - Ⓓ forty-nine thousandths

2. The diamond in Alma's necklace weighs 0.258 carat. What digit is in the hundredths place of 0.258?
   - Ⓐ 0
   - Ⓑ 2
   - Ⓒ 5
   - Ⓓ 8

3. The mass of an ant is about 0.003 gram. What is the value of the digit 3 in 0.003?
   - Ⓐ 3 ones
   - Ⓑ 3 tenths
   - Ⓒ 3 hundredths
   - Ⓓ 3 thousandths

4. A penny has a diameter of 0.019 meter. What is 0.019 written in word form?
   - Ⓐ nineteen thousandths
   - Ⓑ nineteen hundredths
   - Ⓒ nineteen tenths
   - Ⓓ nineteen

Problem Solving

5. In a gymnastics competition, Paige's score was 37.025. What is Paige's score written in word form?

   __thirty-seven and twenty-five thousandths__

6. Jake's batting average for the softball season is 0.368. What is Jake's batting average written in expanded form?

   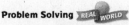
   $3 × (\frac{1}{10}) + 6 × (\frac{1}{100}) + 8 × (\frac{1}{1000})$

www.harcourtschoolsupply.com
© Houghton Mifflin Harcourt Publishing Company
28
Core Standards for Math, Grade 5

---

www.harcourtschoolsupply.com
© Houghton Mifflin Harcourt Publishing Company
207
Core Standards for Math, Grade 5

Answer Key

Name _____

Compare and Order Decimals

You can use a place-value chart to compare decimals.

Compare. Write <, >, or =.

4.375 ◯ 4.382

Write both numbers in a place-value chart. Then compare the digits, starting with the highest place value. Stop when the digits are different and compare.

Ones	Tenths	Hundredths	Thousandths
4	3	7	5
4	3	8	2

The ones digits are the same. The tenths digits are the same. The hundredths digits are different.

The digits are different in the hundredths place.

Since 7 hundredths < 8 hundredths, 4.375 ⟨<⟩ 4.382.

1. Use the place-value chart to compare the two numbers. What is the greatest place-value position where the digits differ?

Ones	Tenths	Hundredths	Thousandths
2	8	6	5
2	8	6	1

thousandths; 2.865 > 2.861

Compare. Write <, >, or =.

2. 5.37 ⟨=⟩ 5.370   3. 9.425 ⟨>⟩ 9.417   4. 7.684 ⟨<⟩ 7.689

Name the greatest place-value position where the digits differ.
Name the greater number.

5. 8.675; 8.654
hundredths
8.675

6. 3.086; 3.194
tenths
3.194

7. 6.243; 6.247
thousandths
6.247

Order from least to greatest.

8. 5.04; 5.4; 5.406; 5.064
5.04; 5.064; 5.4; 5.406

9. 2.614; 2.146; 2.46; 2.164
2.146; 2.164; 2.46; 2.614

Name _____

1. Harry kept a record of how far he ran each day last week.

Day	Distance (in miles)
Monday	4.5
Tuesday	3.9
Wednesday	4.25
Thursday	3.75
Friday	4.2

On which day did Harry run the greatest number of miles?

(A) Monday
(B) Tuesday
(C) Thursday
(D) Friday

2. The four highest scores on the floor exercise at a gymnastics meet were 9.675, 9.25, 9.325, and 9.5. Which shows the order of the scores from least to greatest?

(A) 9.5, 9.25, 9.325, 9.675
(B) 9.25, 9.5, 9.325, 9.675
(C) 9.675, 9.5, 9.325, 9.25
(D) 9.25, 9.325, 9.5, 9.675

3. The table shows the fastest times for the 100-meter hurdles event.

Name	Times (in seconds)
Shakira	15.45
Jameel	15.09
Lindsay	15.6
Nicholas	15.3

Who had the fastest time?

(A) Shakira
(B) Jameel
(C) Lindsay
(D) Nicholas

4. Mary Ann kept a record of how long she practiced the piano each week for a month.

Week	Hours Practiced
Week 1	4.75
Week 2	4.5
Week 3	5.1
Week 4	5.75

During which week did Mary Ann practice the greatest amount of time?

(A) Week 1
(B) Week 2
(C) Week 3
(D) Week 4

Problem Solving REAL WORLD

5. The completion times for three runners in a 100-yard dash are 9.75 seconds, 9.7 seconds, and 9.675 seconds. Which is the winning time?

9.675 seconds

6. In a discus competition, an athlete threw the discus 63.37 meters, 62.95 meters, and 63.7 meters. Order the distances from least to greatest.

62.95 meters, 63.37 meters, 63.7 meters

Name _____

Round Decimals

Rounding decimals is similar to rounding whole numbers.

Round 4.682 to the nearest tenth.

Step 1 Write 4.682 in a place-value chart.

Ones	Tenths	Hundredths	Thousandths
4	◯6	_8_	2

Step 2 Find the digit in the place to which you want to round. Circle that digit.
The digit _6_ is in the tenths place, so circle it.

Step 3 Underline the digit to the right of the circled digit.
The digit _8_ is to the right of the circled digit, so underline it.

Step 4 If the underlined digit is less than 5, the circled digit stays the same. If the underlined digit is 5 or greater, round up the circled digit.
_8_ > 5, so round 6 up to 7.

Step 5 After you round the circled digit, drop the digits to the right of the circled digit.
So, 4.682 rounded to the nearest tenth is _4.7_.

Write the place value of the underlined digit. Round each number to the place of the underlined digit.

1. 0.3_9_2
hundredths
0.39

2. 5._7_14
tenths
5.7

3. 1_6_.908
ones
17

Name the place value to which each number was rounded.

4. 0.825 to 0.83
hundredths

5. 3.815 to 4
ones

6. 1.546 to 1.5
tenths

Name _____

1. It takes the dwarf planet Pluto 247.68 years to revolve once around the sun. What is 247.68 years rounded to the nearest whole number of years?

(A) 247 years
(B) 247.6 years
(C) 247.7 years
(D) 248 years

2. The flagpole in front of Silver Pines Elementary School is 18.375 feet tall. What is 18.375 rounded to the nearest tenth?

(A) 18
(B) 18.38
(C) 18.4
(D) 20

3. Michelle records the value of one Euro in U.S. dollars each day for her social studies project. The table shows the data she has recorded so far.

Day	Value of 1 Euro (In U.S. dollars)
Monday	1.448
Tuesday	1.443
Wednesday	1.452
Thursday	1.458

On which day does the value of 1 Euro round to $1.46 to the nearest hundredth?

(A) Monday
(B) Tuesday
(C) Wednesday
(D) Thursday

4. Jackie found a rock that has a mass of 78.852 grams. What is the mass of the rock rounded to the nearest tenth?

(A) 78.85 grams
(B) 78.9 grams
(C) 79 grams
(D) 80 grams

Problem Solving REAL WORLD

5. The population density of Montana is 6.699 people per square mile. What is the population density per square mile of Montana rounded to the nearest whole number?

7 people per square mile

6. Alex's batting average is 0.346. What is his batting average rounded to the nearest hundredth?

0.35

Lesson 17 (Page 33)

Name _____

Multiply by 1-Digit Numbers

You can use place value to help you multiply by 1-digit numbers.

Estimate. Then find the product. 378×6

Estimate: $400 \times 6 = 2,400$

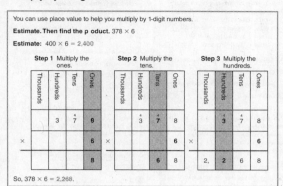

Step 1 Multiply the ones.

Step 2 Multiply the tens.

Step 3 Multiply the hundreds.

So, $378 \times 6 = 2,268$.

Complete to find the product.

1. 7×472 Estimate: $7 \times \underline{500} = \underline{3,500}$

Multiply the ones.	Multiply the tens.	Multiply the hundreds.
1 472 × 7 ‾‾‾ 4	5₁ 472 × 7 ‾‾‾ 04	51 472 × 7 ‾‾‾‾‾ 3,304

Estimate. Then find the product. Possible estimates are given.

2. Estimate: 7,200 863 × 8 ‾‾‾‾ 6,904	3. Estimate: 6,400 809 × 8 ‾‾‾‾ 6,472	4. Estimate: 6,300 932 × 7 ‾‾‾‾ 6,524	5. Estimate: 21,000 2,767 × 7 ‾‾‾‾‾ 19,369

www.harcourtschoolsupply.com
© Houghton Mifflin Harcourt Publishing Company   **33**   Core Standards for Math, Grade 5

Lesson 17 (Page 34)

Name _____

1. A bus driver travels 234 miles every day. How many miles does the bus driver travel in 5 days?
   - (A) 1,050 miles
   - (B) 1,150 miles
   - (C) 1,170 miles
   - (D) 1,520 miles

2. Hector does 165 sit-ups every day. How many sit-ups does he do in 7 days?
   - (A) 1,155
   - (B) 1,145
   - (C) 1,125
   - (D) 725

3. Lara and Chad are both saving to buy cars. So far, Chad has saved $1,235. Lara has saved 5 times as much as Chad. How much has Lara saved?
   - (A) $5,055
   - (B) $6,055
   - (C) $6,075
   - (D) $6,175

4. Mavis drives 634 miles to visit her grandmother in Philadelphia. How many miles does Mavis drive if she visits her grandmother 4 times?
   - (A) 2,426 miles
   - (B) 2,436 miles
   - (C) 2,536 miles
   - (D) 2,836 miles

Problem Solving REAL WORLD

5. Mr. and Mrs. Dorsey and their three children are flying to Springfield. The cost of each ticket is $179. Estimate how much the tickets will cost. Then find the exact cost of the tickets.

   Possible estimate: $1,000; exact cost: $895

6. Ms. Tao flies roundtrip twice yearly between Jacksonville and Los Angeles on business. The distance between the two cities is 2,150 miles. Estimate the distance she flies for both trips. Then find the exact distance.

   Possible estimate: 8,000; exact distance: 8,600 miles

www.harcourtschoolsupply.com
© Houghton Mifflin Harcourt Publishing Company   **34**   Core Standards for Math, Grade 5

Lesson 18 (Page 35)

Name _____

Multiply by 2-Digit Numbers

You can use place value and regrouping to multiply.

Find 29×63.

Step 1 Write the problem vertically. Multiply by the ones.
$$\begin{array}{r} 2 \\ 63 \\ \times\, 29 \\ \hline 567 \end{array} \leftarrow 63 \times 9 = (\underline{60} \times 9) + (\underline{3} \times 9)$$
$$= \underline{540} + \underline{27}, \text{ or } \underline{567}$$

Step 2 Multiply by the tens.
$$\begin{array}{r} \\ 63 \\ \times\, 29 \\ \hline 567 \\ 1,260 \end{array} \leftarrow 63 \times 20 = (\underline{60} \times 20) + (\underline{3} \times 20)$$
$$= \underline{1,200} + \underline{60}, \text{ or } \underline{1,260}$$

Step 3 Add the partial products.
$$\begin{array}{r} 63 \\ \times\, 29 \\ \hline 567 \\ +\, 1,260 \\ \hline 1,827 \end{array}$$

So, $63 \times 29 = 1,827$.

Complete to find the product.

1.
$$\begin{array}{r} 57 \\ \times\, 14 \\ \hline 228 \\ +\, 570 \\ \hline 798 \end{array}$$
$\leftarrow 57 \times \underline{4}$
$\leftarrow 57 \times \underline{10}$

2.
$$\begin{array}{r} 76 \\ \times\, 45 \\ \hline 380 \\ +\, 3040 \\ \hline 3,420 \end{array}$$
$\leftarrow 76 \times \underline{5}$
$\leftarrow 76 \times \underline{40}$

3.
$$\begin{array}{r} 139 \\ \times\, 12 \\ \hline 278 \\ +\, 1390 \\ \hline 1,688 \end{array}$$
$\leftarrow 139 \times \underline{2}$
$\leftarrow 139 \times \underline{10}$

4. Find 26×69. Estimate first.
$$\begin{array}{r} 69 \\ \times\, 26 \\ \hline 1,794 \end{array}$$
Estimate: $\underline{2,100}$

www.harcourtschoolsupply.com
© Houghton Mifflin Harcourt Publishing Company   **35**   Core Standards for Math, Grade 5

Lesson 18 (Page 36)

Name _____

1. Chen burns 354 calories in 1 hour swimming. He swam for 28 hours last month. How many calories did Chen burn in all last month from swimming?
   - (A) 3,010 calories
   - (B) 8,482 calories
   - (C) 9,912 calories
   - (D) 10,266 calories

2. Rachel earns $27 per hour at work. She worked 936 hours last year. How much did Rachel earn working last year?
   - (A) $7,584
   - (B) $24,932
   - (C) $25,272
   - (D) $25,332

3. A company manufactures 295 toy cars each day. How many toy cars do they manufacture in 34 days?
   - (A) 3,065
   - (B) 7,610
   - (C) 10,065
   - (D) 10,030

4. Raul earns $24 per hour painting houses. If he works for 263 hours, how much will Raul earn in all?
   - (A) $6,312
   - (B) $6,112
   - (C) $5,102
   - (D) $1,578

Problem Solving REAL WORLD

5. A company shipped 48 boxes of canned dog food. Each box contains 24 cans. How many cans of dog food did the company ship in all?

   1,152 cans

6. There were 135 cars in a rally. Each driver paid a $25 fee to participate in the rally. How much money did the drivers pay in all?

   $3,375

www.harcourtschoolsupply.com
© Houghton Mifflin Harcourt Publishing Company   **36**   Core Standards for Math, Grade 5

Answer Key

Algebra • Properties

Properties of operations are characteristics of the operations that are always true.

Property	Examples
Commutative Property of Addition or Multiplication	Addition: $3 + 4 = 4 + 3$ Multiplication: $8 \times 2 = 2 \times 8$
Associative Property of Addition or Multiplication	Addition: $(1 + 2) + 3 = 1 + (2 + 3)$ Multiplication: $6 \times (7 \times 2) = (6 \times 7) \times 2$
Distributive Property	$8 \times (2 + 3) = (8 \times 2) + (8 \times 3)$
Identity Property of Addition	$9 + 0 = 9$ $0 + 3 = 3$
Identity Property of Multiplication	$54 \times 1 = 54$ $1 \times 16 = 16$

Use properties to find $37 + 24 + 43$.

$37 + 24 + 43 = 24 + \underline{37} + 43$ Use the <u>Commutative</u> Property of Addition to reorder the addends.

$= 24 + (37 + 43)$ Use the Associative Property of <u>Addition</u> to group the addends.

$= 24 + \underline{80}$ Use mental math to add.

$= \underline{104}$

Grouping 37 and 43 makes the problem easier to solve because their sum, <u>80</u>, is a multiple of 10.

Use properties to find the sum or product.

1. $31 + 27 + 29$
2. $41 \times 0 \times 3$
3. $4 + (6 + 21)$

    _____87_____   _____0_____   _____31_____

Complete the equation, and tell which property you used.

4. $(2 \times \boxed{5}) + (2 \times 2) = 2 \times (5 + 2)$
5. $\boxed{15} \times 1 = 15$

    <u>Distributive Property</u>   <u>Identity Property of Multiplication</u>

---

1. Sherry's family is going to a beach resort. Sherry bought 7 beach towels that cost $13 each to take to the resort. To find the total cost, she added the products of 7×10 and 7×3, for a total of $91. What property did Sherry use?
   - (A) Commutative Property of Multiplication
   - (B) Commutative Property of Addition
   - (C) Associative Property of Multiplication
   - **(D) Distributive Property**

2. Chen bought a basketball for $23, a pair of running shoes for $35, and a baseball cap for $7. He wrote the equation $23 + 35 + 7 = 23 + 7 + 35$. What property did Chen use?
   - (A) Associative Property of Addition
   - **(B) Commutative Property of Addition**
   - (C) Distributive Property
   - (D) Identity Property of Multiplication

3. Nicole baked 9 trays of cookies. Each tray had 5 rows with 4 cookies in each row. Nicole wrote the equation $(9 \times 5) \times 4 = 9 \times (5 \times 4)$. What property did Nicole use?
   - (A) Commutative Property of Multiplication
   - (B) Associative Property of Addition
   - **(C) Associative Property of Multiplication**
   - (D) Distributive Property

4. Ramon has a large collection of marbles. He has 150 clear marbles, 214 blue marbles, and 89 green marbles. Ramon wrote this equation about his marble collection:

   $(150 + 214) + 89 = 150 + (214 + 89)$

   What property did Ramon use?
   - **(A) Associative Property of Addition**
   - (B) Commutative Property of Addition
   - (C) Identity Property of Addition
   - (D) Distributive Property

Problem Solving

5. The Metro Theater has 20 rows of seats with 18 seats in each row. Tickets cost $5. The theater's income in dollars if all seats are sold is $(20 \times 18) \times 5$. Use properties to find the total income.

    _____$1,800_____

6. The numbers of students in the four sixth-grade classes at Northside School are 26, 19, 34, and 21. Use properties to find the total number of students in the four classes.

    _____100_____

Relate Multiplication to Division

Use the Distributive Property to find the quotient of $56 \div 4$.

Step 1
Write a related multiplication sentence for the division problem.

$56 \div 4 = \square$
$4 \times \square = 56$

Step 2
Use the Distributive Property to break apart the product into lesser numbers that are multiples of the divisor in the division problem. Use a multiple of 10 for one of the multiples.

$(40 + 16) = 56$
$(4 \times 10) + (4 \times 4) = 56$
$4 \times (10 + 4) = 56$

Step 3
To find the unknown factor, find the sum of the numbers inside the parentheses.

$10 + 4 = 14$

Step 4
Write the multiplication sentence with the unknown factor you found. Then, use the multiplication sentence to complete the division sentence.

$4 \times 14 = 56$
$56 \div 4 = 14$

Use multiplication and the Distributive Property to find the quotient.

1. $68 \div 4 = \underline{17}$
   $(4 \times 10) +$
   $(4 \times 7) = 68$
   $4 \times 7 = 68$

2. $75 \div 3 = \underline{25}$
   $(3 \times 20) +$
   $(3 \times 5) = 75$
   $3 \times 5 = 75$

3. $96 \div 6 = \underline{16}$
   $(6 \times 10) +$
   $(6 \times 6) = 96$
   $6 \times 6 = 96$

4. $80 \div 5 = \underline{16}$
   $(5 \times 10) +$
   $(5 \times 6) = 80$
   $5 \times 16 = 80$

5. $54 \div 3 = \underline{18}$
   $(3 \times 10) +$
   $(3 \times 8) = 54$
   $3 \times 18 = 54$

6. $105 \div 7 = \underline{15}$
   $(7 \times 10) +$
   $(7 \times 5) = 105$
   $7 \times 15 = 105$

---

1. Francine took 42 photos with her digital camera. She stored an equal number of photos in each of 3 folders on her computer. Which multiplication sentence could Francine use to find the number of photos in each folder?
   - **(A) $3 \times 14 = 42$**
   - (B) $3 \times 40 = 120$
   - (C) $3 \times 42 = 126$
   - (D) $4 \times 42 = 168$

2. Amber baked 120 cookies to give to 5 friends. She wants to put the same number of cookies in each bag. Which of the following can she use to find how many cookies to put in each bag?
   - (A) $(5 \times 20) + (5 \times 4)$
   - (B) $(5 \times 10) + (5 \times 8)$
   - **(C) $(5 \times 60) + (5 \times 2)$**
   - (D) $(5 \times 15) + (5 \times 5)$

3. Shari sent a total of 64 text messages to 4 friends. Each friend received the same number of text messages. Which multiplication sentence could Shari use to find the number of text messages she sent to each friend?
   - (A) $4 \times 64 = 256$
   - (B) $60 \times 4 = 240$
   - (C) $5 \times 64 = 320$
   - **(D) $4 \times 16 = 64$**

4. Jared has 96 books to arrange on 6 shelves of a bookcase. He wants each shelf to have the same number of books. Which of the following **cannot** be used to find how many books Jared can put on each shelf?
   - (A) $(6 \times 10) + (6 \times 6)$
   - (B) $(6 \times 8) + (6 \times 8)$
   - **(C) $(6 \times 4) + (6 \times 4)$**
   - (D) $(6 \times 15) + (6 \times 1)$

Problem Solving

5. Ken is making gift bags for a party. He has 64 colored pens and wants to put the same number in each bag. How many bags will Ken make if he puts 4 pens in each bag?

    _____16 bags_____

6. Maritza is buying wheels for her skateboard shop. She ordered a total of 92 wheels. If wheels come in packages of 4, how many packages will she receive?

    _____23 packages_____

Name _____

Problem Solving • Multiplication and Division

Lesson 21
COMMON CORE STANDARD CC.5.NBT.6
Lesson Objective: Use the strategy *solve a simpler problem to solve problems.*

In Brett's town, there are 128 baseball players on 8 different teams. Each team has an equal number of players. How many players are on each team?

Read the Problem	Solve the Problem
What do I need to find? I need to find **how many players are on each team in Brett's town**	• First, I use the total number of players. **128 players**
What information do I need to use? There are **8 teams** with a total of **128 players**	• To find the number of players on each team, I will need to solve this problem. $128 \div 8 = $ **?** • To find the quotient, I break 128 into two simpler numbers that are easier to divide. $128 \div 8 = (80 + \underline{48}) \div 8$ $= (\underline{80} \div 8) + (\underline{48} \div 8)$ $= \underline{10} + 6$ $= \underline{16}$
How will I use the information? I can **divide** the total number of players by the number of teams. I can use a simpler problem to **divide** .	So, there are **16** players on each team.

1. Susan makes clay pots. She sells 125 pots per month to 5 stores. Each store buys the same number of pots. How many pots does each store buy?

$125 \div 5 = (100 + \underline{25}) \div 5$
$= (100 \div 5) + (\underline{25} \div 5)$
$= \underline{20} + 5$
$= \underline{25}$
25 pots

2. Lou grows 112 rosemary plants. He ships an equal number of plants to customers in 8 states. How many rosemary plants does he ship to each customer?

$112 \div 8 = (80 + \underline{32}) \div 8$
$= (\underline{80} \div 8) + (\underline{32} \div 8)$
$= \underline{10} + 4$
$= \underline{14}$
14 plants

Name _____

Lesson 21
CC.5.NBT.6

1. Marta has 16 postcards from each of 8 different cities in Pennsylvania. She can fit 4 postcards on each page of her scrapbook. How many pages in the scrapbook can Marta fill with postcards?
   - (A) 32
   - (B) 41
   - (C) 128
   - (D) 512

2. Nathan's orchestra has 18 string musicians, 9 percussion musicians, 15 brass musicians, and 12 woodwind musicians. Six of the musicians cannot play in the next performance. If the remaining musicians plan to sit in rows of 6 chairs, how many rows of chairs are needed?
   - (A) 4
   - (B) 6
   - (C) 8
   - (D) 9

3. There are 6 buses transporting students to a baseball game, with 32 students on each bus. Each row at the baseball stadium seats 8 students. If the students fill up all of the rows, how many rows of seats will the students need altogether?
   - (A) 22
   - (B) 23
   - (C) 24
   - (D) 1,536

4. Laura has 24 stamps from each of 6 different countries. She can fit 4 stamps on each display sheet of an album. How many display sheets can Laura fill with stamps?
   - (A) 576
   - (B) 36
   - (C) 34
   - (D) 16

Problem Solving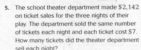

5. Ming's DVD collection includes 16 adventure movies, 7 comedies, 12 westerns, and 8 mysteries. He wants to keep 2 of each type of DVD and give away the rest. Ming says that if he gives an equal number of DVDs to 5 friends, he will give each friend 7 DVDs. Do you agree? Support your answer.

   Yes; Possible explanation: I added $16 + 7 + 12 + 8 = 43$ to find how many DVDs Ming has. Since Ming wants to keep 2 of each of 4 types, I multiplied $2 \times 4 = 8$ DVDs Ming will keep. So, Ming will give away $43 - 8 = 35$ DVDs to 5 friends. I divided 35 by 5 to find how many DVDs each friend will get, which is 7.

Name _____

Place the First Digit

Lesson 22
COMMON CORE STANDARD CC.5.NBT.6
Lesson Objective: Place the first digit in the quotient by estimating or using place value.

When you divide, you can use estimation or place value to place the first digit of the quotient.

Divide.
$6)\overline{1,266}$

• Estimate. $1,200 \div 6 = 200$, so the first digit of the quotient is in the hundreds place.
• Divide the hundreds.
• Divide the tens.
• Divide the ones.

So, $1,266 \div 6 = 211$.

Since 211 is close to the estimate, 200, the answer is reasonable.

```
   211
6)1,266
  -12
   06
   -6
    06
    -6
     0
```

Divide.
$8,895 \div 8$

• Use place value to place the first digit.
• Look at the first digit.
  If the first digit is less than the divisor, then the first digit of the quotient will be in the hundreds place.
  If the first digit is greater than or equal to the divisor, then the first digit of the quotient will be in the thousands place.
• Since 8 thousands can be shared among 8 groups, the first digit of the quotient will be in the thousands place. Now divide.

So, $8,895 \div 8$ is 1,111 r7.

```
  1,111 r7
8)8,895
 -8
  08
  -8
   09
   -8
   15
   -8
    7
```

Divide.

1. $3)\overline{627}$ **209**
2. $5)\overline{7,433}$ **1,486 r3**
3. $4)\overline{5,367}$ **1,341 r3**
4. $9)\overline{6,470}$ **718 r8**

5. $8)\overline{2,869}$ **358 r5**
6. $6)\overline{1,299}$ **216 r3**
7. $4)\overline{893}$ **223 r1**
8. $7)\overline{4,418}$ **631 r1**

Name _____

Lesson 22
CC.5.NBT.6

1. Caleb needs to solve the problem $2,406 \div 6$. In what place is the first digit of the quotient for the problem $2,406 \div 6$?
   - (A) ones
   - (B) tens
   - (C) hundreds
   - (D) thousands

2. Mrs. Tao has 154 books on 7 shelves in her classroom. Each shelf has the same number of books on it. She wants to find out the number of books on each shelf. In what place should Mrs. Tao write the first digit of the quotient for the problem $154 \div 7$?
   - (A) ones
   - (B) tens
   - (C) hundreds
   - (D) thousands

3. The last problem on Jacob's math test was $9,072 \div 9$. In what place should Jacob write the first digit of the quotient for the problem $9,072 \div 9$?
   - (A) ones
   - (B) tens
   - (C) hundreds
   - (D) thousands

4. Raul has 486 baseball cards in 9 albums. Each album has the same number of baseball cards. He wants to find the number of baseball cards in each album. In what place should Raul write the first digit of the quotient for the problem $486 \div 9$?
   - (A) ones
   - (B) tens
   - (C) hundreds
   - (D) thousands

Problem Solving

5. The school theater department made $2,142 on ticket sales for the three nights of their play. The department sold the same number of tickets each night and each ticket cost $7. How many tickets did the theater department sell each night?

   102 tickets

6. Andreus made $625 mowing yards. He worked for 5 consecutive days and earned the same amount of money each day. How much money did Andreus earn per day?

   $125

Answer Key

Name _____

Lesson 23
COMMON CORE STANDARD CC.5.NBT.6
Lesson Objective: Divide 3- and 4-digit dividends by 1-digit divisors.

Divide by 1-Digit Divisors

You can use compatible numbers to help you place the first digit in the quotient. Then you can divide and check your answer.

Divide. $4\overline{)757}$

Step 1 Estimate with compatible numbers to decide where to place the first digit.

$757 \div 4$
$\downarrow$
$800 \div 4 = 200$

The first digit of the quotient is in the hundreds place.

Step 2 Divide.

$$
\begin{array}{r}
189\ r1 \\
4\overline{)757} \\
-4 \\
\hline
35 \\
-32 \\
\hline
37 \\
-36 \\
\hline
1
\end{array}
$$

Step 3 Check your answer.

$$
\begin{array}{r}
189 \leftarrow \text{quotient} \\
\times\ 4 \leftarrow \text{divisor} \\
\hline
756 \\
+\ 1 \leftarrow \text{remainder} \\
\hline
757 \leftarrow \text{dividend}
\end{array}
$$

Since 189 is close to the estimate of 200, the answer is reasonable.

So, $757 \div 4$ is 189 r1.

Check students' work.

Divide. Check your answer.

1. $8\overline{)136}$ **17**

2. $7\overline{)297}$ **42 r3**

3. $5\overline{)8,126}$ **1,625 r1**

4. $7\overline{)4,973}$ **710 r3**

5. $3\overline{)741}$ **247**

6. $7\overline{)456}$ **65 r1**

---

1. During a school fund raiser, the fifth-grade classes sold rolls of wrapping paper. The table shows how many rolls each class sold. The rolls were sold in packages of 4.

Wrapping Paper Sold

Class	Total Rolls
Ms. Lane	672
Mr. Milner	184
Mrs. Jackson	228

How many packages of wrapping paper did Ms. Lane's class sell?

(A) 2,688   (C) 168
(B) 173   (D) 143

2. Sophia wants to buy collector boxes that can hold 6 dolls each. How many boxes will Sophia need to buy for her collection of 168 dolls?

(A) 21   (C) 34
(B) 28   (D) 1,008

3. On a standard week-long space shuttle flight, 175 servings of fresh food are shared equally among 7 crewmembers. How many servings of fresh food does each crewmember receive?

(A) 25   (C) 32
(B) 26   (D) 33

4. A bakery sold croissants to local restaurants. The table shows how many croissants were sold to each restaurant. The croissants were sold 6 to a box.

Croissants Sold

Restaurant	Number of Croissants
The Coffee Counter	546
La Claudette	768
Bon Jour	858

How many boxes of croissants did the bakery sell to La Claudette?

(A) 4,608   **(C) 128**
(B) 143   (D) 96

Problem Solving REAL WORLD

5. Randy has 128 ounces of dog food. He feeds his dog 8 ounces of food each day. How many days will the dog food last?

16 days

6. Angelina bought a 64-ounce can of lemonade mix. She uses 4 ounces of mix for each pitcher of lemonade. How many pitchers of lemonade can Angelina make from the can of mix?

16 pitchers

Name _____

Lesson 24
COMMON CORE STANDARD CC.5.NBT.6
Lesson Objective: Model division with 2-digit divisors using base-ten blocks.

Division with 2-Digit Divisors

You can use base-ten blocks to model division with 2-digit divisors.

Divide. $154 \div 11$

Step 1 Model 154 with base-ten blocks.

Step 2 Make equal groups of 11. Each group should contain **1** ten and **1** one.

You can make 4 groups of 11 without regrouping.

Step 3 Regroup 1 hundred as **10 tens**

Regroup 1 ten as **10 ones**

Step 4 Use the regrouped blocks to make as many groups of 11 as possible. Then count the total number of groups.

There are **14** groups. So, $154 \div 11 = $ **14**

Divide. Use base-ten blocks.

1. $192 \div 12$ **16**

2. $182 \div 14$ **13**

---

1. Emma used a quick picture to help her divide 154 by 11. What is the quotient?

(A) 11   (C) 13
(B) 12   **(D) 14**

2. Garrett used a quick picture to help him divide 182 by 14. What is the quotient?

(A) 11   **(C) 13**
(B) 12   (D) 14

3. Latoya drew a quick picture to solve a division problem. Which division problem does the quick picture show?

(A) $195 \div 15 = 13$
(B) $169 \div 13 = 13$
(C) $180 \div 15 = 12$
(D) $165 \div 15 = 11$

4. Ling has 168 baseball cards. He put the same number of cards into each of 14 piles. How many baseball cards did Ling put in each pile?

(A) 11   **(C) 13**
(B) 12   (D) 14

Problem Solving REAL WORLD

5. There are 182 seats in a theater. The seats are evenly divided into 13 rows. How many seats are in each row?

14 seats

6. There are 156 students at summer camp. The camp has 13 cabins. An equal number of students sleep in each cabin. How many students sleep in each cabin?

12 students

Page 49 (Lesson 25)

Name _____

Lesson 25
COMMON CORE STANDARD CC.5.NBT.6
Lesson Objective: Use partial quotients to divide by 2-digit divisors.

Partial Quotients

Divide. Use partial quotients.

858 ÷ 57

Quotient

Step 1 Estimate the number of groups of 57 that are in 858. You know 57 × 10 = 570. Since 570 < 858, at least 10 groups of 57 are in 858. Write 10 in the quotient column, because 10 groups of the divisor, 57, are in the dividend, 858.

```
    858
  − 570      10
    288
```

Step 2 Now estimate the number of groups of 57 that are in 288. You know 60 × 4 = 240. So at least 4 groups of 57 are in 288. Subtract 228 from 288, because 57 × 4 = 228. Write 4 in the quotient column, because 4 groups of 57 are in 288.

```
    288
  − 228       4
     60
```

Step 3 Identify the number of groups of 57 that are in 60. 57 × 1 = 57, so there is 1 group of 57 in 60. Write 1 in the quotient column.

```
              60
            − 57      + 1
remainder →  3        15
```

Step 4 Find the total number of groups of the divisor, 57, that are in the dividend, 858, by adding the numbers in the quotient column. Include the remainder in your answer.

Answer: 15 r3

Divide. Use partial quotients.

1. 17)476   **28**

2. 14)365   **26 r1**

3. 25)753   **30 r3**

4. 462 ÷ 11   **42**

5. 1,913 ÷ 47   **40 r33**

6. 1,085 ÷ 32   **33 r29**

Page 50 (Lesson 25)

Name _____

Lesson 25
CC.5.NBT.6

1. Jacob divided 976 by 28 using partial quotients. What is missing from Jacob's work?

```
        34 r24
   28)976
      −280   ← 10 × 28     10
       696
      −280   ← 10 × 28     10
       416
      −280   ← 10 × 28     10
       136
      − □    ← 4 × 28      + 4
        24                  34
```

Ⓐ 24   Ⓒ 112
Ⓑ 34   Ⓓ 280

2. Orah takes an 18-day bike tour. She rides 756 miles in all. What is the average number of miles she rides each day?

Ⓐ 32   Ⓒ 90
Ⓑ 42   Ⓓ 92

3. Paloma divided 1,292 by 31 using partial quotients. What is the quotient?

```
   31)1,292
     −930   ← 30 × 31     30
      362
     −310   ← 10 × 31     10
       52
      −31   ← 1 × 31      + 1
       21                  41
```

Ⓐ 21   Ⓒ 41
Ⓑ 21 r41   Ⓓ 41 r21

4. The school library has 2,976 books on its shelves. Each shelf has 48 books on it. How many shelves are in the library?

Ⓐ 42
Ⓑ 52
Ⓒ 62
Ⓓ 192

Problem Solving 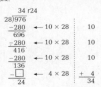 REAL WORLD

5. A factory processes 1,560 ounces of olive oil per hour. The oil is packaged into 24-ounce bottles. How many bottles does the factory fill in one hour?

65 bottles

6. A pond at a hotel holds 4,290 gallons of water. The groundskeeper drains the pond at a rate of 78 gallons of water per hour. How long will it take to drain the pond?

55 hours

Page 51 (Lesson 26)

Name _____

Lesson 26
COMMON CORE STANDARD CC.5.NBT.6
Lesson Objective: Estimate quotients using compatible numbers.

Estimate with 2-Digit Divisors

You can use *compatible numbers* to estimate quotients. Compatible numbers are numbers that are easy to compute with mentally.

To find two estimates with compatible numbers, first round the divisor. Then list multiples of the rounded divisor until you find the two multiples that are closest to the dividend. Use the one less than and the one greater than the dividend.

Use compatible numbers to find two estimates. 4,125 ÷ 49

Step 1 Round the divisor to the nearest ten.
49 rounds to __50__.

Step 2 List multiples of 50 until you get the two closest to the dividend, 4,125.
Some multiples of 50 are:
500   1,000   1,500   2,000   2,500   3,000   3,500   4,000   4,500
__4,000__ and __4,500__ are closest to the dividend.

Step 3 Divide the compatible numbers to estimate the quotient.
4,000 ÷ 50 = __80__   4,500 ÷ 50 = __90__

The more reasonable estimate is 4,000 ÷ 50 = 80, because __4,000__ is closer to 4,125 than 4,500 is.

Use compatible numbers to find two estimates. Accept all reasonable estimates. Possible answers are given.

1. 42)1,578
   1,200 ÷ 40 = 30;
   1,600 ÷ 40 = 40

2. 73)4,858
   4,200 ÷ 70 = 60;
   4,900 ÷ 70 = 70

3. 54)343
   300 ÷ 50 = 6;
   350 ÷ 50 = 7

4. 4,093 ÷ 63
   3,600 ÷ 60 = 60;
   4,200 ÷ 60 = 70

5. 4,785 ÷ 79
   4,000 ÷ 80 = 50;
   4,800 ÷ 80 = 60

6. 7,459 ÷ 94
   7,200 ÷ 90 = 80;
   8,100 ÷ 90 = 90

Use compatible numbers to estimate the quotient. Accept all reasonable estimates. Possible answers are given.

7. 847 ÷ 37
   800 ÷ 40 = 20

8. 6,577 ÷ 89
   6,300 ÷ 90 = 70

9. 218 ÷ 29
   210 ÷ 30 = 7

Page 52 (Lesson 26)

Name _____

Lesson 26
CC.5.NBT.6

1. Lauren bought a television that cost $805. She plans to make equal payments of $38 each month until the television is paid in full. About how many payments will Lauren make?

Ⓐ 20
Ⓑ 30
Ⓒ 38
Ⓓ 40

2. Miss Roja plans to sell tote bags at the art festival for $33 each. She will need to make $265 to pay the rent for the space at the festival. About how many tote bags will she need to sell to pay the rent?

Ⓐ 3
Ⓑ 7
Ⓒ 9
Ⓓ 30

3. Mrs. Ortega bought a dishwasher that cost $579. She will make monthly payments in the amount of $28 until the dishwasher is paid in full. About how many payments will Mrs. Ortega make?

Ⓐ 12
Ⓑ 20
Ⓒ 28
Ⓓ 30

4. Doug plans to sell mugs at the craft fair for $21 each. He will need to make $182 to pay the rent for the space at the fair. About how many mugs will he need to sell to pay the rent?

Ⓐ 2
Ⓑ 6
Ⓒ 9
Ⓓ 20

Problem Solving REAL WORLD

Accept all reasonable estimates. Possible answers are given.

5. A cubic yard of topsoil weighs 4,128 pounds. About how many 50-pound bags of topsoil can you fill with one cubic yard of topsoil?

about 80 bags

6. An electronics store places an order for 2,665 USB flash drives. One shipping box holds 36 flash drives. About how many boxes will it take to hold all the flash drives?

about 70 boxes

Answer Key

Name _____

Lesson 27

COMMON CORE STANDARD CC.5.NBT.6
Lesson Objective: Divide by 2-digit divisors.

Divide by 2-Digit Divisors

When you divide by a 2-digit divisor, you can use estimation to help you place the first digit in the quotient. Then you can divide.

Divide. $53\overline{)2,369}$

Step 1 Use compatible numbers to estimate the quotient. Then use the estimate to place the first digit in the quotient.

$$50\overline{)2,000} = 40$$

The first digit will be in the tens place.

Step 2 Divide the tens.

$$53\overline{)2,369} \quad \begin{array}{r} 4 \\ -212 \\ \hline 24 \end{array}$$

Think:
Divide: 236 tens ÷ 53
Multiply: 53 × 4 = 212 tens
Subtract: 236 tens − 212 tens
Compare: 24 < 53, so the first digit of the quotient is reasonable.

Step 3 Bring down the 9 ones. Then divide the ones.

$$53\overline{)2,369} \quad \begin{array}{r} 44\ r37 \\ -212\downarrow \\ \hline 249 \\ -212 \\ \hline 37 \end{array}$$

Think:
Divide: 249 ones ÷ 53
Multiply: 53 × 4 ones = 212 ones
Subtract: 249 ones − 212 ones
Compare: 37 < 53, so the second digit of the quotient is reasonable.

So, 2,369 ÷ 53 is 44 r37.

Write the remainder to the right of the whole number part of the quotient.

Divide. Check your answer. Check students' work.

1. $52\overline{)612}$ **11 r40**

2. $63\overline{)917}$ **14 r35**

3. $89\overline{)1,597}$ **17 r84**

4. $43\overline{)641}$ **14 r39**

5. $27\overline{)4,684}$ **173 r13**

6. $64\overline{)8,455}$ **132 r7**

Name _____

Lesson 27

CC.5.NBT.6

1. The local concert hall has 48 concerts scheduled this season. Each concert has the same number of tickets available for sale. There is a total of 4,560 tickets. How many tickets are available for each concert?
   - (A) 1,140
   - (B) 950
   - (C) 105
   - (D) 95

2. The director of a pet shelter received a shipment of 1,110 puppy blankets. He put the same number of blankets in each of 27 boxes and put the leftover blankets in the puppy kennels. How many blankets were put in the puppy kennels?
   - (A) 3
   - (B) 18
   - (C) 28
   - (D) 41

3. An airplane has 416 seats arranged in 52 rows. If there is the same number of seats in each row, how many seats are in one row?
   - (A) 21,632
   - (B) 364
   - (C) 8
   - (D) 6

4. Mr. Stephens needs to haul 1,518 tons of rock from a construction site. His dump truck can hold 26 tons per load. How many tons will Mr. Stephens need to haul in the last load to move all of the rock?
   - (A) 10
   - (B) 58
   - (C) 68
   - (D) 1,492

Problem Solving REAL WORLD

5. The factory workers make 756 machine parts in 36 hours. Suppose the workers make the same number of machine parts each hour. How many machine parts do they make each hour?

   21 parts

6. One bag holds 12 bolts. Several bags filled with bolts are packed into a box and shipped to the factory. The box contains a total of 2,760 bolts. How many bags of bolts are in the box?

   230 bags

Name _____

Lesson 28

COMMON CORE STANDARD CC.5.NBT.6
Lesson Objective: Adjust the quotient if the estimate is too high or too low.

Adjust Quotients

When you divide, you can use the first digit of your estimate as the first digit of your quotient. Sometimes the first digit will be too high or too low. Then you have to adjust the quotient by increasing or decreasing the first digit.

Estimate Too High		Estimate Too Low	
Divide. 271 ÷ 48		**Divide.** 2,462 ÷ 27	
Estimate. 300 ÷ 50 = 6		**Estimate.** 2,400 ÷ 30 = 80	
Try 6 ones.	Try 5 ones.	Try 8 tens.	Try 9 tens.
$48\overline{)271}$ $\begin{array}{r}6\\-288\end{array}$	$48\overline{)271}$ $\begin{array}{r}5\ r31\\-240\\\hline 31\end{array}$	$27\overline{)2,462}$ $\begin{array}{r}8\\-216\\\hline 30\end{array}$	$27\overline{)2,462}$ $\begin{array}{r}91\ r5\\-243\\\hline 32\\-27\\\hline 5\end{array}$
You cannot subtract 288 from 271. So, the estimate is too high.	So, 271 ÷ 48 is 5 r31.	30 is greater than the divisor. So, the estimate is too low.	So, 2,462 ÷ 27 is 91 r5.

Adjust the estimated digit in the quotient, if needed. Then divide.

1. $58\overline{)1,325}$ $\overset{2}{}$ **22 r49**

2. $37\overline{)241}$ $\overset{6}{}$ **6 r19**

3. $29\overline{)2,276}$ $\overset{8}{}$ **78 r14**

Divide.

4. $16\overline{)845}$ **52 r13**

5. $24\overline{)217}$ **9 r1**

6. $37\overline{)4,819}$ **130 r9**

Name _____

Lesson 28

CC.5.NBT.6

1. To solve the division problem below, Kyle estimates that 2 is the first digit in the quotient.

   $$29\overline{)556} \quad \begin{array}{r}2\\-58\end{array}$$

   Which of the following is correct?
   - (A) 2 is the correct first digit of the quotient.
   - (B) 2 is too low. The first digit should be adjusted to 4.
   - (C) 2 is too low. The first digit should be adjusted to 3.
   - (D) 2 is too high. The first digit should be adjusted to 1.

2. Alex is saving up to buy a guitar that costs $855. He plans to save $45 a month. How many months will it take him to save enough money to buy the guitar?
   - (A) 19 months
   - (B) 21 months
   - (C) 23 months
   - (D) 25 months

3. An auditorium has 1,224 seats. There are 36 seats in each row. How many rows of seats are in the auditorium?
   - (A) 32
   - (B) 34
   - (C) 42
   - (D) 44

4. Diego estimates that 3 is the first digit in the quotient of the problem below.

   $$16\overline{)4272} \quad \begin{array}{r}3\\-48\end{array}$$

   Which of the following is correct?
   - (A) 3 is the correct first digit of the quotient.
   - (B) 3 is too low. The first digit should be adjusted to 4.
   - (C) 3 is too low. The first digit should be adjusted to 5.
   - (D) 3 is too high. The first digit should be adjusted to 2.

Problem Solving REAL WORLD

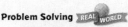

5. A copier prints 89 copies in one minute. How long does it take the copier to print 1,958 copies?

   22 minutes

6. Erica is saving her money to buy a dining room set that costs $580. If she saves $29 each month, how many months will she need to save to have enough money to buy the set?

   20 months

Answer Key

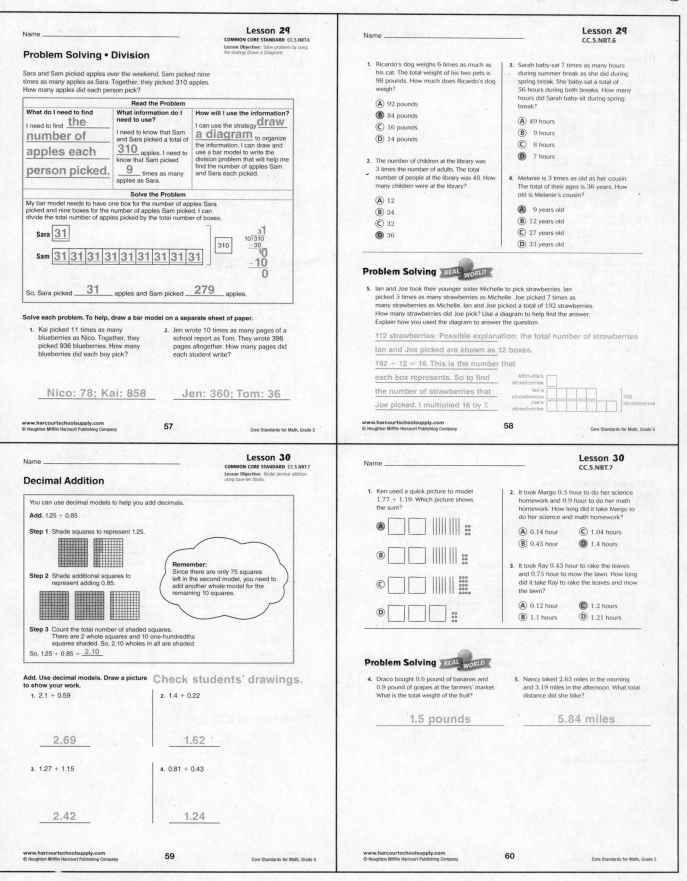

Lesson 29
COMMON CORE STANDARD CC.5.NBT.6
Lesson Objective: Solve problems by using the strategy *Draw a Diagram*.

Problem Solving • Division

Sara and Sam picked apples over the weekend. Sam picked nine times as many apples as Sara. Together, they picked 310 apples. How many apples did each person pick?

Read the Problem

What do I need to find	What information do I need to use?	How will I use the information?
I need to find the number of apples each person picked.	I need to know that Sam and Sara picked a total of 310 apples. I need to know that Sam picked 9 times as many apples as Sara.	I can use the strategy draw a diagram to organize the information. I can draw and use a bar model to write the division problem that will help me find the number of apples Sam and Sara each picked.

Solve the Problem

My bar model needs to have one box for the number of apples Sara picked and nine boxes for the number of apples Sam picked. I can divide the total number of apples picked by the total number of boxes.

Sara 31

Sam 31 31 31 31 31 31 31 31 31

310

```
    31
10)310
   -30
     10
    -10
      0
```

So, Sara picked __31__ apples and Sam picked __279__ apples.

Solve each problem. To help, draw a bar model on a separate sheet of paper.

1. Kai picked 11 times as many blueberries as Nico. Together, they picked 936 blueberries. How many blueberries did each boy pick?

   Nico: 78; Kai: 858

2. Jen wrote 10 times as many pages of a school report as Tom. They wrote 396 pages altogether. How many pages did each student write?

   Jen: 360; Tom: 36

Lesson 29
CC.5.NBT.6

1. Ricardo's dog weighs 6 times as much as his cat. The total weight of his two pets is 98 pounds. How much does Ricardo's dog weigh?

   - (A) 92 pounds
   - **(B) 84 pounds**
   - (C) 16 pounds
   - (D) 14 pounds

2. The number of children at the library was 3 times the number of adults. The total number of people at the library was 48. How many children were at the library?

   - (A) 12
   - (B) 24
   - (C) 32
   - **(D) 36**

3. Sarah baby-sat 7 times as many hours during summer break as she did during spring break. She baby-sat a total of 56 hours during both breaks. How many hours did Sarah baby-sit during spring break?

   - (A) 49 hours
   - (B) 9 hours
   - (C) 8 hours
   - **(D) 7 hours**

4. Melanie is 3 times as old as her cousin. The total of their ages is 36 years. How old is Melanie's cousin?

   - **(A) 9 years old**
   - (B) 12 years old
   - (C) 27 years old
   - (D) 33 years old

Problem Solving REAL WORLD

5. Ian and Joe took their younger sister Michelle to pick strawberries. Ian picked 5 times as many strawberries as Michelle. Joe picked 7 times as many strawberries as Michelle. Ian and Joe picked a total of 192 strawberries. How many strawberries did Joe pick? Use a diagram to help find the answer. Explain how you used the diagram to answer the question.

   112 strawberries; Possible explanation: the total number of strawberries Ian and Joe picked are shown as 12 boxes. 192 ÷ 12 = 16. This is the number that each box represents. So to find the number of strawberries that Joe picked, I multiplied 16 by 7.

Lesson 30
COMMON CORE STANDARD CC.5.NBT.7
Lesson Objective: Model decimal addition using base-ten blocks.

Decimal Addition

You can use decimal models to help you add decimals.

Add. 1.25 + 0.85

Step 1 Shade squares to represent 1.25.

Remember: Since there are only 75 squares left in the second model, you need to add another whole model for the remaining 10 squares.

Step 2 Shade additional squares to represent adding 0.85.

Step 3 Count the total number of shaded squares. There are 2 whole squares and 10 one-hundredths squares shaded. So, 2.10 wholes in all are shaded.

So, 1.25 + 0.85 = __2.10__

Add. Use decimal models. Draw a picture to show your work.   Check students' drawings.

1. 2.1 + 0.59

   2.69

2. 1.4 + 0.22

   1.62

3. 1.27 + 1.15

   2.42

4. 0.81 + 0.43

   1.24

Lesson 30
CC.5.NBT.7

1. Ken used a quick picture to model 1.77 + 1.19. Which picture shows the sum?

   - (A)
   - (B)
   - (C)
   - (D)

2. It took Margo 0.5 hour to do her science homework and 0.9 hour to do her math homework. How long did it take Margo to do her science and math homework?

   - (A) 0.14 hour
   - (B) 0.45 hour
   - (C) 1.04 hours
   - **(D) 1.4 hours**

3. It took Ray 0.45 hour to rake the leaves and 0.75 hour to mow the lawn. How long did it take Ray to rake the leaves and mow the lawn?

   - (A) 0.12 hour
   - (B) 1.1 hours
   - **(C) 1.2 hours**
   - (D) 1.21 hours

Problem Solving REAL WORLD

4. Draco bought 0.6 pound of bananas and 0.9 pound of grapes at the farmers' market. What is the total weight of the fruit?

   1.5 pounds

5. Nancy biked 2.65 miles in the morning and 3.19 miles in the afternoon. What total distance did she bike?

   5.84 miles

Answer Key

www.harcourtschoolsupply.com

Lesson 31
COMMON CORE STANDARD CC.5.NBT.7
Lesson Objective: Model decimal subtraction using base-ten blocks.

Decimal Subtraction

You can use decimal models to help you subtract decimals.

Subtract. $1.85 - 0.65$

Step 1 Shade squares to represent 1.85.

Step 2 Circle and cross out 65 of the shaded squares to represent subtracting 0.65.

Remember:
By circling and crossing out shaded squares, you can see how many squares are taken away, or subtracted.

Step 3 Count the shaded squares that are not crossed out. Altogether, 1 whole square and 20 one-hundredths squares, or 1.20 wholes, are NOT crossed out.

So, $1.85 - 0.65 =$ __1.20__

Subtract. Use decimal models. Draw a picture to show your work.

Check students' drawings.

1. $1.4 - 0.61$

__0.79__

2. $1.6 - 1.08$

__0.52__

3. $0.84 - 0.17$

__0.67__

4. $1.39 - 1.14$

__0.25__

Lesson 31
CC.5.NBT.7

1. Taryn used a quick picture to model $2.34 - 1.47$. Which picture shows the difference?

Ⓐ
Ⓑ
Ⓒ
Ⓓ

2. Jasmine lives 1.25 miles from school and 0.82 mile from the library. How much farther does Jasmine live from school than from the library?

Ⓐ 0.33 mile   Ⓒ 2.07 miles
Ⓑ 0.43 mile   Ⓓ 4.3 miles

3. Avery bought 3.45 pounds of red apples and 1.57 pounds of green apples. How many more pounds of red apples than green apples did Avery buy?

Ⓐ 5.02 pounds
Ⓑ 1.98 pounds
Ⓒ 1.88 pounds
Ⓓ 1.12 pounds

Problem Solving REAL WORLD

4. Yelina made a training plan to run 5.6 miles per day. So far, she has run 3.1 miles today. How much farther does she have to run to meet her goal for today?

__2.5 miles__

5. Tim cut a 2.3-foot length of pipe from a pipe that was 4.1 feet long. How long is the remaining piece of pipe?

__1.8 feet__

Lesson 32
COMMON CORE STANDARD CC.5.NBT.7
Lesson Objective: Make reasonable estimates of decimal sums and differences.

Estimate Decimal Sums and Differences

You can use rounding to help you estimate sums and differences.

Use rounding to estimate $1.24 + 0.82 + 3.4$.

Round to the nearest whole number. Then add.

$1.24 \rightarrow 1$
$0.82 \rightarrow 1$
$+ 3.4 \rightarrow + 3$
$\overline{5}$

Remember:
If the digit to the right of the place you are rounding to is:
• less than 5, the digit in the rounding place stays the same.
• greater than or equal to 5, the digit in the rounding place increases by 1.

So, the sum is about __5__

Use benchmarks to estimate $8.78 - 0.30$.

$8.78 \rightarrow 8.75$
$- 0.30 \rightarrow - 0.25$
$\overline{8.5}$

Think: 0.78 is between __0.75__ and __1__.
It is closer to __0.75__.

Think: 0.30 is between __0.25__ and __0.50__.
It is closer to __0.25__.

So, the difference is about __8.5__

Use rounding to estimate. *Possible estimates are given.*

1. 51.23
-28.4
__23__

2. $\$29.38$
$+\$42.75$
__$72__

3. 7.6
-2.15
__6__

4. 0.74
$+0.20$
__1__

5. 2.08
0.56
$+0.41$
__3__

Use benchmarks to estimate.

6. 6.17
-3.5
__2.75__

7. 1.73
1.4
$+3.17$
__6.5__

8. 3.28
-0.86
__2.5__

9. 15.27
$+41.8$
__57__

10. $\$23.07$
$-\$ 7.83$
__$15.25__

11. $0.427 + 0.711$
__1.25__

12. $61.05 - 18.63$
__42.25__

13. $40.51 + 30.39$
__71__

Lesson 32
CC.5.NBT.7

1. Julie has $16.73. She buys a purse that costs $4.12. About how much money will Julie have left?

Ⓐ $3
Ⓑ $13
Ⓒ $21
Ⓓ $23

2. A vet measured the mass of two birds. The mass of the robin was 76.64 grams. The mass of the blue jay was 81.54 grams. Which is the best estimate of the difference in the masses of the birds?

Ⓐ 5 grams
Ⓑ 10 grams
Ⓒ 15 grams
Ⓓ 20 grams

3. A town plans to add a 3.88-kilometer extension to a road that is currently 5.02 kilometers long. Which is the best estimate of the length of the road after the extension is added?

Ⓐ 1 kilometer
Ⓑ 2 kilometers
Ⓒ 4 kilometers
Ⓓ 9 kilometers

4. Denise has $78.22. She wants to buy a computer game that costs $29.99. About how much money will Denise have left?

Ⓐ $40
Ⓑ $50
Ⓒ $60
Ⓓ $110

Problem Solving REAL WORLD

Possible estimates are given.

5. Elian bought 1.87 pounds of chicken and 2.46 pounds of turkey at the deli. About how much meat did he buy altogether?

__about 4.5 pounds__

6. Jenna bought a gallon of milk at the store for $3.58. About how much change did she receive from a $20 bill?

__$16.50__

Lesson 33
COMMON CORE STANDARD CC.5.NBT.7
Lesson Objective: Add decimals using place value.

Name _____

Add Decimals

Add. $4.37 + 9.8$

Step 1 Estimate the sum.

$$4.37 + 9.8$$
Estimate: $4 + 10 = 14$

Step 2 Line up the place values for each number in a place-value chart. Then add.

Ones	Tenths	Hundredths
4	3	7
+ 9	8	
14	1	7	← sum

Step 3 Use your estimate to determine if your answer is reasonable.

Think: 14.17 is close to the estimate, 14. The answer is reasonable.

So, $4.37 + 9.8 = \underline{14.17}$

Estimate. Then find the sum. Possible estimates are given.

1. Estimate: __1__
$$\begin{array}{r} 1.20 \\ + 0.34 \\ \hline 1.54 \end{array}$$

2. Estimate: __3__
$$\begin{array}{r} 1.52 \\ + 1.21 \\ \hline 2.73 \end{array}$$

3. Estimate: __23__
$$\begin{array}{r} 12.25 \\ + 11.25 \\ \hline 23.50 \text{ or } 23.5 \end{array}$$

4. Estimate: __12__
$$\begin{array}{r} 10.75 \\ + 1.11 \\ \hline 11.86 \end{array}$$

5. Estimate: __41__
$$\begin{array}{r} 22.65 \\ + 18.01 \\ \hline 40.66 \end{array}$$

6. Estimate: __49__
$$\begin{array}{r} 34.41 \\ + 15.37 \\ \hline 49.78 \end{array}$$

Lesson 33
CC.5.NBT.7

Name _____

1. Yolanda's sunflower plant was 64.34 centimeters tall in July. During August, the plant grew 58.7 centimeters. How tall was Yolanda's sunflower plant at the end of August?

(A) 702.1 centimeters
(B) 123.04 centimeters
(C) 70.21 centimeters
(D) 58.7 centimeters

2. Malcolm read that 2.75 inches of rain fell on Saturday. He read that 1.6 inches of rain fell on Sunday. How much rain fell on the two days?

(A) 1.15 inches
(B) 2.91 inches
(C) 3.81 inches
(D) 4.35 inches

3. Olivia bought a beach towel for $9.95 and a beach bag for $13.46. What is the total amount of money Olivia spent on the two items?

(A) $12.31
(B) $23.41
(C) $112.96
(D) $144.55

4. Jon walked 1.75 kilometers on Monday and 3.2 kilometers on Wednesday. What was the total distance that Jon walked on Monday and Wednesday?

(A) 33.75 kilometers
(B) 20.7 kilometers
(C) 4.95 kilometers
(D) 2.07 kilometers

Problem Solving REAL WORLD

5. Marcela's dog gained 4.1 kilograms in two months. Two months ago, the dog's mass was 5.6 kilograms. What is the dog's current mass?

9.7 kilograms

6. During last week's storm, 2.15 inches of rain fell on Monday and 1.68 inches of rain fell on Tuesday. What was the total amount of rainfall on both days?

3.83 inches

Lesson 34
COMMON CORE STANDARD CC.5.NBT.7
Lesson Objective: Subtract decimals using place value.

Name _____

Subtract Decimals

Subtract. $12.56 - 4.33$

Step 1 Estimate the difference.

$$12.56 - 4.33$$
Estimate: $13 - 4 = 9$

Step 2 Line up the place values for each number in a place-value chart. Then subtract.

Ones	Tenths	Hundredths
12	5	6
− 4	3	3
8	2	3	← difference

Step 3 Use your estimate to determine if your answer is reasonable.

Think: 8.23 is close to the estimate, 9. The answer is reasonable.

So, $12.56 - 4.33 = \underline{8.23}$

Estimate. Then find the difference. Possible estimates are given.

1. Estimate: __1__
$$\begin{array}{r} 1.97 \\ - 0.79 \\ \hline 1.18 \end{array}$$

2. Estimate: __3__
$$\begin{array}{r} 4.42 \\ - 1.26 \\ \hline 3.16 \end{array}$$

3. Estimate: __2__
$$\begin{array}{r} 10.25 \\ - 8.25 \\ \hline 2.00 \text{ or } 2 \end{array}$$

Find the difference. Check your answer.

4.
$$\begin{array}{r} 5.75 \\ - 1.11 \\ \hline 4.64 \end{array}$$

5.
$$\begin{array}{r} 25.21 \\ - 19.05 \\ \hline 6.16 \end{array}$$

6.
$$\begin{array}{r} 42.14 \\ - 25.07 \\ \hline 17.07 \end{array}$$

Lesson 34
CC.5.NBT.7

Name _____

1. Juan had a 10.75-pound block of clay. He used 4.6 pounds of clay to make a sculpture of a horse. How much clay does Juan have left?

(A) 6.1 pounds
(B) 6.15 pounds
(C) 10.29 pounds
(D) 15.35 pounds

2. Ella and Nick are meeting at the library. The library is 4.61 kilometers from Ella's house and 3.25 kilometers from Nick's house. How much farther does Ella live from the library than Nick?

(A) 1.36 kilometers
(B) 1.46 kilometers
(C) 7.86 kilometers
(D) 42.85 kilometers

3. Rafael bought 3.26 pounds of potato salad and 2.8 pounds of macaroni salad to bring to a picnic. How much more potato salad than macaroni salad did Rafael buy?

(A) 6.06 pounds
(B) 2.98 pounds
(C) 0.98 pound
(D) 0.46 pound

4. Salvador had 3.25 pounds of dry cement. He used 1.7 pounds to make a paver for his lawn. How many pounds of dry cement does Salvador have left?

(A) 1.55 pounds
(B) 2.08 pounds
(C) 3.08 pounds
(D) 4.95 pounds

Problem Solving REAL WORLD

5. The width of a tree was 3.15 inches last year. This year, the width is 5.38 inches. How much did the width of the tree increase?

2.23 inches

6. The temperature decreased from 71.5°F to 56.8°F overnight. How much did the temperature drop?

14.7°F

Answer Key

Name _____

Lesson 35

COMMON CORE STANDARD CC.5.NBT.7
Lesson Objective: Identify, describe, and
create numeric patterns with decimals.

Algebra • Patterns with Decimals

Marla wants to download some songs from the Internet. The first
song costs $1.50, and each additional song costs $1.20. How much
will 2, 3, and 4 songs cost?

Song 1	Song 1 Song 2	Song 1 Song 2 Song 3	Song 1 Song 2 Song 3 Song 4
1 song $1.50	2 songs ?	3 songs ?	4 songs ?

Step 1 Identify the first term in the sequence.
Think: The cost of 1 song is $1.50. The first term is $1.50.

Step 2 Identify whether the sequence is increasing or decreasing
from one term to the next.
Think: Marla will pay $1.20 for each additional song.
The sequence is increasing.

Step 3 Write a rule that describes the sequence. Start with $1.50 and add $1.20.

Step 4 Use your rule to find the unknown terms in the sequence.

Number of Songs	1	2	3	4
Cost	$1.50	1.50 + 1.20 = $2.70	2.70 + 1.20 = $3.90	3.90 + 1.20 = $5.10

So, 2 songs cost $2.70, 3 songs cost $3.90, and 4 songs cost $5.10.

Write a rule for the sequence.

1. 0.4, 0.7, 1.0, 1.3, …

Rule: _____add 0.3_____

2. 5.25, 5.00, 4.75, 4.50, …

Rule: _____subtract 0.25_____

Write a rule for the sequence, then find
the unknown term.   *Possible rules shown.*

3. 26.1, 23.8, 21.5, __19.2__, 16.9

_____subtract 2.3_____

4. 4.62, 5.03, __5.44__, 5.85, 6.26

_____add 0.41_____

---

1. Students are selling muffins at a school
bake sale. One muffin costs $0.25,
2 muffins cost $0.37, 3 muffins cost $0.49,
and 4 muffins cost $0.61. If this pattern
continues, how much will 6 muffins cost?

   (A) $0.73
   (B) $0.83
   (C) $0.85
   (D) $0.97

2. Bob and Ling are playing a number
sequence game. Bob wrote the following
sequence.

   28.9, 26.8, 24.7, __?__, 20.5

   What is the unknown term in this
sequence?

   (A) 21.6
   (B) 22.6
   (C) 22.7
   (D) 25.8

3. Students are selling handmade magnets
at the school craft fair. One magnet costs
$0.30, 2 magnets cost $0.43, 3 magnets
cost $0.56, and 4 magnets cost $0.69.
If this pattern continues, how much will
6 magnets cost?

   (A) $0.82
   (B) $0.93
   (C) $0.95
   (D) $1.02

4. Kevin and Yasuko are writing number
sequences. Yasuko wrote the following
number sequence.

   35.9, 34.7, 33.5, __?__, 31.1

   What is the unknown term in this
sequence?

   (A) 32.3
   (B) 32.2
   (C) 32
   (D) 31.2

Problem Solving REAL WORLD

5. The Ride-It Store rents bicycles. The cost
is $8.50 for 1 hour, $13.65 for 2 hours,
$18.80 for 3 hours, and $23.95 for 4 hours.
If the pattern continues, how much will it cost
Nate to rent a bike for 6 hours?

   $34.25

6. Lynne walks dogs every day to earn money.
The fees she charges per month are 1 dog,
$40; 2 dogs, $37.25 each; 3 dogs, $34.50
each; 4 dogs, $31.75 each. A pet store wants
her to walk 8 dogs. If the pattern continues,
how much will Lynne charge to walk each of
the 8 dogs?

   $20.75 each

Name _____

Lesson 36

COMMON CORE STANDARD CC.5.NBT.7
Lesson Objective: Solve problems using the
strategy make a table.

Problem Solving •
Add and Subtract Money

At the end of April, Mrs. Lei had a balance of $476.05. Since then
she has written checks for $263.18 and $37.56, and made a deposit
of $368.00. Her checkbook balance currently shows $498.09.
Find Mrs. Lei's correct balance.

Read the Problem	Solve the Problem		

What do I need to find?

I need to find _Mrs. Lei's_
correct checkbook balance

What information do I need to use?

I need to use the _April balance, and_
the check and deposit amounts

How will I use the information?

I need to make a table and use the
information to _subtract the checks_
and add the deposit to find the
correct balance

Balancing Mrs. Lei's Checkbook		
April balance		$476.05
Deposit	$368.00	+$368.00
		$844.05
Check	$263.18	−$263.18
		$580.87
Check	$37.56	−$37.56
		$543.31

Mrs. Lei's correct balance is

$543.31

1. At the end of June, Mr. Kent had a
balance of $375.98. Since then he has
written a check for $38.56 and made a
deposit of $408.00. His checkbook shows
a balance of $645.42. Find Mr. Kent's
correct balance.

   $745.42

2. Jordan buys a notebook for himself and
each of 4 friends. Each notebook costs
$1.85. Make a table to find the cost of
5 notebooks.

   $9.25

---

1. At the end of October, Mr. Diamond had
a balance of $367.38 in his checking
account. Since then, he has written two
checks for $136.94 and $14.75 and made
a deposit of $185.00. What is the balance
in Mr. Diamond's checking account now?

   (A) $30.69
   (B) $334.07
   (C) $400.69
   (D) $704.07

2. Mario has $15. If he spends $6.25 on
admission to the ice skating rink, $2.95
to rent skates, and $1.65 each for 2 hot
chocolates, how much money will he
have left?

   (A) $2.50
   (B) $3.50
   (C) $4.15
   (D) $10.85

3. Miguel has $20 to spend on going to a
movie. If he spends $7.25 on a movie
ticket, $3.95 for snacks, and $1.75 for bus
fare each way, how much money will he
have left?

   (A) $14.70
   (B) $7.05
   (C) $6.30
   (D) $5.30

4. At the end of November, Mrs. Gold had
a balance of $426.83 in her checking
account. Since then, she has written two
checks for $163.49 and $16.85 and made
a deposit of $195.00. What is the balance
in Mrs. Gold's checking account now?

   (A) $51.49
   (B) $412.17
   (C) $441.49
   (D) $802.17

Problem Solving REAL WORLD

5. Each package of stickers that Olivia wants to buy costs $1.25. Olivia has
$10. Explain how you can find the number of packages of stickers Olivia
can buy.

   Possible explanation: I can keep adding the
   cost of one package until I find how many
   packages add up to $10. $1.25 + $1.25 + $1.25
   + $1.25 + $1.25 + $1.25 + $1.25 + $1.25 = $10.
   So Olivia can buy 8 packages of stickers.

Lesson 37 (page 73)

Name _____

Lesson 37
COMMON CORE STANDARD CC.5.NBT.7
Lesson Objective: Choose a method to find a decimal sum or difference.

Choose a Method

There is more than one way to find the sums and differences of whole numbers and decimals. You can use properties, mental math, place value, a calculator, or paper and pencil.

Choose a method. Find the sum or difference.

- Use mental math for problems with fewer digits or rounded numbers.

$$\begin{array}{r} 2.86 \\ - 1.2 \\ \hline 1.66 \end{array}$$

- Use place value for larger numbers.

$$\begin{array}{r} \$15.79 \\ + \$32.81 \\ \hline \$48.60 \end{array}$$

- Use a calculator for difficult numbers or very large numbers.

Find the sum or difference.

1. $\begin{array}{r} 73.9 \\ + 4.37 \\ \hline 78.27 \end{array}$

2. $\begin{array}{r} 127.35 \\ + 928.52 \\ \hline 1{,}055.87 \end{array}$

3. $\begin{array}{r} 10 \\ + 2.25 \\ \hline 12.25 \end{array}$

4. $\begin{array}{r} 0.36 \\ + 1.55 \\ \hline 1.91 \end{array}$

5. $\begin{array}{r} 71.4 \\ + 11.5 \\ \hline 82.9 \end{array}$

6. $\begin{array}{r} 90.4 \\ + 88.76 \\ \hline 179.16 \end{array}$

7. $\begin{array}{r} 3.3 \\ + 5.6 \\ \hline 8.9 \end{array}$

8. $\begin{array}{r} 14.21 \\ 1.79 \\ + 15.88 \\ \hline 31.88 \end{array}$

9. $68.20 - 42.10$ **26.10**

10. $2.25 - 1.15$ **1.10**

11. $875.33 - 467.79$ **407.54**

12. $97.26 - 54.90$ **42.36**

Lesson 37 (page 74)

1. Della's cats weigh 9.8 and 8.25 pounds, and her dog weighs 25 pounds. How much more does her dog weigh than the total weight of both of her cats?
   - (A) 6.95 pounds
   - (B) 15.2 pounds
   - **(C) 16.75 pounds**
   - (D) 18.05 pounds

2. Rob used 4.25 ounces of peanuts, 3.4 ounces of pecans, and 2.75 ounces of walnuts to make a trail mix. How many ounces of nuts did Rob use in the trail mix?
   - (A) 4.1 ounces
   - (B) 4.865 ounces
   - (C) 7.34 ounces
   - **(D) 10.4 ounces**

3. Gina is training for a marathon. She ran 4.6 miles on Friday and 6.75 miles on Saturday. On Sunday, she ran 13 miles. How much farther did she run on Sunday than she did on Friday and Saturday combined?
   - **(A) 1.65 miles**
   - (B) 6.25 miles
   - (C) 11.35 miles
   - (D) 24.35 miles

4. Paul used 1.75 pounds of grapes, 2.6 pounds of bananas, and 3.25 pounds of apples to make fruit salad. How many pounds of fruit did Paul use in the salad?
   - (A) 5.26 pounds
   - (B) 6.6 pounds
   - **(C) 7.6 pounds**
   - (D) 8.6 pounds

Problem Solving REAL WORLD

5. Jill bought 6.5 meters of blue lace and 4.12 meters of green lace. What was the total length of lace she bought?

   10.62 meters

6. Zack bought a coat for $69.78. He paid with a $100 bill and received $26.73 in change. How much was the sales tax?

   $3.49

Lesson 38 (page 75)

Name _____

Lesson 38
COMMON CORE STANDARD CC.5.NBT.7
Lesson Objective: Model multiplication of whole numbers and decimals.

Multiply Decimals and Whole Numbers

You can draw a quick picture to help multiply a decimal and a whole number.

Find the product. 4×0.23

Draw a quick picture. Each bar represents one tenth, or 0.1. Each circle represents one hundredth, or 0.01.

Step 1
Draw **4** groups of **2** tenths and **3** hundredths.

Step 2
Combine the tenths. Then combine the hundredths.

Step 3
There are **12** hundredths. Rename **10** hundredths as **1** tenth. Then you will have **9** tenths and **2** hundredths.

So, $4 \times 0.23 =$ **0.92**

Check students' quick pictures.

Find the product. Use a quick picture.

1. $2 \times 0.19 =$ **0.38**

2. $3 \times 0.54 =$ **1.62**

3. $4 \times 0.07 =$ **0.28**

4. $3 \times 1.22 =$ **3.66**

Lesson 38 (page 76)

1. Callie used a decimal model to help her multiply a decimal by a whole number. What equation does the model show?

   - (A) $3 \times 0.18 = 0.54$
   - (B) $3 \times 0.18 = 5.4$
   - (C) $18 \times 0.3 = 0.54$
   - (D) $18 \times 0.3 = 5.4$

2. The weight of a dime is 0.08 ounce. Amad used a model to find the weight of 7 dimes. What is the weight of 7 dimes?

   - (A) 0.54 ounce
   - **(B) 0.56 ounce**
   - (C) 0.58 ounce
   - (D) 0.78 ounce

3. Miguel used a quick picture to help him multiply a decimal by a whole number. What equation does the model show?

   - (A) $2 \times 5.2 = 1.04$
   - (B) $2 \times 5.2 = 10.4$
   - (C) $2 \times 0.52 = 10.4$
   - **(D) $2 \times 0.52 = 1.04$**

4. One serving of soup contains 0.45 gram of sodium. How much sodium is in 2 servings of the soup? You may use the decimal model to help you answer the question.

   - (A) 0.09 gram
   - **(B) 0.9 gram**
   - (C) 9 grams
   - (D) 90 grams

Problem Solving REAL WORLD

5. In physical education class, Sonia walks a distance of 0.12 mile in 1 minute. At that rate, how far can she walk in 9 minutes?

   1.08 miles

6. A certain tree can grow 0.45 meter in one year. At that rate, how much can the tree grow in 3 years?

   1.35 meters

Answer Key

Lesson 39

COMMON CORE STANDARD CC.5.NBT.7
Lesson Objective: Multiply a decimal and a
whole number using drawings and place value.

Multiplication with Decimals and Whole Numbers

To find the p oduct of a one-digit whole number and a decimal,
multiply as you would multiply whole numbers. To find the
number of decimal places in the product, add the number
of decimal places in the factors.

To multiply 6 × 4.25, multiply as you would multiply 6 × 425.

Step 1	Step 2	Step 3
Multiply the ones.	Multiply the tens.	Multiply the hundreds. Then place the decimal point in the product.

Step 1
Multiply the ones.
```
   3
  425
×   6
   0
```

Step 2
Multiply the tens.
```
  1 3
  425
×   6
   50
```

Step 3
Multiply the hundreds. Then place the decimal point in the product.
```
  1 3
  4.25  ← 2 decimal places
×    6  + 0 decimal places
 25.50  ← 2 decimal places
```

So, 6 × 4.25 = __25.50__

Place the decimal point in the product.

1.
```
  8.23
×    6
4 9.3 8
```
Think: The place value of the decimal factor is hundredths.

2.
```
   6.3
×    4
 2 5.2
    ^
```

3.
```
  16.82
×     5
8 4.1 0
     ^
```

Find the product.

4.
```
 5.19
×   3
15.57
```

5.
```
 7.2
×  8
57.6
```

6.
```
  37.46
×     7
262.22
```

Lesson 39

CC.5.NBT.7

1. Marci mailed 9 letters at the post office. Each letter weighed 3.5 ounces. What was the total weight of the letters that Marci mailed?

(A) 33.5 ounces
(B) 32.5 ounces
(C) 31.5 ounces
(D) 27.5 ounces

2. Laurie is in training for a race. When she trains, Laurie runs on a path that is 1.45 miles long. Last week, Laurie ran on this path 6 times. How many miles did Laurie run on the path last week?

(A) 0.87 mile
(B) 8.7 miles
(C) 87 miles
(D) 870 miles

3. Mari and Rob are making a science poster. They need to write how much a rock that weighs 7 pounds on Earth would weigh on Mars. They know they can multiply weight on Earth by 0.38 to find weight on Mars. What number should they write on their poster?

(A) 0.266 pound
(B) 2.66 pounds
(C) 26.6 pounds
(D) 266 pounds

4. Rhianna made a shelf to store her collection of rocks and shells. She used 5 pieces of wood that were each 3.25 feet long. How much wood did Rhianna use in all to make the shelf?

(A) 6.25 feet
(B) 15.05 feet
(C) 15.25 feet
(D) 16.25 feet

Problem Solving REAL WORLD

5. A half-dollar coin issued by the United States Mint measures 30.61 millimeters across. Mikk has 9 half dollars. He lines them up end to end in a row. What is the total length of the row of half dollars?

__275.49 millimeters__

6. One pound of grapes costs $3.49. Linda buys exactly 3 pounds of grapes. How much will the grapes cost?

__$10.47__

Lesson 40

COMMON CORE STANDARD CC.5.NBT.7
Lesson Objective: Use expanded form and
place value to multiply a decimal and a whole
number.

Multiply Using Expanded Form

You can use a model and partial products to help you find the product
of a two-digit whole number and a decimal.

Find the product. 13 × 6.8

Step 1 Draw a large rectangle. Label its longer side __13__ and its shorter side __6.8__. The area of the large rectangle represents the product, __13__ × __6.8__.

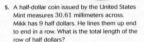

Area = 10 × 6

Step 2 Rewrite the factors in expanded form. Divide the large rectangle into four smaller rectangles. Use the expanded forms to label the smaller rectangles.

13 = __10__ + __3__   6.8 = __6__ + __0.8__

Step 3 Multiply to find the area of each small rectangle.

10 × 6 = __60__   10 × 0.8 = __8__   3 × 6 = __18__   3 × 0.8 = __2.4__

Step 4 Add to find the total area.

__60__ + __8__ + __18__ + __2.4__ = __88.4__

So, 13 × 6.8 = __88.4__

Draw a model to find the p oduct. Check students' models.

1. 18 × 0.25 = __4.5__

2. 26 × 7.2 = __187.2__

Find the product.

3. 17 × 9.3 = __158.1__   4. 21 × 43.5 = __913.5__   5. 48 × 4.74 = __277.52__

Lesson 40

CC.5.NBT.7

1. Ari is setting up a fish tank for his goldfish. The tank holds 15 gallons of water. The weight of a gallon of water rounded to the nearest tenth is 8.3 pounds. Ari used this weight to calculate the weight of the water in his fish tank. Which is the weight that Ari would find for the water in the fish tank?

(A) 12.45 pounds
(B) 16.5 pounds
(C) 124.5 pounds
(D) 165 pounds

2. Paul works at the local grocery store. He worked 15 hours this week. Last week, he worked 2.5 times as many hours as he worked this week. How many hours did Paul work last week?

(A) 30.5 hours
(B) 32.5 hours
(C) 35 hours
(D) 37.5 hours

3. The Barbers are keeping track of their family energy costs. It costs the Barbers $0.16 per week to run their dishwasher. How much will it cost them to run their dishwasher for 52 weeks?

(A) $8.64
(B) $8.32
(C) $3.64
(D) $1.92

4. Mrs. Green needs to store 21 math books on a shelf during school vacation. Each math book is 2.4 centimeters thick. If Mrs. Green stacks the math books on top of each other, how tall does the shelf have to be?

(A) 12.6 centimeters
(B) 40.4 centimeters
(C) 50.4 centimeters
(D) 54 centimeters

Problem Solving REAL WORLD

5. An object that weighs one pound on the moon will weigh about 6.02 pounds on Earth. Suppose a moon rock weighs 11 pounds on the moon. How much will the same rock weigh on Earth?

__66.22 pounds__

6. Tessa is on the track team. For practice and exercise, she runs 2.25 miles each day. At the end of 14 days, how many total miles will Tessa have run?

__31.5 miles__

Name _____

Problem Solving • Multiply Money

Lesson 41
COMMON CORE STANDARD CC.5.NBT.7
Lesson Objective: Solve problems using the
strategy *draw a diagram to multiply money.*

Three students in the garden club enter a pumpkin-growing contest. Jessie's pumpkin is worth $12.75. Mara's pumpkin is worth 4 times as much as Jessie's. Hayden's pumpkin is worth $22.25 more than Mara's. How much is Hayden's pumpkin worth?

Read the Problem	Solve the Problem
What do I need to find? I need to find **how much Hayden's pumpkin is worth**	The amount that Hayden's and Mara's pumpkins are worth depends on how much Jessie's pumpkin is worth. Draw a diagram to compare the amounts without calculating. Then use the diagram to find how much each person's pumpkin is worth.
What information do I need to use? I need to use the worth of **Jessie's** pumpkin to find how much **Mara's** and **Hayden's** pumpkins are worth.	Jessie | $12.75 Mara | $12.75 | $12.75 | $12.75 | $12.75 Hayden | $12.75 | $12.75 | $12.75 | $12.75 | $22.25
How will I use the information: I can draw a diagram to show **how much Jessie's and Mara's pumpkins are worth to find how much Hayden's pumpkin is worth.**	**Jessie:** $12.75 **Mara:** 4 × **$12.75** = **$51.00** **Hayden:** **$51.00** + $22.25 = **$73.25**
So Hayden's pumpkin is worth **$73.25**	

1. Three friends go to the local farmers' market. Latasha spends $3.35. Helen spends 4 times as much as Latasha. Dee spends $7.50 more than Helen. How much does Dee spend?

$20.90

2. Alexia raises $75.23 for a charity. Sue raises 3 times as much as Alexia. Manuel raises $85.89. How much money do the three friends raise for the charity in all?

$386.81

Name _____

Lesson 41
CC.5.NBT.7

1. At a dry cleaning store, it costs $1.79 to clean a man's dress shirt and $8.25 to clean a suit. Thomas brought in 4 shirts and 1 suit to be cleaned. How much will he be charged for the dry cleaning?

- Ⓐ $15.41
- Ⓑ $10.04
- Ⓒ $8.95
- Ⓓ $7.16

2. Mandy, Jeremy, and Lily went to an amusement park during their summer vacation. Mandy spent $16.25 at the amusement park. Jeremy spent $3.40 more than Mandy spent. Lily spent 2 times as much money as Jeremy spent. How much money did Lily spend at the amusement park?

- Ⓐ $6.80
- Ⓑ $19.65
- Ⓒ $32.50
- Ⓓ $39.30

3. Tim wants to rent a bike at the state park. It costs $3.95 per hour for the first 4 hours. After 4 hours, the cost is $2.50 per hour. How much would it cost Tim to rent a bike for 5 hours?

- Ⓐ $19.75
- Ⓑ $18.30
- Ⓒ $15.80
- Ⓓ $12.50

4. Peter spent $32.50 at the ballpark. Marty spent 5 times as much money as Peter. Callie spent $27.25 more than Marty. How much did Callie spend at the ballpark?

- Ⓐ $59.75
- Ⓑ $136.25
- Ⓒ $162.50
- Ⓓ $189.75

Problem Solving REAL WORLD

5. Chris collected $25.65 for a fundraiser. Remy collected $15.87 more than Chris did. Sandy collected 3 times as much as Remy. How much did Sandy collect for the fundraiser? Draw a diagram to solve. Then explain how you found your answer.

Chris   Remy   Sandy

$124.56; Possible explanation: I drew a diagram with one box for Chris showing $25.65 and two boxes for Remy showing $25.65 and $15.87. I added them to get $41.52. Then I drew 3 boxes for Sandy and multiplied 3 × $41.52 to get $124.56.

Name _____

Decimal Multiplication

Lesson 42
COMMON CORE STANDARD CC.5.NBT.7
Lesson Objective: Model multiplication by decimals.

You can use decimal squares to multiply decimals.

Multiply. 0.2 × 0.9

Step 1 Draw a square with 10 equal rows and 10 equal columns.

Step 2 Shade 9 columns to represent **0.9**.

Step 3 Shade 2 rows to represent **0.2**.

Step 4 Count the number of small squares where the shadings overlap: **18** squares, or 0.18.

So, 0.2 × 0.9 = **0.18**

The shadings overlap in 18 squares, or 0.18.

2 rows represent 0.2.
9 columns represent 0.9.

Multiply. Use the decimal model.

1. 0.3 × 0.2 = **0.06**   **2.** 0.9 × 0.5 = **0.45**   **3.** 0.1 × 1.8 = **0.18**

4. 0.4 × 0.4 = **0.16**   **5.** 0.6 × 0.5 = **0.30**   **6.** 0.4 × 1.2 = **0.48**

Name _____

Lesson 42
CC.5.NBT.7

1. Keisha used this decimal model to help her multiply. What equation does the model show?

- Ⓐ 4 × 7 = 28
- Ⓑ 4 × 0.7 = 2.8
- Ⓒ 0.4 × 0.7 = 0.28
- Ⓓ 0.4 × 7 = 2.8

2. Lorenzo had a piece of wire that was 0.6 meter long. He used 0.5 of the wire. How much wire did Lorenzo use?

- Ⓐ 0.03 meter
- Ⓑ 0.1 meter
- Ⓒ 0.3 meter
- Ⓓ 1.1 meters

3. Mickey used a decimal model to help him multiply 0.3 × 0.8. What is the product of 0.3 and 0.8?

- Ⓐ 0.024
- Ⓑ 0.24
- Ⓒ 2.4
- Ⓓ 24

4. One serving of a dried fruit mix contains 0.9 gram of potassium. How much potassium is in 0.5 serving of the dried fruit mix? You may use the decimal model to help you answer the question.

- Ⓐ 0.45 gram
- Ⓑ 1.4 grams
- Ⓒ 4.5 grams
- Ⓓ 45 grams

Problem Solving REAL WORLD

5. A certain bamboo plants grow 1.2 feet in 1 day. At that rate, how many feet could the plant grow in 0.5 day?

0.6 foot

6. The distance from the park to the grocery store is 0.9 mile. Ezra runs 8 tenths of that distance and walks the rest of the way. How far does Ezra run from the park to the grocery store?

0.72 mile

Answer Key

Name _____

Multiply Decimals

Multiply. 9.3×5.27

Step 1 Multiply as with whole numbers.

```
    2 6
     2
    527
 ×   93
  1,581
+ 47,430
  49,011
```

Step 2 Add the number of decimal places in the factors to place the decimal point in the product.

```
   5.27  ←  2  decimal places
 × 9.3   ← +1  decimal place
  1,581
+ 47,430
  49.011 ←  3  decimal places
```

So, $9.3 \times 5.27 = $ __49.011__

Place the decimal point in the product.

1.
```
  1.6
× 0.7
 1.1 2
  ∧
```

2.
```
  14.2
×  7.6
1 0 7.9 2
    ∧
```

3.
```
  3.59
×  4.8
1 7.2 3 2
   ∧
```

Find the product.

4.
```
  5.7
× 0.8
 4.56
```

5.
```
 35.1
×  8.4
294.84
```

6.
```
 2.19
×  6.3
13.797
```

Name _____

1. A scientist at a giant panda preserve in China measured the length of a newborn cub as 15.5 centimeters. The cub's mother was 9.5 times as tall as the length of the cub. How tall is the mother?

   (A) 14.725 centimeters
   (B) 25 centimeters
   (C) 147.25 centimeters
   (D) 1,472.5 centimeters

2. Emily stopped at a produce stand to buy some tomatoes. Tomatoes cost $1.25 per pound at the stand. Emily bought 5 tomatoes that weighed a total of 1.8 pounds. How much did Emily pay for the tomatoes?

   (A) $2.25
   (B) $3.05
   (C) $6.25
   (D) $22.50

3. Mel's father asked Mel to mow his lawn while he was on vacation. Mel bought 1.6 gallons of gas for the lawn mower. The gas cost $2.85 per gallon. How much money did Mel pay for the gas?

   (A) $45.60
   (B) $4.56
   (C) $4.45
   (D) $4.13

4. Mr. Harris has 54.8 acres of land. Mr. Fitz has 0.35 times as many acres as Mr. Harris has. How many acres of land does Mr. Fitz have?

   (A) 4.384 acres
   (B) 19.108 acres
   (C) 19.18 acres
   (D) 43.84 acres

Problem Solving REAL WORLD

5. Aretha runs a marathon in 3.25 hours. Neal takes 1.6 times as long to run the same marathon. How many hours does it take Neal to run the marathon?

   __5.2 hours__

6. Tiffany catches a fish that weighs 12.3 pounds. Frank catches a fish that weighs 2.5 times as much as Tiffany's fish. How many pounds does Frank's fish weigh?

   __30.75 pounds__

Name _____

Zeros in the Product

Sometimes when you multiply two decimals, there are not enough digits in the product to place the decimal point.

Multiply. 0.9×0.03

Step 1 Multiply as with whole numbers.

```
   3
 × 9
  27
```

Step 2 Find the number of decimal places in the product by adding the number of decimal places in the factors.

```
  0.03  ←  2  decimal places
× 0.9   ← +1  decimal place
       ←  3  decimal places
```

Step 3 Place the decimal point.

0.027   There are not enough digits in the product to place the decimal point. Write zeros as needed to the left of the product to place the decimal point.

So, $0.9 \times 0.03 = $ __0.027__

Write zeros in the product.

1.
```
  0.8
× 0.1
0.0 8
```

2.
```
  0.04
×  0.7
0.0 28
```

3.
```
  0.03
×  0.3
0.0 09
```

Find the product.

4.
```
$0.06
× 0.5
$0.03
```

5.
```
 0.09
× 0.8
0.072
```

6.
```
 0.05
× 0.7
0.035
```

Name _____

1. Denise, Keith, and Tim live in the same neighborhood. Denise lives 0.3 mile from Keith. The distance that Tim and Keith live from each other is 0.2 times longer than the distance between Denise and Keith. How far from each other do Tim and Keith live?

   (A) 0.6 mile
   (B) 0.5 mile
   (C) 0.1 mile
   (D) 0.06 mile

2. Tina is making a special dessert for her brother's birthday. Tina's recipe calls for 0.5 kilogram of flour. The recipe also calls for an amount of sugar that is 0.8 times as much as the amount of flour. How much sugar will Tina need to make the dessert?

   (A) 4 kilograms
   (B) 0.4 kilogram
   (C) 0.04 kilogram
   (D) 0.004 kilogram

3. The information booklet for a video console says that the console uses about 0.2 kilowatt of electricity per hour. If electricity costs $0.15 per kilowatt hour, how much does it cost to run the console for an hour?

   (A) $0.03
   (B) $0.30
   (C) $3.00
   (D) $30.00

4. Bruce is getting materials for a chemistry experiment. His teacher gives him a container that holds 0.25 liter of a blue liquid. Bruce needs to use 0.4 of this liquid for the experiment. How much blue liquid will Bruce use?

   (A) 0.001 liter
   (B) 0.01 liter
   (C) 0.1 liter
   (D) 1 liter

Problem Solving REAL WORLD

5. A beaker contains 0.5 liter of a solution. Jordan uses 0.08 of the solution for an experiment. How much of the solution does Jordan use?

   __0.040, or 0.04 liter__

6. A certain type of nuts are on sale at $0.35 per pound. Tamara buys 0.2 pound of nuts. How much will the nuts cost?

   __$0.07__

Answer Key

Lesson 45 — Divide Decimals by Whole Numbers

COMMON CORE STANDARD CC.5.NBT.7
Lesson Objective: Model division of decimals by whole numbers.

Name _____

You can draw a quick picture to help you divide a decimal by a whole number.

In a decimal model, each large square represents one, or 1. Each bar represents one-tenth, or 0.1.

Divide. $1.2 \div 3$

Step 1 Draw a quick picture to represent the dividend, _1.2_.

Step 2 Draw 3 circles to represent the divisor, _3_.

Step 3 You cannot evenly divide 1 into 3 groups. Regroup 1 as 10 tenths. There are _12_ tenths in 1.2.

Step 4 Share the tenths equally among 3 groups.

Each group contains _0_ ones and _4_ tenths.

So, $1.2 \div 3 =$ _0.4_

Divide. Draw a quick picture. *Check students' drawings*

1. $2.7 \div 9 =$ _0.3_ 2. $4.8 \div 8 =$ _0.6_ 3. $2.8 \div 7 =$ _0.4_

4. $7.25 \div 5 =$ _1.45_ 5. $3.78 \div 3 =$ _1.26_ 6. $8.52 \div 4 =$ _2.13_

www.harcourtschoolsupply.com — © Houghton Mifflin Harcourt Publishing Company — 89 — Core Standards for Math, Grade 5

Lesson 45

CC.5.NBT.7

Name _____

1. Emilio used a model to help him divide 2.46 by 2. What is the quotient?

   Ⓐ 1.23
   Ⓑ 1.32
   Ⓒ 3.21
   Ⓓ 12.3

2. Heath bought 1.2 pounds of potato salad. He divided it into 4 containers, each with the same amount. How much potato salad was in each container?

   Ⓐ 0.03 pound
   Ⓑ 0.3 pound
   Ⓒ 0.8 pound
   Ⓓ 4.8 pounds

3. Theo made a model to represent a division statement. What division statement does the model show?

   Ⓐ $3.12 \div 3 = 1.12$
   Ⓑ $3.63 \div 3 = 1.21$
   Ⓒ $2.24 \div 2 = 1.12$
   Ⓓ $3.36 \div 3 = 1.12$

4. Maya practiced the piano for 3.75 hours last week. If she practiced the same amount of time each of 5 days, how long did she practice each day?

   Ⓐ 0.25 hour
   Ⓑ 0.5 hour
   Ⓒ 0.75 hour
   Ⓓ 1.25 hours

Problem Solving REAL WORLD

5. In PE class, Carl runs a distance of 1.17 miles in 9 minutes. At that rate, how far does Carl run in one minute?

   0.13 mile

6. Marianne spends $9.45 on 5 greeting cards. Each card costs the same amount. What is the cost of one greeting card?

   _$1.89_

www.harcourtschoolsupply.com — © Houghton Mifflin Harcourt Publishing Company — 90 — Core Standards for Math, Grade 5

Lesson 46 — Estimate Quotients

COMMON CORE STANDARD CC.5.NBT.7
Lesson Objective: Estimate decimal quotients.

Name _____

You can use multiples and compatible numbers to estimate decimal quotients.

Estimate. $249.7 \div 31$

Step 1 Round the divisor, 31, to the nearest 10.
31 rounded to the nearest 10 is _30_.

Step 2 Find the multiples of 30 that the dividend, 249.7, is between.
249.7 is between _240_ and _270_.

Step 3 Divide each multiple by the rounded divisor, 30.
$240 \div 30 =$ _8_ $270 \div 30 =$ _9_
So, two possible estimates are _8_ and _9_.

Accept all reasonable estimates. Possible answers are given.

Use compatible numbers to estimate the quotient.

1. $23.6 \div 7$
   _21_ ÷ _7_ = _3_

2. $469.4 \div 62$
   _480_ ÷ _60_ = _8_

Estimate the quotient.

3. $338.7 \div 49$
   _7_

4. $75.1 \div 9$
   _8_

5. $674.8 \div 23$
   _30_

6. $61.9 \div 7$
   _9_

7. $96.5 \div 19$
   _5_

8. $57.2 \div 8$
   _7_

www.harcourtschoolsupply.com — © Houghton Mifflin Harcourt Publishing Company — 91 — Core Standards for Math, Grade 5

Lesson 46

CC.5.NBT.7

Name _____

1. Ashleigh rode her bicycle 26.5 miles in 4 hours. Which gives the **best** estimate of how far Ashleigh rode in 1 hour?

   Ⓐ 0.5 mile
   Ⓑ 0.6 mile
   Ⓒ 5 miles
   Ⓓ 7 miles

2. Ellen drove 357.9 miles. Her car gets about 21 miles per gallon. Which is the **best** estimate of how many gallons of gas Ellen used?

   Ⓐ 17 gallons
   Ⓑ 16 gallons
   Ⓒ 1.7 gallons
   Ⓓ 0.17 gallon

3. Landon bought a box of plants for $8.79. There were 16 plants in the box. If Landon had bought only 1 plant, about how much would it have cost?

   Ⓐ about $0.40
   Ⓑ about $0.50
   Ⓒ about $0.60
   Ⓓ about $0.70

4. Josh bought a 34.6-pound bag of dry dog food to feed his dogs. The bag lasted 8 days. About how much dog food did his dogs eat each day?

   Ⓐ about 0.4 pound
   Ⓑ about 0.5 pound
   Ⓒ about 4 pounds
   Ⓓ about 5 pounds

Problem Solving REAL WORLD

5. Taylor uses 645.6 gallons of water in 7 days. Suppose he uses the same amount of water each day. About how much water does Taylor use each day?

   about 90 gallons

6. On a road trip, Sandy drives 368.7 miles. Her car uses a total of 18 gallons of gas. About how many miles per gallon does Sandy's car get?

   about 20 miles per gallon

www.harcourtschoolsupply.com — © Houghton Mifflin Harcourt Publishing Company — 92 — Core Standards for Math, Grade 5

---

www.harcourtschoolsupply.com — © Houghton Mifflin Harcourt Publishing Company — **223** — Core Standards for Math, Grade 5

Answer Key

Name _____

Lesson 47
COMMON CORE STANDARD CC.5.NBT.7
Lesson Objective: Divide decimals by whole numbers.

Division of Decimals by Whole Numbers

Divide. 19.61 ÷ 37

Step 1 Estimate the quotient.
2,000 hundredths ÷ 40 = __50__ hundredths, or 0.50.
So, the quotient will have a zero in the ones place.

$$37\overline{)19.61}$$ with 0

Step 2 Divide the tenths.
Use the estimate. Try 5 in the tenths place.

$$37\overline{)19.61}$$ 0 5

Multiply. __5__ × 37 = __185__

Subtract. 196 − __185__ = __11__   − 18 5 / 1 1

Check. __11__ < 37

Step 3 Divide the hundredths.
Estimate: 120 hundredths ÷ 40 = 3 hundredths.

$$37\overline{)19.61}$$ 0.53

Multiply. __3__ × 37 = __111__   − 18 5 / 1 11

Subtract. __111__ − __111__ = __0__   − 1 11 / 0

Check. __0__ < 37

Place the decimal point in the quotient.

So, 19.61 ÷ 37 = __0.53__

Write the quotient with the decimal point placed correctly.

1. 5.94 ÷ 3 = 198   __1.98__

2. 48.3 ÷ 23 = 21   __2.1__

Divide.

3. 9)61.2   __6.8__

4. 17)83.3   __4.9__

5. 9)7.38   __0.82__

Name _____

Lesson 47
CC.5.NBT.7

1. Grant is making small bags of dried fruit from a large bag of dried fruit that weighs 5.46 pounds. If he puts the same amount of dried fruit in each of 6 bags, how much will each bag weigh?

   Ⓐ 0.0091 pound
   Ⓑ 0.091 pound
   Ⓒ 0.91 pound
   Ⓓ 9.1 pounds

2. Mia has a piece of ribbon that is 30.5 yards long. The length is just enough ribbon to make 5 bows that are the same size. How long is the ribbon that she uses for each bow?

   Ⓐ 6.01 yards
   Ⓑ 6.1 yards
   Ⓒ 6.2 yards
   Ⓓ 6.5 yards

3. A plumber has a piece of copper tubing that is 112.8 inches long. He needs to cut the tubing into 12 equal pieces to repair some leaky pipes. How long will each piece of tubing be?

   Ⓐ 0.094 inch
   Ⓑ 0.94 inch
   Ⓒ 9.4 inches
   Ⓓ 94 inches

4. Matthew bought 13 used video games that were on sale in a store. He paid $84.37 for the games. If each video game cost the same price, how much did 1 video game cost?

   Ⓐ $6.09
   Ⓑ $6.19
   Ⓒ $6.39
   Ⓓ $6.49

Problem Solving REAL WORLD

5. On Saturday, 12 friends go ice skating. Altogether, they pay $83.40 for admission. They share the cost equally. How much does each person pay?

   __$6.95__

6. A team of 4 people participates in a 400-yard relay race. Each team member runs the same distance. The team completes the race in a total of 53.2 seconds. What is the average running time for each person?

   __13.3 seconds__

Name _____

Lesson 48
COMMON CORE STANDARD CC.5.NBT.7
Lesson Objective: Model division by decimals.

Decimal Division

You can use decimal models to divide tenths.

Divide. 1.8 ÷ 0.3.

Step 1 Shade 18 tenths to represent the dividend, __1.8__

18 tenths, or 1.8

Step 2 Divide the 18 tenths into groups of __3__ tenths to represent the divisor, __0.3__

0.3 0.3 0.3 0.3 0.3 0.3

Step 3 Count the groups.
There are __6__ groups of 0.3 in 1.8. So, 1.8 ÷ 0.3 = __6__

You can use decimal models to divide hundredths.

Divide. 0.42 ÷ 0.06

Step 1 Shade 42 squares to represent the dividend, __0.42__

There are 42 shaded squares, or __0.42__

Step 2 Divide the 42 small squares into groups of __6__ hundredths to represent the divisor, __0.06__

There are __7__ groups of __6__ hundredths.

Step 3 Count the groups.
There are __7__ groups of 0.06 in 0.42. So, 0.42 ÷ 0.06 = __7__

Use the model to complete the number sentence.

1. 1.4 ÷ 0.7 = __2__

2. 0.15 ÷ 0.03 = __5__

Divide. Use decimal models. Check students' models.

3. 2.7 ÷ 0.3 = __9__

4. 0.52 ÷ 0.26 = __2__

5. 0.96 ÷ 0.16 = __6__

Name _____

Lesson 48
CC.5.NBT.7

1. Peter used a model to help him divide 0.28 by 0.07. What is the quotient?

   Ⓐ 0.04
   Ⓑ 0.4
   Ⓒ 4
   Ⓓ 28

2. Heather used 1.5 pounds of roast beef. She used it all in sandwiches. She used 0.5 pound in each sandwich. How many sandwiches did she make?

   Ⓐ 0.3
   Ⓑ 3
   Ⓒ 4.5
   Ⓓ 30

3. Fiona made the model below to represent a division statement. What division statement does the model show?

   Ⓐ 1.2 ÷ 0.3 = 4
   Ⓑ 1.2 ÷ 0.4 = 3
   Ⓒ 1.6 ÷ 0.4 = 4
   Ⓓ 0.9 ÷ 0.3 = 3

4. Tyrone used 3.75 cups of hot water to make hot chocolate. He poured 0.75 cup of hot water into each mug of chocolate. How many mugs of hot chocolate did he make?

   Ⓐ 3
   Ⓑ 4
   Ⓒ 5
   Ⓓ 6

Problem Solving REAL WORLD

5. Keisha buys 2.4 kilograms of rice. She separates the rice into packages that contain 0.4 kilogram of rice each. How many packages of rice can Keisha make?

   __6 packages__

6. Leighton is making cloth headbands. She has 4.2 yards of cloth. She uses 0.2 yard of cloth for each headband. How many headbands can Leighton make from the length of cloth she has?

   __21 headbands__

Answer Key

Lesson 49
COMMON CORE STANDARD CC.5.NBT.7
Lesson Objective: Place the decimal point in decimal division.

Divide Decimals

You can multiply the dividend and the divisor by the same power of 10 to make the divisor a whole number. As long as you multiply both the dividend and the divisor by the same power of 10, the quotient stays the same.

Example 1: Divide. 0.84 ÷ 0.07

Multiply the dividend, **0.84**, and the divisor, **0.07**, by the power of 10 that makes the **divisor** a whole number.

0.84 ÷ 0.07 = ?
× 100   × 100
84 ÷ 7 = 12

Since 84 ÷ 7 = 12, you know that 0.84 ÷ 0.07 = **12**

Example 2: Divide. 4.42 ÷ 3.4

Multiply both the dividend and the divisor by 10 to make the divisor a whole number.

3.4)4.42 → Multiply 3.4 and 4.42 both by 10 → 34)44.2

Divide as you would whole numbers. Place the decimal point in the quotient, above the decimal point in the dividend.

$$\begin{array}{r} 1.3 \\ 34\overline{)44.2} \\ -34 \\ \hline 102 \\ -102 \\ \hline 0 \end{array}$$

So, 4.42 ÷ 3.4 = **1.3**

Copy and complete the pattern.

1. 54 ÷ 6 = **9**
   5.4 ÷ **0.6** = 9
   0.54 ÷ 0.06 = 9

2. 184 ÷ 23 = **8**
   18.4 ÷ **2.3** = 8
   1.84 ÷ 0.23 = 8

3. 138 ÷ 2 = **69**
   13.8 ÷ **0.2** = 69
   1.38 ÷ 0.02 = 69

Divide.

4. 1.4)9.8   **7**

5. 0.3)0.6   **2**

6. 3.64 ÷ 1.3   **2.8**

Lesson 49
CC.5.NBT.7

1. Leilani bought tomatoes that cost $0.84 per pound. She paid $3.36 for the tomatoes. How many pounds of tomatoes did she buy?
   - (A) 0.004 pound
   - (B) 0.04 pound
   - (C) 0.4 pound
   - (D) 4 pounds

2. Carly has a piece of yarn that is 7.2 yards long. She needs to cut the yarn into pieces of fringe that each measure 0.3 yard long. How many pieces of fringe can she cut from the piece of yarn?
   - (A) 2,400
   - (B) 240
   - (C) 24
   - (D) 2.4

3. Latisha hiked along a trail that was 9.66 miles long last Saturday. It took her 4.2 hours to complete the trail. What was Latisha's average speed per hour?
   - (A) 0.23 mile per hour
   - (B) 2.3 miles per hour
   - (C) 20.3 miles per hour
   - (D) 23 miles per hour

4. Quan records that his hamster can turn the wheel in its cage to make 1 revolution in 0.5 minute. How many revolutions can the hamster make in 20.5 minutes?
   - (A) 4.1
   - (B) 41
   - (C) 410
   - (D) 4,100

Problem Solving REAL WORLD

5. At the market, grapes cost $0.85 per pound. Clarissa buys grapes and pays a total of $2.55. How many pounds of grapes does she buy?

   3 pounds

6. Damon kayaks on a river near his home. He plans to kayak a total of 6.4 miles. Damon kayaks at an average speed of 1.6 miles per hour. How many hours will it take Damon to kayak the 6.4 miles?

   4 hours

Lesson 50
COMMON CORE STANDARD CC.5.NBT.7
Lesson Objective: Write a zero in the dividend to find a quotient.

Write Zeros in the Dividend

When there are not enough digits in the dividend to complete the division, you can write zeros to the right of the last digit in the dividend. Writing zeros will not change the value of the dividend or the quotient.

Divide. 5.2 ÷ 8

Step 1 Divide as you would whole numbers. Place the decimal point in the quotient above the decimal point in the dividend.

The decimal point in the quotient is directly above the decimal point in the dividend.

$$\begin{array}{r} 0.6 \\ 8\overline{)5.2} \\ -48 \\ \hline 4 \end{array}$$

Step 2 The difference is less than the divisor. Write a 0 in the dividend and continue to divide.

The difference, 4, is less than the divisor.

$$\begin{array}{r} 0.65 \\ 8\overline{)5.20} \\ -48 \\ \hline 40 \\ -40 \\ \hline 0 \end{array}$$

Write a 0 in the dividend. Then continue to divide.

So, 5.2 ÷ 8 = **0.65**

Write the quotient with the decimal point placed correctly.

1. 3 ÷ 0.4 = 75   **7.5**

2. 25.2 ÷ 8 = 315   **3.15**

3. 60 ÷ 25 = 24   **2.4**

4. 8.28 ÷ 0.72 = 115   **11.5**

Divide.

5. 6)43.5   **7.25**

6. 1.4)7.7   **5.5**

7. 30)72   **2.4**

8. 0.18)0.63   **3.5**

Lesson 50
CC.5.NBT.7

1. Tony collected 16.2 pounds of pecans from the trees at his farm. He will give the same weight of pecans to each of 12 friends. How many pounds of pecans will each friend get?
   - (A) 0.135 pound
   - (B) 1.35 pounds
   - (C) 13.5 pounds
   - (D) 135 pounds

2. Trevor drove 202 miles to visit his grandparents. It took him 4 hours to get there. What was the average speed that Trevor drove?
   - (A) 5.05 miles per hour
   - (B) 5.5 miles per hour
   - (C) 50.5 miles per hour
   - (D) 55 miles per hour

3. Denise's mother bought some zucchini for $0.78 per pound. If she paid $2.73 for the zucchini, how many pounds of zucchini did she buy?
   - (A) 0.35 pound
   - (B) 3.5 pounds
   - (C) 35 pounds
   - (D) 350 pounds

4. The students at Winwood Elementary School collected 574 cans of food in 20 days for a food drive. What was the average number of cans of food collected each day?
   - (A) 2.87
   - (B) 27
   - (C) 28
   - (D) 28.7

Problem Solving REAL WORLD

5. Mark has a board that is 12 feet long. He cuts the board into 8 pieces that are the same length. How long is each piece?

   1.5 feet

6. Josh pays $7.59 for 2.2 pounds of ground turkey. What is the price per pound of the ground turkey?

   $3.45

Answer Key

Name _____

Lesson 51

COMMON CORE STANDARD CC.5.NBT.7
Lesson Objective: Solve multistep decimal problems using the strategy work backward.

Problem Solving • Decimal Operations

Rebecca spent $32.55 for a photo album and three identical candles. The photo album cost $17.50 and the sales tax was $1.55. How much did each candle cost?

Read the Problem

What do I need to find	What information do I need to use?	How will I use the information?
I need to find the cost of each candle	Rebecca spent $32.55 for a photo album and 3 candles. The photo album cost $17.50 The sales tax was $1.55	I can use a flowchart and work backward from the total amount Rebecca spent to find the cost of each candle

Solve the Problem

• Make a flowchart to show the information. Then work backward to solve.

Cost of 3 candles	plus	Cost of photo album	plus	Sales tax	equals	Total spent
3 × cost of each candle	+	$17.50	+	$1.55	=	$32.55

Total spent	minus	Sales tax	minus	Cost of photo album	equals	Cost of 3 candles
$32.55	−	$1.55	−	$17.50	=	$13.50

• Divide the cost of 3 candles by 3 to find the cost of each candle.

$13.50 ÷ 3 = **$4.50**

So, each candle cost $4.50.

Use a flowchart to help you solve the problem.

1. Maria spent $28.69 on one pair of jeans and two T-shirts. The jeans cost $16.49. Each T-shirt cost the same amount. The sales tax was $1.62. How much did each T-shirt cost?

   $5.29

2. At the skating rink, Sean and Patrick spent $17.45 on admission and snacks. They used one coupon for $2 off the admission cost. The snacks cost $5.95. What is the admission cost for one?

   $6.75

---

1. Reshawn is buying 3 books in a set for $24.81. He will save $6.69 by buying the set instead of buying individual books. If each book costs the same amount, how much does each of the 3 books cost when purchased individually?
   - (A) $2.23
   - (B) $6.04
   - (C) $8.27
   - (D) $10.50

2. Mackenzie spent a total of $17.50 on Saturday afternoon. She bought a movie ticket for $7.25 and snacks for $4.95. She spent the rest of the money on bus fare to get to the movie and back home. How much was the bus fare each way if each trip cost the same amount?
   - (A) $2.60
   - (C) $5.20
   - (B) $2.65
   - (D) $5.30

3. Corey and Nicole spent $17.00, including sales tax, on 2 sandwiches and 3 slices of pizza. The sandwiches cost $5.25 each and the total sales tax was $0.92. How much did each slice of pizza cost?
   - (A) $1.86
   - (B) $2.47
   - (C) $2.79
   - (D) $5.58

4. Jocelyn bought 2 sweaters for the same price. She paid $23.56, including sales tax of $1.36 and a $5.00 coupon. What was the price of one sweater before the tax and coupon?
   - (A) $8.60
   - (B) $19.96
   - (C) $13.60
   - (D) $14.96

Problem Solving REAL WORLD

5. Samantha bought flowers at a craft store for $14.02. She also bought 4 packages of glass beads and 2 vases. The vases cost $3.59 each and the total sales tax was $1.34. The total amount she paid was $28.50, including sales tax. Explain a strategy you would use to find the cost of one package of glass beads.

   Possible explanation: I would make the following flowchart: cost of 4 packages of glass beads + cost of flowers + cost of 2 vases + sales tax = Total Spent. Then I would work backward to find the cost of the 4 packages of glass beads: Total spent − sales tax − cost of 2 vases − cost of flowers = cost of 4 packages of glass beads. Then I would divide the cost of the 4 packages of glass beads by 4 to find the cost of 1 package.

Name _____

Lesson 52

COMMON CORE STANDARD CC.5.NF.1
Lesson Objective: Find a common denominator or a least common denominator to write equivalent fractions.

Common Denominators and Equivalent Fractions

You can find a common denominator of two fractions.

A **common denominator** of two fractions is a common multiple of their denominators.

Find a common denominator of $\frac{1}{6}$ and $\frac{7}{10}$. Rewrite the pair of fractions using a common denominator.

Step 1 Identify the denominators.
The denominators are 6 and 10.

Step 2 List the multiples of the greater denominator, 10.
Multiples of 10: 10, 20, 30, 40, 50, 60, ...

Step 3 Check if any of the multiples of the greater denominator are evenly divisible by the other denominator.

Both 30 and 60 are evenly divisible by 6.
Common denominators of $\frac{1}{6}$ and $\frac{7}{10}$ are 30 and 60.

Step 4 Rewrite the fractions with a denominator of 30.
Multiply the numerator and the denominator of each fraction by the same number so that the denominator results in 30.

$\frac{1}{6} = \frac{1 \times 5}{6 \times 5} = \frac{5}{30}$ $\frac{7}{10} = \frac{7 \times 3}{10 \times 3} = \frac{21}{30}$

Use a common denominator to write an equivalent fraction for each fraction. Possible answers are given.

1. $\frac{5}{12}, \frac{2}{9}$
   common denominator: __36__
   $\frac{15}{36}, \frac{8}{36}$

2. $\frac{3}{8}, \frac{5}{6}$
   common denominator: __48__
   $\frac{18}{48}, \frac{40}{48}$

3. $\frac{2}{9}, \frac{1}{6}$
   common denominator: __18__
   $\frac{4}{18}, \frac{3}{18}$

4. $\frac{3}{4}, \frac{9}{10}$
   common denominator: __40__
   $\frac{30}{40}, \frac{36}{40}$

---

1. Arturo wants to find the amount of time he spent on his math and science homework combined. He worked $\frac{2}{5}$ hour on math and $\frac{1}{3}$ hour on science. Which is the **best** strategy to find the least common denominator so he can add the time he spent on his homework?
   - (A) Multiply denominators since they share no common factors other than 1.
   - (B) Find all the multiples of each denominator.
   - (C) One denominator is the multiple of the other, so the multiple is the least common denominator.
   - (D) Add the denominators to find the least common multiple.

2. Francine wants to find the total of $\frac{2}{3}$ cup of blueberries and $\frac{5}{8}$ cup of raspberries. What is the least common denominator of the fractions?
   - (A) 10
   - (C) 18
   - (B) 11
   - (D) 24

3. Alana bought $\frac{3}{8}$ pound of Swiss cheese and $\frac{1}{4}$ pound of American cheese. Which pair of fractions **cannot** be used to find how many pounds of cheese she bought in all?
   - (A) $\frac{6}{16}$ and $\frac{4}{16}$
   - (B) $\frac{9}{24}$ and $\frac{6}{24}$
   - (C) $\frac{24}{64}$ and $\frac{8}{64}$
   - (D) $\frac{15}{40}$ and $\frac{10}{40}$

4. Charles bought $\frac{7}{8}$ foot of electrical wire and $\frac{5}{6}$ foot of copper wire for his science project. What is the least common denominator of the fractions?
   - (A) 14
   - (B) 18
   - (C) 24
   - (D) 48

Problem Solving REAL WORLD

5. Ella spends $\frac{2}{3}$ hour practicing the piano each day. She also spends $\frac{1}{2}$ hour jogging. What is the least common denominator of the fractions?

   __6__

6. In a science experiment, a plant grew $\frac{3}{4}$ inch one week and $\frac{1}{2}$ inch the next week. Use a common denominator to write an equivalent fraction for each fraction.

   Possible answer: $\frac{6}{8}$ and $\frac{4}{8}$

Answer Key

Lesson 53

Name _____

COMMON CORE STANDARD CC.5.NF.1
Lesson Objective: Use equivalent fractions
to add and subtract fractions.

Add and Subtract Fractions

To add or subtract fractions with unlike denominators, you need to
rename them as fractions with like denominators. You can do this
by making a list of equivalent fractions.

Add. $\frac{5}{12} + \frac{1}{8}$

Step 1 Write equivalent fractions for $\frac{5}{12}$. $\frac{5}{12} \frac{10}{24} \frac{15}{36} \frac{20}{48}$

Step 2 Write equivalent fractions for $\frac{1}{8}$. $\frac{1}{8} \frac{2}{16} \frac{3}{24}$

Step 3 Rewrite the problem using the equivalent fractions.
Then add.

$\frac{5}{12} + \frac{1}{8}$ becomes $\frac{10}{24} + \frac{3}{24} = \frac{13}{24}$.

> Stop when you find two fractions with the same denominator.

Subtract. $\frac{9}{10} - \frac{1}{2}$

Step 1 Write equivalent fractions for $\frac{9}{10}$. $\frac{9}{10} \frac{18}{20} \frac{27}{30} \frac{36}{40}$

Step 2 Write equivalent fractions for $\frac{1}{2}$. $\frac{1}{2} \frac{2}{4} \frac{3}{6} \frac{4}{8} \frac{5}{10}$

Step 3 Rewrite the problem using the equivalent fractions.
Then subtract.

$\frac{9}{10} - \frac{1}{2}$ becomes $\frac{9}{10} - \frac{5}{10} = \frac{4}{10}$. Written in simplest form, $\frac{4}{10} = \frac{2}{5}$.

Find the sum or difference. Write your answer in simplest form.

1. $\frac{2}{9} + \frac{1}{3}$ 2. $\frac{1}{2} + \frac{2}{5}$ 3. $\frac{1}{4} + \frac{1}{6}$ 4. $\frac{1}{5} + \frac{3}{4}$

   $\frac{5}{9}$ $\frac{9}{10}$ $\frac{5}{12}$ $\frac{19}{20}$

5. $\frac{7}{8} - \frac{1}{4}$ 6. $\frac{3}{4} - \frac{2}{3}$ 7. $\frac{9}{10} - \frac{4}{5}$ 8. $\frac{8}{9} - \frac{5}{6}$

   $\frac{5}{8}$ $\frac{1}{12}$ $\frac{1}{10}$ $\frac{1}{18}$

Lesson 53

Name _____

CC.5.NF.1

1. Brady used $\frac{2}{3}$ gallon of yellow paint and $\frac{1}{4}$ gallon of white paint to paint his dresser. How many gallons of paint did Brady use?

   (A) $\frac{3}{7}$ gallon
   (B) $\frac{3}{4}$ gallon
   (C) $\frac{2}{8}$ gallon
   (D) $\frac{11}{12}$ gallon

2. Mr. Barber uses $\frac{7}{9}$ yard of wire to put up a ceiling fan. He uses $\frac{1}{3}$ yard of wire to fix a switch. How much more wire does he use to put up the fan than to fix the switch?

   (A) $1\frac{1}{9}$ yards
   (B) $\frac{6}{9}$ yard
   (C) $\frac{4}{9}$ yard
   (D) $\frac{1}{3}$ yard

3. Tom jogged $\frac{3}{5}$ mile on Monday and $\frac{2}{6}$ mile on Tuesday. How much farther did Tom jog on Monday than on Tuesday?

   (A) $\frac{1}{30}$ mile
   (B) $\frac{3}{15}$ mile
   (C) $\frac{8}{30}$ mile
   (D) $\frac{4}{15}$ mile

4. Mindy bought $\frac{1}{6}$ pound of almonds and $\frac{3}{4}$ pound of walnuts. How many pounds of nuts did she buy in all?

   (A) $\frac{1}{3}$
   (B) $\frac{7}{12}$
   (C) $\frac{2}{3}$
   (D) $\frac{11}{12}$

Problem Solving REAL WORLD

5. Kaylin mixed two liquids for a science experiment. One container held $\frac{7}{8}$ cup and the other held $\frac{9}{10}$ cup. What is the total amount of the mixture?

   $1\frac{31}{40}$ cups

6. Henry bought $\frac{1}{4}$ pound of screws and $\frac{2}{5}$ pound of nails to build a skateboard ramp. What is the total weight of the screws and nails?

   $\frac{13}{20}$ pound

Lesson 54

Name _____

COMMON CORE STANDARD CC.5.NF.1
Lesson Objective: Add and subtract mixed
numbers with unlike denominators.

Add and Subtract Mixed Numbers

When you add or subtract mixed numbers, you may need to
rename the fractions as fractions with a common denominator.

find the sum. Write the answer in simplest form. $5\frac{3}{4} + 2\frac{1}{3}$

Step 1 Model $5\frac{3}{4}$ and $2\frac{1}{3}$.

Step 2 A common denominator for $\frac{3}{4}$ and $\frac{1}{3}$ is 12, so rename $5\frac{3}{4}$ as $5\frac{9}{12}$ and $2\frac{1}{3}$ as $2\frac{4}{12}$.

Step 3 Add the fractions.
$\frac{9}{12} + \frac{4}{12} = \frac{13}{12}$

Step 4 Add the whole numbers
$5 + 2 = 7$

Add the sums. Write the answer in simplest form.

$\frac{13}{12} + 7 = 7\frac{13}{12}$, or $8\frac{1}{12}$

So, $5\frac{3}{4} + 2\frac{1}{3} = 8\frac{1}{12}$.

Find the sum or difference. Write your answer in simplest form.

1. $2\frac{2}{9} + 4\frac{1}{6}$ 2. $10\frac{5}{6} + 5\frac{3}{4}$ 3. $11\frac{7}{8} - 9\frac{5}{6}$ 4. $18\frac{3}{5} - 14\frac{1}{2}$

   $6\frac{7}{18}$ $16\frac{7}{12}$ $2\frac{1}{24}$ $4\frac{1}{10}$

Lesson 54

Name _____

CC.5.NF.1

1. David practices piano for $1\frac{1}{3}$ hours on Monday and $3\frac{1}{2}$ hours on Tuesday. How much longer does he practice piano on Tuesday than on Monday?

   (A) $1\frac{1}{5}$ hours
   (B) $2\frac{1}{6}$ hours
   (C) $2\frac{2}{5}$ hours
   (D) $2\frac{5}{6}$ hours

2. Roberto's cat weighed $6\frac{3}{4}$ pounds last year. The cat weighs $1\frac{1}{2}$ pounds more now. How much does the cat weigh now?

   (A) $5\frac{1}{4}$ pounds
   (B) $7\frac{1}{4}$ pounds
   (C) $7\frac{3}{4}$ pounds
   (D) $8\frac{1}{4}$ pounds

3. Ken bought $3\frac{3}{4}$ pounds of apples at the farmers' market. Abby bought $2\frac{1}{8}$ pounds of apples. How many pounds of apples did Ken and Abby buy in all?

   (A) $5\frac{5}{8}$ pounds   (C) $5\frac{7}{8}$ pounds
   (B) $5\frac{1}{3}$ pounds   (D) $6\frac{1}{4}$ pounds

4. Three students made videos for their art project. The table shows the length of each video.

Art in Nature	
Video	Length (in hours)
1	$4\frac{3}{4}$
2	$2\frac{7}{12}$
3	$2\frac{1}{6}$

   How much longer is video 1 than video 3?

   (A) $1\frac{5}{12}$ hours   (C) $2\frac{5}{12}$ hours
   (B) $1\frac{7}{12}$ hours   (D) $2\frac{7}{12}$ hours

Problem Solving REAL WORLD

5. Jacobi bought $7\frac{1}{2}$ pounds of meatballs. He decided to cook $1\frac{1}{4}$ pounds and freeze the rest. How many pounds did he freeze?

   $6\frac{1}{4}$ pounds

6. Jill walked $8\frac{1}{8}$ miles to a park and then $7\frac{2}{5}$ miles home. How many miles did she walk in all?

   $15\frac{21}{40}$ miles

Answer Key

Subtraction with Renaming

You can use a common denominator to find the difference of two mixed numbers.

Estimate. $9\frac{1}{6} - 2\frac{3}{4}$

Step 1 Estimate by using 0, $\frac{1}{2}$, and 1 as benchmarks.

$9\frac{1}{6} - 2\frac{3}{4} \rightarrow 9 - 3 = 6$

So, the difference should be close to 6.

Step 2 Identify a common denominator.

$9\frac{1}{6} - 2\frac{3}{4}$ A common denominator of 6 and 4 is 12.

Step 3 Write equivalent fractions using the common denominator.

$9\frac{1}{6} = 9 + \frac{1 \times 2}{6 \times 2} = 9\frac{2}{12}$

$2\frac{3}{4} = 2 + \frac{3 \times 3}{4 \times 3} = 2\frac{9}{12}$

Step 4 Rename if needed. Then subtract.

Since $\frac{2}{12} < \frac{9}{12}$, rename $9\frac{2}{12}$ as $8\frac{14}{12}$.

Subtract. $8\frac{14}{12} - 2\frac{9}{12} = 6\frac{5}{12}$

So, $9\frac{1}{6} - 2\frac{3}{4} = 6\frac{5}{12}$.

Since the difference of $6\frac{5}{12}$ is close to 6, the answer is reasonable.

Possible estimates are given.

Estimate. Then find the difference and write it in simplest form.

1. Estimate: $\underline{5\frac{1}{2} - 4 = 1\frac{1}{2}}$

   $5\frac{1}{3} - 3\frac{5}{6}$ $1\frac{1}{2}$

2. Estimate: $\underline{7 - 2\frac{1}{2} = 4\frac{1}{2}}$

   $7\frac{1}{4} - 2\frac{5}{12}$ $4\frac{5}{6}$

3. Estimate: $\underline{9 - 3 = 6}$

   $8\frac{2}{3} - 2\frac{7}{9}$ $5\frac{8}{9}$

4. Estimate: $\underline{9\frac{1}{2} - 4 = 5\frac{1}{2}}$

   $9\frac{2}{5} - 3\frac{3}{4}$ $5\frac{13}{20}$

5. Estimate: $\underline{7 - 1\frac{1}{2} = 5\frac{1}{2}}$

   $7\frac{3}{16} - 1\frac{5}{8}$ $5\frac{9}{16}$

6. Estimate: $\underline{2\frac{1}{2} - 1\frac{1}{2} = 1}$

   $2\frac{4}{9} - 1\frac{11}{18}$ $\frac{5}{6}$

---

1. Kyle is hanging wallpaper in his bedroom. A roll of wallpaper is $18\frac{3}{8}$ feet long. Kyle cut off a piece of wallpaper $2\frac{5}{6}$ feet long. How much wallpaper is left on the roll?

   (A) $15\frac{13}{24}$ feet

   (B) $15\frac{7}{12}$ feet

   (C) $16\frac{13}{24}$ feet

   (D) $17\frac{3}{8}$ feet

2. Giselle made $24\frac{1}{8}$ ounces of lemonade. She sampled $1\frac{1}{2}$ ounces to make sure it is not too sour. How much lemonade is left?

   (A) $23\frac{9}{8}$ ounces

   (B) $23\frac{5}{8}$ ounces

   (C) $22\frac{5}{8}$ ounces

   (D) $22\frac{5}{16}$ ounces

3. Maria needs a piece of string $4\frac{2}{3}$ feet long for a science project. She cuts it from a piece that is $7\frac{1}{12}$ feet long. How much string does she have left?

   (A) $11\frac{3}{4}$ feet

   (B) $3\frac{5}{12}$ feet

   (C) $2\frac{7}{12}$ feet

   (D) $2\frac{5}{12}$ feet

4. Taylor saw an American alligator at a zoo that measured $12\frac{11}{12}$ feet long. The record length of an American alligator is $19\frac{1}{6}$ feet long. How much longer is the record alligator than the alligator Taylor saw?

   (A) $5\frac{3}{8}$ feet

   (B) $5\frac{7}{8}$ feet

   (C) $6\frac{1}{4}$ feet

   (D) $6\frac{1}{2}$ feet

Problem Solving REAL WORLD

5. Carlene bought $8\frac{1}{16}$ yards of ribbon to decorate a shirt. She only used $5\frac{1}{2}$ yards. How much ribbon does she have left over?

   $2\frac{9}{16}$ yards

6. During his first vet visit, Pedro's puppy weighed $6\frac{3}{8}$ pounds. On his second visit, he weighed $9\frac{5}{16}$ pounds. How much weight did he gain between visits?

   $2\frac{15}{16}$ pounds

Algebra • Patterns with Fractions

You can find an unknown term in a sequence by finding a rule for the sequence.

Find the unknown term in the sequence.

$1\frac{2}{5}, 1\frac{7}{10}, 2, \underline{\hspace{1cm}}, 2\frac{3}{5}$

Step 1 Find equivalent fractions with a common denominator for all of the terms.

The denominators are 5 and 10. A common denominator is 10.

$1\frac{2}{5} = 1\frac{4}{10}$ and $2\frac{3}{5} = 2\frac{6}{10}$

Step 2 Write the terms in the sequence using the common denominator.

$1\frac{4}{10}, 1\frac{7}{10}, 2, \underline{\hspace{1cm}}, 2\frac{6}{10}$

Step 3 Write a rule that describes the pattern.

The sequence increases. To find the difference between terms, subtract at least two pairs of consecutive terms.

$1\frac{7}{10} - 1\frac{4}{10} = \frac{3}{10}$ $2 - 1\frac{7}{10} = \frac{3}{10}$

So, a rule is to add $\frac{3}{10}$.

Step 4 Use the rule to find the unknown term.

Add $\frac{3}{10}$ to the third term to find the unknown term.

$2 + \frac{3}{10} = 2\frac{3}{10}$

Write a rule for the sequence. Then, find the unknown term.

1. $2\frac{2}{3}, 3\frac{1}{2}, \underline{4\frac{1}{3}}, 5\frac{1}{6}, 6$

   Rule: __add $\frac{5}{6}$__

2. $4\frac{1}{2}, 3\frac{7}{8}, 3\frac{1}{4}, \underline{2\frac{5}{8}}, 2$

   Rule: __subtract $\frac{5}{8}$__

---

1. Carrie is given a plant. After one week, it grows to $\frac{7}{8}$ foot tall, and after two weeks it grows to $1\frac{1}{2}$ feet tall. If it keeps growing at the same pace, how tall will it be after 3 weeks?

   (A) $2\frac{1}{4}$ feet

   (B) $2\frac{1}{8}$ feet

   (C) $1\frac{7}{8}$ feet

   (D) $1\frac{3}{8}$ feet

2. Chan ran a race course in $1\frac{3}{5}$ hours. The following month, he ran the same course in $1\frac{3}{10}$ hours. If his time improves by the same amount each month, how long will it take to run the course after another month?

   (A) $\frac{4}{5}$ hour

   (B) $\frac{9}{10}$ hour

   (C) 1 hour

   (D) $1\frac{1}{5}$ hours

3. When Bruce started bowling, he won $\frac{1}{4}$ of the games he played. Within six months, he was winning $\frac{7}{16}$ of his games. If he improves at the same rate, what fraction of his games should he expect to win after another six months?

   (A) $\frac{1}{2}$

   (B) $\frac{9}{16}$

   (C) $\frac{5}{8}$

   (D) $\frac{11}{16}$

4. A farm produced $1\frac{1}{8}$ tons of corn in its first year, $1\frac{3}{8}$ tons in its second year, and $1\frac{10}{16}$ tons in its third year. If the pattern continues each year, how much corn did the farm produce in the fourth year?

   (A) $1\frac{12}{16}$ tons

   (B) $1\frac{7}{8}$ tons

   (C) $1\frac{3}{4}$ tons

   (D) $1\frac{5}{16}$ tons

Problem Solving REAL WORLD

5. Jarett's puppy weighed $3\frac{3}{4}$ ounces at birth. At one week old, the puppy weighed $5\frac{1}{8}$ ounces. At two weeks old, the puppy weighed $6\frac{1}{2}$ ounces. If the weight gain continues in this pattern, how much will the puppy weigh at three weeks old?

   $7\frac{7}{8}$ ounces

6. A baker started out with 12 cups of flour. She had $9\frac{1}{4}$ cups of flour left after the first batch of batter she made. She had $6\frac{1}{2}$ cups of flour left after the second batch of batter she made. If she makes two more batches of batter, how many cups of flour will be left?

   1 cup of flour

Answer Key

Name _____

Lesson 57
COMMON CORE STANDARD CC.5.NF.1
Lesson Objective: Add fractions and mixed numbers with unlike denominators using the properties.

Algebra • Use Properties of Addition

You can use the properties of addition to help you add fractions with unlike denominators.

Use the Commutative Property and the Associative Property.

Add. $\left(3\frac{2}{5} + 1\frac{7}{15}\right) + 2\frac{1}{5}$

$\left(3\frac{2}{5} + 1\frac{7}{15}\right) + 2\frac{1}{5} = \left(1\frac{7}{15} + 3\frac{2}{5}\right) + 2\frac{1}{5}$ ← Use the Commutative Property to order fractions with like denominators.

$= 1\frac{7}{15} + \left(3\frac{2}{5} + 2\frac{1}{5}\right)$ ← Use the Associative Property to group fractions with like denominators.

$= 1\frac{7}{15} + 5\frac{3}{5}$ ← Use mental math to add the fractions with like denominators.

$= 1\frac{7}{15} + 5\frac{9}{15}$ ← Write equivalent fractions with like denominators. Then add.

$= 6\frac{16}{15} = 7\frac{1}{15}$ ← Rename and simplify.

Use the properties and mental math to solve. Write your answer in simplest form.

1. $\left(\frac{5}{7} + \frac{3}{14}\right) + \frac{4}{7}$ ____ $1\frac{1}{2}$

2. $\left(\frac{2}{5} + \frac{5}{9}\right) + \frac{7}{9}$ ____ $1\frac{11}{15}$

3. $\left(3\frac{7}{10} + 5\frac{3}{4}\right) + \frac{3}{4}$ ____ $10\frac{1}{5}$

4. $2\frac{5}{12} + \left(4\frac{2}{3} + 3\frac{7}{12}\right)$ ____ $10\frac{2}{3}$

5. $3\frac{3}{8} + \left(2\frac{1}{5} + 5\frac{1}{8}\right)$ ____ $10\frac{7}{10}$

6. $\left(4\frac{3}{7} + 2\frac{1}{6}\right) + 3\frac{5}{7}$ ____ $10\frac{13}{42}$

Name _____

Lesson 57
CC.5.NF.1

1. Ava hiked a trail that has three sections that are $4\frac{7}{8}$ miles, $3\frac{3}{4}$ miles, and $5\frac{1}{8}$ miles long. Ava wrote this expression to show the total distance that she hiked.

$$\left(4\frac{7}{8} + 3\frac{3}{4}\right) + 5\frac{1}{8}$$

Which shows another way to write the expression using only the Commutative Property of Addition?

Ⓐ $4\frac{7}{8} + \left(3\frac{3}{4} + 5\frac{1}{8}\right)$

Ⓑ $\left(5\frac{1}{8} + 4\frac{7}{8}\right) + 3\frac{3}{4}$

Ⓒ $\left(3\frac{3}{4} + 4\frac{7}{8}\right) + 5\frac{1}{8}$

Ⓓ $(4 + 3 + 5) + \left(\frac{7}{8} + \frac{3}{4} + \frac{1}{8}\right)$

2. Shelley wove three rugs with geometric designs. She wrote this expression to show the total length in feet of all three rugs.

$$\left(8\frac{7}{16} + 11\frac{7}{8}\right) + 15\frac{1}{4}$$

Which shows another way to write the expression using the Associative Property of Addition?

Ⓐ $8\frac{7}{16} + \left(15\frac{7}{8} + 11\frac{1}{4}\right)$

Ⓑ $8\frac{7}{16} + \left(11\frac{7}{8} + 15\frac{1}{4}\right)$

Ⓒ $\left(8\frac{7}{16} + 11\frac{7}{8}\right) + \left(8\frac{7}{16} + 15\frac{1}{4}\right)$

Ⓓ $(8 + 11 + 15) + \left(\frac{7}{16} + \frac{7}{8} + \frac{1}{4}\right)$

3. Larry wrote this expression to show the total number of hours he spent driving during the last three weeks.

$$\left(5\frac{2}{5} + 7\frac{4}{10}\right) + 9\frac{1}{10}$$

Which shows another way to write the expression using the Associative Property of Addition?

Ⓐ $5\frac{2}{5} + \left(7\frac{4}{10} + 9\frac{1}{10}\right)$

Ⓑ $5\frac{2}{5} + \left(9\frac{1}{10} + 7\frac{4}{10}\right)$

Ⓒ $\left(7\frac{4}{10} + 9\frac{1}{10}\right) + 5\frac{2}{5}$

Ⓓ $(5 + 9 + 4) + \left(\frac{2}{5} + \frac{4}{10} + \frac{1}{10}\right)$

4. Marco wrote the following expression to find the total amount of gasoline he bought last month.

$$8\frac{1}{3} + 6\frac{1}{8} + 7\frac{3}{8}$$

Which expression will help make the addition easier for Marco?

Ⓐ $\left(8\frac{1}{3} + 6\frac{1}{8}\right) + 7\frac{3}{8}$

Ⓑ $\left(7\frac{3}{8} + 6\frac{1}{8}\right) + 8\frac{1}{3}$

Ⓒ $\left(8\frac{1}{3} + 7\frac{3}{8}\right) + 6\frac{1}{8}$

Ⓓ $\left(8\frac{1}{3} + 7\frac{3}{8}\right) + 6\frac{1}{8}$

Problem Solving

5. Elizabeth rode her bike $6\frac{1}{2}$ miles from her house to the library and then another $2\frac{3}{5}$ miles to her friend Milo's house. If Carson's house is $2\frac{3}{10}$ miles beyond Milo's house, how far would she travel from her house to Carson's house?
____ $11\frac{2}{5}$ miles

6. Hassan made a vegetable salad with $2\frac{3}{8}$ pounds of tomatoes, $1\frac{1}{4}$ pounds of asparagus, and $2\frac{7}{8}$ pounds of potatoes. How many pounds of vegetables did he use altogether?
____ $6\frac{1}{2}$ pounds

Name _____

Lesson 58
COMMON CORE STANDARD CC.5.NF.2
Lesson Objective: Use models to add fractions with unlike denominators.

Addition with Unlike Denominators

Karen is stringing a necklace with beads. She puts green beads on $\frac{1}{2}$ of the string and purple beads on $\frac{3}{10}$ of the string. How much of the string does Karen cover with beads?

You can use fraction strips to help you add fractions with unlike denominators. Trade fraction strips of fractions with unlike denominators for equivalent strips of fractions with like denominators.

Use fraction strips to find the sum. Write your answer in simplest form.

$\frac{1}{2} + \frac{3}{10}$

Step 1 Use a $\frac{1}{2}$ strip and three $\frac{1}{10}$ strips to model fractions with unlike denominators.

Step 2 Trade the $\frac{1}{2}$ strip for five $\frac{1}{10}$ strips.
$\frac{1}{2} + \frac{3}{10} = \frac{5}{10} + \frac{3}{10}$

Step 3 Add the fractions with like denominators.
$\frac{5}{10} + \frac{3}{10} = \frac{8}{10}$

Step 4 Write the answer in simplest form.
$\frac{8}{10} = \frac{4}{5}$

So, Karen covers $\frac{4}{5}$ of the string with beads.

Use fraction strips to find the sum. Write your answer in simplest form.

Check students' work.

1. $\frac{3}{8} + \frac{3}{4}$

2. $\frac{2}{3} + \frac{1}{4}$

3. $\frac{5}{6} + \frac{7}{12}$

____ $1\frac{1}{8}$ ____ $\frac{11}{12}$ ____ $1\frac{5}{12}$

Name _____

Lesson 58
CC.5.NF.2

Use the information for 1-2.
Addison used $\frac{5}{6}$ yard of ribbon to decorate a photo frame. She used $\frac{1}{3}$ yard of ribbon to decorate her scrapbook.

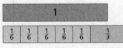

1. Which fraction strips should Addison trade for the $\frac{1}{3}$ strip in order to find how many yards of ribbon she used in all?

Ⓐ $\frac{1}{2}$ Ⓒ $\frac{1}{4}$

Ⓑ $\frac{1}{3}$ Ⓓ $\frac{1}{6}$

2. How many yards of ribbon did Addison use in all?

Ⓐ $1\frac{1}{6}$ yards   Ⓒ $\frac{5}{9}$ yard

Ⓑ 1 yard   Ⓓ $\frac{1}{2}$ yard

Use the information for 3-4.
Gabrielle paints a flower pot to sell at the craft fair. She paints $\frac{2}{5}$ of the pot teal, $\frac{3}{10}$ of the pot yellow, and the rest of the pot white.

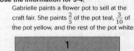

3. Which fraction strips should Gabrielle trade for the $\frac{2}{5}$ strip in order to find how much of the pot is painted teal or yellow?

Ⓐ $\frac{1}{2}$ Ⓒ $\frac{1}{10}$

Ⓑ $\frac{1}{5}$ Ⓓ $\frac{1}{15}$

4. How much of the pot is painted teal or yellow?

Ⓐ $\frac{1}{10}$ Ⓒ $\frac{1}{2}$

Ⓑ $\frac{5}{15}$ Ⓓ $\frac{7}{10}$

Problem Solving

5. Brandus bought $\frac{1}{3}$ pound of ground turkey and $\frac{3}{4}$ pound of ground beef to make sausages. How many pounds of meat did he buy?
____ $1\frac{1}{12}$ pounds

6. To make a ribbon and bow for a hat, Stacey needs $\frac{5}{6}$ yard of black ribbon and $\frac{2}{3}$ yard of red ribbon. How much total ribbon does she need?
____ $1\frac{1}{2}$ yards

Answer Key

Page 117

Name _____

Subtraction with Unlike Denominators

You can use fraction strips to help you subtract fractions with unlike denominators. Trade fraction strips of fractions with unlike denominators for equivalent strips of fractions with like denominators.

Use fraction strips to find the difference. Write your answer in simplest form.

$\frac{1}{2} - \frac{1}{10}$

Step 1 Use a $\frac{1}{2}$ fraction strip to model the first fraction.

Step 2 Trade the $\frac{1}{2}$ strip for five $\frac{1}{10}$ strips.

$\frac{1}{2} - \frac{1}{10} = \frac{5}{10} - \frac{1}{10}$

Step 3 Subtract by taking away $\frac{1}{10}$.

$\frac{5}{10} - \frac{1}{10} = \frac{4}{10}$

So, $\frac{1}{2} - \frac{1}{10} = \frac{4}{10}$. Written in simplest form, $\frac{4}{10} = \frac{2}{5}$.

Use fraction strips to find the difference. Write your answer in simplest form.   *Check students' work.*

1. $\frac{7}{8} - \frac{1}{2}$ $\frac{3}{8}$

2. $\frac{2}{3} - \frac{1}{4}$ $\frac{5}{12}$

3. $\frac{5}{6} - \frac{1}{3}$ $\frac{1}{2}$

4. $\frac{1}{2} - \frac{1}{3}$ $\frac{1}{6}$

5. $\frac{9}{10} - \frac{4}{5}$ $\frac{1}{10}$

6. $\frac{2}{3} - \frac{5}{12}$ $\frac{1}{4}$

Page 118

Name _____

Use the information for 1–2.

Armand lives $\frac{7}{8}$ mile from school. On his way home from school, he rode his skateboard $\frac{5}{16}$ mile and walked the rest of the way.

1. How many $\frac{1}{16}$ fraction strips are equal to $\frac{7}{8}$?
   - (A) 5
   - (B) 7
   - (C) 8
   - (D) 14

2. How far did Armand walk?
   - (A) $\frac{1}{8}$ mile
   - (B) $\frac{1}{2}$ mile
   - (C) $\frac{9}{16}$ mile
   - (D) $1\frac{1}{8}$ miles

Use the information for 3–4.

Kim has a piece of cardboard that is $\frac{5}{6}$ inch long. She cut off a $\frac{5}{12}$-inch piece.

3. How many $\frac{1}{12}$ fraction strips are equal to $\frac{5}{6}$?
   - (A) 5
   - (B) 6
   - (C) 10
   - (D) 12

4. How long is the remaining piece of cardboard?
   - (A) $\frac{10}{12}$ inch
   - (B) $\frac{5}{12}$ inch
   - (C) $\frac{1}{3}$ inch
   - (D) $\frac{1}{6}$ inch

Problem Solving REAL WORLD

5. Amber had $\frac{3}{8}$ of a cake left after her party. She wrapped a piece that was $\frac{1}{4}$ of the original cake for her best friend. What fractional part did she have left for herself?

   $\frac{1}{8}$

6. Wesley bought $\frac{1}{2}$ pound of nails for a project. When he finished the project, he had $\frac{1}{4}$ pound of the nails left. How many pounds of nails did he use?

   $\frac{1}{4}$ pound

Page 119

Name _____

Estimate Fraction Sums and Differences

You can round fractions to 0, to $\frac{1}{2}$, or to 1 to estimate sums and differences.

Estimate the sum. $\frac{4}{6} + \frac{1}{9}$

Step 1 Find $\frac{4}{6}$ on the number line. Is it closest to 0, $\frac{1}{2}$, or 1? The fraction $\frac{4}{6}$ is closest to $\frac{1}{2}$.

Step 2 Find $\frac{1}{9}$ on the number line. Is it closest to 0, $\frac{1}{2}$, or 1? The fraction $\frac{1}{9}$ is closest to 0.

Step 3 To estimate the sum $\frac{4}{6} + \frac{1}{9}$, add the two rounded numbers. $\frac{1}{2} + 0 = \frac{1}{2}$

So, $\frac{4}{6} + \frac{1}{9}$ is about $\frac{1}{2}$.

Estimate the sum or difference.   *Possible estimates are given.*

1. $\frac{4}{6} + \frac{1}{8}$ $\frac{1}{2}$

2. $\frac{2}{6} + \frac{7}{8}$ $1\frac{1}{2}$

3. $\frac{5}{6} - \frac{3}{8}$ $\frac{1}{2}$

4. $\frac{4}{6} + \frac{3}{8}$ 1

5. $\frac{7}{8} - \frac{5}{6}$ 0

6. $\frac{1}{6} + \frac{7}{8}$ 1

Page 120

Name _____

1. Ron walked $\frac{8}{10}$ mile from his grandmother's house to the store. Then he walked $\frac{9}{10}$ mile to his house. About how far did he walk altogether?
   - (A) about $\frac{1}{2}$ mile
   - (B) about 1 mile
   - (C) about $1\frac{1}{2}$ miles
   - (D) about 2 miles

2. Sophia baby-sat for $3\frac{7}{12}$ hours on Friday. She baby-sat $2\frac{5}{6}$ hours on Saturday. Which is the **best** estimate of how many hours Sophia baby-sat altogether?
   - (A) about $5\frac{1}{2}$ hours
   - (B) about 6 hours
   - (C) about $6\frac{1}{2}$ hours
   - (D) about 7 hours

3. Three fences on a ranch measure $\frac{15}{16}$ mile, $\frac{7}{8}$ mile, and $\frac{7}{16}$ mile. Which is the **best** estimate of the total length of all three fences?
   - (A) $1\frac{1}{2}$ miles
   - (B) 2 miles
   - (C) $2\frac{1}{2}$ miles
   - (D) 3 miles

4. Mr. Krasa poured $\frac{5}{16}$ gallon of white paint into a bucket. He then added $\frac{3}{4}$ gallon of blue paint and $\frac{3}{8}$ gallon of red paint. Which is the **best** estimate of the total amount of paint in the bucket?
   - (A) $\frac{3}{4}$ gallon
   - (B) 1 gallon
   - (C) $1\frac{1}{2}$ gallons
   - (D) 3 gallons

Problem Solving REAL WORLD

5. For a fruit salad recipe, Jenna combined $\frac{3}{8}$ cup of raisins, $\frac{7}{8}$ cup of oranges, and $\frac{3}{4}$ cup of apples. About how many cups of fruit are in the salad?

   Accept 2 or $2\frac{1}{2}$ cups

6. Tyler had $2\frac{7}{16}$ yards of fabric. He used $\frac{3}{4}$ yard to make a vest. About how much fabric did he have left?

   about $1\frac{1}{2}$ yards

Lesson 61 (Page 121)

Name _____

COMMON CORE STANDARD CC.5.NF.2
Lesson Objective: Solve problems using the strategy *work backward*.

Problem Solving • Practice Addition and Subtraction

Makayla walks for exercise. She wants to walk a total of 6 miles. On Monday, she walked $2\frac{5}{6}$ miles. On Tuesday, she walked $1\frac{1}{3}$ miles. How many more miles does Makayla need to walk to reach her goal?

Read the Problem	Solve the Problem
What do I need to find	• Start with the equation.
I need to find the distance that Makayla needs to walk.	$6 = 2\frac{5}{6} + 1\frac{1}{3} + x$
	Subtraction is the inverse operation of addition.
What information do I need to use?	• Use subtraction to work backward and rewrite the equation.
I need to use the distance she wants to walk and the distance she has already walked.	$6 - 2\frac{5}{6} - 1\frac{1}{3} = x$
	• Subtract to find the value of x.
How will I use the information?	$\begin{array}{r} 6 = 5\frac{6}{6} \\ -2\frac{5}{6} = -2\frac{5}{6} \\ \hline 3\frac{1}{6} \end{array} \rightarrow \begin{array}{r} 3\frac{1}{6} = 2\frac{7}{6} \\ -1\frac{1}{3} = -1\frac{2}{6} \\ \hline 1\frac{5}{6} \end{array}$
First I can write an equation $6 = 2\frac{5}{6} + 1\frac{1}{3} + x$	Estimate to show that your answer is reasonable.
Then I can work backward to solve the problem.	$3 + 1 + 2 = 6$
	So, Makayla has to walk $1\frac{5}{6}$ more miles to reach her goal.

1. Ben has $5\frac{3}{4}$ cups of sugar. He uses $\frac{2}{3}$ cup of sugar to make cookies. Then he uses $2\frac{1}{2}$ cups of sugar to make fresh lemonade. How many cups of sugar does Ben have left?

$2\frac{7}{12}$ cups

2. Cheryl has 5 ft of ribbon. She cuts a $3\frac{3}{4}$-ft strip to make a hair bow. Then she cuts a $\frac{2}{5}$-ft strip for a border on a scrapbook page. Is there enough ribbon for Cheryl to cut two $\frac{1}{3}$-ft pieces to put on a picture frame? **Explain.**

No, there is only $\frac{5}{12}$ ft. of ribbon left. Two $\frac{1}{3}$-ft pieces is $\frac{2}{3}$ ft, and $\frac{2}{3}$ is more than $\frac{5}{12}$.

Lesson 61 (Page 122)

Name _____

CC.5.NF.2

1. Jacques caught 3 fish weighing a total of $23\frac{1}{8}$ pounds. Two of the fish weighed $9\frac{5}{8}$ and $6\frac{1}{4}$ pounds. How much did the third fish weigh?

- (A) $6\frac{5}{8}$ pounds
- (B) $7\frac{3}{8}$ pounds
- (C) $7\frac{5}{8}$ pounds
- (D) $8\frac{3}{8}$ pounds

2. Maria bought a total of $1\frac{3}{4}$ dozen bagels. Of the total, she bought $\frac{1}{8}$ dozen whole grain bagels, $\frac{3}{4}$ dozen sesame seed bagels, and some plain bagels. How many dozen plain bagels did Maria buy?

- (A) $\frac{5}{8}$ dozen
- (B) 1 dozen
- (C) $1\frac{1}{4}$ dozen
- (D) $2\frac{2}{3}$ dozen

3. A squash, an apple, and an orange weigh a total of $2\frac{3}{4}$ pounds. The squash weighs $1\frac{5}{16}$ pounds, and the apple weighs $\frac{1}{4}$ pound. How much does the orange weigh?

- (A) $\frac{1}{8}$ pound
- (B) $\frac{3}{16}$ pound
- (C) $\frac{1}{4}$ pound
- (D) $\frac{5}{16}$ pound

4. Kelsey entered the triathlon at Camp Meadowlark. The total distance was $15\frac{11}{16}$ miles. The bike segment was $12\frac{1}{4}$ miles, and the running segment was $3\frac{3}{16}$ miles. How long was the swimming segment?

- (A) $\frac{3}{16}$ mile
- (B) $\frac{1}{4}$ mile
- (C) $\frac{5}{16}$ mile
- (D) $\frac{3}{8}$ mile

Problem Solving REAL WORLD

5. In three days this week, Julio worked $18\frac{7}{10}$ total hours. He worked $6\frac{1}{5}$ hours on the first day and $6\frac{2}{5}$ hours on the second day. Explain how you would find the number of hours Julio worked on the third day.

I would add the first two days together: $6\frac{1}{5} + 6\frac{2}{5} = 12\frac{3}{5}$. I would rename $12\frac{3}{5}$ as $12\frac{6}{10}$ and then subtract $12\frac{6}{10}$ from $18\frac{7}{10}$: $18\frac{7}{10} - 12\frac{6}{10} = 6\frac{1}{10}$.

Lesson 62 (Page 123)

Name _____

COMMON CORE STANDARD CC.5.NF.3
Lesson Objective: Solve division problems and decide when to write a remainder as a fraction.

Interpret the Remainder

Erin has 87 ounces of trail mix. She puts an equal number of ounces in each of 12 bags. How many ounces does she put in each bag?

$\begin{array}{r} 7\ r3 \\ 12\overline{)87} \\ -84 \\ \hline 3 \end{array}$

First, divide to find the quotient and remainder. Then, decide how to use the quotient and the remainder to answer the question.

- The dividend, 87, represents the total number of ounces of trail mix.
- The divisor, 12, represents the total number of bags.
- The quotient, 7, represents the whole-number part of the number of ounces in each bag.
- The remainder, 3, represents the number of ounces left over.

Divide the 3 ounces in the remainder by the divisor, 12, to write the remainder as a fraction: $\frac{3}{12}$.

Write the fraction part in simplest form in your answer.

So, Erin puts $7\frac{1}{4}$ ounces of trail mix in each bag.

Interpret the remainder to solve.

1. Harry goes on a canoe trip with his scout troop. They will canoe a total of 75 miles and want to travel 8 miles each day. How many days will they need to travel the entire distance?

10 days

2. Hannah and her family want to hike 8 miles per day along a 125-mile-long trail. How many days will Hannah and her family hike exactly 8 miles?

15 days

3. There are 103 students eating lunch in the cafeteria. Each table seats 4 students. All the tables are full, except for one table. How many students are sitting at the table that is not full?

3 students

4. Emily buys 240 square feet of carpet. She can convert square feet to square yards by dividing the number of square feet by 9. How many square yards of carpet did Emily buy? (Hint: Write the remainder as a fraction.)

$26\frac{2}{3}$ sq yd

Lesson 62 (Page 124)

Name _____

CC.5.NF.3

1. Taylor took 560 photographs during summer vacation. She placed 12 photos on each page of her scrapbook, except the last page. She had fewer than 12 photos to put on the last page. How many photos did Taylor place on the last page of the scrapbook?

- (A) 7
- (B) 8
- (C) 9
- (D) 10

2. Marla filled up her car's gas tank and then went on a trip. After she drove 329 miles, she filled her tank with 14 gallons of gas. If she drove the same number of miles on each gallon of gas, how many miles per gallon did Marla drive?

- (A) 23 miles per gallon
- (B) $23\frac{1}{2}$ miles per gallon
- (C) 24 miles per gallon
- (D) $24\frac{1}{2}$ miles per gallon

3. Kate made 180 ounces of punch for a party. She pours 8 ounces of punch for one serving. How many people can have a full serving?

- (A) 22
- (B) $22\frac{1}{2}$
- (C) 23
- (D) 25

4. The pool director has a list of 123 students who have signed up for swimming lessons. The pool director can register 7 students in each class. What is the **least** number of classes needed for all the students to be registered in a class?

- (A) 16
- (B) 17
- (C) 18
- (D) 19

Problem Solving REAL WORLD

5. Fiona bought 212 stickers to make a sticker book. If she places 18 stickers on each page, how many pages will her sticker book have?

12 pages

6. Jenny has 220 ounces of cleaning solution that she wants to divide equally among 12 large containers. How much cleaning solution should she put in each container?

$18\frac{1}{3}$ ounces

Answer Key

Lesson 63
COMMON CORE STANDARD CC.5.NF.3
Lesson Objective: Interpret a fraction as division and solve whole-number division problems that result in a fraction or mixed number.

Connect Fractions to Division

You can write a fraction as a division expression.

$$\frac{4}{5} = 4 \div 5 \qquad \frac{15}{3} = 15 \div 3$$

There are 8 students in a wood-working class and 5 sheets of plywood for them to share equally. What fraction of a sheet of plywood will each student get?

Divide. $5 \div 8$ **Use a drawing.**

Step 1 Draw __5__ rectangles to represent 5 sheets of plywood. Since there are 8 students, draw lines to divide each piece of plywood into __eighths__.

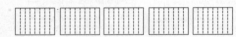

Each student's share of 1 sheet of plywood is $\frac{1}{8}$.

Step 2 Count the total number of eighths each student gets.

Since there are 5 sheets of plywood, each student will get 5 of the __eighths__, or $\frac{5}{8}$.

Step 3 Complete the number sentence.

$5 \div 8 = \frac{5}{8}$

Step 4 Check your answer.

Since $\frac{5}{8} \times \frac{8}{5} = \frac{5}{5}$, the quotient is correct.

So, each student will get $\frac{5}{8}$ of a sheet of plywood.

Complete the number sentence to solve.

1. Ten friends share 6 pizzas equally. What fraction of a pizza does each friend get?

$6 \div 10 = \frac{6}{10}$, or $\frac{3}{5}$

2. Four students share 7 sandwiches equally. How much of a sandwich does each student get?

$7 \div 4 = \frac{7}{4}$, or $1\frac{3}{4}$

Lesson 63
CC.5.NF.3

1. Four friends share 3 apples equally. What fraction of an apple does each friend get?
   - (A) $\frac{2}{3}$
   - (B) $\frac{3}{4}$
   - (C) $1\frac{1}{4}$
   - (D) $1\frac{1}{3}$

2. Ten pounds of rice are distributed equally into 6 bags to give out at the food bank. How many pounds of rice are in each bag?
   - (A) $\frac{3}{5}$ pound
   - (B) $1\frac{1}{3}$ pounds
   - (C) $1\frac{2}{3}$ pounds
   - (D) $1\frac{4}{5}$ pounds

3. Twelve friends share 4 pizzas equally. What fraction of a pizza does each friend get?
   - (A) $\frac{1}{12}$
   - (B) $\frac{1}{4}$
   - (C) $\frac{1}{4}$
   - (D) $\frac{1}{2}$

4. Terry picked 7 pounds of strawberries. She wants to share the strawberries equally among 3 of her neighbors. How many pounds of strawberries will each neighbor get?
   - (A) $\frac{3}{3}$ pound
   - (B) $\frac{7}{10}$ pound
   - (C) $1\frac{3}{7}$ pounds
   - (D) $2\frac{1}{3}$ pounds

Problem Solving

5. There are 12 students in a jewelry-making class and 8 sets of charms. What fraction of a set of charms will each student get?

Each student will get $\frac{2}{3}$ of a set.

6. Five friends share 6 cheesecakes equally. How many cheesecakes will each friend get?

Each friend will get $1\frac{1}{5}$ cheesecakes.

Lesson 64
COMMON CORE STANDARD CC.5.NF.4a
Lesson Objective: Model to find the fractional part of a group.

Find Part of a Group

Lauren bought 12 stamps for postcards. She gave Brianna $\frac{1}{6}$ of them. How many stamps did Lauren give to Brianna?

Find $\frac{1}{6}$ of 12.

Step 1 What is the denominator in the fraction of the stamps Lauren gave to Brianna? 6
So, divide the 12 stamps into 6 equal groups. Circle the groups.

Step 2 Each group represents $\frac{1}{6}$ of the stamps.

How many stamps are in 1 group? 2

So, $\frac{1}{6}$ of 12 is __2__, or $\frac{1}{6} \times 12$ is __2__.
So, Lauren gave Brianna __2__ stamps.

Use a model to solve.   **Check students' models.**

1. $\frac{3}{4} \times 12 = $ __9__

2. $\frac{1}{3} \times 9 = $ __3__

3. $\frac{3}{5} \times 20 = $ __12__

4. $\frac{4}{6} \times 18 = $ __12__

Lesson 64
CC.5.NF.4a

1. Sophie uses 18 beads to make a necklace. Three-sixths of the beads are purple. How many of Sophie's beads are purple?
   - (A) 6
   - (B) 9
   - (C) 12
   - (D) 15

2. Charlotte bought 16 songs. Three-fourths of the songs are pop songs.

How many of the songs are pop songs?
   - (A) 16
   - (B) 12
   - (C) 8
   - (D) 4

3. Mr. Walton ordered 12 pizzas for the art class celebration. One-fourth of the pizzas had only mushrooms.

How many of the pizzas had only mushrooms?
   - (A) 3   (C) 8
   - (B) 4   (D) 9

4. Trisha's mom baked 16 muffins. Two-eighths of the muffins have cranberries.

How many of the muffins have cranberries?
   - (A) 12   (C) 4
   - (B) 8   (D) 2

Problem Solving

5. Marco drew 20 pictures. He drew $\frac{3}{4}$ of them in art class. How many pictures did Marco draw in art class?

15 pictures

6. Caroline has 10 marbles. One half of them are blue. How many of Caroline's marbles are blue?

5 marbles

Answer Key

Lesson 65
COMMON CORE STANDARD CC.5.NF.4a
Lesson Objective: Model the product of a fraction and a whole number.

Multiply Fractions and Whole Numbers

Find the product. $\frac{3}{8} \times 4$

Step 1 Draw 4 rectangles to represent the factor 4.

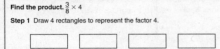

Step 2 The denominator of the factor $\frac{3}{8}$ is 8. So, divide the 4 rectangles into 8 equal parts.

Step 3 The numerator of the factor $\frac{3}{8}$ is 3. So, shade 3 of the parts.

Step 4 The 4 rectangles have 3 shaded parts. Each rectangle is divided into 2 equal parts. So, $\frac{6}{2}$ of the rectangles are shaded.

So, $\frac{3}{8} \times 4$ is $\frac{3}{2}$, or $1\frac{1}{2}$.

Find the product.

1. $\frac{5}{12} \times 4 = \underline{\frac{5}{3}, \text{ or } 1\frac{2}{3}}$ 2. $8 \times \frac{3}{4} = \underline{6}$ 3. $\frac{7}{9} \times 3 = \underline{\frac{7}{3}, \text{ or } 2\frac{1}{3}}$

4. $5 \times \frac{4}{7} = \underline{\frac{20}{7}, \text{ or } 2\frac{6}{7}}$ 5. $\frac{9}{10} \times 5 = \underline{\frac{9}{2}, \text{ or } 4\frac{1}{2}}$ 6. $3 \times \frac{3}{4} = \underline{\frac{9}{4}, \text{ or } 2\frac{1}{4}}$

7. $\frac{7}{12} \times 6 = \underline{\frac{7}{2}, \text{ or } 3\frac{1}{2}}$ 8. $12 \times \frac{2}{9} = \underline{\frac{24}{9}, \text{ or } 2\frac{2}{3}}$ 9. $\frac{2}{9} \times 3 = \underline{\frac{2}{3}}$

Lesson 65
CC.5.NF.4a

1. Gwen uses $\frac{2}{3}$ cup of sugar for one batch of cookies. She used a model to find how much sugar to use in 2 batches of cookies.

How much sugar does Gwen need for 2 batches of cookies?

- (A) $1\frac{1}{3}$ cups
- (B) $1\frac{2}{3}$ cups
- (C) $2\frac{1}{3}$ cups
- (D) $2\frac{2}{3}$ cups

2. Brandon used $\frac{3}{4}$ of an 8-ounce package of blueberries to make muffins. How many ounces of blueberries did he use for the muffins? You may use a model to help you solve the problem.

- (A) 2 ounces
- (B) 4 ounces
- (C) 6 ounces
- (D) $7\frac{1}{4}$ ounces

3. Yoshi wants $\frac{3}{5}$ of his garden to have red flowers. His garden has an area of 3 square yards. He used a model to find the area of his garden that will have red flowers.

What area of Yoshi's garden will have red flowers?

- (A) $1\frac{1}{5}$ square yards
- (B) $1\frac{4}{5}$ square yards
- (C) $2\frac{1}{5}$ square yards
- (D) $3\frac{3}{5}$ square yards

4. Kenya needs $\frac{1}{4}$ yard of material to make a placemat. How much material does she need for 6 placemats? You may use a model to help you solve the problem.

- (A) $1\frac{1}{4}$ yards
- (B) $1\frac{1}{2}$ yards
- (C) $1\frac{3}{4}$ yards
- (D) $6\frac{1}{4}$ yards

Problem Solving

5. Jody has a 5-pound bag of potatoes. She uses $\frac{4}{5}$ of the bag to make potato salad. How many pounds of potatoes does Jody use for the potato salad?

4 pounds

6. Lucas lives $\frac{5}{8}$ mile from school. Kenny lives twice as far as Lucas from school. How many miles does Kenny live from school?

$\frac{10}{8}$, or $1\frac{1}{4}$ **miles**

Lesson 66
COMMON CORE STANDARD CC.5.NF.4a
Lesson Objective: Multiply fractions and whole numbers.

Fraction and Whole Number Multiplication

Find the product. $3 \times \frac{5}{6}$

$3 \times \frac{5}{6} = \frac{3}{1} \times \frac{5}{6}$ Write the whole-number factor, 3, as $\frac{3}{1}$.

$= \frac{3 \times 5}{1 \times 6}$ Multiply the numerators. Then multiply the denominators.

$= \frac{15}{6}$

$= 2\frac{3}{6}$, or $2\frac{1}{2}$ Write the product as a mixed number in simplest form.

So, $3 \times \frac{5}{6}$ is $2\frac{1}{2}$.

Find the product. Write the product in simplest form.

1. $\frac{2}{3} \times 8 = \frac{2}{3} \times \frac{8}{1}$ 2. $4 \times \frac{2}{9} = \underline{\frac{8}{9}}$

$= \frac{2 \times 8}{3 \times 1}$

$= \frac{16}{3}$, or $\underline{5\frac{1}{3}}$

3. $6 \times \frac{3}{4} = \underline{\frac{9}{2}, \text{ or } 4\frac{1}{2}}$ 4. $\frac{4}{9} \times 3 = \underline{\frac{4}{3}, \text{ or } 1\frac{1}{3}}$ 5. $5 \times \frac{3}{8} = \underline{\frac{15}{8}, \text{ or } 1\frac{7}{8}}$

6. $9 \times \frac{2}{3} = \underline{6}$ 7. $2 \times \frac{5}{6} = \underline{\frac{5}{3}, \text{ or } 1\frac{2}{3}}$ 8. $7 \times \frac{4}{10} = \underline{\frac{14}{5}, \text{ or } 2\frac{4}{5}}$

Lesson 66
CC.5.NF.4a

1. Julia has a recipe for salad dressing that calls for $\frac{1}{4}$ cup of sugar. Julia is making 5 batches of the salad dressing. How much sugar will she use?

- (A) $\frac{4}{5}$ cup
- (B) $1\frac{1}{5}$ cups
- (C) $1\frac{1}{4}$ cups
- (D) $5\frac{1}{4}$ cups

2. Taniqua took a test that had 20 questions. She got $\frac{4}{5}$ of the questions correct. How many questions did Taniqua get correct?

- (A) 25
- (B) 16
- (C) 15
- (D) 12

3. In a class book order, $\frac{2}{5}$ of the books are fantasy and $\frac{1}{4}$ of the books are biography. If the order contains 60 books, how many books are either fantasy or biography?

- (A) 15
- (B) 30
- (C) 40
- (D) 55

4. Laurie runs around a track that is $\frac{1}{4}$ mile long. If she does 10 laps around the track, how far does she run?

- (A) $\frac{2}{5}$ mile
- (B) $2\frac{1}{4}$ miles
- (C) $2\frac{1}{2}$ miles
- (D) $10\frac{1}{4}$ miles

Problem Solving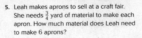

5. Leah makes aprons to sell at a craft fair. She needs $\frac{3}{4}$ yard of material to make each apron. How much material does Leah need to make 6 aprons?

$4\frac{1}{2}$ **yards**

6. The gas tank of Mr. Tanaka's car holds 15 gallons of gas. He used $\frac{2}{3}$ of a tank of gas last week. How many gallons of gas did Mr. Tanaka use?

10 gallons

Answer Key

Lesson 67
COMMON CORE STANDARD CC.5.NF.4a
Lesson Objective: Multiply fractions.

Fraction Multiplication

To multiply fractions, you can multiply the numerators, then multiply the denominators. Write the product in simplest form.

Multiply. $\frac{3}{10} \times \frac{4}{5}$

Step 1 Multiply the numerators. Multiply the denominators.

$$\frac{3}{10} \times \frac{4}{5} = \frac{3 \times 4}{10 \times 5}$$
$$= \frac{12}{50}$$

Step 2 Write the product in simplest form.

$$\frac{12}{50} = \frac{12 \div 2}{50 \div 2}$$
$$= \frac{6}{25}$$

So, $\frac{3}{10} \times \frac{4}{5}$ is $\frac{6}{25}$.

Find the product. Write the product in simplest form.

1. $\frac{3}{4} \times \frac{1}{5}$ $\frac{3}{20}$

2. $\frac{4}{7} \times \frac{5}{12}$ $\frac{5}{21}$

3. $\frac{3}{8} \times \frac{2}{9}$ $\frac{1}{12}$

4. $\frac{4}{5} \times \frac{5}{8}$ $\frac{1}{2}$

5. $\frac{1}{3} \times 4$ $\frac{4}{3}$, or $1\frac{1}{3}$

6. $\frac{3}{4} \times 8$ 6

7. $\frac{5}{8} \times \frac{2}{3}$ $\frac{5}{12}$

8. $\frac{5}{6} \times \frac{3}{8}$ $\frac{5}{16}$

Lesson 67
CC.5.NF.4a

1. Julia has a recipe for salad dressing that calls for $\frac{3}{4}$ cup of vegetable oil. How much vegetable oil should she use to make $\frac{1}{2}$ of the recipe for salad dressing?
   Ⓐ $1\frac{1}{4}$ cups
   Ⓑ $\frac{2}{3}$ cup
   Ⓒ $\frac{1}{2}$ cup
   Ⓓ $\frac{3}{8}$ cup

2. A scientist had $\frac{3}{4}$ liter of solution. He used $\frac{1}{6}$ of the solution for an experiment. How much solution did the scientist use for the experiment?
   Ⓐ $\frac{1}{8}$ liter
   Ⓑ $\frac{3}{8}$ liter
   Ⓒ $\frac{1}{2}$ liter
   Ⓓ $\frac{7}{12}$ liter

3. Of the flowers on Jill's front lawn, $\frac{2}{5}$ are tulips. Of the tulips, $\frac{5}{8}$ are yellow. What fraction of the flowers on Jill's front lawn are yellow tulips?
   Ⓐ $\frac{7}{13}$
   Ⓑ $\frac{1}{2}$
   Ⓒ $\frac{1}{4}$
   Ⓓ $\frac{1}{8}$

4. Otis bought a total of $\frac{7}{10}$ pound of grapes and cherries. The weight of the grapes is $\frac{2}{3}$ of the total weight. What is the weight of the grapes?
   Ⓐ $\frac{3}{10}$ pound
   Ⓑ $\frac{7}{15}$ pound
   Ⓒ $\frac{9}{13}$ pound
   Ⓓ $\frac{20}{21}$ pound

Problem Solving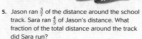

5. Jason ran $\frac{5}{7}$ of the distance around the school track. Sara ran $\frac{4}{5}$ of Jason's distance. What fraction of the total distance around the track did Sara run?

   $\frac{4}{7}$

6. A group of students attend a math club. Half of the students are boys and $\frac{4}{9}$ of the boys have brown eyes. What fraction of the group are boys with brown eyes?

   $\frac{2}{9}$

Lesson 68
COMMON CORE STANDARD CC.5.NF.4b
Lesson Objective: Multiply fractions using models.

Multiply Fractions

You can use a model to help you multiply two fractions.

Multiply. $\frac{1}{3} \times \frac{4}{5}$

Step 1 Draw a rectangle. Divide it into 5 equal columns. To represent the factor $\frac{4}{5}$, shade 4 of the 5 columns.

Step 2 Now divide the rectangle into 3 equal rows. Shade $\frac{1}{3}$ of the $\frac{4}{5}$ you already shaded.

The rectangle is divided into 15 smaller rectangles. This is the denominator of the product.

There are 4 smaller rectangles that contain both types of shading. So, 4 is the numerator of the product.

So $\frac{4}{15}$ of the rectangles contain both types of shading.

Think: What is $\frac{1}{3}$ of $\frac{4}{5}$?

$$\frac{1}{3} \times \frac{4}{5} = \frac{4}{15}$$

Find the product. Draw a model.

1.
   $\frac{1}{4} \times \frac{2}{3} = \frac{2}{12}$, or $\frac{1}{6}$

2.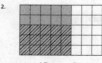
   $\frac{3}{5} \times \frac{5}{8} = \frac{15}{40}$, or $\frac{3}{8}$

3.
   $\frac{2}{5} \times \frac{3}{4} = \frac{6}{20}$, or $\frac{3}{10}$

4.
   $\frac{2}{3} \times \frac{3}{8} = \frac{6}{24}$, or $\frac{1}{4}$

Lesson 68
CC.5.NF.4b

1. Marta breaded $\frac{1}{2}$ of the fish she cooked for dinner. She ate $\frac{1}{3}$ of the breaded fish. She used a model to find how much of the fish she had eaten.

   How much of the fish did Marta eat?
   Ⓐ $\frac{1}{6}$
   Ⓑ $\frac{1}{5}$
   Ⓒ $\frac{2}{15}$
   Ⓓ $\frac{2}{3}$

2. Lawrence bought $\frac{2}{5}$ pound of roast beef. He used $\frac{3}{4}$ of it to make a sandwich. How much roast beef did Lawrence use for his sandwich? You may use a model to help you solve the problem.
   Ⓐ $\frac{5}{12}$ pound
   Ⓑ $\frac{1}{2}$ pound
   Ⓒ $\frac{5}{7}$ pound
   Ⓓ $\frac{6}{7}$ pound

3. Alexa planted tulips in $\frac{2}{5}$ of her garden. Of the tulips, $\frac{2}{3}$ are yellow tulips. She used a model to find what part of her garden has yellow tulips.

   What part of Alexa's garden has yellow tulips?
   Ⓐ $\frac{2}{15}$ Ⓒ $\frac{1}{3}$
   Ⓑ $\frac{4}{15}$ Ⓓ $\frac{1}{2}$

4. A scientist has a bottle that is $\frac{5}{8}$ full of solution. He uses $\frac{2}{5}$ of the solution in the bottle for an experiment. How much of a full bottle of solution does he use? You may use a model to help you solve the problem.
   Ⓐ $\frac{7}{13}$
   Ⓑ $\frac{1}{2}$
   Ⓒ $\frac{1}{4}$
   Ⓓ $\frac{1}{40}$

Problem Solving

5. Nora has a piece of ribbon that is $\frac{3}{4}$ yard long. She will use $\frac{1}{2}$ of it to make a bow. What length of the ribbon will she use for the bow?

   $\frac{3}{8}$ yard

6. Marlon bought $\frac{7}{8}$ pound of turkey at the deli. He used $\frac{2}{3}$ of it to make sandwiches for lunch. How much of the turkey did Marlon use for sandwiches?

   $\frac{7}{12}$ pound

Lesson 69

Name _____

COMMON CORE STANDARD CC.5.NF.4b
Lesson Objective: Use a model to multiply two mixed numbers and find the area of a rectangle.

Area and Mixed Numbers

You can use an area model to help you multiply mixed numbers.

Find the area. $1\frac{4}{5} \times 2\frac{1}{3}$

Step 1 Rewrite each mixed-number factor as the sum of a whole number and a fraction.

$1\frac{4}{5} = 1 + \frac{4}{5}$ and $2\frac{1}{3} = 2 + \frac{1}{3}$

Step 2 Draw an area model to show the original multiplication problem.

Step 3 Draw dashed lines, and label each section to show how you broke apart the mixed numbers in Step 1.

Step 4 Find the area of each section.

$1 \times 2 = \underline{\;2\;}$

$1 \times \frac{1}{3} = \underline{\;\frac{1}{3}\;}$

$\frac{4}{5} \times 2 = \underline{\;\frac{8}{5}\;}$

$\frac{4}{5} \times \frac{1}{3} = \underline{\;\frac{4}{15}\;}$

Step 5 Add the areas of each of the sections to find the total area of the rectangle.

$2 + \frac{1}{3} + \frac{8}{5} + \frac{4}{15} = \boxed{\frac{30}{15}} + \boxed{\frac{5}{15}} + \boxed{\frac{24}{15}} + \frac{4}{15}$

$= \boxed{\frac{63}{15}}$, or $4\frac{1}{5}$

So, $1\frac{4}{5} \times 2\frac{1}{3}$ is $4\frac{1}{5}$.

Use an area model to solve.

1. $1\frac{2}{3} \times 2\frac{1}{4}$ 2. $1\frac{3}{4} \times 2\frac{3}{5}$ 3. $2\frac{1}{2} \times 1\frac{1}{3}$

    $3\frac{3}{4}$ $4\frac{11}{20}$ $3\frac{1}{3}$

Lesson 69

Name _____

CC.5.NF.4b

1. Ana has a poster that is $1\frac{2}{3}$ feet high and $2\frac{1}{4}$ feet wide. She used an area model to find the area of the poster.

What is the area of Ana's poster?

- (A) $3\frac{1}{2}$ square feet
- (B) $3\frac{3}{4}$ square feet
- (C) $3\frac{11}{12}$ square feet
- (D) $4\frac{1}{2}$ square feet

2. The top of Colin's desk is $2\frac{2}{3}$ feet long and $2\frac{1}{4}$ feet wide. What is the area of the top of Colin's desk? You may use an area model to help you.

- (A) $4\frac{1}{6}$ square feet
- (B) $4\frac{11}{12}$ square feet
- (C) $5\frac{11}{12}$ square feet
- (D) 6 square feet

3. Eloise is painting a mural that is $1\frac{3}{4}$ yards long and $1\frac{1}{4}$ yards high. She uses a grid to find the area of the mural.

What is the area of the mural?

- (A) $2\frac{3}{16}$ square yards
- (B) 6 square yards
- (C) $8\frac{3}{4}$ square yards
- (D) 35 square yards

4. A ping pong table is $2\frac{3}{4}$ meters long and $1\frac{1}{2}$ meters wide. What is the area of the ping pong table? You may use an area model to help you.

- (A) $4\frac{1}{8}$ square meters
- (B) $4\frac{1}{4}$ square meters
- (C) $4\frac{3}{8}$ square meters
- (D) $4\frac{1}{2}$ square meters

Problem Solving *REAL WORLD*

5. Ava's bedroom rug is $2\frac{3}{4}$ feet long and $2\frac{1}{2}$ feet wide. What is the area of the rug?

    $6\frac{7}{8}$ square feet

6. A painting is $2\frac{2}{3}$ feet long and $1\frac{1}{2}$ feet high. What is the area of the painting?

    4 square feet

Lesson 70

Name _____

COMMON CORE STANDARD CC.5.NF.5a
Lesson Objective: Relate the size of the product compared to the size of one factor when multiplying fractions.

Compare Fraction Factors and Products

You can use a model to determine how the size of the product compares to the size of one factor when multiplying fractions.

The factor is 1: $\frac{2}{3} \times 1$

- Draw a model to represent the factor 1. Divide it into 3 equal sections.
- Shade 2 of the 3 sections to represent the factor $\frac{2}{3}$.
- $\frac{2}{3}$ of the rectangle is shaded. So, $\frac{2}{3} \times 1$ is $\underline{\text{equal to}}$ $\frac{2}{3}$.

The factor is greater than 1: $\frac{2}{3} \times 2$

- Draw two rectangles to represent the factor 2. Divide each rectangle into 3 equal sections.
- Shade 2 of 3 sections in each to represent the factor $\frac{2}{3}$.

In all, 4 sections are shaded, which is greater than the number of sections in one rectangle. So, $\frac{2}{3} \times 2$ is $\underline{\text{greater than}}$ $\frac{2}{3}$.

The factor is less than 1: $\frac{2}{3} \times \frac{1}{6}$

- Draw a rectangle. Divide it into 6 equal columns. Shade 1 of the 6 columns to represent the factor $\frac{1}{6}$.
- Now divide the rectangle into 3 equal rows. Shade 2 of the 3 rows of the section already shaded to represent the factor $\frac{2}{3}$.

The rectangle is divided into 18 sections. 2 of the sections are shaded twice. 2 sections is less than the 3 sections that represent $\frac{1}{6}$.

So, $\frac{2}{3} \times \frac{1}{6}$ is $\underline{\text{less than}}$ $\frac{1}{6}$.

Complete the statement with *equal to*, *greater than*, or *less than*.

1. $\frac{3}{7} \times \frac{2}{5}$ will be $\underline{\text{less than}}$ $\frac{3}{7}$.

2. $\frac{7}{8} \times 3$ will be $\underline{\text{greater than}}$ $\frac{7}{8}$.

3. $\frac{1}{6} \times \frac{5}{5}$ will be $\underline{\text{equal to}}$ $\frac{1}{6}$.

4. $5 \times \frac{6}{7}$ will be $\underline{\text{less than}}$ 5.

Lesson 70

Name _____

CC.5.NF.5a

1. Doreen lives $\frac{3}{4}$ mile from the library. If Sheila lives $\frac{1}{2}$ as far away as Doreen, which statement below is true?

- (A) Sheila lives closer to the library.
- (B) Doreen lives closer to the library.
- (C) Sheila lives twice as far from the library as Doreen.
- (D) They live the same distance from the library.

2. Mrs. Stephens wrote 4 statements on the board and asked the class which one was true. Which statement below is true?

- (A) $\frac{5}{6} \times \frac{5}{6}$ is equal to $\frac{5}{6}$.
- (B) $\frac{2}{3} \times \frac{1}{3}$ is less than $\frac{2}{3}$.
- (C) $\frac{7}{8} \times 8$ is less than $\frac{7}{8}$.
- (D) $\frac{3}{5} \times 5$ is greater than 5.

3. Nadia needs $\frac{3}{4}$ cup of orange juice for a punch recipe. She will double the recipe to make punch for a party. Which statement below is true?

- (A) She will be using the same amount of orange juice.
- (B) She will be using less orange juice.
- (C) She will be using more orange juice.
- (D) She will be using $\frac{3}{4}$ as much orange juice.

4. It took Mary Lou $\frac{5}{6}$ hour to write a report for her English class. It took Heather $\frac{9}{10}$ as much time to write her report as it took Mary Lou. Which statement below is true?

- (A) It took them both the same amount of time.
- (B) Mary Lou spent less time writing her book report than Heather.
- (C) Mary Lou spent more time writing her book report than Heather.
- (D) It took Heather twice as long to write her book report than it took Mary Lou to write her book report.

Problem Solving *REAL WORLD*

5. Starla is making hot cocoa. She plans to multiply the recipe by 4 to make enough hot cocoa for the whole class. If the recipe calls for $\frac{1}{2}$ teaspoon vanilla extract, will she need more than $\frac{1}{2}$ teaspoon or less than $\frac{1}{2}$ teaspoon of vanilla extract to make all the hot cocoa?

    more than $\frac{1}{2}$ teaspoon
    vanilla extract

6. Miles is planning to spend $\frac{2}{3}$ as many hours bicycling this week as he did last week. Is Miles going to spend more hours or fewer hours bicycling this week than last week?

    fewer hours

Answer Key

Name _____

Lesson 71

COMMON CORE STANDARD CC.5.NF.5a
Lesson Objective: Relate the size of the product to the factors when multiplying fractions greater than one.

Compare Mixed Number Factors and Products

Complete each statement with equal to, greater than, or less than.

$1 \times 1\frac{3}{4}$ is __?__ $1\frac{3}{4}$.

The Identity Property of Multiplication states that the product of

1 and any number is that number. So, $1 \times 1\frac{3}{4}$ is __equal to__ $1\frac{3}{4}$.

$\frac{1}{2} \times 2\frac{1}{4}$ is __?__ $2\frac{1}{4}$.

Draw three rectangles. Divide each rectangle into 4 equal columns.

Shade completely the first two rectangles and one column of the last rectangle to represent $\frac{1}{4}$.

Divide the rectangles into 2 rows. Shade one row to represent the factor $\frac{1}{2}$.

18 small rectangles are shaded. 9 rectangles have both types of shading. 9 rectangles is less than the 18 rectangles that represent $2\frac{1}{4}$.

So, $\frac{1}{2} \times 2\frac{1}{4}$ is __less than__ $2\frac{1}{4}$.

When you multiply a mixed number by a fraction less than 1,

the product will be __less than__ the mixed number.

$1\frac{1}{4} \times 1\frac{3}{4}$ is __?__ $1\frac{1}{4}$.

Use what you know about the product of two whole numbers greater than 1 to determine the size of the product of two mixed numbers.

So, $1\frac{1}{4} \times 1\frac{3}{4}$ is __greater than__ $1\frac{1}{4}$ and __greater than__ $1\frac{3}{4}$.

When you multiply two mixed numbers, their product is __greater than__ either factor.

Complete the statement with equal to, greater than, or less than.

1. $\frac{3}{5} \times 1\frac{2}{7}$ is __less than__ $1\frac{2}{7}$

2. $\frac{6}{6} \times 3\frac{1}{3}$ is __equal to__ $3\frac{1}{3}$

3. $2\frac{1}{5} \times 1\frac{1}{4}$ is __greater than__ $1\frac{1}{4}$

4. $\frac{8}{9} \times 4\frac{3}{4}$ is __less than__ $4\frac{3}{4}$

www.harcourtschoolsupply.com
© Houghton Mifflin Harcourt Publishing Company

141

Core Standards for Math, Grade 5

Name _____

Lesson 71
CC.5.NF.5a

1. Stuart rode his bicycle $6\frac{3}{5}$ miles last week. This week he rode $1\frac{1}{3}$ times as far as he rode last week. Which statement below is true?

   (A) He rode the same number of miles both weeks.

   (B) He rode fewer miles this week.

   (C) He rode more miles this week.

   (D) He rode twice as many miles this week.

2. Mrs. Thompson is buying $1\frac{3}{4}$ pounds of turkey and $\frac{3}{4}$ as much cheese as turkey at a deli. Which statement below is true?

   (A) She is buying the same amount of turkey and cheese.

   (B) She is buying less turkey than cheese.

   (C) She is buying twice as much turkey as cheese.

   (D) She is buying more turkey than cheese.

3. Miss Parks wrote 4 statements on the board and asked the class which one was true. Which statement below is true?

   (A) $3\frac{2}{5} \times \frac{4}{5}$ is greater than $3\frac{2}{5}$

   (B) $1\frac{7}{8} \times 2\frac{1}{3}$ is greater than $2\frac{1}{3}$

   (C) $2\frac{5}{6} \times \frac{8}{8}$ is less than $2\frac{5}{6}$

   (D) $2\frac{3}{8} \times 4$ is less than 4.

4. Diana worked on her science project for $5\frac{1}{3}$ hours. Gabe worked on his science project $1\frac{1}{4}$ times as long as Diana. Which statement below is true?

   (A) Gabe spent more time on his science project than Diana did on hers.

   (B) Diana worked on her science project longer than Gabe worked on his.

   (C) Gabe worked on his science project twice as long as Diana worked on hers.

   (D) They both worked on their science projects the same amount of time.

Problem Solving REAL WORLD

5. Fraser is making a scale drawing of a dog house. The dimensions of the drawing will be $\frac{1}{8}$ of the dimensions of the actual doghouse. The height of the actual doghouse is $36\frac{3}{4}$ inches. Will the dimensions of Fraser's drawing be equal to, greater than, or less than the dimensions of the actual dog house?

   __less than__

6. Jorge has a recipe that calls for $2\frac{1}{3}$ cups of flour. He plans to make $1\frac{1}{2}$ times the recipe. Will the amount of flour Jorge needs be equal to, greater than, or less than the amount of flour his recipe calls for?

   __greater than__

www.harcourtschoolsupply.com
© Houghton Mifflin Harcourt Publishing Company

142

Core Standards for Math, Grade 5

Name _____

Lesson 72
COMMON CORE STANDARD CC.5.NF.5b
Lesson Objective: Solve problems using the strategy guess, check, and revise.

Problem Solving • Find Unknown Lengths

Zach built a rectangular deck in his backyard. The area of the deck is 300 square feet. The length of the deck is $1\frac{1}{3}$ times as long as the width. What are the dimensions of the deck?

Read the Problem

What do I need to find?	What information do I need to use?	How will I use the information?
I need to find __the dimensions of the deck__	The deck has an area of __300__ square feet, and the length is __$1\frac{1}{3}$__ as long as the width.	I will __guess__ the length and width of the deck. Then I will __check__ my guess and __revise__ it if it is not correct.

Solve the Problem

I can try different values for the length of the deck, each that is $1\frac{1}{3}$ times as long as the width. Then I can multiply the length and width and compare to the correct area.

Guess		Check	Revise
Width (in feet)	Length (in feet) ($1\frac{1}{3}$ times the width)	Area of Deck (in square feet)	
12	$1\frac{1}{3} \times 12 = $ __16__	$12 \times 16 = $ __192__ too low	Try a __longer__ width.
18	$1\frac{1}{3} \times 18 = $ __24__	$18 \times 24 = $ __432__ too high	Try a __shorter__ width.
15	$1\frac{1}{3} \times 15 = $ __20__	$15 \times 20 = $ __300__ correct	

So, the dimensions of the deck are __20__ feet by __15__ feet.

1. Abigail made a quilt that has an area of 4,800 square inches. The length of the quilt is $1\frac{1}{3}$ times the width of the quilt. What are the dimensions of the quilt?

   __60 inches by 80 inches__

2. The width of the mirror in Shannon's bathroom is $\frac{4}{9}$ its length. The area of the mirror is 576 square inches. What are the dimensions of the mirror?

   __16 inches by 36 inches__

www.harcourtschoolsupply.com
© Houghton Mifflin Harcourt Publishing Company

143

Core Standards for Math, Grade 5

Name _____

Lesson 72
CC.5.NF.5b

1. Louis wants to carpet the rectangular floor of his basement. The basement has an area of 864 square feet. The width of the basement is $\frac{2}{3}$ its length. What is the length of Louis's basement?

   (A) 24 feet

   (B) 36 feet

   (C) 48 feet

   (D) 576 feet

2. Sally painted a picture that has an area of 480 square inches. The length of the painting is $1\frac{1}{5}$ as long as it is wide. Which of the following could be the dimensions of Sally's painting?

   (A) 20 inches by 24 inches

   (B) 12 inches by 40 inches

   (C) 16 inches by 30 inches

   (D) 15 inches by 32 inches

3. A rectangular park has an area of 6 square miles. The width of the property is $\frac{3}{8}$ the length of the property. What is the width of the property?

   (A) $1\frac{1}{2}$ miles

   (B) $2\frac{1}{4}$ miles

   (C) 3 miles

   (D) 4 miles

4. A pool at a park takes up an area of 540 square yards. The length is $1\frac{2}{3}$ times as long as the width. Which of the following could be the dimensions of the pool?

   (A) 21 yards by 35 yards

   (B) 20 yards by 27 yards

   (C) 15 yards by 36 yards

   (D) 18 yards by 30 yards

Problem Solving REAL WORLD

5. Brianna has a rug that has an area of 24 square feet. The width of the rug is $\frac{2}{3}$ the length of the rug. Explain how you can find the length and the width of the rug.

   Possible explanation: I can use the strategy guess, check, and revise. My first guess would be a length of 8 feet. The width would be $\frac{2}{3} \times 8 = \frac{16}{3}$ or $5\frac{1}{3}$ feet. The area would be $8 \times 5\frac{1}{3} = 42\frac{2}{3}$ square feet, which is more than 24 square feet. My second guess would be a length of 6 feet. The width would be $\frac{2}{3} \times 6 = \frac{12}{3}$ or 4 feet. The area would be $6 \times 4 = 24$ square feet, which is correct. So the length is 6 feet and the width is 4 feet.

www.harcourtschoolsupply.com
© Houghton Mifflin Harcourt Publishing Company

144

Core Standards for Math, Grade 5

---

www.harcourtschoolsupply.com
© Houghton Mifflin Harcourt Publishing Company

236

Core Standards for Math, Grade 5

Answer Key

Lesson 73 — Multiply Mixed Numbers
COMMON CORE STANDARD CC.5.NF.6
Lesson Objective: Multiply mixed numbers.

Name _____

You can use a multiplication square to multiply mixed numbers.

Multiply. $1\frac{2}{7} \times 1\frac{3}{4}$ **Write the product in simplest form.**

Step 1 Write the mixed numbers outside the square.

Step 2 Multiply the number in each column by the number in each row.

Step 3 Write each product inside the square.

×	1	$\frac{2}{7}$
1		
$\frac{3}{4}$		

×	1	$\frac{2}{7}$
1	1×1	$\frac{2}{7} \times 1$
$\frac{3}{4}$	$1 \times \frac{3}{4}$	$\frac{2}{7} \times \frac{3}{4}$

×	1	$\frac{2}{7}$
1	1	$\frac{2}{7}$
$\frac{3}{4}$	$\frac{3}{4}$	$\frac{3}{14}$

Step 4 Add the products inside the multiplication square. $1 + \frac{2}{7} + \frac{3}{4} + \frac{3}{14}$

Find the least common denominator. $\frac{28}{28} + \frac{8}{28} + \frac{21}{28} + \frac{6}{28} = \frac{63}{28}$

Simplify. $\frac{63}{28} = 2\frac{7}{28}$, or $2\frac{1}{4}$

So, $1\frac{2}{7} \times 1\frac{3}{4}$ is $2\frac{1}{4}$.

Find the product. Write the product in simplest form.

1. $2\frac{5}{8} \times 1\frac{1}{7}$ **3**

2. $3\frac{1}{2} \times 12$ **42**

3. $10\frac{5}{6} \times \frac{3}{5}$ **$\frac{13}{2}$, or $6\frac{1}{2}$**

4. $7\frac{7}{10} \times \frac{10}{11}$ **7**

Use the Distributive Property to find the product.

5. $12 \times 2\frac{1}{2}$ **30**

6. $15 \times 5\frac{1}{3}$ **80**

www.harcourtschoolsupply.com
© Houghton Mifflin Harcourt Publishing Company
145
Core Standards for Math, Grade 5

Lesson 73
CC.5.NF.6

Name _____

1. Jared made $12\frac{3}{4}$ cups of snack mix for a party. His guests ate $\frac{2}{3}$ of the mix. How much snack mix did his guests eat?
   - Ⓐ $4\frac{5}{12}$ cups
   - Ⓑ $4\frac{1}{2}$ cups
   - Ⓒ $8\frac{1}{2}$ cups
   - Ⓓ $12\frac{5}{7}$ cups

2. Kayla walks $3\frac{7}{10}$ miles for exercise each day. What is the total number of miles she walks in 31 days?
   - Ⓐ $117\frac{4}{10}$ miles
   - **Ⓑ $114\frac{7}{10}$ miles**
   - Ⓒ $34\frac{7}{10}$ miles
   - Ⓓ $6\frac{4}{5}$ miles

3. Carlos has $7\frac{1}{2}$ acres of farmland. He uses $\frac{1}{3}$ of the acres to graze animals and $\frac{1}{2}$ of the acres to grow vegetables. How many acres does Carlos use for grazing animals or for growing vegetables?
   - Ⓐ $1\frac{1}{2}$ acres
   - Ⓑ $2\frac{1}{2}$ acres
   - Ⓒ 4 acres
   - **Ⓓ $6\frac{29}{30}$ acres**

4. The table shows how many hours some students worked on their math project.

Math Project

Name	Hours Worked
Carl	$5\frac{1}{4}$
Sonia	$6\frac{1}{2}$
Tony	$5\frac{2}{3}$

April worked $1\frac{1}{2}$ times as long on her math project as Carl. For how many hours did April work on her math project?
   - Ⓐ $5\frac{3}{8}$ hours
   - Ⓑ $6\frac{1}{3}$ hours
   - Ⓒ $7\frac{1}{4}$ hours
   - **Ⓓ $7\frac{7}{8}$ hours**

Problem Solving REAL WORLD

5. Jake can carry $6\frac{1}{4}$ pounds of wood in from the barn. His father can carry $1\frac{2}{3}$ times as much as Jake. How many pounds can Jake's father carry?

   $10\frac{5}{7}$ pounds

6. A glass can hold $3\frac{1}{4}$ cups of water. A bowl can hold $2\frac{2}{3}$ times the amount in the glass. How many cups can a bowl hold?

   $8\frac{2}{3}$ cups

www.harcourtschoolsupply.com
© Houghton Mifflin Harcourt Publishing Company
146
Core Standards for Math, Grade 5

Lesson 74 — Divide Fractions and Whole Numbers
COMMON CORE STANDARDS CC.5.NF.7a, CC.5.NF.7b
Lesson Objective: Divide a whole number by a fraction and divide a fraction by a whole number.

Name _____

You can use a number line to help you divide a whole number by a fraction.

Divide. $6 \div \frac{1}{2}$

Step 1 Draw a number line from 0 to 6. Divide the number line into halves. Label each half on your number line, starting with $\frac{1}{2}$.

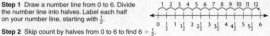

Step 2 Skip count by halves from 0 to 6 to find $6 \div \frac{1}{2}$.

Step 3 Count the number of skips. It takes 12 skips to go from 0 to 6. So the quotient is 12.

$6 \div \frac{1}{2} = \underline{12}$ because $\underline{12} \times \frac{1}{2} = 6$.

You can use fraction strips to divide a fraction by a whole number.

Divide. $\frac{1}{2} \div 5$

Step 1 Place a $\frac{1}{2}$ strip under a 1-whole strip.

Step 2 Find 5 fraction strips, all with the same denominator, that fit exactly under the $\frac{1}{2}$ strip. Each part is $\frac{1}{10}$ of the whole.

Step 3 Record and check the quotient.

$\frac{1}{2} \div 5 = \frac{1}{10}$ because $\frac{1}{10} \times 5 = \frac{1}{2}$.

So, $\frac{1}{2} \div 5 = \frac{1}{10}$.

Divide. Draw a number line or use fraction strips.

1. $1 \div \frac{1}{2} = $ **2**

2. $2 \div \frac{1}{3} = $ **6**

3. $4 \div \frac{1}{4} = $ **16**

4. $\frac{1}{5} \div 3 = $ **$\frac{1}{15}$**

5. $\frac{1}{3} \div 2 = $ **$\frac{1}{6}$**

6. $4 \div \frac{1}{5} = $ **20**

www.harcourtschoolsupply.com
© Houghton Mifflin Harcourt Publishing Company
147
Core Standards for Math, Grade 5

Lesson 74
CC.5.NF.7a, CC.5.NF.7b

Name _____

1. Olivia needs to find the number of $\frac{1}{3}$-cup servings in 2 cups of rice. She used the number line below to find $2 \div \frac{1}{3}$.

   How many $\frac{1}{3}$-cup servings of rice are in 2 cups of rice?
   - Ⓐ 2
   - Ⓑ 3
   - Ⓒ 5
   - **Ⓓ 6**

2. Kwami bought 8 yards of lanyard. He cut the lanyard into $\frac{1}{2}$-yard pieces. How many pieces of lanyard did Kwami make?
   - Ⓐ 2
   - Ⓑ 8
   - **Ⓒ 16**
   - Ⓓ 64

3. Chris divided $\frac{1}{2}$ pound of nails into 6 small bags with the same amount in each bag. He used fraction strips to find the weight of each bag.

   How much does each small bag weigh?
   - Ⓐ $\frac{1}{2}$ pound
   - Ⓑ $\frac{1}{3}$ pound
   - Ⓒ $\frac{1}{6}$ pound
   - **Ⓓ $\frac{1}{12}$ pound**

4. Josie filled a watering can with $\frac{1}{3}$ quart of water. She poured the same amount of water from the can onto each of 3 plants. How much water did Josie pour onto each plant?
   - **Ⓐ $\frac{1}{9}$ quart**
   - Ⓑ $2\frac{2}{3}$ quarts
   - Ⓒ 3 quarts
   - Ⓓ 9 quarts

Problem Solving REAL WORLD

5. Amy can run $\frac{1}{10}$ mile per minute. How many minutes will it take Amy to run 3 miles?

   30 minutes

6. Jeremy has 3 yards of ribbon to use for wrapping gifts. He cuts the ribbon into pieces that are $\frac{1}{4}$ yard long. How many pieces of ribbon does Jeremy have?

   12 pieces

www.harcourtschoolsupply.com
© Houghton Mifflin Harcourt Publishing Company
148
Core Standards for Math, Grade 5

---

www.harcourtschoolsupply.com
© Houghton Mifflin Harcourt Publishing Company
237
Core Standards for Math, Grade 5

Answer Key

Name _____

Lesson 75
COMMON CORE STANDARD CC.5.NF.7b
Lesson Objective: Solve problems using the strategy *draw a diagram.*

Problem Solving • Use Multiplication

Nathan makes 4 batches of soup and divides each batch into halves. How many $\frac{1}{2}$-batches of soup does he have?

Read the Problem	Solve the Problem
What do I need to find? I need to find __the number of__ $\frac{1}{2}$-batches of soup Nathan has	Since Nathan makes 4 batches of soup, my diagram needs to show 4 circles to represent the 4 batches. I can divide each of the 4 circles in half.
What information do I need to use? I need to use the size of each __batch of soup__ and the total number of __batches__ of soup Nathan makes.	
How will I use the information? I can __make a diagram__ to organize the information from the problem. Then I can use the diagram to find __the number of $\frac{1}{2}$-batches of soup Nathan has after he divides the 4 batches of soup__	To find the total number of halves in the 4 batches, I can multiply 4 by the number of halves in each circle. $4 \div \frac{1}{2} = 4 \times \underline{2} = \underline{8}$
	So, Nathan has __8__ one-half-batches of soup.

Draw a diagram to help you solve the problem.

1. A nearby park has 8 acres of land to use for gardens. The park divides each acre into fourths. How many $\frac{1}{4}$-acre gardens does the park have?

   32 $\frac{1}{4}$-acre gardens

2. Clarissa has 3 pints of ice tea that she divides into $\frac{1}{2}$-pint servings. How many $\frac{1}{2}$-pint servings does she have?

   6 one-half-pint servings

Name _____

Lesson 75
CC.5.NF.7b

1. Ben is making a recipe that calls for 5 cups of flour. He only has a $\frac{1}{2}$-cup measuring cup. How many times will Ben need to fill the $\frac{1}{2}$-cup measuring cup to get 5 cups of flour?
   - (A) $\frac{2}{5}$
   - (B) $2\frac{1}{2}$
   - (C) 7
   - (D) 10

2. Lily made 3 pounds of coleslaw for a picnic. Each serving of coleslaw is $\frac{1}{8}$ pound. How many $\frac{1}{8}$-pound servings of coleslaw are there?
   - (A) $2\frac{2}{3}$
   - (B) 12
   - (C) 24
   - (D) 32

3. Kyle shares 3 bananas with some friends. If each person gets $\frac{1}{3}$ of a banana, how many people can share Kyle's bananas?
   - (A) 9
   - (B) 6
   - (C) $1\frac{1}{2}$
   - (D) $\frac{1}{6}$

4. A 6-mile walking trail has a distance marker every $\frac{1}{3}$ mile, beginning at $\frac{1}{3}$ mile. How many distance markers are along the trail?
   - (A) 2
   - (B) 6
   - (C) 9
   - (D) 18

Problem Solving REAL WORLD

5. Aya made 2 pans of brownies to give to some families in her neighborhood. Each family will get $\frac{1}{4}$ of a pan. How many families will share Aya's brownies? Explain how to use a diagram to find your answer.

   8 families; possible explanation: I can draw 2 rectangles, one for each pan of brownies. Then I can divide each pan into fourths and count how many fourths there are in all. There are 8 fourths, so 8 families can share the brownies. $2 \div \frac{1}{4} = 2 \times 4 = 8$.

Name _____

Lesson 76
COMMON CORE STANDARD CC.5.NF.7c
Lesson Objective: Divide a whole number by a fraction and divide a fraction by a whole number.

Fraction and Whole-Number Division

You can divide fractions by solving a related multiplication sentence.

Divide. $4 \div \frac{1}{3}$

Step 1 Draw 4 circles to represent the dividend, 4.

Step 2 Since the divisor is $\frac{1}{3}$, divide each circle into thirds.

Step 3 Count the total number of thirds.
When you divide the __4__ circles into thirds, you are finding the number of thirds in 4 circles, or finding 4 groups of __3__. There are __12__ thirds.

Step 4 Complete the number sentence.
$4 \div \frac{1}{3} = 4 \times \underline{3} = \underline{12}$

Use the model to complete the number sentence.

1. $3 \div \frac{1}{5} = 3 \times \underline{5} = \underline{15}$

2. $\frac{1}{4} \div 2 = \frac{1}{4} \times \underline{\frac{1}{2}} = \underline{\frac{1}{8}}$

Write a related multiplication sentence to solve.

3. $2 \div \frac{1}{5}$ $2 \times 5 = 10$

4. $\frac{1}{3} \div 3$ $\frac{1}{3} \times \frac{1}{3} = \frac{1}{9}$

5. $\frac{1}{6} \div 2$ $\frac{1}{6} \times \frac{1}{2} = \frac{1}{12}$

6. $5 \div \frac{1}{4}$ $5 \times 4 = 20$

Name _____

Lesson 76
CC.5.NF.7c

1. Samara solved $\frac{1}{5} \div 10$ by using a related multiplication sentence. Which multiplication sentence could she have used?
   - (A) $5 \times 10 = 50$
   - (B) $\frac{1}{5} \times 10 = 2$
   - (C) $5 \times \frac{1}{10} = \frac{5}{10}$
   - (D) $\frac{1}{5} \times \frac{1}{10} = \frac{1}{50}$

2. Jawan solved $8 \div \frac{1}{3}$ by using a related multiplication sentence. Which multiplication sentence could he have used?
   - (A) $8 \times \frac{1}{3} = \frac{8}{3}$
   - (B) $\frac{1}{8} \times \frac{1}{3} = \frac{1}{24}$
   - (C) $8 \times 3 = 24$
   - (D) $\frac{1}{8} \times 3 = \frac{3}{8}$

3. Annette has $\frac{1}{4}$ pound of cheese that she is going to cut into 3 chunks of the same size. What fraction of a pound of cheese will each chunk be?
   - (A) $\frac{1}{12}$ pound
   - (B) $\frac{1}{8}$ pound
   - (C) $\frac{1}{2}$ pound
   - (D) $\frac{3}{4}$ pound

4. Eli made 2 peanut butter and jelly sandwiches and cut each one into fourths. How many $\frac{1}{4}$-sandwich pieces did Eli have?
   - (A) $\frac{1}{8}$
   - (B) $2\frac{1}{4}$
   - (C) 4
   - (D) 8

Problem Solving REAL WORLD

5. Isaac has a piece of rope that is 5 yards long. Into how many $\frac{1}{2}$-yard pieces of rope can Isaac cut the rope?

   10 one-half-yard pieces

6. Two friends share $\frac{1}{2}$ of a pineapple equally. What fraction of a whole pineapple does each friend get?

   $\frac{1}{4}$ of the pineapple

Answer Key

Lesson 77

Name _____

Interpret Division with Fractions

You can draw a diagram or write an equation to represent division with fractions.

Beatriz has 3 cups of applesauce. She divides the applesauce into $\frac{1}{4}$-cup servings. How many servings of applesauce does she have?

One Way Draw a diagram to solve the problem.

Draw 3 circles to represent the 3 cups of applesauce. Since Beatriz divides the applesauce into $\frac{1}{4}$-cup servings, draw lines to divide each "cup" into fourths.

To find $3 \div \frac{1}{4}$, count the total number of fourths in the 3 circles.

So, Beatriz has __12__ one-fourth-cup servings of applesauce.

Another Way Write an equation to solve.

Write an equation. $\quad 3 \div \frac{1}{4} = n$

Write a related multiplication equation. $\quad 3 \times \frac{4}{1} = n$

Then solve. $\quad 12 = n$

So, Beatriz has __12__ one-fourth-cup servings of applesauce.

Possible diagram is shown.

1. Draw a diagram to represent the problem. Then solve.

   Drew has 5 granola bars. He cuts the bars into halves. How many $\frac{1}{2}$-bar pieces does he have?

   10 one-half-bar pieces

2. Write an equation to represent the problem. Then solve.

   Three friends share $\frac{1}{4}$ pan of brownies. What fraction of the whole pan of brownies does each friend get?

   $\frac{1}{4} \div 3 = n$; $\frac{1}{4} \times \frac{1}{3} = n$;

   $n = \frac{1}{12}$; $\frac{1}{12}$ **of a whole pan of brownies**

Lesson 77 (page 154)

Name _____

1. Tina has $\frac{1}{2}$ quart of iced tea. She pours the same amount into each of 3 glasses. Which equation represents the fraction of a quart of iced tea, n, that is in each glass?

   (A) $\frac{1}{2} \div \frac{1}{3} = n$

   (B) $\frac{1}{2} \div 3 = n$

   (C) $3 \div \frac{1}{2} = n$

   (D) $3 \div 2 = n$

2. Lucy bought 9 yards of ribbon on a spool. She cut the ribbon into $\frac{1}{2}$-yard pieces. Which equation represents the number of pieces of ribbon, n, Lucy has now?

   (A) $9 \div \frac{1}{2} = n$

   (B) $\frac{1}{2} \div 9 = n$

   (C) $2 \div 9 = n$

   (D) $9 \div 2 = n$

3. Which situation can be represented by $6 \div \frac{1}{3}$?

   (A) Rita has a piece of ribbon that is $\frac{1}{3}$ foot long. She cuts it into 6 pieces, each having the same length. How many feet long is each piece of ribbon?

   (B) Rita has 6 pieces of ribbon. Each piece is $\frac{1}{3}$ foot long. How many feet of ribbon does Rita have in all?

   (C) Rita has a piece of ribbon that is 6 feet long. She cuts it into pieces that are $\frac{1}{3}$ foot long. How many pieces of ribbon does Rita have?

   (D) Rita has a piece of ribbon that is 6 feet long. She cuts it into 3 pieces. How many feet long is each piece of ribbon?

Problem Solving REAL WORLD

4. Spencer has $\frac{1}{3}$ pound of nuts. He divides the nuts equally into 4 bags. What fraction of a pound of nuts is in each bag?

   $\frac{1}{12}$ pound

5. Humma has 3 apples. She slices each apple into eighths. How many $\frac{1}{8}$-apple slices does she have?

   24 one-eighth-apple slices

Lesson 78

Name _____

Customary Length

You can convert one customary unit of length to another customary unit of length by multiplying or dividing.

<u>Multiply</u> to change from <u>larger</u> to smaller units of length.

<u>Divide</u> to change from <u>smaller</u> to larger units of length.

Customary Units of Length
1 foot (ft) = 12 inches (in.)
1 yard (yd) = 3 feet
1 mile (mi) = 5,280 feet
1 mile = 1,760 yards

Convert 3 feet to inches.

Step 1
Decide: (Multiply) or Divide

feet → inches
larger → smaller

Step 2
Think:
1 ft = 12 in., so
3 ft = (3 × 12) in.

Step 3
Multiply.
3 × 12 = 36

So, 3 feet = __36__ inches.

Convert 363 feet to yards.

Step 1
Decide:
Multiply or (Divide)

feet → yards
smaller → larger

Step 2
Think:
3 ft = 1 yd,
so 363 ft = (363 ÷ 3) yd.

Step 3
Divide.
363 ÷ 3 = 121

So, 363 feet = __121__ yards.

Convert.

1. 33 yd = __99__ ft
2. 300 mi = __528,000__ yd
3. 46 in. = __3__ ft __10__ in.
4. 96 yd = __288__ ft
5. 48 ft = __16__ yd
6. 2 mi 20 yd = __3,540__ yd

Compare. Write <, >, or =.

7. 2 yd $<$ 7 ft
8. 67 mi $=$ 117,920 yd
9. 250 yd $<$ 800 ft
10. 14 yd 2 ft $>$ 16 ft
11. 34 ft 10 in. $<$ 518 in.
12. 5 mi 8 ft $>$ 8,800 yd

Lesson 78 (page 156)

Name _____

1. The first stop on a bus route is 4 miles from school. How many yards are in 4 miles?

   (A) 48 yards
   (B) 144 yards
   (C) 7,040 yards
   (D) 21,120 yards

2. Anoki bought 36 yards of fabric to make costumes for the school play. What is that length in inches?

   (A) 3 inches
   (B) 12 inches
   (C) 108 inches
   (D) 1,296 inches

3. Sarah is 53 inches tall. Sarah's brother Luke is 4 inches taller than she is. What is Luke's height in feet and inches?

   (A) 4 feet 7 inches
   (B) 4 feet 9 inches
   (C) 5 feet 7 inches
   (D) 5 feet 8 inches

4. The distance between a football field and a parking lot is 135 feet. What is that length in yards?

   (A) 36 yards
   (B) 45 yards
   (C) 405 yards
   (D) 1,620 yards

Problem Solving REAL WORLD

5. Marita orders 12 yards of material to make banners. If she needs 1 foot of fabric for each banner, how many banners can she make?

   36 banners

6. Christy bought an 8-foot piece of lumber to trim a bookshelf. Altogether, she needs 100 inches of lumber for the trim. Did Christy buy enough lumber? Explain.

   No. She bought only 96 inches of trim.

Answer Key

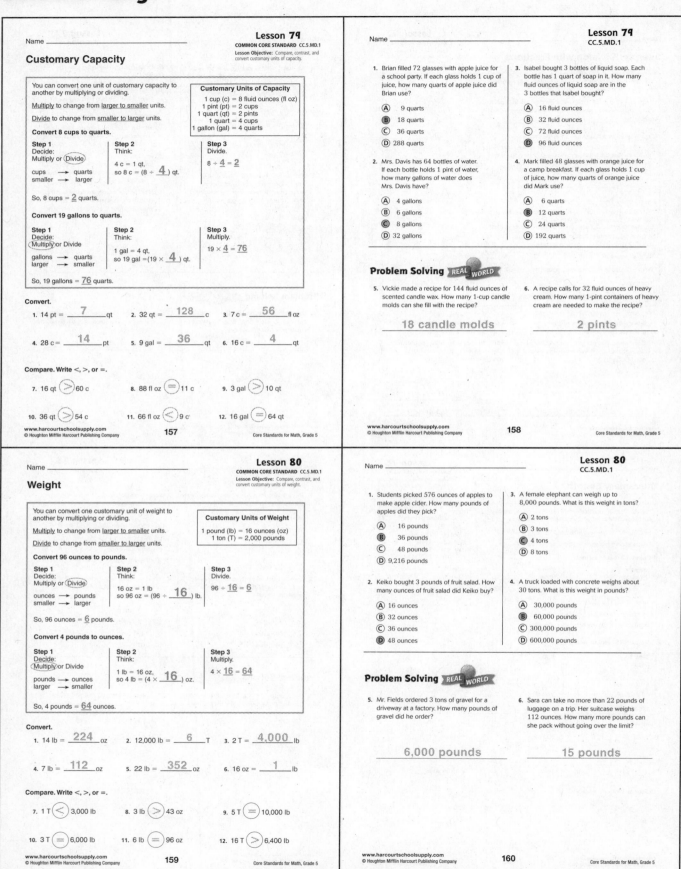

Name _____

Customary Capacity

You can convert one unit of customary capacity to another by multiplying or dividing.

<u>Multiply</u> to change from <u>larger to smaller</u> units.

<u>Divide</u> to change from <u>smaller to larger</u> units.

Customary Units of Capacity
1 cup (c) = 8 fluid ounces (fl oz)
1 pint (pt) = 2 cups
1 quart (qt) = 2 pints
1 quart = 4 cups
1 gallon (gal) = 4 quarts

Convert 8 cups to quarts.

Step 1	Step 2	Step 3
Decide: Multiply or (Divide)	Think: 4 c = 1 qt, so 8 c = (8 ÷ 4) qt.	Divide. 8 ÷ 4 = 2
cups → quarts smaller → larger		

So, 8 cups = 2 quarts.

Convert 19 gallons to quarts.

Step 1	Step 2	Step 3
Decide: (Multiply) or Divide	Think: 1 gal = 4 qt, so 19 gal = (19 × 4) qt.	Multiply. 19 × 4 = 76
gallons → quarts larger → smaller		

So, 19 gallons = 76 quarts.

Convert.

1. 14 pt = __7__ qt   2. 32 qt = __128__ c   3. 7 c = __56__ fl oz

4. 28 c = __14__ pt   5. 9 gal = __36__ qt   6. 16 c = __4__ qt

Compare. Write <, >, or =.

7. 16 qt ⊚> 60 c   8. 88 fl oz ⊚= 11 c   9. 3 gal ⊚> 10 qt

10. 36 qt ⊚> 54 c   11. 66 fl oz ⊚< 9 c   12. 16 gal ⊚= 64 qt

---

Name _____

1. Brian filled 72 glasses with apple juice for a school party. If each glass holds 1 cup of juice, how many quarts of apple juice did Brian use?
   - Ⓐ 9 quarts
   - **Ⓑ 18 quarts**
   - Ⓒ 36 quarts
   - Ⓓ 288 quarts

2. Mrs. Davis has 64 bottles of water. If each bottle holds 1 pint of water, how many gallons of water does Mrs. Davis have?
   - Ⓐ 4 gallons
   - Ⓑ 6 gallons
   - **Ⓒ 8 gallons**
   - Ⓓ 32 gallons

3. Isabel bought 3 bottles of liquid soap. Each bottle has 1 quart of soap in it. How many fluid ounces of liquid soap are in the 3 bottles that Isabel bought?
   - Ⓐ 16 fluid ounces
   - Ⓑ 32 fluid ounces
   - Ⓒ 72 fluid ounces
   - **Ⓓ 96 fluid ounces**

4. Mark filled 48 glasses with orange juice for a camp breakfast. If each glass holds 1 cup of juice, how many quarts of orange juice did Mark use?
   - Ⓐ 6 quarts
   - **Ⓑ 12 quarts**
   - Ⓒ 24 quarts
   - Ⓓ 192 quarts

Problem Solving REAL WORLD

5. Vickie made a recipe for 144 fluid ounces of scented candle wax. How many 1-cup candle molds can she fill with the recipe?

   18 candle molds

6. A recipe calls for 32 fluid ounces of heavy cream. How many 1-pint containers of heavy cream are needed to make the recipe?

   2 pints

Name _____

Weight

You can convert one customary unit of weight to another by multiplying or dividing.

<u>Multiply</u> to change from <u>larger to smaller</u> units.

<u>Divide</u> to change from <u>smaller to larger</u> units.

Customary Units of Weight
1 pound (lb) = 16 ounces (oz)
1 ton (T) = 2,000 pounds

Convert 96 ounces to pounds.

Step 1	Step 2	Step 3
Decide: Multiply or (Divide)	Think: 16 oz = 1 lb so 96 oz = (96 ÷ 16) lb.	Divide. 96 ÷ 16 = 6
ounces → pounds smaller → larger		

So, 96 ounces = 6 pounds.

Convert 4 pounds to ounces.

Step 1	Step 2	Step 3
Decide: (Multiply) or Divide	Think: 1 lb = 16 oz, so 4 lb = (4 × 16) oz.	Multiply. 4 × 16 = 64
pounds → ounces larger → smaller		

So, 4 pounds = 64 ounces.

Convert.

1. 14 lb = __224__ oz   2. 12,000 lb = __6__ T   3. 2 T = __4,000__ lb

4. 7 lb = __112__ oz   5. 22 lb = __352__ oz   6. 16 oz = __1__ lb

Compare. Write <, >, or =.

7. 1 T ⊚< 3,000 lb   8. 3 lb ⊚> 43 oz   9. 5 T ⊚= 10,000 lb

10. 3 T ⊚= 6,000 lb   11. 6 lb ⊚= 96 oz   12. 16 T ⊚> 6,400 lb

---

Name _____

1. Students picked 576 ounces of apples to make apple cider. How many pounds of apples did they pick?
   - Ⓐ 16 pounds
   - **Ⓑ 36 pounds**
   - Ⓒ 48 pounds
   - Ⓓ 9,216 pounds

2. Keiko bought 3 pounds of fruit salad. How many ounces of fruit salad did Keiko buy?
   - Ⓐ 16 ounces
   - Ⓑ 32 ounces
   - Ⓒ 36 ounces
   - **Ⓓ 48 ounces**

3. A female elephant can weigh up to 8,000 pounds. What is this weight in tons?
   - Ⓐ 2 tons
   - Ⓑ 3 tons
   - **Ⓒ 4 tons**
   - Ⓓ 8 tons

4. A truck loaded with concrete weighs about 30 tons. What is this weight in pounds?
   - Ⓐ 30,000 pounds
   - **Ⓑ 60,000 pounds**
   - Ⓒ 300,000 pounds
   - Ⓓ 600,000 pounds

Problem Solving REAL WORLD

5. Mr. Fields ordered 3 tons of gravel for a driveway at a factory. How many pounds of gravel did he order?

   6,000 pounds

6. Sara can take no more than 22 pounds of luggage on a trip. Her suitcase weighs 112 ounces. How many more pounds can she pack without going over the limit?

   15 pounds

Name _____

Lesson **81**
COMMON CORE STANDARD CC.5.MD.1
Lesson Objective: Convert measurement units to solve multistep problems.

Multistep Measurement Problems

An ice cream parlor donated 6 containers of ice cream to a local elementary school. Each container holds 3 gallons of ice cream. If each student is served 1 cup of ice cream, how many students can be served?

Step 1 Record the information you are given.

There are __6__ containers of ice cream.

Each container holds __3__ gallons of ice cream.

Step 2 Find the total amount of ice cream in the 6 containers.

6 × 3 gallons = __18__ gallons of ice cream

Step 3 Convert from gallons to cups.

There are __4__ quarts in 1 gallon, so 18 gallons = __72__ quarts.

There are __2__ pints in 1 quart, so 72 quarts = __144__ pints.

There are __2__ cups in 1 pint, so 144 pints = __288__ cups.

So, __288__ students can be served 1 cup of ice cream.

Solve.

1. A cargo truck weighs 8,750 pounds. The weight limit for a certain bridge is 5 tons. How many pounds of cargo can be added to the truck before it exceeds the weight limit for the bridge?

    1,250 pounds

2. A plumber uses 16 inches of tubing to connect each washing machine in a laundry to the water source. He wants to install 18 washing machines. How many yards of tubing will he need?

    8 yards

3. Larry has 9 gallons of paint. He uses 10 quarts to paint his kitchen and 3 gallons to paint his living room. How many pints of paint will be left?

    28 pints

4. Ketisha is practicing for a marathon by running around a track that is 440 yards long. Yesterday she ran around the track 20 times. How many miles did she run?

    5 miles

Name _____

Lesson **81**
CC.5.MD.1

1. At the bulk food store, Stacey bought 7 pounds of nuts. She used 8 ounces of nuts in a recipe and then made small bags to use for snacks. If each small bag contained 4 ounces of nuts, how many small bags of nuts did Stacey make?

    (A) 15
    (B) 19
    (C) 26
    (D) 29

2. Keisha is walking around a track that is 400 yards long. She has walked around the track 5 times so far. How many more yards does she need to walk around the track to do 2 miles?

    (A) 1,520 yards
    (B) 3,120 yards
    (C) 3,280 yards
    (D) 8,560 yards

3. Devon uses 64 inches of ribbon to make 1 bow. How many yards of ribbon does Devon need to make 9 bows?

    (A) 8 yards
    (B) 16 yards
    (C) 24 yards
    (D) 48 yards

4. Brandon bought a 5-gallon container of paint to paint his house. After he finished painting, he had 2 quarts of paint left over. How many quarts of paint did Brandon use?

    (A) 3 quarts
    (B) 8 quarts
    (C) 18 quarts
    (D) 23 quarts

Problem Solving REAL WORLD

5. A pitcher contains 40 fluid ounces of iced tea. Shelby pours 3 cups of iced tea. How many pints of iced tea are left in the pitcher?

    1 pint

6. Olivia ties 2.5 feet of ribbon onto one balloon. How many yards of ribbon does Olivia need for 18 balloons?

    15 yards

Name _____

Lesson **82**
COMMON CORE STANDARD CC.5.MD.1
Lesson Objective: Compare, contrast, and convert metric units.

Metric Measures

The metric system is based on place value. To convert between units, you multiply or divide by a power of 10. You **multiply** to change larger units to smaller units, such as liters to centiliters. You **divide** to change smaller units to larger units, such as meters to kilometers.

Convert 566 millimeters to decimeters.

• Think about how the two units are related.

1 decimeter = 100 millimeters

• **Think:** Should I multiply or divide?

Millimeters are smaller than decimeters.

So divide, or move the decimal point left for each power of 10.

566 ÷ 100 = __5.66__
millimeters   *mm in 1 dm*   *total decimeters*

So, 566 mm = __5.66__ dm.

Metric Units of Length
1 centimeter (cm) = 10 millimeters (mm)
1 decimeter (dm) = 10 centimeters (cm)
1 meter (m) = 1,000 millimeters (mm)
1 kilometer (km) = 1,000 meters (m)

kilo-(k)	hecto-(h)	deka-(da)	meter liter gram	deci-(d)	centi-(c)	milli-(m)
				5	6	6

Complete the equation to show the conversion.

1. 115 km ⊗ 10 = __1,150__ hm

    115 km ⊗ 100 = __11,500__ dam

    115 km ⊗ 1,000 = __115,000__ m

2. 418 cL ÷ 10 = __41.8__ dL

    418 cL ÷ 100 = __4.18__ L

    418 cL ÷ 1,000 = __0.418__ daL

Convert.

3. 40 cm = __400__ mm

4. 500 mL = __5.00__ dL

5. 6 kg = **5, or** __6,000__ g

6. 5,000 cL = **50, or** __50.00__ L

7. 4 kg = __40__ hg

8. 200 mm = **20, or** __20.00__ cm

Name _____

Lesson **82**
CC.5.MD.1

1. Ed bought 3 liters of water, 2,750 milliliters of sports drink, and 2.25 liters of juice. Which statement is true?

    (A) Ed bought 50 milliliters more sports drink than juice.
    (B) Ed bought 1.25 liters more water than juice.
    (C) Ed bought 75 milliliters more water than juice.
    (D) Ed bought 250 milliliters more water than sports drink.

2. Roland's dog has a mass of 2,500 dekagrams. What is the dog's mass in kilograms?

    (A) 0.25 kilogram
    (B) 2.5 kilograms
    (C) 25 kilograms
    (D) 250 kilograms

3. Sofia bought 3.25 meters of fabric to make a costume. How many centimeters of fabric did she buy?

    (A) 0.325 centimeter
    (B) 3.25 centimeters
    (C) 32.5 centimeters
    (D) 325 centimeters

4. Lorena's backpack has a mass of 10,000 grams. What is the mass of Lorena's backpack in kilograms?

    (A) 1 kilogram
    (B) 10 kilograms
    (C) 100 kilograms
    (D) 1,000 kilograms

Problem Solving REAL WORLD

5. Bria ordered 145 centimeters of fabric. Jayleen ordered 1.5 meters of fabric. Who ordered more fabric?

    Jayleen

6. Ed fills his sports bottle with 1.2 liters of water. After his bike ride, he drinks 200 milliliters of the water. How much water is left in Ed's sports bottle?

    1 L, or 1,000 mL

Answer Key

Name _____

Problem Solving • Customary and Metric Conversions

COMMON CORE STANDARD CC.5.MD.1
Lesson Objective: Solve problems about customary and metric conversions using the strategy make a table.

You can use the strategy *make a table* to help you solve problems about customary and metric conversions.

Jon's faucet is dripping at the rate of 24 centiliters in a day. How many milliliters of water will have dripped from Jon's faucet in 24 hours?

Read the Problem

What do I need to find

I need to find how many milliliters of water will have dripped from Jon's faucet in 24 hours.

What information do I need to use?

I need to use the number of cL that have dripped in 24 hr and the number of mL in a cL.

How will I use the information?

I will make a table to show the relationship between the number of centiliters and the number of milliliters

Conversion Table

	L	dL	cL	mL
1 L	1	10	100	1,000
1 dL	$\frac{1}{10}$	1	10	100
1 cL	$\frac{1}{100}$	$\frac{1}{10}$	1	10
1 mL	$\frac{1}{1,000}$	$\frac{1}{100}$	$\frac{1}{10}$	1

I can use the Conversion Table to find the number of milliliters in 1 centiliter. There are **10** milliliters in 1 centiliter.

cL	1	2	4	24
mL	10	20	40	240

So, **240** milliliters of water will have dripped from Jon's faucet in 24 hours.

Make a table to help you solve the problems. *Check students' tables.*

1. Fernando has a bucket that holds 3 gallons of water. He is filling the bucket using a 1-pint container. How many times will he have to fill the pint container in order to fill the bucket?

24 times

2. Lexi has a roll of shelf paper that is 800 cm long. She wants to cut the paper into 1-m strips to line the shelves in her pantry. How many 1-meter strips can she cut?

8 strips

Name _____

1. When it is full, a fish tank holds 15 gallons of water. Jordan is using a 1-pint container to fill the fish tank. How many times will he need to fill the 1-pint container to fill the fish tank?
   - (A) 30
   - (B) 60
   - (C) 90
   - (D) 120

2. An art teacher has a roll of art paper 5 meters long. She needs to cut it into 1-decimeter long pieces for a collage project. How many 1-decimeter pieces can she cut from the roll of art paper?
   - (A) 5
   - (B) 50
   - (C) 500
   - (D) 5,000

3. Mickey needs to cut pieces of ribbon that are each 1 meter long to tie onto balloons. If he has 8 pieces of ribbon that are each 1 dekameter long, how many 1-meter pieces of ribbon can he cut?
   - (A) 80
   - (B) 800
   - (C) 8,000
   - (D) 80,000

4. The largest known carnivorous dinosaur, Spinosaurus, weighed about 18,000 pounds. How many tons did the Spinosaurus dinosaur weigh?
   - (A) 9 tons
   - (B) 18 tons
   - (C) 36 tons
   - (D) 90 tons

Problem Solving REAL WORLD

5. A Komodo dragon lizard can grow up to about 30 decimeters in length. Toni says that this is 300 centimeters. Do you agree? Explain how you can use a table to support your answer.

   Yes. Possible answer: a table can show the relationship between centimeters and decimeters. 1 decimeter equals 10 centimeters, 2 decimeters equals 20 centimeters, 3 decimeters equals 30 centimeters, and so on. The pattern shows to multiply the number of decimeters by 10 to find the number of centimeters. So there are 300 centimeters in 30 decimeters.

Name _____

Elapsed Time

COMMON CORE STANDARD CC.5.MD.1
Lesson Objective: Convert units of time to solve elapsed time problems.

You can solve elapsed time problems by converting units of time.

Starting at 4:20 P.M., Connie practiced piano for 90 minutes. At what time did Connie stop practicing piano?

Convert 90 minutes to hours and minutes. Then find the end time.

Units of Time
60 seconds (s) = 1 minute (min)
60 minutes = 1 hour (hr)
24 hours = 1 day (d)
7 days = 1 week (wk)
52 weeks = 1 year (yr)
12 months (mo) = 1 year
365 days = 1 year

Step 1 To convert minutes to hours, divide.

90 ÷ 60 is 1 with a remainder of 30

90 min = **1** hr **30** min

Step 2 Count forward by hours until you reach 1 hour.

4:20 → 5:20 = 1 hour

Step 3 Count forward by minutes until you reach 30 minutes.

5:20 → 5:30 = 1 hour 10 minutes
5:30 → 5:40 = 1 hour 20 minutes
5:40 → 5:50 = 1 hour 30 minutes

Connie stops practicing piano at **5:50 P.M.**

Convert.

1. 480 min = **8** hr   2. 4 d = **96** hr   3. 125 hr = **5** d **5** hr

Find the start, elapsed, or end time.

4. Start time: 7:15 A.M.
   Elapsed time: 2 hr 20 min
   End time: **9:35 A.M.**

5. Start time: 6:28 A.M.
   Elapsed time: **3 hr 40 min**
   End time: 10:08 A.M.

6. Start time: **2:05 P.M.**
   Elapsed time: 5 hr 50 min
   End time: 7:55 P.M.

7. Start time: 5:24 P.M.
   Elapsed time: 6 hr
   End time: **11:24 P.M.**

Name _____

1. The high school football game started at 7:15 P.M. and ended at 10:44 P.M. How long did the game last?
   - (A) 2 hours 9 minutes
   - (B) 2 hours 29 minutes
   - (C) 3 hours 9 minutes
   - (D) 3 hours 29 minutes

2. Betsy spent 26 days traveling in Europe. How many weeks and days did Betsy travel in Europe?
   - (A) 2 weeks 6 days
   - (B) 3 weeks 5 days
   - (C) 4 weeks 2 days
   - (D) 5 weeks 1 day

3. Students arrived at the science museum at 1:15 P.M. They stayed at the museum for 2 hours 51 minutes. What time did the students leave the museum?
   - (A) 3:06 P.M.
   - (B) 4:00 P.M.
   - (C) 4:06 P.M.
   - (D) 4:44 P.M.

4. It takes Kate 10 minutes to walk to the bus stop. How many seconds does it take her to walk to the bus stop?
   - (A) 6,000 seconds
   - (B) 600 seconds
   - (C) 60 seconds
   - (D) 6 seconds

Problem Solving REAL WORLD

5. Kiera's dance class starts at 4:30 P.M. and ends at 6:15 P.M. How long is her dance class?

   1 hr 45 min

6. Julio watched a movie that started at 11:30 A.M. and ended at 2:12 P.M. How long was the movie?

   2 hr 42 min

Lesson 85 (page 169)

Name _____

Lesson 85
COMMON CORE STANDARD CC.5.MD.2
Lesson Objective: Make and use line plots with fractions to solve problems.

Line Plots

A **line plot** is a graph that shows the shape of a data set by placing Xs above each data value on a number line. You can make a line plot to represent a data set and then use the line plot to answer questions about the data set.

Students measure the lengths of several seeds.
The length of each seed is listed below.

$\frac{1}{2}$ inch, $\frac{3}{4}$ inch, $\frac{1}{2}$ inch, $\frac{1}{4}$ inch, $\frac{3}{4}$ inch, $\frac{3}{4}$ inch, $\frac{3}{4}$ inch, $\frac{1}{4}$ inch, $\frac{1}{2}$ inch

What is the combined length of the seeds that are $\frac{1}{4}$ inch long?

Step 1 To represent the different lengths of the seeds, draw and label a line plot with the data values $\frac{1}{4}$, $\frac{1}{2}$, and $\frac{3}{4}$. Then use an X to represent each seed. The line plot has been started for you.

Step 2 There are ___2___ Xs above $\frac{1}{4}$ on the line plot.

Multiply to find the combined length of the seeds:

$\frac{2}{}$ × $\frac{1}{4}$ = $\frac{2}{4}$, or $\frac{1}{2}$ inch

The combined length of the seeds that are $\frac{1}{4}$ inch long is $\frac{1}{2}$ inch.

You can use the same process to find the combined lengths of the seeds that are $\frac{1}{2}$ inch long and $\frac{3}{4}$ inch long.

Length of Seeds (in inches)

Use the data and the line plot above to answer the questions.

1. What is the total length of all the seeds that the students measured?

   5 inches

2. What is the average length of one of the seeds that the students measured?

   $\frac{5}{9}$ inch

Lesson 85 (page 170)

Name _____

Lesson 85
CC.5.MD.2

Use the line plot for 1–2.

Maya measured the heights of the seedlings she was growing. She made a line plot to record the data.

Seedling Growth (in inches)

1. What was the total growth, in inches, of Maya's seedlings?
   - (A) 3 inches
   - (B) $3\frac{1}{2}$ inches
   - (C) 7 inches
   - (D) 10 inches

2. What was the average height, in inches, of the seedlings she measured?
   - (A) $\frac{11}{16}$ inch
   - (B) $\frac{7}{10}$ inch
   - (C) $\frac{3}{4}$ inch
   - (D) $\frac{7}{8}$ inch

Use the line plot for 3–4.

A builder is buying property where she can build new houses. The line plot shows the sizes of the lots for each house.

House Lots (in acres)

3. How many acres does the builder buy?
   - (A) 3 acres
   - (B) 4 acres
   - (C) 6 acres
   - (D) 12 acres

4. What is the average size of the lots?
   - (A) $\frac{1}{12}$ acre
   - (B) $\frac{1}{6}$ acre
   - (C) $\frac{1}{4}$ acre
   - (D) $\frac{1}{3}$ acre

Problem Solving REAL WORLD

5. Shia measured the thickness of the buttons in her collection. She graphed the results in a line plot.

   What steps could Shia use to find the average thickness of her buttons?

   Button Thicknesses (in inches)

   Shia could add the total for each thickness. Then she would add those amounts and divide by the number of buttons, 9.

Lesson 86 (page 171)

Name _____

Lesson 86
COMMON CORE STANDARD CC.5.MD.3
Lesson Objective: Identify, describe, and classify three-dimensional figures.

Three-Dimensional Figures

A **polyhedron** is a solid figure with faces that are polygons. You can identify a polyhedron by the shape of its faces.

A **pyramid** is a polyhedron with one polygon base. The lateral faces of a pyramid are triangles that meet at a common vertex.

A **prism** is a polyhedron with two congruent polygons as bases. The lateral faces of a prism are rectangles.

triangular pyramid	The base and faces are triangles.	triangular prism	The two bases are triangles.
rectangular pyramid	The base is a rectangle.	rectangular prism	All faces are rectangles.
square pyramid	The base is a square.	square prism or cube	All faces are squares.
pentagonal pyramid	The base is a pentagon.	pentagonal prism	The two bases are pentagons.
hexagonal pyramid	The base is a hexagon.	hexagonal prism	The two bases are hexagons.

A solid figure with curved surfaces is **not a polyhedron.**

| cone | The one base is a circle. | cylinder | The two bases are circles. |
| sphere | There is no base. | | |

Classify the solid figure. Write prism, pyramid, cone, cylinder, or sphere.

The solid figure has one base.

The rest of its faces are triangles.

So, the solid figure is a ___pyramid___

Classify each solid figure. Write prism, pyramid, cone, cylinder, or sphere.

1. cylinder
2. pyramid
3. rectangular prism
4. cone

Lesson 86 (page 172)

Name _____

Lesson 86
CC.5.MD.3

1. Koji is building a tower out of paper. He starts by making 2 congruent circular bases. He then makes 1 curved surface for the body of the tower. What three-dimensional figure does Koji build?
   - (A) cone
   - (B) cylinder
   - (C) prism
   - (D) sphere

2. Which of the following **best** classifies this solid figure?
   - (A) triangular pyramid
   - (B) triangular prism
   - (C) square pyramid
   - (D) square prism

3. Tanya drew this solid figure on her notebook.

   What solid figure did Tanya draw?
   - (A) hexagonal prism
   - (B) pentagonal prism
   - (C) hexagonal pyramid
   - (D) pentagonal pyramid

4. Min Soo is making solid figures in the shape of party hats. He starts by making 1 circular base. He then makes 1 curved surface for the figure. What three-dimensional figure does Min Soo make?
   - (A) prism
   - (B) sphere
   - (C) cylinder
   - (D) cone

Problem Solving REAL WORLD

5. Darrien is making a solid figure out of folded paper. His solid figure has six congruent faces that are all squares. What solid figure did Darrien make?

   cube

6. Nanako said she drew a square pyramid and that all of the faces are triangles. Is this possible? **Explain.**

   No. The base of the pyramid is a square that has 4 sides, not 3.

Answer Key

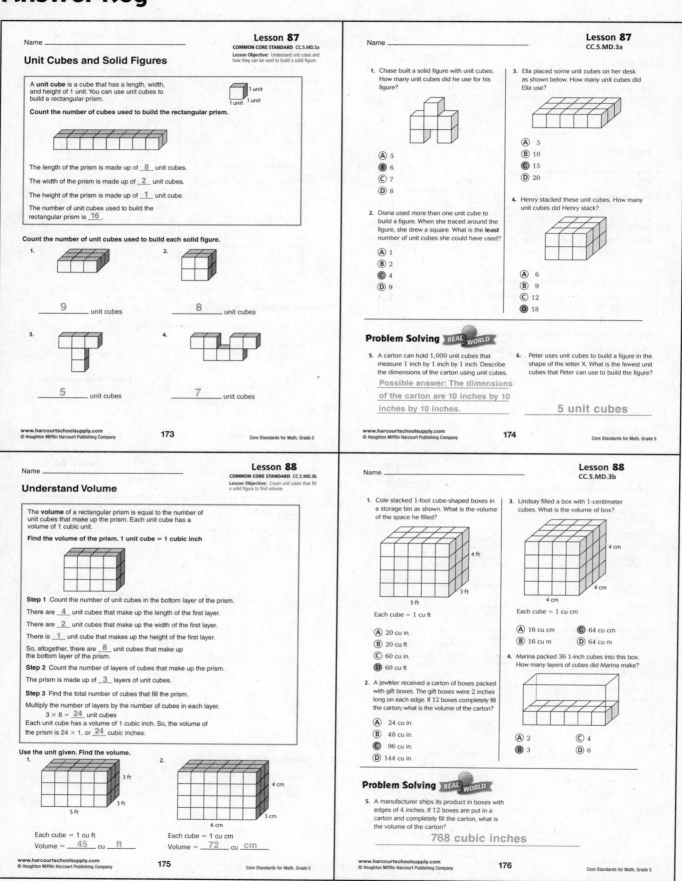

Unit Cubes and Solid Figures

Name _____

A **unit cube** is a cube that has a length, width, and height of 1 unit. You can use unit cubes to build a rectangular prism.

1 unit 1 unit 1 unit

Count the number of cubes used to build the rectangular prism.

The length of the prism is made up of __8__ unit cubes.

The width of the prism is made up of __2__ unit cubes.

The height of the prism is made up of __1__ unit cube.

The number of unit cubes used to build the rectangular prism is __16__.

Count the number of unit cubes used to build each solid figure.

1. _____9_____ unit cubes

2. _____8_____ unit cubes

3. _____5_____ unit cubes

4. _____7_____ unit cubes

Name _____

1. Chase built a solid figure with unit cubes. How many unit cubes did he use for his figure?
   - Ⓐ 5
   - Ⓑ 6
   - Ⓒ 7
   - Ⓓ 8

2. Diana used more than one unit cube to build a figure. When she traced around the figure, she drew a square. What is the **least** number of unit cubes she could have used?
   - Ⓐ 1
   - Ⓑ 2
   - Ⓒ 4
   - Ⓓ 9

3. Ella placed some unit cubes on her desk as shown below. How many unit cubes did Ella use?
   - Ⓐ 5
   - Ⓑ 10
   - Ⓒ 15
   - Ⓓ 20

4. Henry stacked these unit cubes. How many unit cubes did Henry stack?
   - Ⓐ 6
   - Ⓑ 9
   - Ⓒ 12
   - Ⓓ 18

Problem Solving REAL WORLD

5. A carton can hold 1,000 unit cubes that measure 1 inch by 1 inch by 1 inch. Describe the dimensions of the carton using unit cubes.

   Possible answer: The dimensions of the carton are 10 inches by 10 inches by 10 inches.

6. Peter uses unit cubes to build a figure in the shape of the letter X. What is the fewest unit cubes that Peter can use to build the figure?

   5 unit cubes

Understand Volume

Name _____

The **volume** of a rectangular prism is equal to the number of unit cubes that make up the prism. Each unit cube has a volume of 1 cubic unit.

Find the volume of the prism. 1 unit cube = 1 cubic inch

Step 1 Count the number of unit cubes in the bottom layer of the prism.

There are __4__ unit cubes that make up the length of the first layer.

There are __2__ unit cubes that make up the width of the first layer.

There is __1__ unit cube that makes up the height of the first layer.

So, altogether, there are __8__ unit cubes that make up the bottom layer of the prism.

Step 2 Count the number of layers of cubes that make up the prism.

The prism is made up of __3__ layers of unit cubes.

Step 3 Find the total number of cubes that fill the prism.

Multiply the number of layers by the number of cubes in each layer.

$3 \times 8 = $ __24__ unit cubes

Each unit cube has a volume of 1 cubic inch. So, the volume of the prism is 24×1, or __24__ cubic inches.

Use the unit given. Find the volume.

1. Each cube = 1 cu ft
   Volume = __45__ cu __ft__

2. Each cube = 1 cu cm
   Volume = __72__ cu __cm__

Name _____

1. Cole stacked 1-foot cube-shaped boxes in a storage bin as shown. What is the volume of the space he filled?

   Each cube = 1 cu ft
   - Ⓐ 20 cu in.
   - Ⓑ 20 cu ft
   - Ⓒ 60 cu in.
   - Ⓓ 60 cu ft

2. A jeweler received a carton of boxes packed with gift boxes. The gift boxes were 2 inches long on each edge. If 12 boxes completely fill the carton, what is the volume of the carton?
   - Ⓐ 24 cu in.
   - Ⓑ 48 cu in.
   - Ⓒ 96 cu in.
   - Ⓓ 144 cu in.

3. Lindsay filled a box with 1-centimeter cubes. What is the volume of box?

   Each cube = 1 cu cm
   - Ⓐ 16 cu cm
   - Ⓑ 16 cu m
   - Ⓒ 64 cu cm
   - Ⓓ 64 cu m

4. Marina packed 36 1-inch cubes into this box. How many layers of cubes did Marina make?
   - Ⓐ 2
   - Ⓑ 3
   - Ⓒ 4
   - Ⓓ 6

Problem Solving REAL WORLD

5. A manufacturer ships its product in boxes with edges of 4 inches. If 12 boxes are put in a carton and completely fill the carton, what is the volume of the carton?

   768 cubic inches

Answer Key

Lesson 89
COMMON CORE STANDARD CC.5.MD.4
Lesson Objective: Estimate the volume of a rectangular prism.

Estimate Volume

Name _____

You can estimate the volume of a larger box by filling it with smaller boxes.

Mario packs boxes of markers into a large box. The volume of each box of markers is 15 cubic inches. Estimate the volume of the large box.

The volume of one box of markers is __15__ cubic inches.

Use the box of markers to estimate the volume of the large box.

- The large box holds __2__ layers of boxes of markers, a top layer and a bottom layer. Each layer contains __10__ boxes of markers. So, the large box holds about 2 × 10, or __20__ boxes of markers.
- Multiply the volume of 1 box of markers by the estimated number of boxes of markers that fit in the large box.
  __20__ × __15__ = __300__

So, the volume of the large box is about __300__ cubic inches.

Estimate the volume.

1. Each box of toothpaste has a volume of 25 cubic inches.

   There are __30__ boxes of toothpaste in the large box.
   The estimated volume of the large box is __30__ × 25 = __750__ cubic inches.

2. Volume of CD case: 80 cu cm

   Volume of large box: __about 4,800 cu cm__

www.harcourtschoolsupply.com
© Houghton Mifflin Harcourt Publishing Company
177
Core Standards for Math, Grade 5

Lesson 89
CC.5.MD.4

Name _____

1. The volume of a box of coloring pencils is 250 cubic centimeters. Which is the best estimate of the volume of the box that the coloring pencils came packed in?

   (A) 750 cu cm (C) 7,500 cu cm
   (B) 3,750 cu cm (D) 75,000 cu cm

2. Joe packed boxes of staplers into a larger box. If the volume of each stapler box is 400 cubic centimeters, which is the best estimate for the volume of the box that Joe packed with staplers?

   (A) 800 cu cm (C) 4,000 cu cm
   (B) 2,000 cu cm (D) 8,000 cu cm

3. The volume of a pencil box is 80 cubic inches. Which is the best estimate of the volume of the box that the pencil boxes came packed in?

   (A) 9,600 cu in. (C) 960 cu in.
   (B) 3,840 cu in. (D) 384 cu in.

4. Joe packed tissue boxes into a larger box. If the volume of each tissue box is 90 cubic inches, which is the best estimate for the volume of the box that Joe packed with tissue boxes?

   (A) 360 cu in. (C) 720 cu in.
   (B) 540 cu in. (D) 1,080 cu in.

Problem Solving REAL WORLD

5. Theo fills a large box with boxes of staples. The volume of each box of staples is 120 cu cm. Estimate the volume of the large box.

   __3,600 cu cm__

www.harcourtschoolsupply.com
© Houghton Mifflin Harcourt Publishing Company
178
Core Standards for Math, Grade 5

Lesson 90
COMMON CORE STANDARD CC.5.MD.5a
Lesson Objective: Find the volume of rectangular prisms.

Volume of Rectangular Prisms

Name _____

Jorge wants to find the volume of this rectangular prism. He can use cubes that measure 1 centimeter on each side to find the volume.

Step 1 The base has a length of 2 centimeters and a width of 3 centimeters. Multiply to find the area of the base.
Base = __2__ × __3__
Base = __6__ cm²

Step 2 The height of the prism is 4 centimeters. Add the number of cubes in each layer to find the volume.

Remember: Each layer has 6 cubes.

Step 3 Count the cubes. __24__ cubes
Multiply the base and the height to check your answer.
Volume = __6__ × __4__
Volume = __24__ cubic centimeters

So, the volume of Jorge's rectangular prism is __24__ cubic centimeters.

Find the volume.

1. Volume: __18 cm³__
2. Volume: __20 ft³__
3. Volume: __32 in.³__
4. Volume: __54 cm³__

www.harcourtschoolsupply.com
© Houghton Mifflin Harcourt Publishing Company
179
Core Standards for Math, Grade 5

Lesson 90
CC.5.MD.5a

Name _____

1. Claudine filled a box with smaller boxes shaped like cubes. What is the volume of the box Claudine filled?

   (A) 15 cubic inches
   (B) 25 cubic inches
   (C) 100 cubic inches
   (D) 120 cubic inches

2. Luke keeps his art supplies in a shoe box that is 12 inches long, 7 inches wide, and 5 inches high. What is the volume of the shoe box?

   (A) 420 cubic inches
   (B) 358 cubic inches
   (C) 240 cubic inches
   (D) 24 cubic inches

3. Barbie stacked small cubes into a box until it was full. What is the volume of the box?

   (A) 18 cubic inches
   (B) 40 cubic inches
   (C) 120 cubic inches
   (D) 158 cubic inches

4. A storage bin in the shape of a rectangular prism has a volume of 5,400 cubic inches. The base area of the storage bin is 450 square inches. What is the height of the storage bin?

   (A) 9 inches
   (B) 11 inches
   (C) 12 inches
   (D) 15 inches

Problem Solving REAL WORLD

5. Aaron keeps his baseball cards in a cardboard box that is 12 inches long, 8 inches wide, and 3 inches high. What is the volume of this box?

   __288 in.³__

6. Amanda's jewelry box is in the shape of a cube that has 6-inch edges. What is the volume of Amanda's jewelry box?

   __216 in.³__

www.harcourtschoolsupply.com
© Houghton Mifflin Harcourt Publishing Company
180
Core Standards for Math, Grade 5

---

www.harcourtschoolsupply.com
© Houghton Mifflin Harcourt Publishing Company
245
Core Standards for Math, Grade 5

Answer Key

Name _____

Lesson **91**

COMMON CORE STANDARD CC.5.MD.5b
Lesson Objective: Use a formula to find the volume of a rectangular prism.

Algebra • Apply Volume Formulas

You can use a formula to find the volume of a rectangular prism.

$$Volume = length \times width \times height$$
$$V = (l \times w) \times h$$

Find the volume of the rectangular prism.

Step 1 Identify the length, width, and height of the rectangular prism.

length = _9_ in. width = _3_ in. height = _4_ in.

Step 2 Substitute the values of the length, width, and height into the formula.

$$V = (l \times w) \times h$$
$$V = (\_9\_ \times \_3\_) \times \_4\_$$

Step 3 Multiply the length by the width.

$$V = (9 \times 3) \times 4$$
$$V = \_27\_ \times 4$$

Step 4 Multiply the product of the length and width by the height.

$$V = 27 \times \_4\_$$
$$= \_108\_$$

So, the volume of the rectangular prism is _108_ cubic inches.

Find the volume.

1.

$V = $ _240 ft³_

2.

$V = $ _512 cm³_

---

1. Antonio found an antique chest in his grandfather's attic.

What is the volume of the chest?

- (A) 6 cubic feet
- (B) 9 cubic feet
- (C) 12 cubic feet
- (D) 24 cubic feet

2. When Emma went to college, her mother packed up all her old skiing trophies into a box with the dimensions shown.

What is the volume of the box?

- (A) 7 cubic feet
- (B) 8 cubic feet
- (C) 9 cubic feet
- (D) 10 cubic feet

3. Kristin keeps paper clips in a box that is the shape of a cube. Each edge of the cube is 3 inches. What is the volume of the cube?

- (A) 6 cubic inches
- (B) 9 cubic inches
- (C) 18 cubic inches
- (D) 27 cubic inches

4. Will moved a box of old newspapers from the back room of the library.

What is the volume of the box?

- (A) 10 cubic feet
- (B) 15 cubic feet
- (C) 30 cubic feet
- (D) 40 cubic feet

Problem Solving REAL WORLD

5. A construction company is digging a hole for a swimming pool. The hole will be 12 yards long, 7 yards wide, and 3 yards deep. How many cubic yards of dirt will the company need to remove?

252 yd³

6. Amy rents a storage room that is 15 feet long, 5 feet wide, and 8 feet. What is the volume of the storage room?

600 ft³

Name _____

Lesson **92**

COMMON CORE STANDARD CC.5.MD.5b
Lesson Objective: Use the strategy make a table to compare volumes.

Problem Solving • Compare Volumes

A company makes aquariums that come in three sizes of rectangular prisms. The length of each aquarium is three times its width and depth. The depths of the aquariums are 1 foot, 2 feet, and 3 feet. What is the volume of each aquarium?

Read the Problem	Solve the Problem
What do I need to find? I need to find the _volume_ of each aquarium.	**Think:** The depth of an aquarium is the same as the height of the prism formed by the aquarium
What information do I need to use? I can use the formula for volume, $V = l \times w \times h$, or $V = B \times h$, I can use _1 ft, 2 ft, and 3 ft_ as the depths. I can use the clues _the length is three times_ _the width and depth_	

Length (ft)	Width (ft)	Depth, or Height (ft)	Volume (cu ft)
3	1	1	3
6	2	2	24
9	3	3	81

How will I use the information? I will use the _volume formula_ and a _table_ to list all of the possible combinations of lengths, widths, and depths.	So, the volumes of the aquariums are 3 cubic feet, 24 cubic feet, and 81 cubic feet.

1. Jamie needs a bin for her school supplies. A blue bin has a length of 12 inches, a width of 5 inches, and a height of 4 inches. A green bin has a length of 10 inches, a width of 6 inches, and a height of 5 inches. What is the volume of the bin with the greatest volume?

_300 in.³_

2. Suppose the blue bin that Jamie found had a length of 5 inches, a width of 5 inches, and a height of 12 inches. Would one bin have a greater volume than the other? **Explain.**

No. Both bins have the
same volume; 300 in.³

---

1. Ben is filling a box that has the shape of a rectangular prism with 1-inch cubes. A layer of 7 rows with 8 cubes in each row filled the bottom of the box. The volume of the box is 224 cubic inches. How many layers of cubes can Ben fit in the box?

- (A) 2
- (B) 4
- (C) 8
- (D) 10

2. Mary bought a puzzle in a box that has a width of 3 inches, a length of 10 inches, and a height of 8 inches. She put it in a box that has a volume of 576 cubic inches so she could mail it with some other things. How many cubic inches of space were left in the box?

- (A) 816 cu in.
- (B) 597 cu in.
- (C) 336 cu in.
- (D) 240 cu in.

3. Sylvia can buy a blue box or a green box to store her markers. Both boxes have a base that measures 8 inches by 4 inches. The height of the blue box is 2 inches. The height of the green box is 1 inch. How much greater is the volume of the blue box than the green box?

- (A) 96 cu in.
- (B) 64 cu in.
- (C) 35 cu in.
- (D) 32 cu in.

4. Mr. McDonald is designing a cabinet to store sports equipment in the gym. The length and width of one design cannot be the same as the length or width of another design. He wants the cabinet to be 5 feet high with a volume of 60 cubic feet. How many different designs, all with whole number dimensions, can he make?

- (A) 2
- (B) 3
- (C) 6
- (D) 12

Problem Solving REAL WORLD

5. Margie is packing 108 small boxes into a large carton. The small boxes will fill all of the space inside the large carton. Each small box is 3 inches long, 2 inches wide, and 1 inch high. The width of the base and the height of the large carton are the same. The length of the base is less than 36 inches. All of the dimensions are whole numbers. Explain how to find possible dimensions for the large carton.

Possible explanation: the volume of each of the boxes is 6 in.³: 3 × 2 × 1.
There are 108 boxes, so the volume of the carton is 6 × 108, or 648 in.³.
Make a table to find that if the width and the height could both be 6 inches,
the length would be 648 ÷ (6 × 6), or 648 ÷ 36 = 18 inches. The dimensions
of the carton could be 6 inches high, 6 inches wide, and 18 inches long.
Note: Other possible dimensions are: 9 × 9 × 8 and 18 × 18 × 2.

Lesson 93

COMMON CORE STANDARD CC.5.MD.5c
Lesson Objective: Find the volume of combined rectangular prisms.

Name _____

Find Volume of Composed Figures

A composite figure is a solid made up of two or more solids. To find the volume of a composite figure, first find the volume of each solid that makes up the figure. Then find the sum of the volumes of the figures.

Find the volume of the composite figure at right.

Step 1 Break apart the composite figure into two rectangular prisms. Label the dimensions of each prism.

Prism 1   Prism 2

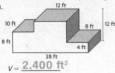

Step 2 Find the volume of each prism.

Prism 1
$V = (l \times w) \times h$
$V = \underline{4} \times \underline{8} \times \underline{4}$
$V = 128 \text{ in.}^3$

Prism 2
$V = (l \times w) \times h$
$V = \underline{20} \times \underline{8} \times \underline{4}$
$V = 640 \text{ in.}^3$

Step 3 Find the sum of the volumes of the two prisms.

Volume of Prism 1 + Volume of Prism 2 = Volume of Composite Figure
$\underline{128}$ + $\underline{640}$ = Volume of Composite Figure
$\underline{768}$ = Volume of Composite Figure

So, the volume of the composite figure is 768 in.³

Find the volume of the composite figure.

1.

$V = \underline{2,400 \text{ ft}^3}$

2.
$V = \underline{105 \text{ in.}^3}$

Lesson 93

CC.5.MD.5c

Name _____

1. Dmitri built a step out of blocks. What is the volume of the step?

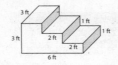

(A) 360 cu in.   (C) 540 cu in.
(B) 450 cu in.   (D) 750 cu in.

2. Latoya built some new steps up to the front of her house. What is the volume of the steps?

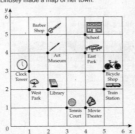

(A) 18 cu ft   (C) 48 cu ft
(B) 36 cu ft   (D) 54 cu ft

3. Maksim built a scratching toy for his cat. What is the volume of the scratching toy?

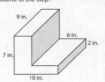

(A) 85 cu in.   (C) 210 cu in.
(B) 180 cu in.   (D) 1,800 cu in.

4. Jacinda made some steps for her deck. What is the volume of the steps?

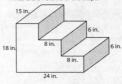

(A) 432 cu in.   (C) 4,320 cu in.
(B) 3,240 cu in. (D) 6,480 cu in.

Problem Solving REAL WORLD

5. As part of her shop class, Jules made the figure below out of pieces of wood. How much space does the figure she made take up?

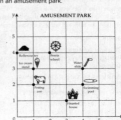

$\underline{2,916 \text{ cu cm}}$

Lesson 94

COMMON CORE STANDARD CC.5.G.1
Lesson Objective: Graph and name points on a coordinate grid using ordered pairs.

Name _____

Ordered Pairs

A coordinate grid is like a sheet of graph paper bordered at the left and at the bottom by two perpendicular number lines. The **x-axis** is the horizontal number line at the bottom of the grid. The **y-axis** is the vertical number line on the left side of the grid.

An ordered pair is a pair of numbers that describes the location of a point on the grid. An ordered pair contains two coordinates, x and y. The **x-coordinate** is the first number in the ordered pair, and the **y-coordinate** is the second number.

$(x, y) \longrightarrow (10, 4)$

Plot and label (10, 4) on the coordinate grid.

To graph an ordered pair:

• Start at the origin, (0, 0).
• Think: The letter x comes before y in the alphabet. Move across the x-axis first.
• The x-coordinate is 10, so move 10 units right.
• The y-coordinate is 4, so move 4 units up.
• Plot and label the ordered pair (10, 4).

Use the coordinate grid to write an ordered pair for the given point.

1. G $\underline{(3, 4)}$ 2. H $\underline{(8, 10)}$
3. J $\underline{(4, 6)}$ 4. K $\underline{(1, 2)}$

Plot and label the points on the coordinate grid.

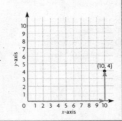

5. A (1, 6)   6. B (1, 9)
7. C (3, 7)   8. D (5, 5)
9. E (9, 3)   10. F (6, 2)

Lesson 94

CC.5.G.1

Name _____

Use the coordinate grid for 1–2.

Lindsey made a map of her town.

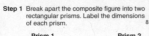

1. Which place in Lindsey's town is located at (4, 5)?

(A) East Park   (C) Barber Shop
(B) West Park   (D) School

2. Which point describes the location of the Art Museum?

(A) (2, 4)   (C) (4, 4)
(B) (2, 5)   (D) (5, 2)

Use the coordinate grid for 3–4.

The map shows the location of the attractions in an amusement park.

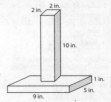

3. Which attraction is located at (2, 4)?

(A) Rollercoaster
(B) Ferris Wheel
(C) Water Slide
(D) Haunted Houses

Problem Solving REAL WORLD

Use the map for 4–5.

4. Which building is located at (5, 6)?

$\underline{\text{Price Slicer Mart}}$

5. What is the distance between Kip's Pizza and the bank?

$\underline{\text{6 units}}$

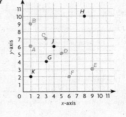

Answer Key

Name _____ **Lesson 95**
COMMON CORE STANDARD CC.5.G.2
Lesson Objective: Collect and graph data
on a coordinate grid.

Graph Data

Graph the data on the coordinate grid.

Plant Growth				
End of Week	1	2	3	4
Height (in inches)	4	7	10	11

- Choose a title for your graph and label it. You can use the data categories to name the x- and y-axis.
- Write the related pairs of data as ordered pairs.

(1 , 4), (2 , 7)
(3 , 10), (4 , 11)

- Plot the point for each ordered pair.

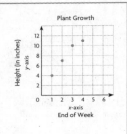

Plant Growth

Graph the data on the coordinate grid. Label the points.

1.

Distance of Bike Ride				
Time (in minutes)	30	60	90	120
Distance (in miles)	9	16	21	27

Write the ordered pair for each point.

(30 , 9), (60 , 16)
(90 , 21), (120 27)

2.

Bianca's Writing Progress				
Time (in minutes)	15	30	45	60
Total Pages	1	3	9	11

Write the ordered pair for each point.

(15 , 1), (30 , 3)
(45 , 9), (60 , 11)

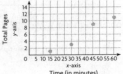

Distance of Bike Ride

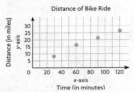

Bianca's Writing Progress

Use the graph for 1–3.

Sunil made this graph to show the weight of his new puppy.

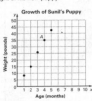

Growth of Sunil's Puppy

1. At what age did the puppy weigh 26 pounds?

- (A) 2 months
- (B) 4 months
- (C) 3 months
- (D) 5 months

2. What information is represented by the point labeled A?

- (A) The puppy weighed 4 pounds at age 35 months.
- (B) The puppy weighed 40 pounds at age 4 months.
- (C) The puppy weighed 35 pounds at age 4 months.
- (D) The puppy weighed 35 pounds at age 5 months.

3. What was the weight of the puppy at age 5 months?

- (A) 40 pounds
- (B) 43 pounds
- (C) 47 pounds
- (D) 50 pounds

Problem Solving REAL WORLD

Possible graph is shown.

4.

Windows Repaired					
Day	1	2	3	4	5
Total Number Repaired	14	30	45	63	79

a. Write the ordered pairs for each point.

(1, 14), (2, 30), (3, 45),
(4, 63), (5, 79)

b. What does the ordered pair (2, 30) tell you about the number of windows repaired?

Possible answer: After 2 days, a total of 30 windows had been repaired.

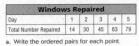

Windows Repaired

Name _____ **Lesson 96**
COMMON CORE STANDARD CC.5.G.2
Lesson Objective: Analyze and display
data in a line graph.

Line Graphs

A **line graph** uses a series of line segments to show how a set of data changes over time. The **scale** of a line graph measures and labels the data along the axes. An **interval** is the distance between the numbers on an axis.

Use the table to make a line graph.

- Write a title for your graph. In this example, use **Average Monthly High Temperature in Sacramento**.

Average Monthly High Temperature in Sacramento, California					
Month	Jan.	Feb.	Mar.	April	May
Temperature (°F)	53	60	65	71	80

- Draw and label the axes of the line graph. Label the horizontal axis **Month**. Write the months. Label the vertical axis **Temperature (°F)**.
- Choose a scale and an interval. The range is 53–80, so a possible scale is 0–80, with intervals of 20.
- Write the related pairs of data as ordered pairs:
(Jan, 53); (Feb, 60); (Mar, 65); (April, 71); (May, 80).

1. Make a line graph of the data above.

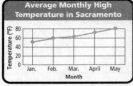

Average Monthly High Temperature in Sacramento

Use the graph to determine between which two months the least change in average high temperature occurs.

February and March

2. Make a line graph of the data in the table.

Average Low Temperature in San Diego, California					
Month	Mar.	April	May	June	July
Temperature (°F)	51	51	60	62	66

Average Low Temperature in San Diego

Use the graph to determine between which two months the greatest change in average low temperature occurs.

April and May

---

1. Kareem made a table showing how much he earned each month mowing lawns.

Lawn Mowing Earnings					
Month	April	May	June	July	August
Amount Earned	$40	$55	$60	$75	$50

What are the most appropriate scale and interval for Kareem to use to make a line graph of the data?

- (A) Scale: 0 to 50, Interval: 2
- (B) Scale: 0 to 50, Interval: 5
- (C) Scale: 0 to 100, Interval: 10
- (D) Scale: 0 to 100, Interval: 20

2. A scientist made a line graph that showed how a bear's average heart rate changes over time.

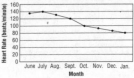

CHANGE IN AVERAGE HEART RATE OF BEAR

Based on the graph, which statement is true?

- (A) A bear's average heart rate rarely changes.
- (B) A bear's average heart rate starts to decrease at the end of the summer.
- (C) A bear's average heart rate increases over time.
- (D) A bear's average heart rate is at its lowest in the summer.

Problem Solving REAL WORLD

3. Randy makes a table that shows how long it takes her to run different distances.

Running Time and Distance				
Number of miles	1	2	3	4
Time (in minutes)	10	20	28	35

Randy uses the data to make a line graph. Describe the line graph.

Possible description: the graph will increase by the same amount for the first 2 miles. It will increase less between 2 and 3 miles and still less between 3 and 4 miles.

Answer Key

Name _____

Lesson 97
COMMON CORE STANDARD CC.5.G.3
Lesson Objective: Identify and classify polygons.

Polygons

A **polygon** is a closed plane figure formed by three or more line segments that meet at points called vertices. You can classify a polygon by the number of sides and the number of angles that it has.

Congruent figures have the same size and shape. In a **regular polygon,** all sides are congruent and all angles are congruent.

Classify the polygon below.

Polygon	Sides	Angles	Vertices
Triangle	3	3	3
Quadrilateral	4	4	4
Pentagon	5	5	5
Hexagon	6	6	6
Heptagon	7	7	7
Octagon	8	8	8
Nonagon	9	9	9
Decagon	10	10	10

How many sides does this polygon have? __5 sides__

How many angles does this polygon have? __5 angles__

Name the polygon. __pentagon__

Are all the sides congruent? __no__

Are all the angles congruent? __no__

So, the polygon above is a pentagon. It is *not* a regular polygon.

Name each polygon. Then tell whether it is a *regular polygon* or *not a regular polygon.*

1. __quadrilateral; not a regular polygon__
2. __triangle; not a regular polygon__
3. __pentagon; regular polygon__
4. __octagon; regular polygon__

Name _____

Lesson 97
CC.5.G.3

1. Mr. Delgado sees this sign while he is driving.

Which **best** describes the sign?

- (A) triangle; regular polygon
- (B) triangle; not a regular polygon
- (C) hexagon; regular polygon
- (D) hexagon; not a regular polygon

2. Mr. Diaz is building a fence around his yard. He drew a sketch of the fence line.

Which **best** describes the fence line?

- (A) pentagon; regular polygon
- (B) pentagon; not a regular polygon
- (C) hexagon; regular polygon
- (D) hexagon; not a regular polygon

3. A stained glass window at the town library is the shape of a regular octagon. Which of the following describes a regular octagon?

- (A) a figure with 6 congruent sides and 6 congruent angles
- (B) a figure with 6 sides that are not congruent
- (C) a figure with 8 sides that are not congruent
- (D) a figure with 8 congruent sides and 8 congruent angles

4. Beth drew four quadrilaterals. Which of the quadrilaterals that she drew is a regular polygon?

- (A)
- (C)
- (B)
- (D)

Problem Solving REAL WORLD

5. Sketch nine points. Then, connect the points to form a closed plane figure. What kind of polygon did you draw?

__Check students' drawings; nonagon.__

6. Sketch seven points. Then, connect the points to form a closed plane figure. What kind of polygon did you draw?

__Check students' drawings; heptagon.__

Name _____

Lesson 98
COMMON CORE STANDARD CC.5.G.3
Lesson Objective: Classify and draw triangles using their properties.

Triangles

You can classify triangles by the length of their sides and by the measure of their angles. **Classify each triangle.**

Use a ruler to measure the side lengths.

- **equilateral triangle**
  All sides are the same length.
- **isosceles triangle**
  Two sides are the same length.
- **scalene triangle**
  All sides are different lengths.

Use the corner of a sheet of paper to classify the angles.

- **acute triangle**
  All three angles are acute.
- **obtuse triangle**
  One angle is obtuse. The other two angles are acute.
- **right triangle**
  One angle is right. The other two angles are acute.

Classify the triangle according to its side lengths.
It has two congruent sides.
__The triangle is an isosceles triangle.__

Classify the triangle according to its angle measures.
It has one right angle.
__The triangle is a right triangle.__

Classify each triangle. Write *isosceles*, *scalene*, or *equilateral*. Then write *acute*, *obtuse*, or *right*.

1. __scalene; acute__
2. __equilateral; acute__
3. __isosceles; acute__
4. __isosceles; obtuse__
5. __scalene; right__
6. __isosceles; right__

Name _____

Lesson 98
CC.5.G.3

1. Which kind of triangle has no congruent sides?

- (A) equilateral
- (B) horizontal
- (C) isosceles
- (D) scalene

2. Nathan drew this triangle.

Which of the following **best** classifies the triangle?

- (A) scalene, acute
- (B) scalene, obtuse
- (C) isosceles, acute
- (D) isosceles, obtuse

3. What is the **least** number of acute angles that a triangle can have?

- (A) 0
- (B) 1
- (C) 2
- (D) 3

4. Amanda drew this triangle.

Which of the following **best** classifies the triangle?

- (A) equilateral, acute
- (B) isosceles, acute
- (C) scalene, acute
- (D) isosceles, right

Problem Solving REAL WORLD

5. Mary says the pen for her horse is an acute right triangle. Is this possible? **Explain.**

__No. It can be right or acute, but not both.__

6. Karen says every equilateral triangle is acute. Is this true? **Explain.**

__Yes. All the angles in an equilateral triangle are acute.__

Answer Key

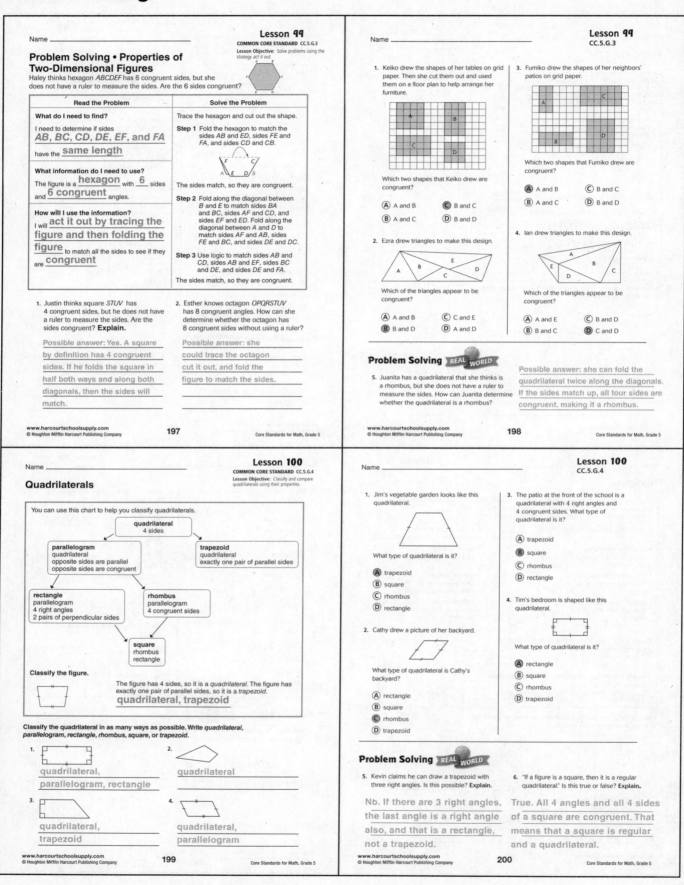

Name _____

Problem Solving • Properties of Two-Dimensional Figures

Haley thinks hexagon *ABCDEF* has 6 congruent sides, but she does not have a ruler to measure the sides. Are the 6 sides congruent?

Read the Problem	Solve the Problem
What do I need to find?	Trace the hexagon and cut out the shape.
I need to determine if sides *AB, BC, CD, DE, EF,* and *FA* have the ~~same length~~	**Step 1** Fold the hexagon to match the sides *AB* and *ED,* sides *FE* and *FA,* and sides *CD* and *CB.*
What information do I need to use? The figure is a ~~hexagon~~ with ~~6~~ sides and ~~6 congruent~~ angles.	The sides match, so they are congruent.
How will I use the information? I will ~~act it out by tracing the figure and then folding the figure~~ to match all the sides to see if they are ~~congruent~~	**Step 2** Fold along the diagonal between *B* and *E* to match sides *BA* and *BC,* sides *AF* and *CD,* and sides *EF* and *ED.* Fold along the diagonal between *A* and *D* to match sides *AF* and *AB,* sides *FE* and *BC,* and sides *DE* and *DC.*
	Step 3 Use logic to match sides *AB* and *CD,* sides *AB* and *EF,* sides *BC* and *DE,* and sides *DE* and *FA.* The sides match, so they are congruent.

1. Justin thinks square *STUV* has 4 congruent sides, but he does not have a ruler to measure the sides. Are the sides congruent? **Explain.**

   Possible answer: Yes. A square by definition has 4 congruent sides. If he folds the square in half both ways and along both diagonals, then the sides will match.

2. Esther knows octagon *OPQRSTUV* has 8 congruent angles. How can she determine whether the octagon has 8 congruent sides without using a ruler?

   Possible answer: she could trace the octagon cut it out, and fold the figure to match the sides.

Name _____

1. Keiko drew the shapes of her tables on grid paper. Then she cut them out and used them on a floor plan to help arrange her furniture.

   Which two shapes that Keiko drew are congruent?

   Ⓐ A and B   **Ⓒ** B and C
   Ⓑ A and C   Ⓓ B and D

2. Ezra drew triangles to make this design.

   Which of the triangles appear to be congruent?

   Ⓐ A and B   Ⓒ C and E
   Ⓑ B and D   Ⓓ A and D

3. Fumiko drew the shapes of her neighbors' patios on grid paper.

   Which two shapes that Fumiko drew are congruent?

   Ⓐ A and B   Ⓒ B and C
   Ⓑ A and C   Ⓓ B and D

4. Ian drew triangles to make this design.

   Which of the triangles appear to be congruent?

   Ⓐ A and E   Ⓒ B and D
   Ⓑ B and C   Ⓓ C and D

Problem Solving REAL WORLD

5. Juanita has a quadrilateral that she thinks is a rhombus, but she does not have a ruler to measure the sides. How can Juanita determine whether the quadrilateral is a rhombus?

   Possible answer: she can fold the quadrilateral twice along the diagonals. If the sides match up, all four sides are congruent, making it a rhombus.

Name _____

Quadrilaterals

You can use this chart to help you classify quadrilaterals.

- **quadrilateral** 4 sides
  - **parallelogram** quadrilateral opposite sides are parallel opposite sides are congruent
    - **rectangle** parallelogram 4 right angles 2 pairs of perpendicular sides
    - **rhombus** parallelogram 4 congruent sides
      - **square** rhombus rectangle
  - **trapezoid** quadrilateral exactly one pair of parallel sides

Classify the figure.

The figure has 4 sides, so it is a *quadrilateral*. The figure has exactly one pair of parallel sides, so it is a *trapezoid*.

quadrilateral, trapezoid

Classify the quadrilateral in as many ways as possible. Write *quadrilateral, parallelogram, rectangle, rhombus, square,* or *trapezoid*.

1. quadrilateral, parallelogram, rectangle

2. quadrilateral

3. quadrilateral, trapezoid

4. quadrilateral, parallelogram

Name _____

1. Jim's vegetable garden looks like this quadrilateral.

   What type of quadrilateral is it?

   Ⓐ trapezoid
   Ⓑ square
   Ⓒ rhombus
   Ⓓ rectangle

2. Cathy drew a picture of her backyard.

   What type of quadrilateral is Cathy's backyard?

   Ⓐ rectangle
   Ⓑ square
   Ⓒ rhombus
   Ⓓ trapezoid

3. The patio at the front of the school is a quadrilateral with 4 right angles and 4 congruent sides. What type of quadrilateral is it?

   Ⓐ trapezoid
   Ⓑ square
   Ⓒ rhombus
   Ⓓ rectangle

4. Tim's bedroom is shaped like this quadrilateral.

   What type of quadrilateral is it?

   Ⓐ rectangle
   Ⓑ square
   Ⓒ rhombus
   Ⓓ trapezoid

Problem Solving REAL WORLD

5. Kevin claims he can draw a trapezoid with three right angles. Is this possible? **Explain.**

   No. If there are 3 right angles, the last angle is a right angle also, and that is a rectangle, not a trapezoid.

6. "If a figure is a square, then it is a regular quadrilateral." Is this true or false? **Explain.**

   True. All 4 angles and all 4 sides of a square are congruent. That means that a square is regular and a quadrilateral.

Common Core State Standards

Operations and Algebraic Thinking

Write and interpret numerical expressions.

1. Use parentheses, brackets, or braces in numerical expressions, and evaluate expressions with these symbols.

2. Write simple expressions that record calculations with numbers, and interpret numerical expressions without evaluating them.

Analyze patterns and relationships.

3. Generate two numerical patterns using two given rules. Identify apparent relationships between corresponding terms. Form ordered pairs consisting of corresponding terms from the two patterns, and graph the ordered pairs on a coordinate plane.

Common Core State Standards

Number and Operations in Base Ten

Understand the place value system.

1. Recognize that in a multi-digit number, a digit in one place represents 10 times as much as it represents in the place to its right and 1/10 of what it represents in the place to its left.

2. Explain patterns in the number of zeros of the product when multiplying a number by powers of 10, and explain patterns in the placement of the decimal point when a decimal is multiplied or divided by a power of 10. Use whole-number exponents to denote powers of 10.

3. Read, write, and compare decimals to thousandths.

   a. Read and write decimals to thousandths using base-ten numerals, number names, and expanded form, e.g., $347.392 = 3 \times 100 + 4 \times 10 + 7 \times 1 + 3 \times (1/10) + 9 \times (1/100) + 2 \times (1/1000)$.

   b. Compare two decimals to thousandths based on meanings of the digits in each place, using $>$, $=$, and $<$ symbols to record the results of comparisons.

4. Use place value understanding to round decimals to any place.

Perform operations with multi-digit whole numbers and with decimals to hundredths.

5. Fluently multiply multi-digit whole numbers using the standard algorithm.

6. Find whole-number quotients of whole numbers with up to four-digit dividends and two-digit divisors, using strategies based on place value, the properties of operations, and/or the relationship between multiplication and division. Illustrate and explain the calculation by using equations, rectangular arrays, and/or area models.

7. Add, subtract, multiply, and divide decimals to hundredths, using concrete models or drawings and strategies based on place value, properties of operations, and/or the relationship between addition and subtraction; relate the strategy to a written method and explain the reasoning used.

Number and Operations – Fractions CC.5.NF

Use equivalent fractions as a strategy to add and subtract fractions.

1. Add and subtract fractions with unlike denominators (including mixed numbers) by replacing given fractions with equivalent fractions in such a way as to produce an equivalent sum or difference of fractions with like denominators.

2. Solve word problems involving addition and subtraction of fractions referring to the same whole, including cases of unlike denominators, e.g., by using visual fraction models or equations to represent the problem. Use benchmark fractions and number sense of fractions to estimate mentally and assess the reasonableness of answers.

Apply and extend previous understandings of multiplication and division to multiply and divide fractions.

3. Interpret a fraction as division of the numerator by the denominator $(a/b = a \div b)$. Solve word problems involving division of whole numbers leading to answers in the form of fractions or mixed numbers, e.g., by using visual fraction models or equations to represent the problem.

4. Apply and extend previous understandings of multiplication to multiply a fraction or whole number by a fraction.

   a. Interpret the product $(a/b) \times q$ as a parts of a partition of q into b equal parts; equivalently, as the result of a sequence of operations $a \times q \div b$.

   b. Find the area of a rectangle with fractional side lengths by tiling it with unit squares of the appropriate unit fraction side lengths, and show that the area is the same as would be found by multiplying the side lengths. Multiply fractional side lengths to find areas of rectangles, and represent fraction products as rectangular areas.

5. Interpret multiplication as scaling (resizing), by:

   a. Comparing the size of a product to the size of one factor on the basis of the size of the other factor, without performing the indicated multiplication.

   b. Explaining why multiplying a given number by a fraction greater than 1 results in a product greater than the given number (recognizing multiplication by whole numbers greater than 1 as a familiar case); explaining why multiplying a given number by a fraction less than 1 results in a product smaller than the given number; and relating the principle of fraction equivalence $a/b = (n \times a)/(n \times b)$ to the effect of multiplying a/b by 1.

Common Core State Standards

Number and Operations – Fractions (cont'd)   CC.5.NF

6. Solve real world problems involving multiplication of fractions and mixed numbers, e.g., by using visual fraction models or equations to represent the problem.

7. Apply and extend previous understandings of division to divide unit fractions by whole numbers and whole numbers by unit fractions.

    a. Interpret division of a unit fraction by a non-zero whole number, and compute such quotients.

    b. Interpret division of a whole number by a unit fraction, and compute such quotients.

    c. Solve real world problems involving division of unit fractions by non-zero whole numbers and division of whole numbers by unit fractions, e.g., by using visual fraction models and equations to represent the problem.

Core Standards for Math, Grade 5

Measurement and Data   CC.5.MD

Convert like measurement units within a given measurement system.

1. Convert among different-sized standard measurement units within a given measurement system (e.g., convert 5 cm to 0.05 m), and use these conversions in solving multi-step, real world problems.

Represent and interpret data.

2. Make a line plot to display a data set of measurements in fractions of a unit (1/2, 1/4 , 1/8). Use operations on fractions for this grade to solve problems involving information presented in line plots.

Geometric measurement: understand concepts of volume and relate volume to multiplication and to addition.

3. Recognize volume as an attribute of solid figures and understand concepts of volume measurement.

   a. A cube with side length 1 unit, called a "unit cube," is said to have "one cubic unit" of volume, and can be used to measure volume.

   b. A solid figure which can be packed without gaps or overlaps using n unit cubes is said to have a volume of n cubic units.

4. Measure volumes by counting unit cubes, using cubic cm, cubic in, cubic ft, and improvised units.

5. Relate volume to the operations of multiplication and addition and solve real world and mathematical problems involving volume.

   a. Find the volume of a right rectangular prism with whole-number side lengths by packing it with unit cubes, and show that the volume is the same as would be found by multiplying the edge lengths, equivalently by multiplying the height by the area of the base. Represent threefold whole-number products as volumes, e.g., to represent the associative property of multiplication.

   b. Apply the formulas $V = l \times w \times h$ and $V = b \times h$ for rectangular prisms to find volumes of right rectangular prisms with whole-number edge lengths in the context of solving real world and mathematical problems.

   c. Recognize volume as additive. Find volumes of solid figures composed of two non-overlapping right rectangular prisms by adding the volumes of the non-overlapping parts, applying this technique to solve real world problems.

Common Core State Standards

Geometry CC.5.G

Graph points on the coordinate plane to solve real-world and mathematical problems.

1. Use a pair of perpendicular number lines, called axes, to define a coordinate system, with the intersection of the lines (the origin) arranged to coincide with the 0 on each line and a given point in the plane located by using an ordered pair of numbers, called its coordinates. Understand that the first number indicates how far to travel from the origin in the direction of one axis, and the second number indicates how far to travel in the direction of the second axis, with the convention that the names of the two axes and the coordinates correspond (e.g., *x*-axis and *x*-coordinate, *y*-axis and *y*-coordinate).

2. Represent real world and mathematical problems by graphing points in the first quadrant of the coordinate plane, and interpret coordinate values of points in the context of the situation.

Classify two-dimensional figures into categories based on their properties.

3. Understand that attributes belonging to a category of two-dimensional figures also belong to all subcategories of that category.

4. Classify two-dimensional figures in a hierarchy based on properties.